Women and Crime in Post-Transitional South African Crime Fiction

Costerus New Series

Editors

C.C. Barfoot (*Leiden University, The Netherlands*)
Michael Boyden (*Uppsala University, Sweden*)
Theo D'haen (*Leiden University, The Netherlands
and Leuven University, Belgium*)
Raphaël Ingelbien (*Leuven University, Belgium*)
Birgit Neumann (*Heinrich-Heine-Universität Düsseldorf*, Germany)

VOLUME 230

The titles published in this series are listed at *brill.com/cos*

Women and Crime in Post-Transitional South African Crime Fiction

A Study of Female Victims, Perpetrators and Detectives

By

Sabine Binder

BRILL

RODOPI

LEIDEN | BOSTON

This work was accepted as a PhD thesis by the Faculty of Arts and Social Sciences, University of Zurich in the fall semester 2017 on the recommendation of the Doctoral Committee: Prof. Dr. Therese Steffen (main supervisor), Prof. Dr. Elisabeth Bronfen, and Prof. Dr. Sally-Ann Murray.

The open access version of this publication was funded by the Swiss National Science Foundation.

This is an open access title distributed under the terms of the CC-BY-NC-ND 4.0 license, which permits any non-commercial use, distribution, and reproduction in any medium, provided no alterations are made and the original author(s) and source are credited. Further information and the complete license text can be found at https://creativecommons.org/licenses/by-nc-nd/4.0/

The terms of the CC license apply only to the original material. The use of material from other sources (indicated by a reference) such as diagrams, illustrations, photos and text samples may require further permission from the respective copyright holder.

Cover illustration: Tobias Binder.

Library of Congress Cataloging-in-Publication Data
Names: Binder, Sabine, author.
Title: Women and crime in post-transitional South African crime fiction :
    a study of female victims, perpetrators and detectives / by Sabine Binder.
Description: Leiden ; Boston : Brill Rodopi, [2021] | Series: Costerus new
    series, 0165-9618 ; volume 230 | Includes bibliographical references and index.
Identifiers: LCCN 2020036513 (print) | LCCN 2020036514 (ebook) |
    ISBN 9789004437432 (hardback) | ISBN 9789004437449 (ebook)
Subjects: LCSH: Detective and mystery stories, South African (English)–History
    and criticism. | Women in literature. | Victims of crimes in literature. | Female
    offenders in literature. | Women detectives in literature.
Classification: LCC PR9362.6.D48 B56 2021 (print) | LCC PR9362.6.D48 (ebook) |
    DDC 823/.087209968–dc23
LC record available at https://lccn.loc.gov/2020036513
LC ebook record available at https://lccn.loc.gov/2020036514

Typeface for the Latin, Greek, and Cyrillic scripts: "Brill". See and download: brill.com/brill-typeface.

ISSN 0165-9618
ISBN 978-90-04-43743-2 (hardback)
ISBN 978-90-04-43744-9 (e-book)

Copyright 2021 by Sabine Binder. Published by Koninklijke Brill NV, Leiden, The Netherlands.
Koninklijke Brill NV incorporates the imprints Brill, Brill Hes & De Graaf, Brill Nijhoff, Brill Rodopi, Brill Sense, Hotei Publishing, mentis Verlag, Verlag Ferdinand Schöningh and Wilhelm Fink Verlag.
Koninklijke Brill NV reserves the right to protect this publication against unauthorized use. Requests for re-use and/or translations must be addressed to Koninklijke Brill NV via brill.com or copyright.com.

This book is printed on acid-free paper and produced in a sustainable manner.

Contents

Acknowledgements VII

Introduction 1
1. Choice of Texts and Approach 4
2. Post-Transitional Literature 7
3. Post-Transitional Crime Fiction and Crime Discourse 13
4. Post-Transitional Gender Conflicts 16
5. Preview of Chapters 19

1 The Female Victim: Whose Story is Written on Her Dead Body? Exploring the Gender Politics of Writing Female Victims and Their Traumas 22
1. The Female Victim: Introduction 22
2. Boniswa Sekeyi and Lulu: Witnesses of Systemic and Sexual Violence in Penny Lorimer's *Finders Weepers* 28
3. Resisting Arrest: Amahle Matebula, Female Victim in Malla Nunn's *Blessed Are the Dead* 38
4. Serial Female Victimhood: Margie Orford's Clare Hart Series 49
5. The Female Victim: Conclusion 72

2 The Female Perpetrator: Doing and Undoing Masculinity Through Crime—Exploring the Meanings and Politics of Female Counter-Violence 75
1. The Female Perpetrator: Introduction 75
2. Mike Nicol's Femme Fatale Sheemina February: Empowered Female Agent or Symptom of Male Fears? 84
3. Jassy Mackenzie's Renegade Detective Jade de Jong: Exploring Femininity and Justice 99
4. Angela Makholwa's Black Widow Society: Collective Female Terror against Gender Norms 112
5. The Female Perpetrator: Conclusion 128

3 The Female Detective: Agent of (Gender) Justice? Exploring Female Detective Agency and Investigating 133
1. The Female Detective: Introduction 133
2. Not That Kind of Cop: Michéle Rowe's Detective Constable Persy Jonas 139

    3   Not What South Africans Expect: Hawa Jande Golakai's Investigator
        Vee Johnson   168
    4   Renegade Contained: Charlotte Otter's Investigative Journalist
        Maggie Cloete   190
    5   The Female Detective: Conclusion   210

Conclusion   213

Works Cited   223
Index   241

Acknowledgements

This journey would have been an impossible one to undertake without the warm and dependable support of so many people. I am profoundly grateful for the amazing help I have received.

My deep and heartfelt appreciation goes to my three supervisors, my "Doktormütter" or "doctoral mothers" (as they are known in German). First of all, to Therese Steffen: It is safe to say that without your encouragement from the very earliest stages, without your unfailing intellectual and emotional support, your far-reaching expertise, strategic advice and full understanding of my situation, my thesis and the book that it has now become would not have seen the light of day. I am thankful to you beyond words. Second, Elisabeth Bronfen: I want to thank you for your truly long-term academic support. You have safely seen me through my master's thesis, my teaching qualification and, finally, my doctoral project. You and your work have been a source of enormous inspiration to and a lasting influence on me. Third, Sally-Ann Murray: You have kept me firmly anchored in South Africa and in the loop long after my departure and I am tremendously grateful to you for this. Your enthusiasm, your generous sharing of crucial articles with me as well as your ongoing and incisive feedback have played a vital role in shaping and improving this work up its very final stages.

The University of Stellenbosch, in particular the English Department, were a place of warm hospitality and my academic home whilst I was doing research in South Africa in 2013/2104. The year spent in Stellenbosch was crucial in conceptualising this study. I would like to thank you all for your support, advice and time taken to discuss. Beyond the university, in the Western Cape at large I could not have coped without the gentle, kind and ever so generous assistance of many. Thank you all for making a home away from home for me and my son, for friendship, practical support and child care. In the field of South African crime writing, I owe special thanks to Andrew Brown, Jassy Mackenzie, Angela Makholwa and Mike Nicol not only for writing blood-curdling crime novels, but also for interviews, lively conversations and hospitality.

Bridging the continents, the wider circle of the Swiss South African Joint Research Programme warrants special mention for creating opportunities to present my work both in South Africa and in Switzerland, and for lively discussions and friendship. I am further indebted to the Doctoral Programme Gender Studies at the Institute of Asian and Oriental Studies and to the English Seminar at the University of Zürich. My work substantially benefitted from these intellectually stimulating institutional frameworks as well as from the feedback and encouragement of my fellow doctoral students.

I am greatly indebted to Paddy Clark for patiently and meticulously proofreading my entire thesis. Your engagement with my work – reaching far beyond the written page – your generosity and friendship remain very special to me. When my thesis became the book it is now, Mark Taplin subjected it to expert copyediting. Thank you for your diligence and for working your magic on many of my phrases. At this stage, I owe further thanks to the anonymous peer reviewers for their useful comments as well as to the editors at Brill for their professional guidance throughout the publication process.

The help and encouragement of my friends has been incredible. You have been my role models and my sounding boards, you have lifted me up, you have read my work and honestly voiced your views, you have assisted me practically and technically, you have lovingly cared for my son, you have been my extended family: Karin Athanasiou, Judith Binder, Thomas Büchi, Marianne Bauer, Karima Geitlinger, Regula Keller, Amani Kilewo, Monica Lienin, Ciro Miniaci, Sabina Müller, Maria Nänny, Martina Padmanabhan, Tyrone Savage and Jörg Simmler. Thank you for giving me more than you could possibly imagine.

I am blessed with the most wonderful of families. I cannot thank you, my parents, my brothers and my sister together with your loved ones enough for your unfailing love and constant care. You have carried me both in Switzerland and in South Africa. Tobias, my son, you have been so patient. Thank you for always keeping me firmly rooted in the reality of everyday life and also for fullheartedly sharing the South African adventure with me. It is to you that I dedicate this book and to my late father, who understood my thirst for knowledge.

∴

For this study, I received generous financial support from the following institutions:

Swiss National Science Foundation (grant number PBZHP1_147227: research grant (Stipendium für angehende Forschende), August 2013 to July 2014 and grant number 10BP12_198037: open access publication grant, June 2020)

Kathrin-Hunziker Bieri Stiftung, Bern (research grant, December 2015)

Salomon David Steinberg-Stipendien-Stiftung, Zürich (Promotionsstipendium, July to October 2016)

Introduction

> The bad news – and it is indeed very bad news – is that post-apartheid South Africa remains a country at war with itself. Only this time, it is nothing less than a gender civil war.
> HELEN MOFFETT (2008, 110)

∴

> The threat of rape is an effective way to remind women that they are not safe and that their bodies are not entirely theirs. [...] It is an effective way to keep women in check ...
> PUMLA GQOLA (2015, 79)

∴

> [U]nder the comfortable cover of genre, writers can display narratives that would not otherwise see the light of day, and, indeed, reach audiences who would not otherwise be reached. Quite what those narratives actually are, however, is rather less easy both to discern and to control.
> GILL PLAIN (2001, 94)

∴

> [To] challenge [oppression] ... would be to re-imagine the oppressed as multidimensional, complex human beings.
> – NJABULO NDEBELE (ANDERSSON 2004, 16)

∴

Since the transition from apartheid to democracy in 1994, crime fiction in South Africa has taken on an unprecedented significance. Far from being escapist or trivial, this popular genre has resonated with the country's real experience of crime in singular ways, assuming an almost seismographic quality and continuing the political engagement that has long been a feature of South African literature. In the face of alarming levels of gender-based violence, a number of South African crime writers have begun to use the genre to address crimes against women, gender inequality and gender conflict. When asked about their motivations for writing crime, South African crime writers unequivocally refer to real-life crime in the country. Margie Orford reports being driven by a "deep sense of moral outrage" and a desire to go beneath the mere facts of violence, closer to the "truth of violence, resilience and revenge" (2010b, 191). Angela Makholwa devised her crime novel *Black Widow Society* in order to bring the taboo subject of domestic violence into the open (Binder 2015, 267). Malla Nunn calls her detective's adventures "retrospective justice" (2010a, par. 23) and Jassy Mackenzie writes out of a need to do something against crime and to imbue female readers with a sense of empowerment (Binder 2015, 271). These authors are making a claim that is actually quite extraordinary: to be writing against *real* violence in a genre that is invested in and depends on violence like no other. The aesthetics of violence on which the genre draws make it particularly prone to violent – or, at least, problematic – representational practices. The aesthetics of violence may all too easily lead to the violence of aesthetics, especially when we recall the gendered and racialised parameters within which the genre operates. Its commercial modes of production potentially add further constraints.[1]

Women and Crime in Post-Transitional South African Crime Fiction (hereinafter referred to as *Women and Crime*) sets out to critically examine this seemingly paradoxical fictional recreation and reflection of a real social ill in present-day South Africa. Drawing on a wide range of South African crime novels written over the last decade, it interrogates their mimetic reflections of gender and racial dynamics against the backdrop not only of South Africa's violent colonial and apartheid legacy, but of broader processes of social and political transformation. The study is guided first and foremost by the questions asked and issues raised in and by the texts and their authors themselves. It is based on the assumption that to a certain extent a text predefines the ways in which it is to be read – a view of literature as inherently conceptual. It traces the paths carved out by three generic stock figures – the victim, the perpetrator and the detective – in their female forms and explores how crime novels use these figures to a number of ends: to highlight the nexus between women and

---

[1] Here, "genre fiction" or "genre literature", sometimes also called "popular" or "formula" fiction, is understood as fiction that relates to a set of recognisable yet flexible conventions in terms of content, characterisation and structure. Examples of genre fiction include crime fiction, romance, chick-lit, horror, western, etc. Stephen Knight argues that genre fiction "draws its popularity – and importance – from dynamic variations on compulsive patterns and from its own rapid responses to changing sociocultural concerns" (2010, xii). According to Priscilla L. Walton and Manina Jones, works of genre fiction "provide audiences with a cheap and readily available source of entertainment, and they draw on iconographies, narrative patterns, and conventions of characterization that become familiar through frequent repetition" (1999, 227).

crime in South Africa, to expose the many forms of real violence with which South African women are confronted, to reveal gendered and racial "truths" [2] and to offer explanations and modes of resistance to women.

At the same time, the study subjects the "theories" outlined by the texts to critical scrutiny by asking several key questions. What gendered and racialised subjectivities are constructed and contested, and what assumptions and genealogies underlie these constructions? How are female figures framed by generic, gender and racial norms? Where do they reproduce the norms and expectations laid out for them? What modes of resistance do they adopt? What new forms of agency do they explore for women? Postcolonial[3] feminists such as Chandra Talpade Mohanty (1984) insist on the importance of attending to such questions in order to lay bare the politics of representation, especially of women of colour from the global South. Representational practices and discourses must be examined carefully lest they perpetuate the marginalisation and oppression of women in general, and women of colour in particular. Kimberlé Crenshaw coined the term "intersectionality" to denote multiple and simultaneous oppression based on gender and race. In a seminal essay, she notes that Black women are rendered invisible by "feminist theory and antiracist policy discourse because both are predicated on a discrete set of experiences that often does not accurately reflect the intersection of race and gender" (1989, 140).[4] This problem was first identified by Sojourner Truth in 1851 in her speech

---

2 I use the word "truth" either in quotation marks or in the plural in order to signal absence of objectivity – to signal that "truth" is necessarily biased, controversial, contested, that there are always multiple truths. When I talk about "truth-finding" or "truth-telling", it always denotes a version of the truth. Deborah Posel and Graeme Simpson call it "one of the striking historical ironies of the late twentieth century" that the "philosophical angst about the pursuit of truth has been accompanied by a newfound political confidence in exactly this project." They view the "growing global enthusiasm for truth commissions," which "evoke high expectations of the power of truth," as evidence of this (2002, 1).

3 In this study the "post" in postcolonial is understood not as a temporal, but as a critical perspective that denotes a challenge or alternative to colonial, Eurocentric views and epistemologies.

4 A note on racial terminology is essential at this point. Like gender, race is a construct – or a metaphor, as Henry Louis Gates Jr. calls it (1985, 4). Any racial terminology therefore refers to the specific historical and socio-political power constellations under which, or in contestation of which, it was constructed. References to people as "Black", "Coloured", "Indian" or "White" in my study denote racial categories created under apartheid. This is highly problematic, as it repeats apartheid's racist, segregationist practices. Unfortunately, these categories are still very much in place and in use in South Africa, and they continue to have meaning and value. I will use them whenever this meaning is important. In order to signify their constructed nature, I have chosen to capitalise these terms, including the term "White". As Richard Dyer reminds us, it is precisely as an unmarked term, by seeming not to be anything in particular, that White has secured its hegemonic power (1988, 1).

"Ain't I a Woman?" In *Black Feminist Thought,* Patricia Hill Collins speaks of interconnected "systems of oppression" (of race, social class, gender, sexuality, ethnicity, nation and age) (2000, 18, 299). She further names and challenges "controlling images" that originate in slavery and colonialism, but still serve to dominate women of colour (69–96). Some of these images and stereotypes are at play in the representation of female victims, perpetrators and detectives of colour, as I will show. By applying a decolonial feminist lens, my study reveals subjectivities, practices and performances that draw on what María Lugones – with recourse to Gloria Anzaldúa – terms "feminist border thinking": "[W]here the liminality of the border is a ground, a space, a borderland" (2010, 753). Such "Third Spaces" – along with strategies of disidentification and resignification that destabilise dominant power structures[5] – assume significance in decoding, for example, South African Coloured subjectivities in crime fiction.

1 Choice of Texts and Approach

My analysis, which is undergirded by post- and decolonial as well as Black feminist theory, involves a close reading of 21 crime novels that have received little critical attention to date. All are set in South Africa and written by South African authors in the post-transitional period. Their authors include South African citizens as well as residents and diasporic voices[6], and all are written in English.[7] All feature female victims, perpetrators or detectives as protagonists or as prominent figures who react to and engage with the social and political pressures facing real South African women.

The figure of the *female victim* is given particular prominence in Penny Lorimer's first-time crime novel *Finders Weepers* (2014), as well as in Malla Nunn's expat view *Blessed Are the Dead* (2012). The tradition of attending to female victimisation in South African crime fiction was initiated by Margie Orford – often called South Africa's "queen of krimi" – in her Clare Hart series, which started in 2006 and is still ongoing, but Lorimer departs from Orford's

---

5 This link is established by Gabriele Dietze. For Dietze, this is the point where the critical subgenre that she dubs "Queer Intersectionality" can be connected to "the decolonial imperative of 'knowledges otherwise'" (2014, 261–2).

6 Malla Nunn is from eSwatini, but her parents lived in South Africa before emigrating to Australia, where Nunn still lives. Charlotte Otter is a South African living in Germany. Hawa Jande Golakai is Liberian, but she has lived in South Africa and offers the perspective of the many immigrants from other African countries in South Africa.

7 There is a growing body of crime fiction in other languages, most notably in Afrikaans. The best-known Afrikaans crime writer internationally is Deon Meyer.

agenda in two important ways. First, her detective is not White, like Orford's Clare Hart, but Xhosa/German. Secondly, unlike Orford's host of victims of sexual violence, Lorimer's female victims Boniswa and Lulu are as much victims of the South African education system as they are of more event-based forms of violence. Nunn, as an expat and writer of historical crime novels, introduces a further variation. Her detective is not only male and of uncertain racial origins, but Amahle, the victim, is a Zulu girl killed by her father's wife. Foregrounding their victims' trauma, as these crime novels do, they lend themselves to being regarded as trauma novels. Drawing from studies on the gender dimensions of bearing witness in South Africa, as well as postcolonial trauma theory, I examine how the novels, both process the trauma of past and present real violence against women and chart the resources that women are able to deploy in response to such violence. Female victims in the crime genre, particularly if they are of colour, have traditionally been simultaneously invisible and hypervisible. Questions of representation are therefore pertinent, as post- and decolonial and Black feminist theorists emphasise. This study reads the novels in the light of scholarship on the ethics and aesthetics of representing the violated female body in order to assess their politics and, ultimately, their success in doing justice to women.

Novels featuring *female perpetrators* as protagonists are as rare as they are conspicuous. The obvious starting point is Mike Nicol's Coloured femme fatale Sheemina February. She features in his Revenge Trilogy (2010a, 2010b and 2011), which marks the beginning of Nicol's turn to crime writing. February is joined by Jassy Mackenzie's White killer heroine Jade de Jong. Mackenzie, who started her thriller series featuring Jade de Jong, which is still ongoing, in 2008. My third perpetrator is the Black Widow Society, an interracial group of murderous women created by Angela Makholwa in her novel of the same name (2013). All three novelists write female perpetrators who are intent on redressing the power balance for women. Drawing from theories on gender performativity and masculinity studies, my study delineates the ways in which performing the male role of the killer enables these women to move to a place of power and to do justice. What is at stake is their "offence" against both the law and gender norms. By attending to questions of representation and reading fictional female perpetrators against the background of existing discursive constructions of violent women in the crime genre and in South Africa I show that these characters have the potential to prize open gender norms as constructs, to transform the way in which readers of crime fiction view women and to probe issues of retribution and alternative notions of justice from a female perspective.

Because of their diverse backgrounds and origins, the *female detectives* in the novels that I have chosen are confronted with a wide variety of types of crime.

The Coloured police detective Persy Jonas features in Michéle Rowe's crime series of the same name, which began in 2013. Vee Johnson, a Liberian journalist-investigator, is the protagonist of a series by Hawa Jande Golakai in which the detective scrutinises South African society from an immigrant's perspective. Charlotte Otter, like Malla Nunn, is a South African emigrant. Her protagonist is the Afrikaner journalist-investigator Maggie Cloete, who is based in South Africa. Even though these investigators are licensed and empowered by institutions such as the police or the media, the novels examined here also show that their agency is constrained by those same institutions, which marginalise them as women. The feminist potential of the female detective has been debated by feminist literary scholars ever since explicitly feminist crime fiction first appeared in the 1970s. My analysis will engage with these controversies and the question they ultimately touch on: namely, how much change is possible from within the patriarchal system. Taking cues from feminist political and legal scholars from both South Africa and further afield, I will identify the creative and unconventional agentic strategies employed by the detectives in South African crime novels. My reading will also attend to the particular aspects of the South African real that the female detective subjects to female investigation, the kinds of truths that she brings to light and the kind of justice that she is able to administer for women. Finding and exposing the truths about past crimes was institutionalised in South Africa's Truth and Reconciliation Commission (TRC), as were restorative forms of justice. I will therefore read the female detective in conversation with feminist scholarship on the TRC.

As my intention is to critically map the cultural and gender/racial-political contribution of South African crime fiction, I am guided in my choice of theory by the crime novels themselves: by the ways in which they negotiate the problematics of law and justice for women faced with crime in South Africa from the diverse viewpoints of their female victim, perpetrator and/or detective figures. What *Women and Crime* offers is a cross-cultural perspective, a *regard croisé*, a view from Europe shaped not only by a full year of living in South Africa and doing research at a South African university, but by numerous conversations with South African writers and an ongoing dialogue with friends and academics in South Africa and beyond over many years. My looking and researching both "here" in Europe and "there" in South Africa is also reflected in the scholarship that informs the study.

Although the crime genre's ability to shed light on social change and the state of the nascent democratic order in South Africa has been recognised in numerous scholarly articles, few book-length treatments of the subject – let alone of novels by female writers – have appeared to date. One notable exception is Leon de Kock's comprehensive study *Losing the Plot: Crime, Reality and Fiction in Postapartheid Writing* (2016a), which, however barely touches on questions of gender. Although Samantha Naidu's and Elizabeth Le Roux's recent volume *A Survey of South African Crime Fiction* (2017) does include a chapter on the subject, this does not consider the intersection between gender and race. Largely under-researched are the crime genre's singular reverberations with trauma, truth-finding, justice and the restoration of order in South Africa, especially from a female perspective. Focusing on the period following the South African Truth and Reconciliation Commission (TRC), *Women and Crime* traces the various ways in which crime fiction is still in conversation with the endeavours of the TRC and, arguably, provides a response to the TRC's alleged failure to develop a full understanding of women's suffering under apartheid. Ewald Mengel's and Michela Borzaga's collection of essays *Trauma, Memory, and Narrative in the Contemporary South African Novel* (2012b) is an in-depth examination of the role of literature in reclaiming and transcending the country's traumatic past. *Women and Crime* continues this line of research with a focus on crime narratives and an intersectional perspective. In doing so, it takes cue from a long line of work on the consequences of disregarding violations of women's rights in contemporary South Africa by writers such as the literary scholars Desiree Lewis and Pumla Dineo Gqola, the sociologist Nthabiseng Motsemme, the political scientist Sheila Meintjes, the legal scholar Beth Goldblatt, the anthropologist Fiona Ross and the journalist Redi Tlhabi. Beyond South Africa, the book represents an important contribution to the study of what Chris Andrews and Matt McGuire term "post-conflict literature" (2016). In this newly established field, *Women and Crime* is the first work to examine crime fiction. It also fills a critical gap by examining the figure of the detective alongside those of the victim and the perpetrator, who have received insufficient attention in studies of crime fiction more generally. The study demonstrates that, by tapping into violence, misogyny and racism, the crime genre provides a vibrant platform for social, cultural and ethical debates. Its innovative and interdisciplinary theoretical approach sheds new light on the complex ways in which crime fiction resonates with the real and on the genre's potential as a tool of political and cultural intervention from a feminist perspective.

2 Post-Transitional Literature

The crime novels examined here are a product of the so-called post-transitional moment in South Africa's history. Although crime novels are not an entirely new phenomenon in South Africa, they were relatively uncommon before

1994.[8] Especially during apartheid, as crime writer Mike Nicol puts it, "no self-respecting writer was going to set up with a cop as the main protagonist of a series. It was akin to sleeping with the enemy" (2015c, par. 1). In the "new" South Africa, particularly with the onset of the new millennium, crime fiction started to burgeon. It is important, therefore, to take a closer look at this post-transitional moment in time and the literary landscape associated with it. As Ronit Frenkel and Craig MacKenzie note, "the term 'post-transitional' is not primarily a temporal marker but rather a widening of the scope of what characterizes current cultural formations" (7). In fact, not all scholars see it as necessary to draw a line between the transitional and post-transitional periods.[9] For my study, however, which looks at novels that were all written some time after the transition to a new dispensation, and that speak to and reflect the transition and its promises in various ways, it remains a useful distinction.

The period of change, which the *post*-transitional period both refers back to and sets itself apart from, is the *transitional* period as such, which designates the time from 1990 to around 2000. After the country's narrow escape from a civil war, the unbanning of the liberation movements and Nelson Mandela's release from prison in early 1990 initiated a process of negotiation. Eventually, a peaceful shift to democracy was secured, culminating in the first non-racial democratic election in 1994, which saw Nelson Mandela elected president. According to Meg Samuelson, the literatures of transition were "invested and implicated in national, often nation-building, processes which found their symbolic and moral centre in the hearings of the Truth and Reconciliation Commission (TRC)" (2010, 113).

If the transitional period was about "turning inward," as Samuelson puts it, the post-transitional years are marked by a turn towards "scripting connections," both within the national entity and beyond (113–114). As Frenkel and MacKenzie explain, such connections have come to be theorised in terms of "complicities (Sanders), foldedness, conviviality (Gilroy), improvisation (Titlestad) or hybridity [...] and mutual 'entanglement' (Nuttall) [...]" (2010, 6). What this idiom denotes is an orientation towards the complexity of points of social and temporal contact and intersection. Sarah Nuttall captures it with the notion of "entanglement". She writes, "Entanglement is a condition of being

---

8 Elizabeth le Roux provides a bibliography of South African crime fiction written in English up to 1994 (2013). A good and regularly updated map of the current crime fiction landscape, which includes South African crime novels written in other languages, can be found on Mike Nicol's *Crime Beat* website/blog (Nicol 2016). The article by Lindy Stiebel adds Black crime writers of the 1990s (2002).

9 See, for example, Leon de Kock's study on post-apartheid crime writing (2016a, 9–15).

twisted together or entwined, involved with; it speaks of an intimacy gained, even if it was resisted, or ignored or uninvited" (2009, 1). In post-transitional literature, Frenkel and MacKenzie note an increase in transnational allegiances and diasporic connections (2010, 2). With regard to the connections inside the country, they observe that apartheid-era racial categorisations are being complicated or ignored altogether in the post-transition period and that the interrogation of South Africa's painful history, which started during the transition, is being continued, although much literature "disavows the past altogether" (2). On a more cautious note, Samuelson warns that violations of both the apartheid and the colonial past continue to harm the post-transitional present, a fact to which the growing crime genre bears witness (2010, 114). "Crime fiction too," she emphasises, "draws into its bloody maw a range of unfinished business from the past even as it increasingly inserts the national into various transnational networks" (114). Just as the past remains influential, so does the political. Contrary to expectations, post-transitional literature has not turned away from the kind of political engagement South African literature was renowned for during apartheid. Sam Naidu and Elizabeth Le Roux find the status of crime fiction elevated "to the 'new political novel'" (2017, 162). Its significantly increased presence within the South African literary landscape is the result of a general post-transitional opening up, to which the genre has contributed in important ways. This should come as no surprise, given the close association between popular literature and social change.

In very different cultural contexts, two pioneering theorists of popular culture, John G. Cawelti and Karin Barber, have independently postulated that popular forms are both a *sign* of processes of transformation and a *means* of negotiating them. For Cawelti, popular genres facilitate the assimilation of new interests and values into conventional imaginative structures (1976, 36). Barber notes, "New popular cultural forms not only emerge out of historical change, but also participate in it, embody it and comment upon it" (2018, 3).[10] Having said that, the term "popular" is by no means uncontested – Barber calls it a "slippery" term. Given its reverberations with Western class relations, it creates unease when applied to an African context (2018, 7). It is defined as belonging to "ordinary people" by the *Oxford English Dictionary* (2020), as opposed to the elite, which raises further problems. Neither group is a fixed entity, boundaries are porous. What is more, as Barber points out, "'Popular' is a term laden with contradictory values, attracting both championship ('the voice of the people') and disdain ('low-class trash')" (2018, 11). South African crime fiction displays a

---

10   See also Barber 1987 (13–15).

number of characteristics that Barber deems typical of African popular forms (12). First, ambiguity – even contradiction at times – is pervasive, especially when it comes to gender politics. Secondly, South African crime fiction features voices that pit the "us" (the poor, the marginalised) against the "them" (the rich, the powerful, the privileged), albeit while acknowledging complicities and fault lines. Finally, the genre clearly expresses "sarcasm, outrage and challenge," asserts the dignity of those who are less privileged and exposes inequality, another typical feature of African popular forms according to Barber (12). The ways in which African popular cultural productions negotiate change with regard to questions of gender are outlined by Lynda Gichanda Spencer, Dina Ligaga and Grace A Musila, who make a strong case for the impact that such productions have on perceptions of gender in Africa. They perceive "manifestations of change and continuity in gender scripts," as well as "alternative ways to re-imagine gender within popular imaginaries in Africa" (2018, 4). Among the elements that they identify as inherent to African popular culture is its capacity to function as a democratic platform to probe gender issues in both transgressive and conservative ways (4).

Intricately linked to the ways in which South African crime fiction mediates social and political change in the years following the transition – not least in the area of gender – is the South African Truth and Reconciliation Commission (TRC). If, as Frenkel and MacKenzie declare, the literature of the transition years is "inextricable from the spectacle of the TRC" (2010, 4), the post-transitional period can be regarded as one of prolonged and critical engagement with the TRC in the genre that, like no other literary form, is (explicit) about crime, the "truth" about crime, justice and the restoration of order – epitomised in the victim, the perpetrator and the detective. In fact, I find each of these three figures in conversation with the TRC, so, inter alia, I read post-transitional crime novels as still engaged with – or as "rearranging," to use Samuelson's terminology – the endeavours of the country's Truth Commission. The foundations of the TRC were laid in the final clause of the South African Interim Constitution, which recognised the injustice of the past and stated that amnesty would be granted to perpetrators (Hayner 2001, 41). Following the 1995 Promotion of National Unity and Reconciliation Act, the TRC began its work in 1996 (41). Its threefold mandate included, first, investigating and reporting on human rights violations during the apartheid era;[11] secondly, granting amnesty to violators of human rights provided that

---

11 To be precise, the TRC was charged with investigating human rights violations between 1 March 1960, the day of the Sharpeville Massacre, and 10 May 1994, the day of Nelson Mandela's inauguration as president (Krüger 2007, 40).

they fully confessed and their acts had been politically motivated; and thirdly, making recommendations for reparations to victims (Hayner 2001, 41–43, Butler 2009, 53).[12] The commission submitted its final report in 2003. According to Anthony Butler, "[t]he TRC's principal achievement was to elicit and record the testimony of thousands of victims of human rights violations, and to establish on the historical record the extent and nature of such abuses committed during the era of political struggle" (53). Over 21,000 victims and witnesses testified and told their own versions of the "truth", 2,000 of them in public hearings; over 7,000 perpetrators applied for amnesty, as Priscilla B. Hayner notes (2001, 42–43). The TRC's aim to facilitate reconciliation through truth-telling was informed by psychological tenets and the Christian/spiritual principles of compassion and forgiveness: For the victims, telling their story and having its truth value acknowledged was thought of as a way of processing their pain to bring about healing. The perpetrators' confessions were supposed to have a cathartic effect and to foster forgiveness on the part of the victim (Posel and Simpson 2002, 2, 9). Given the scale of the South African TRC, the most ambitious of its kind to date, it is impossible to measure exactly how successful the Commission was in achieving these aims. Gesine Krüger gives the consensus view: namely, that the TRC played a seminal role in averting a war (2007, 41). For her, it testifies to South Africa's high awareness of the explosive force a violent history can develop if it remains unreviewed (41). Taking stock, Deborah Posel maintains, "The TRC remains, in several respects, a remarkable achievement" (2002, 166). In particular, she emphasises its role as "historical 'lie detector'": enough human rights violations were revealed "to debunk any lingering attempts either to sanitise apartheid or to romanticise the struggle against it" (167).[13]

The TRC has been the subject of widespread debate and criticism, which may be perceived not only as necessary, but as part and parcel of its reconciliation project. With regard to gender, it has been criticised for failing to uncover a full understanding of women's sufferings under apartheid (Ross 2003a, b, 2008, Borer 2009).[14] Beth Goldblatt and Sheila Meintjes summarise this critique as follows:

---

12   The commission's mandates are mirrored in its three committees: the Human Rights Violations Committee, the Amnesty Committee and the Reparations and Rehabilitation Committee (Hayner 2001, 41–42).
13   Posel quotes Michael Ignatieff, who stated, "All that a truth commission can achieve is to reduce the number of lies that can be circulated unchallenged in public discourse" (2002, 167).
14   See "The female victim: Introduction" for details.

> The TRC's narrow interpretation of "severe ill-treatment" means that women who bore the brunt of oppression through forced removals, pass arrests and other acts of systemic apartheid violence have not been identified as victims of gross human rights violations. We have also argued that women's evidence as wives and mothers of victims has cast them as secondary victims rather than as primary agents in a struggle against injustice. A third dimension of a gender analysis [...] is the lack of testimony to the TRC from women victims of sexual violence to the TRC [sic].
> 1997, 8

In my analysis of individual crime novels, I will show in detail how they respond to these perceived shortcomings, but at this point I would like to highlight some views on the relationship and commonalities between the TRC and literature. Thinking about the role of literature vis-à-vis the country's violent history and the work of the TRC, South African writer André Brink attributes a key function to it. He famously maintains that "unless the enquiries of the Truth and Reconciliation Commission (TRC) are extended, complicated, and intensified in the imaginings of literature, society cannot sufficiently come to terms with its past to face the future" (1998, 30). Brink claims that, because it is based on memory, which is necessarily unreliable, history – even the kind of history that the TRC has written – will always be fallible, will always have its "blind spots and silences" (37). It is therefore literature, as "imagined rewriting of history" (37), that is better suited to the task of attending to the "silent or silenced landscape of the past" (32). Shane Graham makes a similar argument in his study of literature after the TRC, in which he describes the TRC as "merely the opening chapter" in the process of South Africa's transformation: "[R]ather than allowing South Africa to 'close the book on the past,' as many of the commission's proponents suggested would follow from its work, the TRC helped make possible the continual writing and rewriting of that book" (2009, 3).[15] The past, in Graham's understanding, is not monolithic or final (20).[16] This study and the crime novels analysed in it form part of the on-going process initiated by the TRC. It will employ some of the conceptual tools and vocabulary of the human rights discourse introduced by the TRC (restorative justice,

---

15   For nuance, see, for example, Tyrone Savage (2011).
16   Graham identifies a number of prominent South African writers as participants in this process of (re)writing the past, notably Achmat Dangor, K. Sello Duiker, Antjie Krog, Sindiwe Magona, Zakes Mda and Zoë Wicomb. The process continues to the present day with writers such as Nadia Davids, Niq Mhlongo, Lebogang Mashile, Koleka Putuma and Makhosazana Xaba to mention but a few.

"truth" and reconciliation, gendered peace, discourses of victimhood) in seeking to trace where and how crime fiction responds to the TRC. It will also critically examine the paradox, if not outrageousness, of a potentially violent genre continuing in the vein of a TRC that explicitly advocated non-violent means of conflict resolution.

3   Post-Transitional Crime Fiction and Crime Discourse

This study follows Worthington's definition of crime fiction as fiction "that has crime, or the appearances of crime, at its centre and as its *raison d'être*" (xi). The exact nature of "crime fiction" is notoriously hard to determine. Charles J. Rzepka mentions the vagueness of the term (2010, 2), while Stephen Knight and Heather Worthington discuss in detail the difficulties of defining what constitutes crime fiction (2010, xiii, 2011, xi). South African crime fiction written in the post-transitional period draws from European and American genre traditions originating in both the 19th-century detective novel and the 20th-century hard-boiled and noir thriller. However, it has significantly adapted, transformed and, at times, subverted those traditions. In particular, it shares the notion of "postcolonial 'genre-bending'" (Matzke and Mühleisen 2006a, 5) which entails social detection, an investigation into power and authority, and a questioning of the social order, often "through alternative notions of justice" (5), with other crime fiction that has emerged in colonial and postcolonial contexts around the globe. The crime novels analysed here largely fall into what Sam Naidu regards as the two main sub-genres being written in South Africa today: namely, the thriller and the detective novel (2013a, 127). Modelled on the US-American hard-boiled novel and its derivatives, as well as on spy or noir thrillers, the South African thriller as Naidu describes it "is formulaic, fast-paced, plot-driven, contains more action than detection, is quite violent, and usually ends with a climactic chase or physical show-down" (127). I use the term "thriller" in this way, with the slight adaptation that it prominently includes the perpetrator's perspective. The focus of the detective novel, by contrast, is on the – often somewhat eccentric – detective. He or she is the driving force behind the investigation of the murder mystery around which the novel revolves. The detective novel can be traced back to tales by Edgar Allan Poe, Arthur Conan Doyle and Agatha Christie, although it also borrows from the police procedural of the late 20th century. It can include action, but is slower paced and has more psychological depth than the thriller. Having said that, sub-generic boundaries are notoriously difficult to draw in the crime genre, so I will use the terms "thriller" and "detective fiction" as very broad points of reference only. As sub-generic distinctions are not central to my argument, most of the time I will refer simply to "crime fiction".

The recent phenomenon of crime fiction in South Africa was first taken seriously outside academic circles – most notably by Mike Nicol, who in 2007 began documenting the South African crime fiction scene and sparking off critical debates on his website and in his blog *Crime Beat*.[17] As Naidu points out, "Nicol's reviews, interviews, and research have performed a vital role in creating and sustaining interest in this field" (2013a, 125). In the past few years, South African crime fiction has since developed into an important field of academic study. A key milestone in this development was the 2013 special edition of *Current Writing*, which placed contemporary South African crime fiction in a historical context and brought together scholarly contributions on the subject for the first time. This was followed in 2014 by a special issue of *Scrutiny2*. Since then, numerous publications have appeared in scholarly journals and a lively debate has evolved. If South African crime fiction has begun to attract academic attention, this is largely on account of its capacity for socio-political analysis. As Naidu observes,

> For South African crime fiction, which entertains, provides a form of escapism *and* yet manages to engage with suffering on various levels, the question of artistic merit is closely linked to socio-political analysis. The question is no longer whether crime fiction is "highbrow" or "lowbrow", but one of how this genre, and its sub-genres, manage to entertain and simultaneously perform a much-needed hermeneutic function.
> 2013b, 731

While crime writers themselves are attracted by this tension between entertainment and analysis (Nicol 2012a), a substantial body of critical work has focused on the genre's politics. This includes crime novels' potential as "state of the nation" narratives, to use Jonathan Amid's term (2011, par. 1). Within the arena of the socio-political, questions of gender and gender-based violence have attracted significant critical interest. My study forms part of and continues this line of critical enquiry.

Just as crime fiction in South Africa cannot be isolated from real-life crime, so it must be viewed within the context of the country's pervasive discourse on crime. Rosalind Morris notes, "Crime is the phantom that haunts the new nation's imaginary" (2006, 60). Jonathan Amid and Leon de Kock identify

---

[17] The few crime novels written during apartheid did receive some scholarly attention, however (Green 1994, Stiebel 2002, Davis 2006).

"'crime' as the dominant discourse that encompasses many forms of lawbreaking, violence and violation that have taken on 'mythic' proportions in the current sociopolitical climate" (2014, 60). In fact, crime fiction occupies a rather complex place as both within and outside such discourse, both feeding into it and reflecting it.[18] On the one hand, crime fiction partakes in these discourses about crime, which encompass dinner-table conversations, news reports, television series and crime films,[19] as well as investigative journalism and the very popular true-crime books.[20] John and Jean Comaroff argue that "there seems to be more to the public obsession with criminality and disorder than the mere *fact* of its reality. South Africans of all stripes are also captivated by *images* of crime and policing [...]" (2004, 801, original emphasis). In a society that is threatened by real crime, while faced with an unreliable criminal justice system, crime fiction has a restorative function, "iterating an order that remains distinctly fragile" (Comaroff and Comaroff 2006, 20). Warnes relates "[t]he fact that the detective arm of the South African police is felt to be a key to solving the country's crime problem" to Meyer's and Orford's crime fictional detectives and concludes that "the post-apartheid crime thriller should be read as negotiating – in the ambivalent sense of the word – the threat and uncertainty that many feel to be part of South African life, creating fantasies of control, restoration and maintenance [...]" (2012, 991). Thus crime fiction reproduces the larger discourse about crime, the "criminal obsessions," which the Comaroffs read as an "effort to *produce* social order" (2004, 822, original emphasis). On the other hand, crime fiction can serve to critique discourses about crime. In her analysis of Truth Commission thrillers, Shameem Black demonstrates how crime fiction reveals the limits of the national narrative of disclosure and healing in its attempt to overcome the atrocities of apartheid (2011). De Kock offers another example of the critical stance that crime fiction can take, namely that of bringing to light "'crime' and disorder in the public

---

18 This section is derived in part from an article published in *The Journal of Commonwealth Literature* December 29, 2015, available online: http://jcl.sagepub.com, DOI: 10.1177/0021989415619466.

19 Examples of South African crime films include *Hijack Stories* (2000), *Tsotsi* (2005), *Jerusalema* (2008), *A Small Town Called Descent* (2010), *Menda City* (2011), *State of Violence* (2011), *How To Steal 2 Million* (2011), *Four Corners* (2014) and *iNumber Number* (2014) (Nicol 2014). Jean and John Comaroff discuss South African crime drama as part of the discourse on crime (2016, 83–98).

20 Prominent true-crime writers include the investigative journalists Antony Altbeker, Jonny Steinberg, Mandy Wiener, Barry Bateman, Alex Eliseev and Julian Rademeyer, among others. See Nicol's article for a discussion and for interviews with some of these writers (Nicol 2014).

body itself" (2015, 35). Doing "the work of social detection," crime fiction exposes the new social and moral economy of the country, in which "the borderlines of legitimate and illegitimate, now far less clear or identifiable, are under erasure" and which, ultimately, has compromised the democratic ideal (36). With reference to the early crime novels by Meyer, Nicol and Roger Smith, De Kock argues that the plotting of crime fiction repeats, and thereby reveals, the plotting of the "agents of self-enrichment and public-sphere corruption" (34) in the South African real. Under these circumstances, he maintains, "[t]he task of the writer (and the critic), then, is to make the transition – or the fiction of the transition – visible and tractable by plotting its characters, their sphere of operation, their motives and modus operandi, and ultimately, their deeds and the social meaning thereof" (35).

Crime fiction can occupy yet another place in relation to the larger crime discourse; it can be itself a discourse of resistance and empowerment. Matthew Christensen demonstrates how it can teach us ways to behave and survive in a world governed by neo-liberal rationales. Crime fiction manoeuvres "the chasm between popular and official narratives of collective justice in moments of acute transformation in the relationship between the individual and the state" (2015, 315). What is more, by creating fictional characters who refuse to give in to the threat and terror created both by real crime and by the discourse about it, who refuse to reproduce the awareness of powerlessness and resolve to act against all the odds, such crime fiction offers coping strategies, as Marla Harris notes (2013, 124). This is, of course, a form of mediating fears, but it goes a step further by countering debilitating stereotypes and creating fantasies of empowerment, notably with regard to gender.

4 Post-Transitional Gender Conflicts

When it comes to gender, the transition and the post-transition periods in South Africa are characterised by a seeming contradiction: "women are legislatively empowered, and yet we do not feel safe in our streets or homes," as Pumla Dineo Gqola, a South African public intellectual and gender activist, summarises it (2007, 116). In the midst of the country's hyper-awareness of race, this contrast has brought into sharp focus the importance of attending to issues of gender, too. A large amount of post-transitional South African writing, and certainly all the crime writing discussed here, focuses on gender dynamics, gender inequalities and gender-based violence.

On the one hand, South African women's rights and protection are constitutionally guaranteed. Women were at the forefront of protest and organisation against apartheid from at least the 1950s, and they took up arms in the struggle for democracy (Meintjes 2001, 64; 69). After the end of apartheid, women were able to sustain political influence and managed to secure their interests and protection in the country's new constitution (69–70). In Cheryl McEwan's words, "This is one of the most progressive constitutions in the world and its guarantees are potentially revolutionary [...]" (2000, 633). And yet, Gqola protests that "women are denied the very freedom that 'empowerment' suggests, the very freedom the Constitution protects," as their "bodies are seen as accessible for consumption – touching, raping, kidnapping, commenting on, grabbing, twisting, beating, burning, maiming – and control" (2007, 120). "A genuinely gender-progressive country," Gqola emphasises, "is without the gender based violence statistics that South Africa has, making South African women collectively a majority (at 52 per cent) under siege" (117). Exactly what these statistics are able to reveal is questionable. For various reasons, including underreporting, accurate statistics about gender-based violence are hard to come by. However, it is said that up to 40% to 50% of women in South Africa have experienced sexual violence (Snodgrass 2015, par. 4). Based on official crime statistics, Rachel Jewkes and Robert Morrell report that South Africa's rape rate ranks as "the highest of any INTERPOL member country, with more than 55,000 rapes reported to the police annually" (2010, 2). The website of Rape Crisis South Africa states:

> Rape in South Africa has emerged as a crime of extreme violence. Commentators liken the types of rape they see in South Africa to those perpetrated during armed conflict, in terms of the degradation, ritual humiliation and the extent of injuries, such as mutilation, that are involved. [...] A recent national mortuary-based study concluded that in South Africa a woman is killed every six hours by an intimate partner, another record-setting statistic.
> RAPE CRISIS SOUTH AFRICA 2017, par. 6

Such extremely widespread gender-based violence, including the various forms of structural violence that facilitate it, has given rise to numerous attempts at explaining and theorising across a wide range of disciplines. Recurring modes of explanation refer to the colonial and apartheid past and the ways in which it fostered violent masculinities; to the impact on men of the transition and its *de jure* female empowerment and continuing high rates of unemployment and poverty; and, with increasing urgency, to a pervasive culture of tolerance and impunity of gender-based violence (Meintjes 1998, Morrell 2001, Moffett 2006, Hamber 2007, Meintjes 2011, Gqola 2015). Louise du Toit provides a useful overview of the field, which she organises and discusses in four interpretative frames. The first two, which she observes as prevalent and dominant in both academic and popular discourse, she calls the "past perpetrator trauma" and the "current social exclusion" interpretative frames (2014, 102). They have in common that they explain men's violent behaviour as a result of colonial/apartheid-oppression or post-transitional socioeconomic marginalisation to the point of emasculation (103, 108). Du Toit criticises both of these frames for othering the phenomenon and the perpetrators on the basis of either race or class (110). She also maintains that neither of these oppressive factors has been limited to men (105, 108). Besides standing in contradiction to the statistical fact that most acts of gender-based violence occur within the perpetrators' own communities (108), these frames also serve to reduce a perpetrator's accountability (107). The third interpretative frame, which Du Toit labels "feminist", is the "patriarchal-politics" frame (112). It denotes what is generally referred to as a patriarchal backlash, often in the aftermath of violent conflict. Thus Sheila Meintjes, Anu Pillay and Meredeth Turshen argue that "the gender violence women experience in wartime increases when the fighting dies down" (2001, 4). They consider that the new power relations women have established during the struggle, and now seek to maintain, are met with the violence of men who want to reassert the old status quo (11–13). Helen Moffett shares this view. She states that "in post-apartheid, democratic South Africa, sexual violence has become a socially endorsed punitive project for maintaining patriarchal order" (2006, 129). In similar vein, Desiree Lewis describes acts of sexual violence directed against Black lesbians as "a backlash against individual sexual freedoms [which] have increased in the face of constitutional and legislative rights to sexual freedoms" (2009, 130). Du Toit favours this interpretative frame over the previous two because it acknowledges the political function of sexual violence and helps to explain its intracommunal and gendered nature, as well as the fact that it is not confined to certain ethnic groups or social classes (2014, 115). Still, she finds fault with a frame that sees sexual violence as a result of a patriarchal crisis, as a symptom of "too much democracy" (114). Not only is it unhelpful in accounting for the fact that a lot of violence against women takes a specifically sexual form – given that "[t]here are many forms of violence that can serve the purpose of terrorizing a subordinate group" (116–117) – but it wrongly "presumes that women in South Africa [...] are already included as the political opponents of men. This is to claim too much" (117). Du Toit therefore prefers a fourth approach, namely an "ontological-violence" interpretative frame. Within this frame, sexual violence is less an instrument for women's oppression, with a message directed at women, than an instrument to perform and produce male dominance, with a message directed at other men (118). This specific display of male dominance via sexual violence – which, ultimately, is a perpetuation of patriarchal culture – is particularly tempting for men in present-day South Africa, Du Toit argues, because it is illegal and thus considered daring, but still relatively risk-free, given the low conviction rates, the dysfunctional criminal justice system and the pervasive myths that put the blame for rape on victims (119). A further temptation for the perpetrator, according to Du Toit, lies in the fact that the sexual nature of the crime targets the very world of the victim and thereby bestows power on the perpetrator (120). She concludes that, through an ontological-violence interpretative frame, "we can hold men accountable for rape, even as we address the patriarchal frame and social complicity that heighten the attractiveness of rape for them. Whereas talk of injured masculinities seems to imply that the realisation of women's rights must be curbed, the current frame indicates the opposite" (121). The importance of exposing and countering social complicity – be it in the form of victim-blame, looking away or trivialising sexual violence – is underscored by Gqola too, particularly since it facilitates a culture of impunity.[21] She claims, "It is time to apply pressure on men who rape, those who make excuses for rapists, those who make rape 'jokes', and to pressure our government to create a criminal justice system that works to bring the possibility of justice to rape survivors and all other survivors of violence" (2015, 15–16). Crime fiction raises these issues of complicity, impunity and justice for women time and again. It makes plain that the law is not (enough) for women: legal rights alone do not suffice, while the criminal justice system is biased.

5 Preview of Chapters

The study falls into three parts, focusing in turn on the figures of the female victim, the female perpetrator and the female detective. Each figure offers a very specific view not only on female experience, but on the fictional construction and contestation of gendered and racialised subjectivities and the scope of their agency in the field of crime, law and justice in South Africa. At the same time, the boundaries between the three figures are not always as clear-cut as they might appear. Victims may turn into detectives, or, alternatively, into perpetrators. Some detectives, too, take up their guns and kill – and not only in self-defence, thus blending with the perpetrators. They are also frequently

---

21 In her decolonial analysis of media reportage on the life and death of Anene Booysen, Floretta Boonzaier finds the media reproducing victim blaming discourse (2017, 476).

attacked, becoming victims themselves. In addition, they sometimes become the victims' advocates – or even, unwittingly, the perpetrators'. Blurring the figures of victim, perpetrator and detective allows authors to mirror the complexities of contemporary South Africa – in business and politics, the law, ethics and female subjectivities.

The first part of *Women and Crime* analyses the crime novels of Penny Lorimer, Malla Nunn and Margie Orford, all of which give unusual prominence to the victim and her story, be it as dead body or as survivor. If, according to Judith Butler, "grievability is a presupposition for the life that matters" (2010, 14), these novels are concerned with those lives that are not recognised as "grievable." This part of the book revolves around the question of whether and under what circumstances the crime generic frame allows for an emergence – or facilitates the effacement/silencing – of the victim's story and her trauma. It asks whether the South African crime novel can function as an extension or corrective of the TRC by providing a platform for female victims. This is pertinent, given the potential for violence inherent in the representation of the violated female body.

Part two of the study focuses on the female perpetrator figure, who may be read as a radical answer to female victimhood. If the works discussed in part one are about doing justice to female victims by acknowledging their stories of pain, the female perpetrators in the novels of Mike Nicol, Jassy Mackenzie and Angela Makholwa stand for retributive justice; the kind of justice that the TRC sought to avert. The central question here is what happens if women resort to violent means and take the weapons of revenge into their own hands. It is a question that points to both the threat that fictional female violence poses and the empowerment that lies in this masculine gender performance for a woman.

While the female detective shares some of the female perpetrator's frustration with the biased legal and gender system, she seeks to bring about change from within, as an agent and critic of the law. In part three, I examine the female detective who appears in the novels of Michéle Rowe, Hawa Jande Golakai and Charlotte Otter. I interrogate how they navigate the tensions to which they are subjected as female professionals in male-dominated institutions and how they resist and negotiate the law's construction of gender and race.

Pumla Gqola laments the fact that in South Africa gender-based violence is often made women's responsibility. Women are advised to take precautions against violence by being vigilant, dressing conservatively or avoiding deserted areas, especially at night: in short, they should modify *their* behaviour, as they are expected to play by the rules of dominant patriarchy (2007, 120–121). In the workplace too, Gqola contends, it is expected that "women should adapt to the current system, being 'empowered' into position, rather than transforming the formal workplace into a space that is more receptive to women's contributions, needs and wants" (115–116). Each in her own ways, and from a great diversity of subject positions, the three female figures examined in this study react to and engage with the social and political pressures that Gqola describes.

CHAPTER 1

The Female Victim

Whose Story Is Written on Her Dead Body? Exploring the Gender Politics of Writing Female Victims and Their Traumas

1   The Female Victim: Introduction

Crime novels are either narratives of investigators or narratives of criminals – rarely are they narratives of victims. While the murderer and, subsequently, the detective in some sense write their stories on the victim's body, the victim, often conventionally female, seldom gets the chance to tell her story. If she does, her tale risks being hijacked by the audience as pornographic spectacle, especially if it is one of sexual violence (Du Toit 2005, 257–258). Reading crime fiction through the lens of the female victim, thereby foregrounding her traumas as well as the potential for violence inherent in the representation of femaleness, is therefore a novel approach. My analysis of the female victim is based on a selection of contemporary South African crime novels that not only give unusual prominence to the female victim, but do so with a view to emphasising via fictional narration the real crimes that South African women suffer. The authors thereby become the female victims' advocates. I contend that, in so far as they give narrative shape to the female victim's story, these crime novels can be read as trauma novels that function to testify to and process through fiction the trauma of past and present real violence against women. At the same time, this fictional reworking of trauma constitutes a political act, as it exposes and revises – and at times reiterates – gendered and racial assumptions about women as victims, and of women's suffering and its representation in a local, South African – as well as in a global, generic – context. This raises some important questions. First, to what extent is it possible, within the generic frame of crime fiction and with a focus on the female victim – both as dead body and as survivor – to write against empirical gender violence? Secondly, can this be done in ethical as well as gender-revisionist ways that do justice to the victim's own trauma, in ways that have the potential to counterbalance the danger of sacrificing the female victim anew in narrative? For possible strategies, if not answers, I will examine *Finders Weepers* (2014) by Penny Lorimer, *Blessed Are the Dead* (2012) by Malla Nunn and Margie Orford's Clare Hart Series. Before doing so, however, I will discuss the complexities inherent in

© SABINE BINDER, 2021 | DOI:10.1163/9789004437449_003
This is an open access chapter distributed under the terms of the CC-BY-NC-ND 4.0 license.

writing the female victim in a South African crime novel and then suggest a theoretical approach.[1]

1.1   The Female Victim in Crime Fiction and in South Africa

Closely looked at, but not seen, the victim is both the spectacular beginning of the crime novel and its invisible centre. Gill Plain calls it the "deep structural irony" within the crime fiction genre that "'the body' is both crucial to and yet often overlooked by the fictional process" (2001, 12). Martin Edwards perceives a move in the genre's treatment of the victim from a mere "cipher" and a "signal for a battle [...] between murderer and sleuth" during the Golden Age (1999, 478) towards today's "realistic depiction of those destroyed by crime" (479). Kathleen Gregory Klein argues that, in the course of a crime novel, the victim becomes less visible and fades almost into irrelevance, as "the narrative of investigation supersedes the narrative of crime" (1995, 173).

The victim shares this paradoxical position of invisibility despite high visibility with people of colour. Beginning with W.E.B. Du Bois, African American authors have repeatedly problematised the experience of the racially different subject as simultaneously attracting and deflecting the gaze, and being rendered invisible in the process (Steffen 2012, 195, 199). The arrival of feminist crime writing in the 1980s and 1990s brought with it an attention to female victimhood, especially in relation to sexual violence. Its major concern, according to Priscilla Walton, was with "the thorny issue of the relationship between woman's victimization and woman's agency," between her "endangerment and empowerment" (2013, 23). However, this tension was mostly negotiated through the figure of the female detective and the female detective as victim.[2] In addition to her relative invisibility, the female victim comes with the baggage of the gender stereotype. Traditionally, the role of the victim is ascribed to women. Klein goes so far as to argue that "the victim – or [...] 'the body' in the library – is, despite biology, always female" (1995, 173). She finds support for this in the victim's occupying the second position in the criminal/victim binary and in the victim's gradual disappearance as, in the course of the investigation, the detective gains ascendancy over the criminal.

---

1   This chapter is derived in part from an article published in *Current Writing: Text and Reception in Southern Africa* October 2017, copyright the Editorial Board *Current Writing*, available online: http://www.tandfonline.com, DOI: 10.1080/1013929X.2017.1347424.

2   Until very recently, this focus on the female detective and her agency has been reflected in feminist scholarship on crime fiction (Walton and Jones 1999, Kinsman 2010, to name but a few examples).

In the South African context, when we leave the crime site of the fictional for that of the real, the female victim is no less fraught. In a society long characterised by violent crime, the need to acknowledge the victim seems crucial, whether this entails a symbolic acknowledgement of those female victims who are dead and can no longer bear witness, or an acknowledgement of those victims who survive to tell their stories. The need to listen to a woman's story of the pain inflicted, to trust its truth value, could be considered a precondition for reconciliation, for reparation as well as for individual healing. Indeed, these are the foundational assumptions of the TRC. As the experience of South African women with the TRC has made evident, attending to victims and their narratives of trauma is not a gender-neutral practice. Writing the female victim is a risky endeavour – made even riskier when she is a woman of colour – since the necessity of protecting the victim from further, secondary trauma is set in difficult relation to the necessity of exposing injustices and precipitating change. The necessity of acknowledging her as a victim is opposed to the danger of fixing her, almost as a cipher, in victim status and of perpetuating racial and gender stereotypes of invisibility, passivity, subordination and inferiority.[3] Moreover, as the historian Svenja Goltermann reminds us, the very category of "victim" is by no means a stable one. Who is defined as a victim in the first place, and who is not, depends on power structures, as well as the victim's personal perception (2015).[4]

1.2 *Theoretical Preliminaries*

Chris van der Merwe and Pumla Gobodo-Madikizela point out that " 'translating' trauma into the structure of a language and a narrative is a way of bringing order and coherence into the chaotic experience" (2008, 15). For this reason, I propose to read the crime novels examined in this section as trauma novels and the victim's story as both a – necessarily mediated – testimony of gendered "truth" and a feminist-political act. This approach is informed both by postcolonial literary trauma theory and by scholarship on the gendered dimensions of bearing witness following the work of the South African TRC. In addition, I will focus on interrelated questions of ethics and aesthetics in representing female victims. This part of my discussion is informed by Elisabeth Bronfen's studies on death and femininity and by Michele Aaron's work on the ethics of spectatorship.

---

3   With regard to speaking about rape, Du Toit, drawing on Plato and Derrida, alerts us to the notion of language as *pharmakon*, as having the capacity to act as either medicine or poison, a capacity that cannot be controlled easily (Du Toit 2005, 257).

4   Goltermann bases this last point on Ashraf Kagee's research on political prisoners in South Africa. The prisoners see themselves not only as victims of the apartheid regime, but as heroes in the struggle for democracy (2015, 89–90).

At this point, I want to clarify what I mean by the term "postcolonial literary trauma theory" and highlight three pivotal respects in which it overlaps with South African feminist criticism of the TRC. The term "postcolonial literary trauma theory" does not exist *per se*, nor does it refer to a unified theoretical body of ideas. Instead, I use it to draw together various postcolonial critics of the early scholarship on trauma in the field of literature, such as Michelle Balaev, Barry Stampfl, Irene Visser, Ewald Mengel and Michela Borzaga.[5] Although these scholars' views vary considerably,[6] all of them criticise the Eurocentricity of the early trauma model and are sceptical of its ability to account for trauma as it is represented in literature emerging from postcolonial situations. In particular, they take issue with the Caruthian notion of trauma as unknowable, unclaimable and unrepresentable (Balaev 2014, 1). Mengel and Borzaga state:

> Notably, Western theorists of trauma like Cathy Caruth, Dori Laub or Geoffrey Hartman, whose theories are informed by deconstruction, have treated trauma as an unclaimed (and unclaimable) experience. By putting trauma at the centre of a theory of representation, their *melancholic* vocabulary is one marked by notions of absence, holes, deferral, crises of meanings, unknowing, and dissociation, in this way precluding any possibility of healing for individuals or entire nations.
>
> 2012a, xiii, original emphasis

While Balaev concedes that "amnesia, dissociation, or repression *may* be responses to trauma," she does not consider them "exclusive responses" (2014, 6, original emphasis). She shares the claim of postcolonial literary trauma theorists that traumatic experience can be known and claimed, and that transformation

---

5   Michelle Balaev coins an umbrella term for the diverse body of criticism of classic trauma models, namely "the pluralistic model of trauma" (2014, 3). Barry Stampfl uses the term "revisionist trauma studies" (2014, 37). Both Balaev (2014, 1–8) and Stampfl (2014, 15–22) offer a detailed discussion and criticism of the work of Shoshana Feldman, Dori Laub, Cathy Caruth and other early trauma scholars. Stampfl further provides an overview of the revisionist literature, starting with Dominick LaCapra and Ruth Leys and extending beyond the postcolonial perspective (2014, 16; 36–37). Irene Visser offers a criticism of the early scholarship as well as an overview of existing work from a specifically postcolonial perspective (2011, 2015).

6   While some critics consider it necessary to decolonise, or adapt and modify the tenets of classic trauma theory in order to render it fruitful for postcolonial situations, Mengel and Borzaga seek to incorporate existing but long-excluded studies by thinkers such as Frantz Fanon, Albert Memmi and Ashis Nandy, which link trauma, colonialism and racism (2012a, xii-xiii).

and healing are therefore possible, at least to some extent. In her reading of South African literature, which draws on Mengel's and Borzaga's essays, Visser demonstrates that the collective traumatisation of generations of South Africans is neither "an unclaimed nor unclaimable experience, but rather is reclaimed in narrative" and that "the characters find ways of coming to terms with the past and moving on with their lives in new and creative ways" (2014, 117). In a similar vein, Fiona Ross alerts us to the ways in which the TRC framed female victims of apartheid as "unable to move beyond the experience of violence," thus freezing them in victimhood (2003a, 92). This is in stark contrast to her own research, which testifies to women's ability to recuperate and to remake their lives not only for themselves, but for those around them (Ross 2003a, 20, 139–141, 161).

As well as according victims the potential for healing and transformation of the traumatic experience, postcolonial literary trauma theory and South African studies on women and the TRC agree on two more pivotal points. First, they call for a widening of the scope of trauma to include the effects of long-term structural or systemic violence emanating from conditions such as patriarchy, colonialism or apartheid.[7] Christopher J. Colvin (2008, 230), Mengel and Borzaga (2012a, xi) and Stampfl (2014, 24, 37) all point to the need to move away from an event-based notion of trauma in situations like the South African one, not least because it "'medicalises' and 'privatises' suffering" and thereby "remove[s it] from the world of political and moral debate" (Colvin 2008, 230). In her critique of the TRC's narrow focus on bodily harm, Ross concurs:

> The physical experience of pain is but a part of a far wider destruction. By focusing too closely on bodily experience, we run the danger of failing to attend to the experiences of which women speak. A focus solely on the body and its violation fixes experience in time, in an event, and draws attention away from ways of understanding of that experience as *a process that endures across bodies and through time.*
>
> ROSS 2003a, 49, my emphasis

Besides offering a limited account of women's suffering and eliding harmful social consequences, such a reductive understanding of trauma reinscribes

---

7   "Structural" or "systemic" violence refers to the systematic continual and continuing harm to individuals that results from social, economic and political structures. Colonialism, patriarchy, apartheid, poverty, sustained police harassment, persistent discrimination and humiliation, confiscation of land, constant surveillance or racially formulated education are often cited as examples of this type of violence in a South African context (Ross 2003a, 21–22; 30, Van der Merwe and Gobodo-Madikizela 2008, 10–11, Colvin 2008, 230).

gender differences, Ross argues (2003b, 176). This point is emphasised by Tristan Anne Borer, who notes that women have been shown to suffer from structural violence even more than men (2009, 1174).

Secondly, literary scholarship on trauma in the post-colony and studies on women and the TRC agree on the need to highlight victims' agency, resistance and resilience in the face of trauma. Colvin warns against ignoring traumatised individuals' coping strategies and resources, including local ones, as well as their capacity to assign culturally specific meaning to trauma (2008, 231). Similarly, Visser maintains that "agency and empowerment might need to be incorporated as modes of theorizing trauma's aftermath" (2011, 279). Balaev sees early trauma scholars as removing agency from survivors by "disregarding a survivor's knowledge of the experience and the self" (2014, 6), while Ross's research on the violations that women suffered during apartheid reveals how the TRC's definition of women as victims tends to downplay their agency and resistance (Ross 2003b, 175). She, too, opposes a limiting view of victims that disregards women's other roles, resilience, survival strategies and agency amidst and despite suffering (Ross 2003b, 175).

The contribution of gendered criticism of the TRC to postcolonial literary trauma theory makes clear that gender matters when attending to victims and their trauma – be they real or fictional. The TRC's failure to uncover the full extent of women's sufferings under apartheid (Ross 2003a, b, 2008, Borer 2009) has had severe and lasting consequences for women. The women who did not testify were not able to take advantage of either the psychological support services provided to statement makers or reparation grants (Goldblatt and Meintjes 1997, 15–16). What is more, the widespread use of sexual violence during apartheid and the way in which it functioned as a weapon of war have been left unacknowledged. Worst of all, the perpetrators of these crimes have not been held accountable (Borer 2009, 1179). This unacknowledged legacy of past violence has led to an acceptance of violence against women in the present (Goldblatt and Meintjes 1997, 14) or, in Borer's terms, to "a culture of sexual violence in South Africa" rather than "a culture of rights" (2009, 1180). Ultimately, the way in which patriarchy served as a means of supporting racial discrimination has remained off the record (1180). While the nexus between trauma, memory and narrative has been the object of considerable attention in South African literary studies more generally,[8] so far, postcolonial literary trauma

---

8 Contributions include the essay collections edited by Jaspal K. Singh and Rajendra Chetty (2010), Mengel and Borzaga (2012b) and Chris Andrews and Matt McGuire (2016, Section II: South Africa) as well as individual essays by Chris van der Merwe and Pumla Gobodo-Madikizela (2008, chapters four and five), Mengel (2009), Rosalind C. Morris (2011) and Visser (2014).

theory – let alone with a focus on gender – has not been applied to an in-depth reading of South African crime fiction. This is surprising, given the fact that the enactment, re-enactment or at least recapitulation of a traumatic event, and often also the quest for "truth", are part and parcel of the crime genre. What is more, the genre's serial nature lends itself both to a fictional compulsive repetition of trauma and/or a working through of trauma. In his essay on trauma and genre in the South African novel, Mengel lists crime among the genres with an "inherent suitability for and special affinity with the representation of trauma" (2012, 146) and notes the common concern with truth-finding of both crime fiction and the South African TRC (160–162). These connections will be explored further in my analysis of the crime novels of Penny Lorimer, Malla Nunn and Margie Orford.

2   Boniswa Sekeyi and Lulu: Witnesses of Systemic and Sexual Violence in Penny Lorimer's *Finders Weepers*

> "I want to charge him," said Lulu. Her voice tightened.
> She had been fiercely insistent on reporting Nyumbane, despite my warning that she in turn might be accused of instigating a flirtation.
> […]
> "What I will say is just the truth," she stated. "If people want to doubt, then they can doubt, but I will know. Miss S always told us to be honest."
>
>   LULU in *Finders Weepers* (156–157)

Miss S – Boniswa Sekeyi – is the principal of Girdwood College, a once-illustrious mission school in South Africa's poverty-stricken Eastern Cape, and the murder victim in Penny Lorimer's debut detective novel *Finders Weepers*. Her promising student and protégé Lulu falls prey to South Africa's education system and to sexual abuse. This chapter argues that, with Boniswa and Lulu, Lorimer pursues alternative approaches to writing female victims and their traumas within the frame of the crime genre. Not only does she resist existing representational practices of violated female bodies that deflect from the individual woman's pain, but she effectively addresses the structural violence of the South African education system and the ways in which it perpetuates gender inequality and gender violence.

In *Finders Weepers,* the I-narrator Nix Mniki, who is of mixed Xhosa/German parentage and a broadcast journalist, recounts the story of her investigation into the murder of her mother's best friend's daughter, Boniswa Sekeyi, newly appointed principal of Girdwood College. Nix's narrative is interspersed at regular intervals with the emails Boniswa had been sending to her American friend and mentor, Dr Pauline Wilson, from the moment she took over as principal of Girdwood College until the day before she died. Boniswa's emails provide a kind of fictional documentation of the state crime that is South Africa's education crisis. Together with the journalistic piece on the history of South African mission schools that concludes *Finders Weepers*, the emails lend a touch of the documentary to Lorimer's detective novel. They are testament to an urge on the part of the author to supplement the crime fictional "truth" with a more factual kind of truth. The "documentary turn", or the "desire (or need) to document," as Leon de Kock terms it, is commonly found in South African literature following the TRC (2016a, 179).

Published in 2014, *Finders Weepers* is Lorimer's debut adult detective novel. Previously, the White author had written school textbooks, short stories and young adult crime fiction. Born in England, Lorimer has lived in South Africa from the age of six months. A trained actress, she has been a union administrator and a PA to an archbishop, and has had various jobs in the media. She is currently working in the education sector (Lorimer 2015, par. 2). In my discussion of Lorimer's novel, I will focus first on its ethics and aesthetics of representation. Next, I will look at the testimonial content of *Finders Weepers* and its gendered implications.

2.1 *Absent in Presence—Present in Absence: Representational Practices of (Dead) Female Bodies*

The case of journalist-investigator Nix Mniki is triggered by a female victim – true to genre conventions. Boniswa Sekeyi is missing and her mother fears the worst. It is the absence, rather than the presence, of the female body that marks the opening of the detective novel. Only a few pages later, however, we read the first of Boniswa's many emails to her American friend. Boniswa's sudden, spectral and unmitigated presence as murder victim through her own voice in her emails comes as a complete surprise to readers of crime fiction. I argue here – following Elisabeth Bronfen – that, by rendering Boniswa as both absent and present in the narrative, the author stages sacrificial representational practices, as femininity in stereotypical representation is characterised by simultaneous presence and absence (1992, 1995).

An intriguing absence is contained in the novel's very title. Derived from the adage "finders keepers, losers weepers," the title encloses a lacuna. Ending on "weepers," it merely echoes the "keepers" that are lost, thus emphasising what is not actually there, what is missing. For Nix, Boniswa has been an absent presence all her life. Their mothers are close friends, but the girls, although of almost the same age, have never met, as Boniswa grew up with her grandparents and later went abroad to study. Boniswa has always been a rather begrudged barometer in Nix's life: "As long as I could remember, my mother had held up Princess' daughter as the epitome of intellectual brilliance, a model of all that a truly dutiful child should be" (Lorimer 2014, 8). Understandably, Nix harbours no kind feelings for Boniswa, whom she resentfully names "Perfect Example Girl" or "PE Girl" (9, 10). To Nix, Boniswa is the one who is already lost before she actually finds her in more ways than one. By the time Nix finally encounters Boniswa's dead body (about halfway into the novel), Nix has paradoxically come to feel that she knows her and experiences her loss. Through her investigation, Nix has discovered a young woman whom she might actually have liked, and Boniswa in death becomes somebody she has come to admire and sympathise with. Even in death, Boniswa is there and not there, hidden in plain sight. Boniswa's dead body literally remains hidden in the midst of the frenzy of Girdwood College – precisely where Nix has come to look for her, but fails to see her for a large part of the novel. With reference to Bronfen's work, I will show how Lorimer's simultaneous absenting and presenting of the female victim and her body can be read as a reflection of representational practices of both femininity and death. Viewed in this light, what is literally missing in the title – "keepers, losers" – is a nod to the presence/absence specifically of *women*.

Taking a semiotic, aesthetic and psychoanalytical perspective in her work on femininity and representation, Bronfen shows that in stereotypical cultural representations – and the female victim is such a stereotype – woman is always a representative of something other than herself and hence not represented as a subject (1995, 412). Bronfen bases her claim on Teresa de Lauretis's differentiation between *woman* and *women*. The stereotypical *woman* is the object of representation, whom we look at. She is the purpose and origin of male desire and, as such, a construction. *Women* on the other hand are real, historical, physically existing women in De Lauretis's understanding. *Woman* and *women* do not coincide, yet *women* cannot be defined outside this discursive formation (410). While *woman* is pervasive as a signifier, what she signifies is not *women*. In representations, *woman* is present precisely in absenting real *women*. She is a representative, a proxy, a lacuna, her body a screen. Bronfen thus cautions us always to ask what ideological purpose lies behind the extinction of empirical women in the process of representation (420). Whose norms and whose interests are represented by *woman*, and what is it that she actually signifies (421)? If read psychoanalytically, cultural representations for Bronfen become collective symptoms, moments where suppressed material finds expression.

As such, representations become leftovers, traces of what has been relegated to the unconscious, of what otherwise is unspeakable or unacceptable (425–427). According to psychoanalytically informed work by feminist film scholars, the woman in representation becomes a means to negotiate male sexuality – the position of the spectator being coded as masculine. It is assumed that, when the male spectator looks at a woman, he sees a castrated version of his own body. The female body is a reminder of loss and evokes feelings of threat and anxiety in him. However, he also sees a maternal body reminding him of a primordial, now lost, state of wholeness. According to Lacanian logic, this female body offers comfort to the male spectator at the same time as it sets his desire in motion, as he futilely attempts to regain this state of wholeness and unity (429–431). Since woman thus signifies both threat *and* safety, Bronfen terms her position an impossible, if not uncanny one: woman stages male rule[9] and its impossibility at the same time (432).

Importantly, besides being coded as male, the spectator is coded as White. In her reading of W.E.B. Du Bois's concept of the veil, Therese Steffen shows how the veil, in the eyes of the dominant White viewer, negates the individuality of the person of colour, silencing and transforming him or her into a mere screen (2012, 190). If whatever woman signifies is not about her as a subject, such that her subjectivity is completely effaced, the woman of colour is doubly effaced in representation.[10] As Bronfen notes in her seminal work on death and femininity, "death is at work in the cultural construction of femininity" (1992, 208). She argues that, in representation, femininity and death function in analogous ways. Like femininity, death is ungraspable and lacks any empirical object: "Placed beyond the register of images that the living body can know, '[d]eath' can only be read as a trope, as a signifier with an incessantly receding, ungraspable signified, invariably always pointing back self-reflexively to other signifiers" (54). Bronfen demonstrates how representations of both femininity and death culturally work to "appease the threat of real mortality, of sexual insufficiency, of lack of plenitude and wholeness" (xii). The death of a woman thus becomes a "social sacrifice" (181), aimed at arresting in representation what cannot be arrested in reality – i.e. the dual threat of femininity and mortality – so as to preserve cultural norms. In the case of the death of a woman

---

9   Bronfen uses the German word "Herrschaft", which means male dominance, but also male rule and male control.
10 Chandra Talpade Mohanty bases her critique of Western feminist theory on De Lauretis's distinction between *woman* and *women*. She sees Western feminists as producing the "Third World Woman", an arbitrary construction that discursively colonises "the material and historical heterogeneities of the lives of women in the third world" (1984, 334).

of colour, we can add, the sacrifice becomes a twofold one, stemming from the added threat of the racially other. It is this theoretical frame that helps to explain why *real women*'s testimonies of sexual abuse are so prone to being appropriated by the audience as pornography. As Louise du Toit observes, "The attempt to represent an *experience of female pain* with the aim of fighting or stopping it, [may be] hijacked by an audience who reads it [...] as a *spectacle of male pleasure*" (2005, 257–258, original emphasis). Fiona Ross recounts the example of a woman who testified before the TRC. While she spoke out about the many different harms that she had suffered, one of which was sexual violation, she found herself framed by the TRC solely as a victim of sexual violence. This was reinforced by subsequent media reports that exploited the very graphic details of her testimony (2003a, 82–92), in effect positioning her through the sexual violence wrought upon her female body. Here *woman* is clearly revealed as a culturally circulated construct. Real *women* and their complex pain remain invisible.

Besides mirroring this simultaneous presence and absence of femininity through the figure of Boniswa, Lorimer draws attention to the inherent dangers for a victim who publicly speaks out about her sexual violations through the Xhosa girl Lulu. When Lulu, a student of Boniswa's and a survivor of sexual abuse by a well-known teacher, is about to address the church congregation, Nix warns readers of the risks that she is taking. Nix, the I-narrator, tells us: "Lulu rose [...] [h]er white choir robe gave her a look of radiant purity, but I felt my hands gripping each other in my lap, fearful that all she would do was open herself to disbelief and rejection from her neighbours" (Lorimer 2014, 229). For the duration of Lulu's public testimony – which is conveyed in direct speech – the tension and uncertainty as to its effect on the audience is palpable. Only once the listeners acknowledge Lulu's testimony as truthful and express their determination to fight this crime can Lulu and Nix – and, by extension, we reader-spectators – relax: "They believed her. I let out a breath I seemed to have been holding for aeons" (230). Setting a counter-example to both exploitative representational practices and to the South African reality, which more often than not sees sexual offenders walk free, Lorimer has Lulu's testimony protected by the audience and acknowledged for what it is, resulting in the arrest of the perpetrator.

In representing the dead victim Boniswa, Lorimer offers two more resistant practices. First, she makes Boniswa resist the White male gaze and thus prevents her from functioning as a signifier that preserves the dominant norm.[11]

---

11 It is important to note that the "male gaze" can be adopted by anyone. "Male" here denotes an exploitative gaze that is originally coded as masculine, but can be adopted by spectators of any gender.

Secondly, she features the victim's own voice via her emails. The way in which we first get to see her is through Nix's eyes. Nix is alerted to the presence of Boniswa's dead body by cawing crows jostling around it and by the smell of decomposing flesh. Stepping closer, she notices insects and then finally sees this:

> As I parted the foliage a black buzz of flies lifted off some dark, swollen, disgusting thing. I reeled back and heard myself whimper [...] again, I squatted down and peered through the tangle of twigs and branches. First I saw a large-faced watch with a broken brown leather strap. Then a square-bladed garden spade. Finally, hair still woven in neat, intricate braids. There was no room for even the slightest doubt.
> LORIMER 2014, 136–137

What we see here is nothing but fragments. First, there is the flesh, which cannot yet be identified as human. In fact, Nix is hoping that it belongs to an animal carcass. Then we see the watch, which a neighbour later confirms to be Boniswa's: "I always tease her with her man's watch. She says she needs it to be big so that she is never late" (137). With the watch, gender comes into play, but in unconventional ways: for the neighbour, it is a man's watch, while for Boniswa it is a sign of professionalism. Next, we see a gardening tool, which may or may not be the murder weapon. Finally, there is the victim's braided hair, which serves as a racial marker. Only now is it confirmed: this is a Black female body. Nix's gaze narrows down, through a process of gradual accretion, ever more closely on to the specific human femaleness of what she discovers. And yet, we do not actually see Boniswa, not now and not later, when she is examined by a woman doctor. This is both a logical continuation of Lorimer's tactics of making us aware of the absence of the female subject, and a way of shielding Boniswa's dead body from the preying male gaze that is in search of reassurance. Fragmentation as a strategy here does not serve to fetishise the female body in order to disavow its threatening quality; rather, it functions to resist feeding the White male gaze.

Lorimer troubles this male gaze in a second way: namely, by having her victim "speak" beyond her death, beyond victimhood and beyond the confines of Nix's crime narrative. Boniswa's emails to her American friend are interspersed among and visibly set apart from the detective's account, appearing in every second or third chapter. For us as readers, therefore, Boniswa is present through her emails not only independently of Nix, but much earlier than for Nix. Nix retrieves the emails only once she finds Boniswa's laptop and manages to access her email account, about one third of the way into the novel. Because there are 28 emails in total, they carry substantial weight. They make

Boniswa a prominent presence inside and outside the detective's account and thus arguably function to break the White male gaze and to work against the effacement of Black femininity. Moreover, Lorimer's strategy has ethical reverberations. Boniswa's emails interrupt the crime narrative at regular intervals and thereby serve as an "artful reminder" to the reader of his/her ethical involvement in the representation of violence to others. According to film scholar Michele Aaron, taking pleasure in unpleasure, or in the suffering of others as a spectator, can be ethical only if "the spectator's removal and innocence with regard to the spectacle" is challenged (2007, 92), only if "the cinematic contract that sustains the safety of the spectator, licensing a safe indulgence in the unreal, with the promise that it is only temporary" (92) is broken. One way to break the cinematic contract for her is through so-called "artful reminders" (94). If we apply Aaron's cinematic concept to readers of crime fiction, the email-voice of the victim that interrupts and disrupts the crime narrative can perform this function. It removes the distance between the reader and the pain of the victim that is being represented on the page. Through Boniswa's emails, we readers learn long before Nix about her problems with her poorly performing teaching staff. We can therefore rule out the possibility that Boniswa has simply forgotten to inform her colleagues and her mother that she is on leave from school much earlier than Nix can. This, and the information about the dismal state of the South African public education system we receive, propels the reader's own ethical judgement. If we read Aaron alongside Bronfen, we can extend the argument further. The artful reminder then also serves to make tangible the reader's complicity with the gendered practices in representation, with the way in which *women* are sacrificed. It allows for an alternative gaze on the female victim that does not sacrifice her anew in representation.

To sum up, Lorimer must be credited for finding means to sustain her focus on the trauma about which she seeks to testify. Nevertheless, Boniswa remains invisible to some extent. In her emails, she gives voice less to her own pain than to the way in which her students, the wider Girdwood community and, indeed, the country are suffering as a consequence of the education crisis. Boniswa thus becomes a "secondary victim", which is problematic, particularly because she is a Black woman. Here, Lorimer may be repeating a pattern for which the TRC was heavily criticised: eliciting testimonies from women who speak as mothers and as wives and who concentrate primarily on the sufferings of their family members, remaining silent about the violence inflicted on themselves. In fact, this is another recreation of the absent female victim. As much as Boniswa's emails are testament to her agency, they recreate her, at least to some extent, as the invisible Black female victim, who serves as a screen for a story that points to a larger social ill and away from the trauma of her own death.[12]

2.2 A Testimony Uncovering Gendered Aspects of Structural Violence in State Education

The story that is partly written on Boniswa's dead body by Nix, the investigator-journalist, and partly recounted by Boniswa herself in her emails testifies to "the full horror of the effects of apartheid on the education of Black South Africans, which is something we have still not managed to correct" (Lorimer 2015, par. 7). Although the provocative subject of female pain – which Lorimer does not limit to sexual violence – is addressed in *Finders Weepers*, the narrative's main concern is with the less spectacular but historically traumatising effects of South African state education. These are mainly detailed in Boniswa's emails. Her account of the shabby, dirty, dilapidated buildings that she finds on her first day at Girdwood, with their broken stairs and windows and empty flowerbeds (Lorimer 2014, 14–15), read like a description of the current state and bleak outlook of South African education. Besides other shortcomings in the school's facilities – non-existent toilets and libraries, and a dearth of books, textbooks, photocopying machines and computers – the teachers themselves and their under-performance are described by Boniswa as a major obstacle to quality education. Not only do they lack methodical training and adequate qualifications for the subjects that they teach (64, 85), but they have a serious attitude problem, lacking both passion and interest (64, 85, 93, 117). Rampant absenteeism of teachers and students due to the shortage of transport and food, alcohol and sexual harassment further contribute to low performances and high dropout rates, as do poverty, HIV and teenage pregnancies (21, 64, 132, 148, 189, 252, 274). The appalling state education that Girdwood exemplifies in the post-transitional present is repeatedly contrasted with the college's former glory. Before apartheid, Girdwood was a famous mission school. As "the leading school for blacks in the whole country" (9), it produced many of today's leaders. Boniswa and other voices in the novel blame Girdwood's decline on several factors: the apartheid legacy of Bantu education, the powerful teachers' union, which protects underperforming teachers, petty politics and a lack of government support (64, 93, 117, 204, 257, 297–299). The salience of Lorimer's account in present-day South Africa is emphasised when we recall the stance of two prominent South African public intellectuals, Hlumelo Biko and Alex

---

[12] What is more, as a recipient of a relatively privileged education, Boniswa herself is subjected to the trauma of South African state education to a lesser extent than her students.

Boraine. Their analyses support elements of the narrative focus of *Finders Weepers*: namely, that the present flood of unqualified teachers is a legacy of Bantu education,[13] which Biko terms an "intellectual genocide of indigenous South African people" (2013, 171). Boraine, too, points to the lack of training and/or commitment of teachers (2014, 115). This reinforces inequalities because state schools in poor areas, such as the one Girdwood is modelled on, are disproportionally affected. The influential South African Democratic Teachers' Union (Sadtu) prevents change. It "has protected the majority of teachers from the harsh realities of normal competition and has facilitated the retention of a large cadre of poorly trained, de-motivated teachers" (Biko 2013, 179). As an affiliate of the influential Cosatu – the Congress of South African Trade Unions – Sadtu participates in the ANC government. Since then President "Zuma needs their support and their vote, he is unlikely to act against them" (Boraine 2014, 115). Thus, the systemic violence stemming from the legacy of Bantu education under apartheid has been actively perpetuated by the democratic South African government. "[W]ho knew," Biko accuses, "that under a black-led government, the chief casualties of bad policy making would be black children?" (2013, 187). Here the novel clearly succeeds in testifying to long-term damage and acknowledging the consequences of systemic violence, as called for by postcolonial literary trauma theory. While both Lulu and Boniswa suffer event-based trauma when having their bodies violated, the novel demonstrates that these physical violations have their genesis in structural violence: Combined with the systemic violence of an unreliable criminal justice system and public health system (251, 246–248), and unleashed on a community that is already weakened by rampant HIV, addiction and fragmented family structures (36, 55, 77), the South African education system robs children of any occupational prospects. In this way, it sustains and cements racial and gender inequalities.

Lorimer can be credited for attending expressly to the gendered dimensions of trauma founded in structural violence. Both Boniswa's sharp analysis in her emails and Nix's findings in the course of her murder investigation expose the effect of structural forms of violence on gender equality and gender relations. Boniswa describes how teenage pregnancies and a lack of sanitation facilities at school lead to poor attendance and high dropout rates among girls, further limiting an already poor education and diminishing girls' prospects (133, 164). Lulu's story illustrates the particular impact of structural violence on girls. Losing both her parents and her brother (to AIDS-related illnesses, Boniswa

---

[13] For an in-depth discussion of Bantu education and its continuing effects, as well as of the relative benefits of missionary schools, see Biko (2013, 171–197).

presumes (176)) within one year leaves Lulu particularly vulnerable and at risk of sexual violence (77, 121). Her character exemplifies the claim made by research on women and the TRC – that women suffer from structural violence in specific and aggravated ways. In addition, Boniswa points out how systemic violence harbours violence against women. She views male violence as resulting from a lack of male role models and from the way in which mothers take out their anger at being deserted on their sons (55, 148–149). Her own death is framed in these terms. Her eventual killer, the 17-year-old Sizwe, "is one of the very few students who has the academic potential to get a place at university" (148), but he lacks a male role model and is thus insecure and desperate for peer acceptance, as Boniswa recounts in her emails. When Sizwe arrives at school drunk and belligerent, she loses her temper with him and sends him home (265). This makes him feel so angry that he later kills her. When Nix finds him as the killer, he tells her that " 'she talk to me like I'm nothing. [...] I am a man. She must not talk to me like that.' " (280). Sizwe's reason for killing Boniswa is linked to gender. He kills a woman of authority for what he experiences as a humiliation of his masculinity. This is particularly ironic, since Boniswa in fact meant well. Perceiving Sizwe's potential, she wanted to make him head of the Student Representative Council and planned to help him to apply for a university bursary (148). Lorimer's explanation for Sizwe's violence against Boniswa falls within two of Du Toit's four interpretative frames, the "patriarchal-politics" frame and the "current social exclusion" frame. On the one hand, what Sizwe seems to resent here is "too much democracy," as Du Toit puts it (2014, 114): the fact that a woman exercises her lawful authority over him, which in his eyes is an act of humiliation that requires an apology (Lorimer 2014, 280). On the other hand, his sense of degradation is depicted as originating in his own victimhood. As Boniswa's mother phrases it, " 'His life was too hard. His mother was dead and I think his father beat him. He had no one to give him any direction, no values, no identity. A lot of the children here are like that. They have no self-control. They cannot grow up as they should because they are so focused on surviving [...]' " (285). By making us aware of Sizwe's own vulnerability as a young male, the novel puts the blame less on the individual Sizwe than on the larger structures responsible for his victimisation. While this serves to foreground the ways in which structural violence impacts on gender relations, and although Sizwe, through his suicide, pays a price, too, the novel nevertheless excuses Sizwe's violence, at least in parts. This is problematic if we follow Du Toit. It reduces Sizwe's accountability for the murder of Boniswa – which, after all, for him was a kind of punishment of a woman more powerful than him. There is a certain tension here between Lorimer's successful foregrounding of the traumatic effects of long-term systemic violence, the necessity for individual men's accountability and, possibly, the crime genre's preference for event-based death.

Finally, the novel rewrites female victims by depicting them as agents despite and against the oppressive structures. This is best exemplified by Lulu and her courageous decision to make her sufferings public, notwithstanding the risks of shame and vilification. Lulu is a victim, but she does not remain one. *Finders Weepers* manages to depict the agency, resilience and resourcefulness of the various victims, which allows them to go on beyond and in the midst of traumatisation. The novel is a story not just of Boniswa and Lulu, but of traumatised mothers like Nix's, who raise their daughters single-handedly (16–18); of mothers like Princess, who lose their children and still find the strength to go on and help others in need (214); of hard-working mothers who earn money far away from their children to sustain them (91–92) and of dedicated grandmothers who manage to support children and grandchildren on their tiny pensions (149). Although the victimhood of these women is by no means downplayed in the novel, the way in which they are endowed with agency prevents us from reading them as stereotypically passive and helpless. They are survivors, rather than victims. Boniswa, though, does die in the end – and she dies for having exerted her female agency and authority as a school principal. At the same time, she remains a powerful presence throughout the novel. Her emails, as well as the findings of Nix's investigation, are a testament to and celebration of her agency, her resolution to restore Girdwood to its former glory and her – in many ways, successful – mission to improve the education of her students. At the end of the novel, Nix decides to take over from her as foster mother of the orphaned student Lulu. Similar strategies of resistant agency are exemplified by Amahle, the victim at the centre of Malla Nunn's novel *Blessed Are the Dead*.

3 Resisting Arrest: Amahle Matebula, Female Victim in Malla Nunn's *Blessed Are the Dead*

> From the day my daughter was born her eyes were on the horizon and what was beyond it. I should have kept her by my side but she did not like to be watched over. Now she is gone …
>
> NOMUSA in *Blessed Are the Dead* (16)

Grief-stricken Nomusa has to acknowledge both her daughter Amahle Matebula's death and Amahle's refusal to be contained by any set boundaries, be they racial or gendered. In making the 17-year-old Zulu Amahle the focus of her fictional investigation into the past in her historical detective novel *Blessed Are the Dead*, Malla

Nunn works against arresting her victim in genre conventions.[14] Amahle's dead body refuses arrest in a very literal way, being restlessly on the move throughout the novel. From the crime site, her friend Gabriel moves her to the hill where the detectives first see her. She is then taken to the town doctor's cellar for the postmortem, from where she is stolen by her half-brother Mandla and eventually buried in her father's kraal, sitting upright. According to Zulu belief, such a position prevents her spirit from finding rest (202) – as might her bus ticket to freedom, which remains valid after her burial (254, 299). This chapter aims to elucidate the novel's revisionist potential. I argue that Nunn erodes the sacrificial male detective's gaze on Amahle's dead body, thereby revising representational practices and allowing us to see *women* beyond the construct of *woman*. By depicting Black women, specifically, as agents in the face of trauma, Nunn further revises practices of bearing witness to South African women's sufferings under early apartheid.[15] This allows Nunn to fictionally revisit and work through women's multiple traumas of patriarchal and racial oppression during that time.

Blessed Are the Dead is the third novel in Nunn's Detective Emmanuel Cooper series. Set in 1953, it takes Detective Sergeant Emmanuel Cooper and his colleague Detective Constable Samuel Shabalala of the Durban Detective Branch to the farming hamlet of Roselet in the foothills of the Drakensberg Mountains, where they investigate the murder of Amahle Matebula. the daughter of a local Zulu chief.[16] Nunn is an internationally renowned novelist, screenwriter and

---

14   Pan Macmillan Australia published *Blessed Are the Dead* as *Silent Valley* in 2012.
15   Although Nunn's account of apartheid in the early 1950s falls outside the time frame covered by the TRC, I still consider the scholarship on women and the TRC to be relevant because it reveals the gendered dimensions of bearing witness in general and sheds light on the mechanisms that silence women's agency and sustain gender inequalities in that process.
16   The novel is set in the early years of apartheid (Butler 2009, 17). In its 1948 electoral campaign, the Afrikaner National Party used the slogan of "apartheid", which soon rose to prominence. The slogan drew attention to fears of urbanisation of the country's Black population and job competition. After its victory, the National Party enacted a body of racist laws (often termed "petty apartheid") that were all in effect at the time the novel is set: the *Population Registration Act* (enforced racial classification into four categories: White, Coloured, Indian/Asiatic and Native), the *Immorality Act* (prohibiting any sexual contacts between white people and people from the other three groups) and the *Group Areas Act* (enforced residential segregation). The *Reservation of Separate Amenities Act* (segregated transport, cinemas, restaurants and sporting facilities) was enacted in 1953 (Butler 2009, 16–17). While it laid much of the groundwork, according to Butler, " 'petty' apartheid legislation was not designed to reshape South Africa's structures of economic opportunity but was distinguished by its undisguised racial malevolence" (17). It was later, in the 1960s, during "high apartheid" that social engineering assumed a comprehensive, qualitatively distinct scale (20).

film director and has won numerous awards for both her writing and her films. She has published four detective novels in the Detective Emmanuel Cooper series, all of which are set in South Africa: *A Beautiful Place to Die* (2009), *Let the Dead Lie* (2010), *Blessed Are the Dead* (2012) and *Present Darkness* (2014), as well as the young adult novel *When the Ground is Hard* (2019). Her filmography includes *Fade to White* (1991), *Sweetbreeze* (1992) and *Servant of the Ancestors* (1998). *Blessed Are the Dead*, the novel discussed in this chapter, was nominated for the Edgar Award, was short-listed for an Anthony Award and a Ned Kelly Award and was a 2013 Publishers' Weekly Top Ten Summer Crime Read. Nunn was born and schooled in Swaziland (now eSwatini) before emigrating to Australia. She attended universities in Australia and America and currently lives in Sydney (Krimi-Couch 2016, par. 1, 3, Nunn 2010a, par. 6, Key West Literary Seminar 2016, par. 1–3). In my analysis of *Blessed Are the Dead*, I will begin by identifying the novel's ways of remembering and reworking trauma as both individual healing processes and political interventions. Next I will explore the novel's politics of representing the female dead body, especially its negotiation of the male detective gaze. I will conclude with a discussion of women's sufferings and resistance in the South Africa of the 1950s, highlighting the novel's importance as a testament to women's agency in the midst of trauma across colour lines.

3.1 Acting *Out and Working Through: Revisiting, Reliving and Revising Trauma as Observer and Observed in Nunn's Crime Fiction Project*

Given that both the author's and the detective protagonist's backgrounds suggest at least a potential for trauma not dissimilar from those that are given narrative form in the novel, I argue that *Blessed Are the Dead* offers a space not only for testimony, but for the processing of trauma,[17] which in this case enables the author to take a political stance. It must be noted that neither the author nor her protagonist Cooper testify about their own trauma in any direct way. Both are witnesses of other people's traumas, but, since they share certain similarities in background with the people they testify for, they can be viewed as implicated in it to some extent. In contrast, in *Finders Weepers*, neither the author nor the detective were directly subjected to the structural violence to which the novel bears witness i.e. the South African education system (Lorimer 2014, 238).

---

17   To some extent this can be said of the whole of Nunn's Detective Emmanuel Cooper Series. Since *Blessed Are the Dead* is the novel in the series which gives most prominence to female victims, my analysis focuses on this novel.

Dominick LaCapra's notions of "acting out" and "working through" trauma are particularly useful for understanding the processes at work in *Blessed Are the Dead*, since both Nunn and Cooper engage in the process of "working through" trauma. LaCapra elaborates the Freudian notion of "working through" in his book *Writing History, Writing Trauma*. He relates "working through" to "acting out" as forms of remembering trauma in a way that reveals not only the implication of the one in the other, but "the implication of the observer in the observed" (2001, 141). Acting out, as LaCapra explains, is a repetitive, compulsive way of reliving the past trauma as if it were happening now, in the form of flashbacks, nightmares or a sense of being haunted by ghosts. This can happen to victims, as well as to secondary witnesses and observers (141–143). Working through, on the contrary, is a desirable process, a "countervailing force," insofar as "the person tries to gain critical distance on a problem and to distinguish between past, present, and future" (143). While the two processes are distinct, LaCapra sees them as intimately related. For example, both are based on repetition. While "[a]cting out is compulsively repetitive, [...] [w]orking through involves repetition with significant difference" (148). It is precisely in this *difference* in the act of repeating that not only the potential for healing, but the potential for feminist interventions and revisions lies.

Nunn's narrative project is closely linked to her own childhood and to her family's history. However, while she draws from this source, she also renders it with significant difference. In a radio interview, she states that she used childhood memories alongside oral accounts from her relatives as a basis for her Detective Emmanuel Cooper series (Nunn 2012a). Nunn was born in Swaziland, as a child of a racially-mixed marriage. At the time her novel is set, in the 1950s, Swaziland was a British protectorate, but economically it was dependent on South Africa (Butler 2009, 20). Apartheid policies did not apply in Swaziland, but, as in all of southern Africa at the time, varying degrees of de facto racial segregation were in place. As Nhlanhla Dlamini explains, the racial hierarchy placed people of European origin on top and people of African origin at the bottom of the social pyramid (2007, 150). People of mixed European and African origins, referred to as "EuroAfrican" or "Coloured" in Swaziland, occupied an intermediary space. Dlamini details how people of mixed racial origins were excluded from the social, economic and political life of the country (34). Nunn herself attended a boarding school for mixed-race children, and her parents lived in Durban for many years before emigrating to Australia to escape apartheid (Key West Literary Seminar 2016, par. 2–3, Nunn 2012a).

Because of her background, Nunn has first-hand experience of the degrading effects of racial discrimination and segregation. In an interview, she speaks about the courage that it took for her to tackle southern Africa in fiction. "One major obstacle to writing a novel about Southern Africa was the fact that I never felt 'at home' there. I was uncomfortable in my own skin because I wasn't white or black but somewhere in-between" (Nunn 2010a, par. 13). It was only after making a trip with her mother back to her home in Swaziland – which became the basis for her award-winning documentary *Servant of the Ancestors* – that she "found the guts" to write the first Emmanuel Cooper novel. She maintains that this way of reconnecting with her ancestors "made me realize that I was (and am) an African woman" (par. 13). In her crime writing project, set in apartheid South Africa, Nunn, significantly, moves away from the documentary mode that she employed in her film work. While she continues to rely on factual knowledge and personal experience, she chooses to mediate it through fiction, albeit in a genre that relies heavily on the real. Repetition with difference in LaCapra's sense can also be discerned in the way in which she portrays the effect of apartheid legislation in her crime fiction, but refuses to reproduce its segregationist practices. Roselet's social network is highly complex and only appears to abide by the law. Nunn paints a cross-section view of this society, with the legally induced racial and sexual boundaries intact in the upper half of the painting and with a very different network of paths, connections and divisions in the bottom half. Throughout her series, Nunn is at pains to demonstrate the myriad ways in which individuals are interconnected and entangled with, similar to, influenced by, dependent on and complicit with each other, across the lines of race and gender set by the law. For example, *Blessed Are the Dead* features Karen Paulus, a White Afrikaner woman who speaks flawless Zulu and is in love with an English woman. A love of gossip unites the different racial groups as much as the common belief that "members of their own tribe were more trustworthy than outsiders" (Nunn 2012b, 94, 190). By emphasising such commonalities and transgressions of set boundaries, Nunn not only challenges segregationist practices, but repeats their traumatic effect with a difference. She works through in LaCapra's sense, combining the psychological with the political, and demonstrates how, by working through, one can become an ethical and political agent (2001, 144). Finally, Nunn performs repetition with a difference and feminist political intervention through her fictional reintegration of Black women into the historical record. Back in 1953, incidents of Black-on-Black violence were low-priority cases for the police (Nunn 2012b, 31, 168). This may have been especially true of Black female-on-Black female violence. "[T]he hard truth [was]: reputations were not built on solving black homicides" (39). White detectives called it "[p]icking up the garbage" (39). A murder such as Amahle's would have gone uninvestigated and unnoticed by the official records; the story of the resistance of a young Black woman would have been lost to memory, constituting one of the "myriad hidden experiences of women" referred to by Anne McClintock (1995, 313). Though mediated by genre conventions and time, Nunn's historical detective novel reintegrates Zulu women such as Amahle into the South African cultural memory.[18]

In a similar fashion, Nunn's protagonist, who shares his author's racially mixed origins,[19] witnesses and investigates traumatic experiences that are not, or are only partly, his own. Working his cases confronts Cooper with alcohol-addicted husbands, dysfunctional marriages, domestic violence and forbidden interracial love, all of which have played a part in his own life.[20] What is more, the combat, violence, blood and death that are part and parcel of his job as a detective trigger his war trauma from his days as a soldier in World War Two. The war dead constantly haunt his dreams and come "to warm their hands at his fire" (Nunn 2012b, 174) as do memories of "firestorms or missiles or swollen rivers washing the dead out to sea" (74). Detective work for Cooper thus very much entails being implicated in others' traumas and acting out as well as working through his own. Returning from the war, "he'd switched soldiering for policing because he needed to create order out of chaos and to uphold some notion of good regardless of the consequences" (222). His job has not merely a restorative function, but a redeeming one: "He could do nothing for the war dead. This death on a Natal hillside, however, he could do something about" (17). Even though Cooper is not able – and probably never will be – to leave his traumatic past behind him completely, in the end the voices of the dead and memories that resurface in dreams, triggered by his investigation, help him to grow and find his family (309). Processes of acting out and working through can never be entirely separated in *Blessed Are the Dead*, and neither do they happen independently of the act of witnessing and testifying to the trauma of others.

---

18   In his essay on trauma and genre in the South African novel, Ewald Mengel credits the popularity of the historical novel in post-apartheid South Africa to the fact that this genre offers a means of rewriting and reappropriating history from various formerly neglected perspectives (2012, 147).

19   Cooper has an English mother and an Afrikaner father, but there is a possibility that he is part Cape Malay (Nunn 2012b, 123). In *A Beautiful Place to Die*, we learn that his paternal origins are contested. His mother had an affair with a man who was part Malay (Nunn 2009, 354). With Cooper's convoluted lineage, Nunn deliberately disrupts apartheid's racial categories and counters any simplistic polarities.

20   Growing up a "white kaffir child" (Nunn 2012b, 35) in extreme poverty in Sophiatown, Johannesburg, Cooper was subjected to a violent father who was also an alcoholic. His father killed his mother because he thought "a half-caste shopkeeper had fathered his children" and was acquitted of manslaughter (Nunn 2009, 354). He and his sister were then adopted by a "staunch, God-loving Afrikaner family" (Nunn 2012b, 74). Later Cooper escaped to Europe to fight with the British military in World War Two.

3.2   *Challenging the Power of Looking On: Contesting the Male Gaze*

"Amahle" means "the beautiful one" (Nunn 2012b, 15). This corresponds with her function in the novel as a "a looker", as somebody whose attractive physique draws attention. Based on Elisabeth Bronfen's work on femininity and representation, I argue that Amahle appears to feed the male gaze and to be arrested by it. At the same time, however, the control of the male gaze itself is undercut and called into question.

Unlike Penny Lorimer's female victim Boniswa, Amahle is not looked at by a female detective. Because Cooper is the main focaliser in the third-person narrative, it is through his eyes and investigation that we see Amahle, so it is important to examine exactly what Cooper's eye focalises and to what effect.[21] Cooper and Shabalala are guided to Amahle's dead body by a maternal relative of hers and by the wailing sound of the grieving women who surround the corpse.

> One of the women shuffled to the side to make a gap in the circle through which Emmanuel could approach the body. A black girl lay on the sweet spring grass, gazing up at the soft blue sky and the shapes of darting birds in the air. Her head rested on a rolled-up tartan blanket and tiny red and yellow wildflowers were scattered over the ground. Three or four flowers had fallen into her mouth, which was slightly open.
> NUNN 2012b, 9

From her face, Emmanuel's attention next moves to her hands, arms and feet. He finds a small bruise on her inner thigh, but no visible injuries. Only when he rolls Amahle's body over does he spot a small hole puncturing her white dress, which is speckled with spots of blood (13). With Shabalala's attentive support, Emmanuel's gaze works slowly and methodically. Although pornographic detail is lacking, it is nonetheless a preying, objectifying gaze – the gaze of the investigator scanning the body for clues. "Under normal circumstances [...] Emmanuel would have pushed aside the neckline of the girl's dress and checked for bruising on the shoulders and under the armpits" (10), but the presence of Amahle's relatives keeps him in check, so that all he can do is frantically read the dressed body and its surroundings for signs and take notes. Amahle's dead body is an object to be examined for clues by the detectives, a signifier. Moreover, Amahle's corpse, as pictured here, is an

---

21   Nunn states that she had to make Cooper male for plausibility's sake: in the 1950s, police work was a male game (2012a).

aestheticised death, beautified – in keeping with the meaning of her name. Absorbed into the natural world as she is, Amahle the individual is effaced. As *woman*, Amahle is a representative of something other than herself and, heeding Bronfen, we must examine whose norms and whose interests she represents (1995, 412; 420–421; see also my previous discussion of representational practices in Lorimer's novel). To begin with, as the object of a murder investigation, she serves to further Cooper's and Shabalala's careers in the police service. This case is going to get them "out of the dogbox and back in the kitchen" (Nunn 2012b, 306), as a relieved Cooper notices in the end. It also feeds Cooper's need for heroism. "Solving a homicide is the closest we come to being heroes. You'd have to be lazy or stupid to give up the chance" (77). However, this bolstering of male hegemony is more complicated than it first appears, since Nunn challenges or at least mitigates Cooper's exploitative gaze. First, he and his team display a high degree of self-reflection with regard to their own professional roles and explicitly acknowledge and empathise with different perspectives. This is exemplified by the Jewish doctor Daniel Zweigman, who understands why the child Gabriel would want to take revenge on him for cutting Amahle during the post-mortem (148–149). As Cooper notes, "Without the law and the promise of justice for the victims, Zweigman was just a charnel-house sawbones and he and Shabalala mere undertakers" (83). This is an artful reminder – to use Michele Aaron's term – that serves to qualify the predominance of Cooper's perspective. Secondly, by rendering Cooper as himself a victim, Nunn dismantles the hegemony of his gaze. The numerous flashbacks he experiences in the course of his murder investigation, especially when being confronted with the pain of others, leave him exposed and vulnerable. He is himself in crisis, his control vitiated.

Next to the male detective team, Amahle's male next of kin fight over the way in which her dead body is "represented," wanting to secure their norms and interests. With his nubile daughter's death, Chief Matebula has lost a prized possession, a commodity. Cheated out of his lobola (bride price), he makes Amahle's mother and sister suffer for it and punishes Amahle by burying her sitting upright like a criminal (201–202). This offends the men of Amahle's mother's clan, who in turn wage war against Chief Matebula. Amahle's burial place turns into a battleground (202–205). Her contested dead body becomes a pawn in a war between men: brothers and fathers fight for male sovereignty over her dead body. Like that of the detective, the familial power of her father and brothers over her body is disputed. As an alternative to Amahle's biological, patriarchal family, her self-chosen "adoptive brother" Gabriel Reed functions as a qualifier. Gabriel is Amahle's intimate friend and the youngest son of the influential English Reed family, Amahle's employers. Gabriel also claims Amahle's dead body, but he does so in order to care for, to protect and to commemorate it, as Cooper immediately understands (10–11). The White boy is mentally challenged yet highly intelligent, speaks Zulu better than English, has a pale blue and a dark brown eye (161, 205, 210), is still childlike at sixteen and has been nick-named "Nyonyane" or "little bird" by Amahle.[22] He defies any categorisation and refuses to be caught up in the net of any patriarchal power. According to Ella Reed, Amahle saw herself as Gabriel's big sister. While "[a]ll the native men in the valley were after Amahle [...] she let Gabriel get close because he didn't want her that way. They made their own little world together" (271). When she is dead, Gabriel grieves for Amahle the individual, the soul sister, the fellow transgressor, the accomplice, beyond Amahle the object of desire, or *woman*. So, even if Amahle functions to sustain male hegemony, be it that of the detective or that of the patriarchal family, that hegemony is always already undermined by Nunn, constituting an unstable representational hold.

3.3 Cooper's Testimony of South African Women in the 1950s: Patriarchal and Apartheid Violence Revisited and Resisted

Thanks to Cooper's gaze being undercut in its hegemony, it allows for a testimony of women's trauma. What is revealed are the effects for women of the systemic violence of patriarchy, particularly the institution of marriage, and the racial politics of early apartheid in rural South Africa in the 1950s. Remarkably, though, Cooper's testimony foregrounds female victims' agency, especially their transgressive agency and the ways in which they resist arrest resulting from violence. Across the boundaries of race and class, women are watched over and kept in place by their violent husbands. The English, middle-class town doctor Margaret Daglish has a bruised wrist (2012b, 36, 79), fears the alcohol-fuelled anger of her husband and says with regard to her marriage: "I am living in the dark" (222). Amahle's battered mother Nomusa, too, lives "in the shadow of the great chief" (66) who controls even who she is allowed to speak to (60). Cooper sees these women in their sufferings, not least because he recognises his own broken mother in them, a mother he was unable to save from his father's violence (53, 66). Amahle's story, by contrast, is not framed as

---

22   Gabriel's illness is not specified. Several times he is called "befok" (Nunn 2012b, 137), which is crude Afrikaans for "crazy". The Zulu call his illness "ukuthwasa" (297), a disturbance of the mind. Gabriel is "a habitual runaway and thief" (139) and has a habit of "roam[ing] the hills by day and night, talking to the trees and the animals" (297). He can "outfox" watch dogs (138) and compulsively names and catalogues the world (214): people by their nicknames and plants and animals by their scientific names (213, 225).

a narrative of brokenness, focusing instead on her active resistance to victimhood and to the precarity conveyed to women by marriage. Cooper's account reveals that the intelligent and independent-minded Amahle had been making secret plans to escape Roselet and her father's plans to marry her off to another local chief for twenty cows. What is more, the fact that as a Black woman she is doubly discriminated against does not necessarily turn her into a victim. The following contrast between Amahle and another Black girl with whom Cooper crosses paths makes this evident: "The National Party split the population into groups based entirely on skin color but Amahle Matebula and this meek Zulu girl with a half smile on her mouth had nothing in common *but* color. Amahle, the beautiful one, could detect male weakness and possessed the audacity to dream of a future bathed in bright, saturated colors" (252). More than anything, it is implied here, the difference lies in Amahle's "audacity to dream," in the ability to create a mental space in which the set gender boundaries are imaginatively transcended.

Even if the actual crossing of the boundaries fails, as in Amahle's case, the dream does not remain without effect on the way in which a woman perceives herself. In her work on the power of silence, Nthabiseng Motsemme points out that it is the retreat into an inner, imaginative space that allows the self to transcend existing "oppressive representations" (2004, 924), since it allows women to reimagine themselves (924–925). Motsemme perceives this as "an act of women's agency" (925). Moreover, any real or imagined transgression of the confines of gender and race in the novel renders the very existence of those confines visible. Significantly, Amahle, and other female victims Cooper testifies for bring patriarchal and apartheid law into focus the moment they transgress against it. Amahle knows full well the prospects of a married Zulu woman: "Married off young, a wife, then a mother and finally a widow without a home to shelter her children: Amahle had looked ahead, seen her own future and said no" (Nunn 2012b, 260). How completely a Zulu wife is at the mercy of her husband is illustrated by Nomusa's impending fate. Blaming Amahle's murder on her, the chief threatens to cast Nomusa and her other daughter out. If that happens, "[n]o clan will give them shelter. They will live like ghosts out on the veldt, drifting and hungry" (258–259). Even in the case of the chief's death, there is no relief, for then, like cattle, his "wives and children will be split up and given to other chiefs or to men who can afford to keep them" (260). Amahle, instead, was in pursuit of "life" (70), seeking to cross "the river," to use men "like stepping-stones to be skipped over lightly until you reached the other side" (70), rather than being exploited by them. In terms of race, too, for Amahle boundaries were there to be crossed. The Afrikaner Karin Paulus complains to Cooper how "[Amahle] forgot she was a kaffir and treated everyone like they were the servants" (121).[23] She even turned the power tables on the White male town constable Bagley in terms of race and gender. Knowing that he was sexually attracted to her, she satisfied him in order to then blackmail him for hush money and to ensure his silence about her escape (238–244).[24] This allowed her to buy herself a bus ticket to Durban and plan her getaway.

Amahle is not punished for her numerous transgressions. Rather, she is killed by a woman who is trying to overcome the same traumatising structures of hegemonic patriarchy, especially matrimony. Chief Matebula's fifth and youngest wife murdered Amahle to save her own skin. She killed Amahle in order to prevent the chief from collecting a bride price and marrying another wife with it, an action that would have resulted in her loss of privileges and – as a childless woman – of social security. (288). As a murder weapon, she chose a poisoned porcupine quill used by married Zulu women as decoration in their head coverings (14). Amahle was literally killed by a signifier of the institution she had been trying so hard to flee. Ironically, had her murderer known of her plan to run away, she would have had no need to kill her.

Besides Amahle's and her murderer's agency, Cooper's testimony includes White women's resistance to patriarchal hegemony. The town doctor Margaret Daglish refuses to "[p]lay [h]appy" (221) and keep up the façade of White, respectable middle-class life any longer, stepping out of her oppressive marriage to a violent ex-Air Force pilot turned alcoholic (230, 306). Ella Reed, an English woman, and Karin Paulus, an Afrikaner woman, manage to keep out of the institution of marriage – at least for the moment. By having a sexual relationship with each other, they secretly undermine the patriarchal hold of Ella's brother, "a South African king of the veldt" (90), and Karin's father, as well as the class divisions between English and Afrikaner in South Africa. Ella further attempts to undermine her brother's power by anonymously reporting Amahle's murder to the Durban police. Given that Amahle was employed by the Reed family, Cooper views Ella's act as akin to "lobbing a hand grenade into the family living room" (270). Overall, Cooper's testimony allows us to witness women's trauma, but neither we nor the victims themselves are arrested there. In LaCapra's terms, trauma is not made contagious; it is not simply repeated, it is worked through (2001, 142). LaCapra is adamant that, in an ethical sense, this does not equate to harmonisation of the past. Rather, "[i]t means coming to terms with the trauma, including its details, and critically engaging the tendency to act

---

23 A "kaffir" is a derogatory term for a Black person (*Oxford English Dictionary* 2017).
24 Amahle made Bagley break the law. As Cooper tells us, "a sexual dalliance with a black juvenile, no matter how brief, meant the loss of his job, his reputation and his family if it was made public" (Nunn 2012b, 243).

out the past" (144). Nunn makes the traumatic conditions visible, while probing them for spaces of transgressive agency. She thereby complicates rigid constructions of victimhood, as advocated by feminist critics of the TRC.

The cultural and political achievement of *Blessed Are the Dead* lies in its revisiting and reworking both of a traumatic past and of representational and testimonial practices. Placing Amahle at the centre of her novel allows Nunn to focus not just on vulnerability, but on gendered and racial invisibility and effacement, historical as well as generic. Even though Amahle herself remains silent about her suffering, she is not silenced. Her dead body unsettles the male detective gaze and – like Boniswa's – "speaks" of women's traumas, without limiting them to sexual violence and without cementing women in victimhood. The nexus between trauma work and investigative work is also central to Margie Orford's detective novels. This time, though, the investigator is a woman.

4   Serial Female Victimhood: Margie Orford's Clare Hart Series

> How must I tell my secret if I stay hidden?
> PEARL in *Daddy's Girl* (36)

Pearl, daughter of gangster and serial rapist Graveyard de Wet, decides to tell her secret. She undresses in front of the camera, revealing the scars and cut marks inflicted by her father. Intent on not perpetuating her mother's and her grandmother's silence, she goes public, but is promptly subject to her father's brutal revenge. Whether or not she survives, whether or not her father becomes her graveyard, we never learn.

Pearl's scars, like the wounds of most female victims in Margie Orford's Clare Hart Series, speak of sexual violence. Like many of them, she remains arrested in victimhood, suspended between life and death, living yet not, unable to move beyond the frame that is the trauma of sexual violence, despite all the agency with which Orford invests her. Sexual violence is depicted by Orford as extending way beyond the singular event of crime. It is rooted in and perpetuated by a "culture of violence against women" that reaches back in time. Based on this understanding of sexual violence, Orford renders her heroine Clare's investigative work as a form of the trauma work that features in post-apartheid literature more widely. By attending to victims and becoming a victim herself, Clare uses her investigations to face and retrieve – even to repeat – the pain, to give it a narrative shape, and to alter how women relate to victimhood. In essence, Orford's storytelling is feminist political work. Pitting these ethical narrative achievements against the series' politics of representing the violated female body reveals complexities and contradictions, however. Orford employs a wide range of representational strategies, not all of which can be reconciled with her feminist project. Some succeed in drawing attention to and ethically engaging with women's sufferings. Others work to undermine this endeavour by not only sacrificing *women* anew in representation, but by distracting from their traumas.

Orford's Clare Hart detective novels quickly earned her the title "Queen of South African crime fiction". Born in London, Orford is a White writer who grew up in Namibia and South Africa. She left South Africa in 1988, subsequently living in London, Namibia and New York. On returning to Cape Town with her husband and three daughters in 2001, Orford "felt besieged by the extravagant violence of the place" (2010b, 186), especially the high levels of gender violence. They were the reason why she, as a journalist, started working on crime. Orford reported crime in order to "find the voices of the brutalised and the dead" (187), but soon became frustrated. As a journalist, she felt that all you can do is "list a never-ending series of facts" (187). She therefore turned to crime fiction, which allowed her to "at least start to scratch at the truth" (187), "the truth of violence, resilience or revenge" (191). Orford's crime fiction has earned her national and international acclaim and been translated into many languages. Besides being a successful crime writer, she is an award-winning journalist, a filmmaker, a writer of children's books, academic books, school text books and non-fiction,[25] an editor,[26] a university lecturer, a campaigner against sexual violence, a board member of PEN South Africa and the patron of Rape Crisis and the children's book charity the Little Hands Trust (Fletcher 2013, 196, PEN South Africa 2015, par. 11–15, Pretorius 2014, 7, Vale 2010, 6, Vincent and Naidu 2013, 50). My analysis is based on all but one of Orford's Clare Hart novels: *Like Clockwork*, originally published in 2006 (I use the 2010 edition), *Daddy's Girl*, first published in 2009 (I use the 2011 edition), *Gallows Hill* (2011) and *Water Music* (2013). I do not discuss *Blood Rose* (2007) as female victims are peripheral to the novel's main plot, which centres on male juvenile victims.

---

25 These include *The Magic Fish* (2012), *The Little Red Hen* (2011), *Fifteen Men: Words and Images from Behind Bars* (2008), *Fabulously 40 And Beyond: Coming Into Your Power And Embracing Change* (2006), *Busi's Big Idea* (2006), *Dancing Queen* (2004), *Climate Change and the Kyoto Protocol's Clean Development Mechanism: Stories from the Developing World* (2004), *Rural Voice: The Social Change Assistance Trust, 1984–2004, Working in South Africa* (2004).

26 She co-edited *Coming on Strong: Writing by Namibian Women* (1996) and *Women Writing Africa: The Southern Region* (2003).

All the novels examined here feature the White private investigator-cum-investigative journalist Dr Clare Hart as detective protagonist and give prominence to female victims. Each novel focuses on a particular aspect of violence against women, in line with Orford's claim that each of her novels is a response to a particular, real crime (2013b, 226). In *Like Clockwork*, businessman Otis Tohar sexually assaults, brutally murders and spectacularly exhibits the bodies of three beautiful young women along the affluent Cape Town waterfront. His fourth victim manages a counter-attack and is saved with Clare's help. While Tohar's murder motives are located in his own traumatic childhood and are thus of a personal nature, his crimes against young women are greatly facilitated by his associates, human traffickers for the flourishing video porn industry. *Daddy's Girl*[27] centres on the abduction of Yasmin, daughter of Captain Riedwaan Faizal, head of the SAPS's Organised Crime and Drug Unit, a Coloured man and Clare's professional and romantic partner-to-be. Yasmin, whose disappearance is one in a series of disappearances and murders of schoolgirls, is finally rescued unscathed. The other young female victims are less fortunate: they all lose their lives through sexual violence and/or shootings in gang warfare. It transpires that Yasmin's abduction was instigated by Superintendent Clinton van Rensburg, a colleague of Riedwaan's, in order to force Riedwaan to take revenge on the members of the Numbers gang who have been ruining Van Rensburg's daughter's life. Like Otis Tohar's motives, Van Rensburg's are ultimately personal, but similarly dependent on larger structures that condone crimes against women. Orford locates these crimes primarily within Louise du Toit's fourth or "ontological-violence interpretative frame". While "past perpetrator trauma" (Du Toit 2014, 103 (first frame)) does play a role, Tohar's aim is to destroy the victims' worlds in an attempt to produce dominance (118, 120). The same is true of the male perpetrator in *Water Music*. In *Daddy's Girl*, Van Rensburg's violence, as well as that of the Numbers gang, is a message directed at other men in a (gang) war between men, which Du Toit sees as characteristic of the fourth interpretative frame. Of a different kind are the crimes in *Gallows Hill*, where Clare's murder investigation coincides with her documentary on slavery in the Cape. The death of Eva Africa leads to the discovery of a mass slave grave in Cape Town's Gallows Hill and of a female victim murdered 25 years previously, Suzanne le Roux. Clare's investigation of Suzanne's killing leads her to Suzanne's daughter Lilith, who lives in Cape Town under threat from

---

27 *Daddy's Girl*'s narrative time precedes *Like Clockwork*'s, even though it was published afterwards. It describes the beginnings of Clare's relationship with Riedwaan.

her mother's murderer, Gilles Osman. His crimes, as well as the larger past and present crimes that come under scrutiny in this novel, are not of a sexual nature; rather, they point to a criminal web of politicians and business people. In her most recent novel, *Water Music*, Orford returns to sexual crimes against women and children, which she terms a modern form of slavery (2013b, 229). Under the pretext of religious chastisement, Noah Stern keeps women and girls imprisoned as his sex slaves on his secluded Paradys farm. His most recent victim is the beautiful young cellist Rosa Wagner. Although the novel revolves around the individual cases of Noah Stern's female victims, it suggests that crimes against children have assumed epidemic proportions in South Africa. As part of Clare's work for Section 28, an SAPS unit named after clause 28 of the South African constitution and set up to guarantee children's rights, she has created a "chart of horror" (Orford 2013c, 39), a map with a whole forest of red and black pins. The red pins stand for injured, the black pins for dead children.

As is evident from these plot summaries, Orford tends to generate hyperspectacularised crimes in her fiction. By doing so, she panders to the public obsession with crime that exceeds the facts of crime, as described by John and Jean Comaroff (2004, 801; see also "Introduction"). With regard to the facts of crime locations, for example, the Comaroffs report that the Cape Flats, "that high-density, low-income part of Cape Town contains six of the seven worst microzones in the country for both murder and attempted murder" (153). The Cape Flats figure prominently as a criminal location in Orford's fiction, but many of the crimes we actually get to witness in her narratives occur in more affluent and Whiter areas, where, according to the Comaroffs, the real crime rates are low even by global standards (153). However, the Comaroffs' findings confirm the prevalence of sexual violence in South Africa, as reflected in Orford's crime fiction. Although international comparisons are difficult to establish, the Comaroffs report that the country "[b]y most accounts [...] comes up first in comparative measures of rape" (155, see also "Introduction"). For this reason, I will begin my discussion of the Clare Hart series with female victims' testimonies of sexual violence.

4.1   *Testifying to a Culture of Sexual Violence: the Stories Told by Scars on Women's Bodies*

For Orford, it was J.M. Coetzee's novel *Disgrace* that "opened a space for [her] to think of writing crime as fiction" (Orford 2013b, 224). The epiphany came one cold Monday morning, when she was standing next to the raped and stabbed body of a twelve-year-old girl. Recounting that moment in a Cape Town mortuary, Orford notes that

> the crimes represented in *Disgrace* are, in essence, violent conversations between men about land, possession, revenge, and access to women. The bodies of women are, in a profound sense, incidental, the women themselves either silenced or inaudible. And yet, as Lurie insists, "There must be a niche in the system for women and what happens to them" (Coetzee 1999:98). I wanted to locate that niche.
>
> 2013b, 225

Locating that niche and narrating the women's traumas is the task Orford sets herself as writer, intending to give a voice to, or at least to speak for, the otherwise "silenced or inaudible." In this way, her writing becomes an act of testifying – albeit, arguably, a paradoxical one, if evaluated against the backdrop of postcolonial literary trauma theory and feminist critical engagement with the TRC.

Despite giving unusual prominence to female victims in her crime fiction, Orford explores female agency mainly through the figure of Clare. It must be noted, with Sam Naidu, that "it is not only the detective figure that determines the feminist status of the text" (2014, 8). Orford invests her victims with substantial agency; however, by focusing on the traumatic moment, she fixes them not only in victimhood, but in that moment in time. Many of Orford's victims fight fiercely for their lives. In the hands of the killers, entirely at their mercy, their fates seemingly sealed, Teresa Angelo in *Like Clockwork*, Yasmin Faizal in *Daddy's Girl*, and Rosa Wagner and little Esther in *Water Music* all remain agents and fight to stay alive in situations that appear utterly hopeless. All of them survive. The same goes for Clare's twin sister Constance and Whitney Ruiters, two victims who not only survive but singlehandedly avenge the violations that they have suffered by killing the perpetrator, Kelvin Landman, in *Like Clockwork* (313–314). Another victim in the same novel, Nathalie Mwanga, as well as Pearl de Wet in *Daddy's Girl*, decide to speak out about the abuse that they have suffered over an extended period, while Lilith le Roux in *Gallows Hill*, severely traumatised by her mother's early disappearance, displays agency in her use of art as coping strategy.

Given that these women play an active role in their survival, it would be wrong to say that Orford portrays them as without agency, thus perpetuating the stereotype of the passive female victim. There are other criticisms that can be made of her approach, however. First, the survivors remain pitted against all those who precede them, of whose struggles we learn little and who have found death at the hands of the very same serial killers. Taking into account the sea of victims of similar crimes who populate the novels via Clare's documentary film projects, the parallels to other victims that she establishes in the course of each investigation, and the way in which, time and again, the epidemic proportions of sexual violence in South Africa are emphasised, the nine surviving women listed above appear like the chosen few. Secondly, the sheer impossibility of escaping victimhood is epitomised by the physical marks that it leaves. Strikingly, Orford's female victims have the stories of the violence committed against them literally and indelibly written on their bodies. Trauma in Orford's novels leaves physical traces inscribed in the female body, in the form of wounds, bruises, scars or brittle bones. In *Like Clockwork*, Kelvin Landman marks "his girls" (145) with an x-shaped tattoo (93), thus conferring victim and distinctive object status. Noah Stern's victims in *Water Music* bear his signature in the form of sjambok[28] scars and signs of malnourishment (150, 183) while Lilith has her mother's death certificate – faked by her murderers, we later learn – tattooed on her body in *Gallows Hill*. " '[…] It's what made me,' " Lilith says (174). It made her an artist, mentored by her mother's murderer. And it has made her remain under his power. Clearly, Orford intends the visible signs of violence to be seen and acknowledged by the public, to be read (like a language), understood and made sense of by the trained eye and sharp mind of her female investigator. According to Caitlin Martin, the visible scars in Orford's crime writing mirror invisible psychological damage. For her, this points to the dissociation of or duality between mind and body that violence can inflict on human beings (2013, 110–111). Kate Every views the scars and tattoos in *Like Clockwork* as testament to the lasting effects of violence on victims and society as a whole (2016, 39). While she reads them specifically as stigmata pointing to the stigma (in its meaning of "shame" and "discredit") that is attached to sexual violence (36–37), she also finds them to be markers of shared visible victimhood, facilitating a community of victims (38). These are convincing arguments, but the fact remains that the victims will never be able to shed the perpetrator's stamp, making it impossible for them to move beyond the traumatic event. Despite functioning to draw attention to the huge injustice of these crimes, indelible scars are suggestive of lifelong victimhood, particularly if they mirror psychological damage. Victimhood here is reproduced and perpetuated, despite the best of intentions. In this, the novels reiterate the effects of the TRC, which, as Fiona Ross argues, tended to freeze victims as such (2003a, 92–93).

This framing and freezing of the survivors in Orford's novels as victims is underscored by the fact that we part with them rather abruptly at the end of the narrative, and often uncertain as to their ultimate fate. It is as if they are

---

28　A "sjambok" is a strong and heavy whip made of rhinoceros or hippopotamus hide, used in South Africa for driving cattle and sometimes for administering chastisement (*Oxford English Dictionary* 2017).

made to function as sacrificial outcasts, hovering in a zone that is neither life nor death. For example, in *Like Clockwork* we leave Teresa Angelo safely ensconced in an ambulance and are taken back to witness Riedwaan's final struggle with the perpetrator in the subterranean tunnels. However, our gratification at Riedwaan's success in arresting Tohar is dampened by the film scenes of rape and mutilation of female bodies that continue to be played out on Tohar's screens – and, by implication, on many others all around the globe. Even if the individual, particular perpetrator is apprehended, his violent enterprise seems impossible to curtail and female victimhood is perpetuated. In *Daddy's Girl*, the last we learn of Yasmin is that her father has signed the document permitting her to embark on a new, safer life with her mother in Canada, but the other surviving victim, Pearl de Wet, remains in intensive care with life-threatening injuries (311). Lilith is similarly suspended between life and death in *Gallows Hill*: "sliced up like a halaal lamb" (341), she is awaiting the ambulance.[29] Only in *Water Music* do we get to see the two surviving victims, Rosa and Esther, alive and happy six months after their spectacular rescue. Rosa is playing her beloved cello again, and they are able to scatter Esther's mother's ashes on the ocean (329). Through this symbolic act of release, they can let go of their victimhood and move on with their lives together. None of Orford's other female victims are able to leave the shadows of their victimhood, however. Victimhood, it is implied, is unlikely to end for women.

The indelible marks and tattoos on Orford's victims' bodies tell stories of a veritable war against women and girls, waged mainly with the weapon of sexual violence. Jessica Murray provides a detailed description of the gender violence in Orford's novels. She concludes that "Orford's Clare Hart novels succeed in representing the pervasive presence of gender violence in the lives of South African women and they give the lie to the persistent illusion that these instances of violence are aberrations that emanate from strangers" (2013, 76). However, Louise Vincent and Samantha Naidu question whether Orford paints a realistic picture of violence against women in South Africa (2013, 56). Real violence, they state, follows banal plotlines and "for many South African women their brutalisation is more mundane and as a result all the more baffling and debilitating" (55), although they acknowledge the value of Orford's depictions as a political gesture and counter-discourse. As Ross argues in her critique of the TRC, the limiting of violence against women to sexual violence – as understandable as it may be, given the extreme prevalence of sexual violence

---

29 "Halal" in this context means to kill an animal in the way prescribed by Muslim law (*Oxford English Dictionary* 2017).

in South Africa – runs the risk of obscuring the effects of structural violence. Although Orford is less explicit in her exploration of structural violence and its effects on women than either Penny Lorimer or Malla Nunn, the role played by such violence is acknowledged in the stories written on the bodies of Orford's victims. Social structures are depicted as variously complicit in and/or facilitating, if not engendering, individual criminal acts. According to Murray, Orford's novels "suggest just how deeply gender violence is embedded in various social institutions, including the family, the state and the police force" (2013, 69). What is more, sexual violence as it is experienced by South African women can be characterised as a systematic continual and continuing harm resulting from what Tristan Anne Borer terms "a *culture* of sexual violence in South Africa" (2009, 1180, my emphasis). In her critique of the TRC, Borer notices the absence of applicants for amnesty for the crime of rape or other sexual violence before the TRC, and asks whether "raping women was simply not deemed a serious enough crime to warrant opening oneself up to public exposure" (2009, 1179). Helen Moffett contends that this sentiment is widespread among men in South Africa (2006, 138), which tends to support Borer's claim that the failure of men to apply for amnesty for sexual crimes has had repercussions for the human rights of women beyond the Truth Commission period. Notably, the fact that "no one was held accountable for these crimes [...] may well contribute to a climate of impunity – which is the antithesis of a human-rights-respecting culture based on respect for the rule of law" (Borer 2009, 1179). Such a climate, according to Borer, may explain why, arguably, "[a]t the moment [...] rather than a culture of rights, there is a culture of sexual violence in South Africa" (Borer 2009, 1180).

Whatever the limits of fictional efficacy, Orford must be credited for depicting this "culture",[30] its pervasiveness and the fact that it is sustained by men from all walks of life, independent of their social class and skin colour. She exposes the social complicity that allows for the culture of impunity criticised by South African feminists. As Teresa, the surviving victim in *Like Clockwork* is quick to notice, the film featuring another woman being gang raped that Tohar forces her to watch "had been through post-production. Someone had watched it before her, had seen whatever she was going to see, had edited and tweaked it. Teresa wouldn't be here if this person had said something, had done something" (296). *Like Clockwork* portrays trafficking women as a low-risk, high-return investment (36). Women are also a relatively risk-free means

---

[30] In her analysis of *Daddy's Girl*, Elizabeth Fletcher also points to this "culture of abuse and violence" (2013, 202–204).

of enabling men to wage a psychopathic or religious crusade, as in *Like Clockwork* and *Water Music*, to rise up the gang hierarchy, to fight a gang turf war or to blackmail a colleague in the police, as in *Daddy's Girl*, or to protect their illegal business activities, as in *Gallows Hill*.[31]

Orford's crime fiction suggests that the culture of sexual violence does not stop at the door of the family. On the contrary – the family is depicted as damaged, disintegrating, dysfunctional, even lethal. Regardless of whether it is housed in wealthy suburbs or on the Cape Flats, the family fails to provide for and to care for children. It is not only a violent place of destruction and death for girls and women, but the breeding ground for an even more violent next generation of men. Change, Orford seems to imply, must be bottom up, beginning in the family. In the few visions of new family forms that she offers, she envisages a move away from the patriarchal family. Pearl de Wet in *Daddy's Girl* regards a total breaking of family ties as the only option for her daughter Hope. She has given her child up for adoption and "[n]ow her name is Hope Pennington. Her mother's a lawyer who lives with another woman in a nice, smart flat. Two mommies. Completely safe" (149). *Water Music* is suggestive of a future for the strong emotional bond between Rosa and little Esther born out of shared suffering. Rosa's fading grandfather and Esther's maimed brother, who are literally in the same boat with them in the novel's final scene, may well be part of that alternative family arrangement (329). Yet when Riedwaan asks Clare – their three-week-old son Ishmael in her arms – if she wants to marry him. Clare refuses politely: " 'Marriage. Being two, becoming one. That's a step too far' " (330). Despite Orford's hopes, however, the queer family, the family of survivors, the rainbow family, will find it difficult to thrive as long as structural violence persists. Before the non-violent, nurturing South African family can materialise, a good deal of working through of the pain of the female victim is required.

4.2 *Breaking the Cycle of Trauma: Writing and Investigating Crime As Trauma Work and Politics*

Orford's focus on the victim in her fiction turns her crime writing into a privileged (in its dual meaning) site of engagement with trauma. Nowhere does

---

31   Despite her focus on sexual violence, Orford does not explore the issue of sexual violence against men, as has been done by K. Sello Duiker in his novel *Thirteen Cents* (2000), for example. The issue of sexual violence against men in prisons is alluded to just once, in *Like Clockwork*, when Riedwaan maliciously reminds Tohar that a dislocated shoulder will be "the least of your worries, where you're going. A handsome fellow like you is going to have lots of fun" (310).

she dissect and exemplify the historical and psychological processes of facing and working through trauma more masterfully than in *Gallows Hill*. The novel's title refers to an actual location in Cape Town's Green Point where a mass slave grave was found in 2003 during construction work for a shopping centre and offices.[32] I argue that, through the methods and strategies that Orford employs to retrieve and work through trauma in *Gallows Hill*, both writing and investigating crime become trauma work in Dominick LaCapra's sense. Trauma work, in addition to its psychological benefits, is in this way mobilised as a political act that aims to break the cycle of violence against women.

Like Lorimer and Nunn, Orford contests the traditional notion of trauma as an irretrievable and thus unsurmountable event, challenging proponents of trauma theory who regard traumatic experience as being beyond verbal expression. As the patron of Rape Crisis in South Africa, she notes:

> I have observed that survivors who, through counselling, therapy and their own courage, could turn the obliterating experience of rape into a narrative – their own – would heal much faster, would reclaim their lost agency, their assaulted self, far more quickly. And they would be able to move on: they would be the same person, but also a profoundly different one.
> 2013b, 223

As well as illustrating Orford's understanding of trauma as retrievable, these remarks are testament to Orford's awareness of victims' ability to "move on" after trauma in real life. However, as I have already shown, this is a step that she rarely permits her fictional victims to taken. In *Gallows Hill*, it is Riedwaan who, on digging up the bones of Cape Town's past, perceives the need to contain this trauma in a narrative. He is convinced that Clare is the right person to "find a way to tell this story [...] the violence of it. Where these people came from" (24) so that "[i]t won't be so easy to hide" (25). Riedwaan's words point to the inseparability of the victims' stories from stories of historical perpetrators and stories of present perpetrators who wish to obliterate the past in the interest of business. This last point is particularly pressing given the fact that his crime scene is a prime building site that investors want to see developed.[33]

---

32 Ra'eesa Pather describes this and subsequent discoveries of slave bones in Cape Town, as well as the ensuing debates (2015). The same events are referred to by Mike Nicol in *Payback* (see my discussion of his novels in my chapter on female perpetrators).

33 "Who cares about people nobody even knew they'd forgotten" (Orford 2011b, 37), as the ruthless Hond Williams puts it. Hond ("Dog") is the new owner of the Gallows Hill building site. He "used to run Woodstock – tik, abelone, girls, guns, protection for brothels, later for politicians," Riedwaan remembers (34).

The past is excavated in the narrative layer by layer. The process of retrieval starts with the death of a homeless woman, Eva Africa, on the Gallows Hill construction site. While Eva is suffering a heart attack, clutching the 300-year-old VOC[34] slave disc handed down to her by her mother and grandmother, her hungry dog Jennie scavenges the ground and digs up a human bone (10). Called to the scene, Riedwaan digs deeper and discovers a mass grave of far older bones (18–19). In the course of further excavations, a small packing crate is found containing the remains of a woman who died approximately 25 years ago (30–31). The story of this privileged White woman, Suzanne le Roux, becomes the focus of Clare's investigation. With her name and the slave disc that Eva is clutching at her death, Orford establishes an obvious link to past female victimhood. At the same time, she effaces Eva as an individual. Eva is *woman*, who functions as a trigger for other stories. With her dead body comes the unravelling of a chain of bodies and bones of older victims, a catena that establishes links between various stages of Cape Town's traumatic past. Suzanne's body brings to life the violent days of apartheid in the 1980s, while the slave bones point to the crimes of slavery committed in the Cape 200 to 300 years earlier. Clare is determined to ascertain the identity and story of Suzanne in order to have Suzanne's trauma literally resur*face* in a potentially legible representation. Based on her skull, a forensic artist reconstructs the victim's face in a clay model. Not only does this facilitate her identification as Suzanne le Roux, but it leads Clare to her surviving daughter Lilith (144), who is her mother's "living image" (162).[35] Even more faces are appearing all over town now: Lilith, who has been turning the pain of being abandoned by her mother into art,[36] is advertising her current exhibition with posters picturing a face. " 'I've seen a face, a haunting face, it's up everywhere,' " Clare suddenly realises (151). In a process of gradual identification and piecing together of fragments of evidence, Clare is now intent on reconstructing Suzanne's life, particularly the days around her disappearance. Knowing that Lilith is her only key, Clare convinces her to "pick the lock" (310) to the painful memories of the night when her mother disappeared. It is at this stage that Clare's murder investigation turns into psychotherapy, into working through trauma. During an interview, which could just as well be a trauma

---

34   VOC stands for "Vereenigde Oost-Indische Compagnie" (Orford 2011b, 68), the Dutch East India Company, which was instrumental in formalising the slave trade as an industry in the Cape.
35   The name Lilith, like Eva, is a *woman*-name in Teresa de Lauretis's sense. It refers to woman as a cultural construct and functions to absent empirical women (Bronfen 1995, 412).
36   Clare is eventually able to reveal that Suzanne did not disappear for political reasons, as her daughter was made to believe, but was in fact murdered.

counselling session, Clare takes Lilith back to that night, when she was only four years old, and coaches her body and mind into remembering the details. Clare urges Lilith to "[f]ocus on the senses [...] [s]mell, taste, texture – those are the details that anchor the bigger things. They are the tiny things that jog the involuntary memory" (312). As additional "anchors" Clare uses the physical evidence she has so far gathered in the murder investigation, such as the stone inside Lilith's teddy bear and her mother's sketchbooks. Thus, fragment after fragment of memory is triggered and emerges either on paper – Lilith starts to sketch rapidly: "Colour and shape. Images returning from the other side of time" (312) – or as a sensory memory: " 'How did you cut your feet, Lilith?' She shook her head. 'Think back,' said Clare, 'your feet. The pain in your feet –' 'Slippery,' she whispered. 'The rocks, they were wet.' Clare waited. Lilith closed her eyes. 'She was with the man' " (315). Continuing her journey into that night, Lilith suddenly remembers how she felt a stone in her throat, " 'blocking the words. [...] It also blocked the pain.' 'And when it slips?' asked Clare. Lilith turned her scarred wrists upwards. 'You see, Clare, if I remember too much, maybe I'll lose the ability to speak again,' Lilith said. 'And I'm afraid that if I remember everything I'll die' " (316).

Retrieving trauma is a painful, terrifying and dangerous process that repeatedly threatens to overwhelm the traumatised. For Lilith, it is dangerous in yet another sense, as it will identify her mentor, art gallerist Gilles Osman, as her mother's killer. Constrained by the generic demand for speed as it is, Orford's account of trauma therapy is somewhat simplistic, while relying on metaphors like lock and key or likening the retrieval of trauma to an archaeological excavation is clichéd when compared with the slow toil of real psychotherapy. However, because the crime genre lives off and invokes the existential threat that the facing of trauma poses, it must be taken seriously as a platform to negotiate this threat. The genre is also well suited to treading the thin, often permeable line that separates acting out from working through. Orford lets the female detective, rather than the female victim, walk the final steps along this line, which is her investigation. If the female investigator Clare acted the therapist for the female victim Lilith, in the final stages of the process she herself acts and becomes the victim. It is she who finally turns the process into a clear working through, a working through that for LaCapra entails a "repetition with significant difference" (2001, 148). It is precisely in this difference in the act of repeating that not only the potential for healing and the resolution of the murder case, but the potential for interventions and revisions in the field of gender lies. In this difference, a space for gender transformation opens up. In the denouement of *Gallows Hill*, Suzanne's murderer Gilles Osman takes Clare captive. Intent on a precise repetition of his murderous act, this time with Clare as victim, Gilles leads Clare up to the quarry on Cape Town's Signal Hill, to the exact spot where he killed Suzanne all those years ago. On the way, Clare hears "the sigh of the grass against [her] legs" and instantly remembers the sounds in Lilith's gallery installation (343), confirming her suspicion that the evidence of Suzanne's murder "was all there, hidden in plain sight" (337) in Lilith's art.[37] She now realises that she is being led along the same path as Suzanne, awaiting the same fate – namely, to be killed by Gilles with a black rock (344–345). By this time, Clare has completely identified with the original victim Suzanne. She is repeating, acting out the trauma of her violent death. At some point, though, "Clare's mind shifted gear, turned the terror back. [...] She was alive. And she knew this man. She knew him far better than he thought she did. She had a chance" (344). Clare the victim finds her agency – thanks to the knowledge that she has gained as a detective – and she laughingly mocks Gilles in the same way Suzanne mocked him, intent on triggering his memory and thus provoking him into an acting out, into replicating the same script. It works: "Osman stared at Clare. This woman was uncowed. Suzanne le Roux's laughter, her threats to expose him, were caught in the echo chamber of the quarry" (346). Clare keeps the upper hand and is now able to anticipate his next step. This, and her certainty that Gilles was caught unawares by the return of his memories, allows Clare to slip away from him, to hide in the darkness and to kick him over the edge of the cliff (348). Thus, in *Gallows Hill* Clare, the detective, takes the victim's place, reproduces the original victim's story and suffers some of the same violations, at the hands of the same perpetrator, only to add a twist of significant difference at the end: Clare the victim turns into Clare the perpetrator who kills in self-defence. Here, she embodies all three figures: the victim, the perpetrator and the detective.

The similarities between Clare and the victims whose interests she protects are made evident before this final scene up at the quarry.[38] What is more, the same pattern of the detective turning into the victim and then into the

---

[37] This scene is reminiscent of an installation by crime artist Kathryn Smith, who inspired Orford while she was working on *Gallows Hill* (Orford 2012, par. 15).

[38] Clare herself is conscious of the resemblances between herself and Suzanne (48) and between herself and Lilith, who, like her, lost her mother prematurely (173). Furthermore, she instantly recognises her twin sister Constance's scars in Lilith's "symmetrical row of cuts and scars on the inside of her thighs" (170). These similarities are also perceived by the perpetrators – Basson sees both Suzanne's beauty and stubbornness in Clare (234), while Gilles hears both Suzanne's and Clare's mocking laughter at the same time (346) – and even by Riedwaan, who first mistakes the injured Lilith for Clare (341).

perpetrator is employed by Orford in her next novel, *Water Music*.[39] Caitlin Martin and Sally-Ann Murray highlight a related incident where Clare becomes one with the victims of slavery during her visit to the slave quarters in *Gallows Hill*. They view Clare's physical reactions to the traumas that played out at this place as "an effect of emotional transference" (2014, 44) and read her response along ethical lines, as a resistant practice to "packaging exploitation as distant legacy, separate from current complicity and emotional claim" (43). For Antoinette Pretorius, on the other hand, Clare's ability to morph into victimhood is "an alternative mode of embodied investigation" (2014, 15), which, among other things, serves to value intuition in detection (13). Although Pretorius is right to see the way in which Clare steps into the victims' shoes as a feminist political strategy, it is important to emphasise that Clare becomes a victim but does not stay one, that she is a victim who regains her agency. For me, the moment of difference in Clare's repetition is crucial. Managing to transform the acting out of trauma into a working through facilitates both healing and the restoration of justice. Furthermore, it is a strategy that revises both gender and generic scripts of female victimhood. As a female victim herself, Clare taps into the cycle of violence against women, but is then able to break that cycle and reverse the roles. Not only does she thereby upset the victim-perpetrator binary, but she is able to achieve what is often not achieved in reality, certainly not by the TRC: namely, the arrest of the male perpetrator of violence against women. Thus, Every's reading of *Like Clockwork* as the re-enactment of a "counter-narrative to the closed nature of the TRC" (2016, 35) can be extended to Orford's novels as a whole. In *Gallows Hill*, for example, there is an emphasis on the incomplete or premature closure offered by the TRC. The novel provides us with a brief glimpse of the sufferings during apartheid and post TRC of Sophie Xaba, Lilith's other, "paid-for mother" (172). As Lilith's carer, Sophie, like countless other Black mothers, had to split her loyalty between the child she was paid to look after and her own son. The night Lilith's mother disappeared, Sophie's own house was burnt down and her own son Scipio disappeared (226). Sophie later tells Lilith, " '[...] That's why I could not help you, my Lily. I had to get home' " (225). Scipio's remains were never found: " 'Not even in the TRC. All the files were gone, they said. And no witnesses [...]' " (227). Sophie is still waiting for her son's bones, so

---

39   In *Water Music*, Clare follows Rosa's steps as part of her investigation only to end up, like and with Rosa, as Noah's captive. Intending to kill his victims, Noah is killed by Clare. On a platform servicing a water tunnel, Clare fights Noah and plunges a porcupine quill into his eye. They both fall into the water. While Noah drowns, Clare is pulled out and saved by Riedwaan (Orford 2013c, 325–327).

that she can bury him (228). Orford offers a further hint at too-sudden closure of unfinished apartheid business in the figure of Jacques Basson, the former apartheid general with whom "nothing stuck" at the TRC. As he hastens to tell Clare, his case " 'was dealt with by the TRC. Disclosed, forgiven, forgotten. Case closed, end of story. Nothing there [...]' " (235). It is against such socially pressurised closure, against a hasty closing of the books on the past, that Orford has Clare work, by reopening cold cases and by returning to, retrieving and working through past trauma. Orford demonstrates – albeit simplistically, perhaps – that detective fiction can function as trauma fiction. In the difference of the re-enactment that crime fiction produces lies political, revisionist potential. An important caveat must be added here, however. As a White, middle-class and well-educated woman, Clare is enormously privileged, and it is questionable how far the symbolic power of her agency can extend to less advantaged women. In South Africa, the women most affected by the trauma of violent crime are Black women who live in precarious socioeconomic conditions. Unlike Clare, these women are barely protected by public and private infrastructure. Viewed in this light, Clare's is a less inclusive political act than it might otherwise appear.

4.3 "How Must I Tell My Secret If I Stay Hidden?" Representing Violence and the Violence of Representation

Orford's success in using detective fiction as a means of attending to trauma cannot be properly assessed, however, without considering the ethics and politics of her aesthetics. Orford's sexy, violated female bodies have attracted a fair amount of scholarly attention. Christopher Warnes claims that, in her first three crime novels, Orford renders violence against women as a spectacle and thereby "runs the risk of reinforcing some of the very delusions that impede the feminist struggle she is claiming to wage" (2012, 990). Warnes does not develop this claim any further though. Focusing on *Daddy's Girl*, Elizabeth Fletcher recognises the fine line that Orford walks in her representations of the dead female body by "eliciting voyeurism and complicity on the part of the reader" (2013, 206). However, she regards this as a feminist strategy in order to draw "the reader into a state of collusion with the culture of abuse and thus a sense of responsibility" (208). Building on Fletcher's point, Naidu engages with the tension between the supposed generic requirement for sensationalised violence and Orford's stated and, in many ways, successful feminist agenda. Naidu reads *Like Clockwork*, *Daddy's Girl* and *Water Music* against the backdrop of *écriture féminine* and Julia Kristeva's notion of the abject. She argues that Orford represents the violated female body as abject – i.e. as both attractive and repulsive – and that, as a consequence, "the reader of crime fiction is interpellated as both voyeur and sympathizer, and the author and reader are both critic of gender-based violence and complicit peddler or consumer of a 'thrilling' genre" (2014, 71). She finds that the potential violence in Orford's representational practices might be read either as impeding her feminist project or as suggesting "a shared responsibility, a shared abjection on the part of author, detective, victim, perpetrator and reader" (78). Given the fact that the author is aware of the dangers inherent in representation, Naidu concludes by according Orford's representational practices a *bona fide* feminist status (78). Finally, in her reading of *Like Clockwork*, Every sees Orford as gesturing to the trope of the beautiful dead woman, but argues that this is counterbalanced by the agency of Orford's women (or, more precisely, some of Orford's women) (2016, 38).

Orford is well aware of the complex relationship between violence and representation. She states, "Edgar Allan Poe's formulation that the most poetic subject is the death of a beautiful woman holds true, and I am less and less convinced that one can short-circuit the erotic charge of the damaged female body, the building block of pornography, desire and crime fiction" (2013b, 227). In what follows, I will examine these tensions and contradictions in Orford's texts and their implications for the reader. I will show how widely Orford's treatment of the violated female body varies, both within and across her novels, and explore what this means for her feminist mission. Frequently, Orford sacrifices her victims anew in representation without granting the reader any opportunity to disengage from the narrative violence. At other times, her representational practices are highly self-reflexive and encourage readers to face their own complicities. On occasion, she effects an awkward merging of these strategies. Drawing on Elisabeth Bronfen's work on the cultural construction of femininity, Griselda Pollock's notion of aesthetic wit(h)nessing and Michele Aaron's concept of ethical spectatorship, I argue against any reconciliation of Orford's very different ways of dealing with the female victim. Contrary to Fletcher, Naidu and Every, I contend that Orford clearly undermines her own feminist project at times.

I will begin by highlighting where and how Orford's female victims are subjected to a decidedly heterosexual, predatory male gaze, which objectifies and thus efficiently effaces them as subjects and deflects from their traumas. The first dead female body in *Like Clockwork*, Charnay Swanepoel, "[...] lay spreadeagled on the promenade in full view of anyone who cared to look. Her face was child-like in death, dark hair rippling in the breeze. Blood, pooled and dried in the corners of her eyes, streaked her right cheek like tears. Her exposed breasts gestured towards womanhood" (3). Charnay's body is eroticised, as we look at her through the eyes of an elderly male passer-by. The bodies of the next two victims – Amore Hendricks (97) and India King (181–182) – are represented in similarly spectacular, sexualised ways. The man who discovers India's body even expresses his desire for her through touch. "[C]upping her breasts in his hands," he finds them "as full as the moon" (182) before he notices her slit throat and the fact that she is dead. Even Riedwaan and Clare, who generally approach female victims from a forensic perspective, can adopt the male gaze at times. When called to the scene of the murder of two schoolgirls in *Daddy's Girl*, Riedwaan notices that "[p]uberty had just settled, light as a butterfly, on the child's body – glossing and thickening her hair, swelling the exposed nipple" (28). Likewise, when Cassie reveals her discovery of the emaciated child she has been keeping warm under her fleece in *Water Music*, Clare's gaze immediately fixes on Cassie's "newly budded breasts" (16). And when Clare first meets the battered DesRay, she sees "the cold wind moulding her pink nylon nightie against her breasts, the tight curve of her belly, her bare legs. Bambi-eyes, full mouth, her bleached hair windblown" (115). At times, Clare becomes a voyeur, thus repeating "the lazy-gaze wander: lips, breasts, hips" (77) to which she knows she herself is often subjected by men. As Bronfen reminds us, such representational practices cater to heterosexual male desire and work to efface the woman as a represented subject (1992, 208). They seek to arrest the dual threat of femininity and mortality and thereby sacrifice the woman as a subject. This effect is intensified when the victim is a woman of colour. Although Orford's female bodies are always clearly gendered, they are seldom characterised in terms of race, at least not directly. However, given their names, the location of their homes and their socioeconomic status, we can infer that their racial backgrounds vary greatly. Orford wants to emphasise that gender-based violence cuts across lines of race and class, but her international readers, at least, who are possibly less well versed in deciphering the more subtle local markers of race, may misread this as a signal that race does not matter (any more) in South Africa. Moreover, leaving a female victim's racialised subjectivity to the imagination of the reader does not work to expose racial categories as constructs. Rather, it reinforces the problematic ways in which a woman's body functions as a screen and skips over the very real effects that racial categorisations have for South African women, not least in terms of vulnerability to sexual violence.[40]

---

40   Louise Vincent demonstrates that race "continues to have an often unacknowledged and unseen power to determine perceptions, experiences and relationships" in South Africa (2008, 1427–1428). According to the Comaroffs, "the incidence of crime and victimhood typically follows lines of race and class," with poor and Black precincts disproportionally affected (2016, 153).

Griselda Pollock's critique of Alain Resnais' film *Nuit et Brouillard/Night and Fog* illustrates why Orford's representational strategy is irreconcilable with a real concern for female victims of violence. Taking her cue from Bronfen, Pollock criticises Resnais' politics of representation of women being killed in his 1955 film, which seeks to commemorate Nazi atrocities. She disapproves of the way in which he reproduces real photographs depicting naked/humiliated women and children just before they were killed because "[…] the relations between violence and eroticism are re-enacted in ways that *deflect from the human trauma of what we are seeing*. They stem from, and reabsorb the event into pre-existing tropes which use eroticised or humiliated femininity to deflect from the encounter with death" (2010, 853, my emphasis). If we apply this argument to Orford's use of the male gaze, two things become apparent. First, Orford performs and perpetuates the very sexual politics that she seeks to contest. Secondly, her practice diverts the reader from the very phenomenon to which she wants to draw attention: women's experience of pain. In other words, "the niche" for what happens to women, which Orford wants her crime fiction to point to (2013b, 225), is obscured, leaving the women inside unheard. Indeed, with regard to the complicity of the spectator (or, for that matter, the reader), Pollock emphasises that there is no escaping the sacrificial, (hetero-)sexualised gaze – what she terms "phallocentric voyeurism" (2010, 852). For "[…] our encounter with the images […] momentarily aligns us with the originating perpetrator position […]. Even if we begin to recoil once realizing what we are seeing, making sense of the image's denotation already aligns us with that perpetrating gaze" (850). This brings us back to Naidu's argument suggesting a complicity and shared responsibility between author and reader, with which I agree in principle. However, this does not apply to the examples that I have just discussed, because here Orford effectively prevents the reader from critically engaging with his/her complicity. Rather than giving the reader a chance to reflect on the problematics of what is being represented, Orford turns him/her into a perpetrator, too. As a consequence, the only ethical choice that a reader is given is simply to refrain from reading her novels – a choice that again forecloses critical engagement. As long as Orford renders the female dead body erotically charged and sensationalises women's pain, her and her readers' attempts to bear witness to women's traumas will be thwarted. Since the male gaze is aimed precisely at not seeing the double package of femininity and death, it is utterly useless as a form of ethical engagement with the female victim. As we have seen in Lorimer's and Nunn's depictions of female victims, there are ways of raising awareness of both female pain and the problematics of representing it in crime fiction. Orford, too, understands how to do this.

While perpetuating phallocentric voyeurism, Orford employs various means to reflect on and disrupt this practice in her crime fiction. Again, Aaron's notion of ethical spectatorship helps to illustrate the point. For Aaron, the spectator is neither passive nor impartial, but complicit with and hence responsible for the representation of the socially unacceptable and the sufferings of others. Films and texts that allow for ethical spectatorship are "contra-disavowal" by adopting an "anti-forgetting strategy": "They deliberately break that cinematic contract between spectator and screen [...] by aggravating the act of 'artful forgetting' at the heart of the spectacle-real dynamic" (Aaron 2007, 92). Orford makes spectatorship as such an issue through the pervasive presence of film in her crime fiction. Clare's own documentaries, alongside the porn videos and strip shows, work to conscientise the reader of (her/his) spectatorship. Orford's novels also feature representations of pain and exploitation that are contra-disavowal, in Aaron's sense, in two distinct ways. First, Orford does allow female victims to speak for themselves at times – although not as often as Lorimer does – thus impeding "artful forgetting". *Daddy's Girl* is interspersed with the thoughts and physical experiences of the captured girl Yasmin (see, for example, chapters 15 and 26). Yasmin's voice is set apart by the use of italic print, visually signalling an interruption of the narrative flow and creating the impression of a voice that is independent of the narrator's, even of polyphony. In *Water Music*, Orford employs a similar technique, inserting the transcript of the testimony of a real-life victim who, much like her fictional protagonists Esther and Rosa, was buried alive underground (187–189; 331).[41] In a similar vein, *Like Clockwork* features fictional trafficking victim Nathalie Mwanga's verbal testimony, including both parts that she recounts in front of Clare's camera and parts that she decides to keep to herself (38–41). The fact that we watch

---

41   When working on the same novel, Orford apparently deleted, or at least chose not to include, large sections written from Rosa's perspective. Her explanation for this decision illustrates both her awareness and the divergent ways in which she represents the female victim: "Rosa posed the problem of the absent female victim – the staple of so much crime fiction. I felt I had to imagine her fully and, in the earlier drafts, I had written several chapters from her point of view. So I got to know her and understand her by writing her – by making her very much a real person who tries her best to survive what has happened to her. This did not work well for the tension in the way that I had structured the plot. It did not work for the revelation at the end as the mystery is unfolded very much from Clare Hart's investigative point of view. However, it meant that getting other characters to tell the story of Rosa was easy because I had written so much from her perspective. It was a matter of distilling that sense of her – and of her absence. A way, I suppose, of trying to work out how to solve the problem of the erasure of the female victims of crime" (Orford 2013a, par. 8). While I understand the genre's requirement for suspense, I would question the validity of Orford's last point.

both Clare filming and asking questions and Nathalie "adjust[ing] her hair [...] [sitting] straight up in her chair and pull[ing] her skirt over her knees" (38–39) before answering in front of the camera reminds us that this is a performance and that we, like Clare, are spectators.[42] In all these examples, we are given access to the female victim's voice and thoughts. This allows Orford to open up a space for her readers' own ethical reflections and, in so doing, to foster the reader's agency. By having the victim speak to the reader in the first person, Orford creates the effect of testimony, with the victim exposing her sufferings in a way that removes the safe distance between character and reader – almost with the assumption of a bond of trust being established, similar to the autobiographical pact.

For Aaron, these features are all markers of ethical spectatorship. A second contra-disavowal strategy to be found in Orford's fiction is what Aaron terms consistent "artful reminders" (2007, 94). When Clare and Charlie Wang visit the Winter Palace in *Daddy's Girl*, they are rendered as observers of and commentators on male customers observing and interacting with female sex workers in the club. Clare as focaliser of the scene contrasts the women's seductive behaviour with their blank eyes and likens a customer's "cupping the woman's breast in his hand" to a butcher who is "weighing fresh meat" (173). When a mesmerised Charlie breathes, "This is like a movie," Clare says matter-of-factly, "Not people you want to get to know, Charlie" (173). Clare's sardonic reminders turn this representation of female victims[43] into a self-reflexive and thus ethical one. The sex workers' scantily clad bodies are just as sensationalised and sexualised as the dead female victims displayed on the Sea Point promenade in *Like Clockwork*, but they are pictured in this way for the gaze of the onlooking male customers only, not for Clare's benefit, or for the reader's. They are presented to us together with Clare's disapproving response, thus giving us clear ethical guidelines on how to react to the spectacle.[44] An analogous scene in a strip club in *Like Clockwork* displays a quite different level of reflexivity. When Clare interviews Landman in his Isis Club and "[t]he lights [were] suddenly dimmed"

---

42 In an analogous scene in *Daddy's Girl*, we see only Clare's documentary film version of Pearl de Wet's testimony (35–37). With the production process by and large omitted, Pearl is rendered indirectly, making artful forgetting easier for us as spectators.

43 The sex workers are depicted as victims. They are immigrants who are dependent on their gangster owners and addicted to the drugs that they sell. This reminds us that sexual victimhood is implicated in wider forms of global commerce in the service of a violence that masquerades as business.

44 The same successful strategy is used in *Water Music*, when we watch the porn video featuring Rosa on Jonny's phone through Clare's eyes and are shown her disgusted reactions (211–212).

(154), she is released not only from her interview, but from her duty of functioning as an artful reminder to us as readers. Clare watches the strip show, which is rendered in explicitly erotic terms, completely fascinated over an extended period of time, until "Landman touched the inside of her knee. 'That is Justine. I see you like it [...]'" (155). It is only now, by qualifying the spectacle as a "degradation," that she dis-aligns herself – and us as readers – from the sexually predating male gaze that she has been adopting. After the interview, Clare feels both complicit with Landman's misogyny and defiled by her own sexual arousal (157). What we get here is first Clare's unethical disavowal – and, by extension, the reader's – and then her "artful reminder", which characterises ethical spectatorship. However, this reminder is belated and is further undermined by what follows: Clare's road home takes her "without thinking" straight into Riedwaan's bed, where his passionate love-making "obliterat[ed] from her mind what she had watched all evening" (157). We are left wondering whether Clare's act of self-protection is not obliterating her previous act of contra-disavowal along with it. As Naidu concludes on reading this scene, both Clare and the reader are being compromised here (2014, 76), I am not persuaded by Naidu's argument that Clare's belated artful reminder in the scene – which is subsequently "obliterated" – has the effect of encouraging reflexivity in the reader, but, in any case, self-reflexivity can cut both ways. As Aaron points out, it is "capable of being either conservative or transgressive" (2007, 94), and the "line between a representation perpetuating or critiquing conventional myths [...] is a thin one" (98). This brings me to the third type of representational practice that Orford employs: those instances in which she simultaneously both sacrifices the female victim in representation and exposes and contests the practice.

When Clare is close to solving the case of Suzanne's murder in *Gallows Hill*, she goes in search of Lilith, whom she knows to be in danger from her mother's killers. Once she is inside Lilith's house, Clare is guided to a curtained alcove at the end of Lilith's studio by the faint odour of blood:

> Clare pushed the curtains aside and recoiled at the form sprawled on the floor, pale as marble. Lilith. Her lovely head turned away from the door where Clare had entered the room. Clare's eyes were led from the delicate shoulders, rib by rib, to the angle of her hip, the gentle slope of her thighs. The knees. The feet still in heels. Almost the pose of a reclining nude. Her limbs were small and compact, the hips flaring from a narrow waist, her breasts exposed. Above the gash of red lipstick, her face was wan, her hair matted. Blood pooled around her. Both wrists were slashed, with long deep cuts to the bone.
> 328

Clare's slow gaze here in semi-darkness creates the dying Lilith as a piece of art – recalling the stock imagery of the beautiful "reclining nude" cast in "marble," imbuing her with erotic charge, setting her off against a dark pool of blood. Thus, step by step, she activates and reconstructs the aesthetic conventions that link femininity and death. Only after this long-drawn-out moment does Clare attend to Lilith's sufferings. She finally feels for her "moth-breath," diagnoses her as just alive and bandages her wrists (328) before she herself falls into the hands of the perpetrators. What is replicated and perpetuated here is the sacrificial male gaze on the dead/dying female body: the gaze that renders the woman invisible as a subject and distracts from her trauma, as Bronfen and Pollock maintain. Discussing Edgar Allan Poe's famous proposition that "the death of a beautiful woman is, unquestionably, the most poetical topic in the world" (1992, 59), Bronfen claims, "The equation between femininity and death is such, that while in cultural narratives the feminine corpse is treated like an artwork, or the beautiful woman is killed to produce an artwork, conversely, artworks emerge only at the expense of a beautiful woman's death and are treated like feminine corpses" (1992, 72–73). In Orford's text, Clare's prolonged predatory gaze both "kills" the beautiful woman that is Liliths and, by slowing down the narrative pace and creating suspense, serves to create the artwork that is the comforting detective novel.[45] The absence of Orford's usual mission – Lilith is one of Orford's rare female victims who is not subjected to sexual violence – corroborates the impression that Lilith is sacrificed for art's sake alone.

However, this is only one part of the story. We must not forget that, before sacrificing Lilith, Orford had Clare push the curtain aside, thus turning the alcove into a stage. Here, it can be argued, Orford breaks the contract with the spectator by self-reflexively framing the victim's sacrifice as an artistic performance – a performance that is followed by potentially self-reflective echoes of the sacrifice in various languages and cultural spheres. Riedwaan finds the dying Lilith later on and likens her to a "halaal lamb" (Orford 2011b, 341), while Gilles up on Signal Hill replies to Clare's reference to "[a] human sacrifice" with "Muti" and "muti murder" (346).[46] In *Like Clockwork*, Orford uses a different strategy to a similar both/and effect. The prologue starts off with the as yet

---

45   By contrast, an analogous scene in *Daddy's Girl* is much more fast paced and refrains from sacrificing the violated victim in art. Here, Clare springs into action straightaway when she finds the dying Pearl in her house following a brutal assault by her father: "Pearl on the floor. Clare dropped to her knees, her face close to Pearl's. Still breathing. Maybe. She put her hands against her neck. The flicker of a pulse [...] Clare called an ambulance" (303).
46   "Muti" is derived from the Zulu noun "umuthi" and means traditional medicine. A "muti murder" refers to a murder with the purpose of acquiring body parts for use in muti (*Oxford English Dictionary* 2017).

anonymous perpetrator (Kevin Landman) as focaliser and torturer of the as yet anonymous victim (Whitney Ruiters). We see him sadistically burn the palm of her hand with his cigarette and then arrange for her to be picked up by one of his partners in crime as a "[f]resh delivery" (2). After a change of scene that is not instantly recognisable as such, "[m]any hours later" we see the victim again, alone and naked, "huddled in the corner of a room, unaware of the unblinking eye of the camera watching her" (2). The focus is first on her physical pain, caused by various wounds, and then on her thoughts of revenge: "to survive, she thinks of ways of killing. The door opens. 'Dinner, sir,' announces the maid, transfixed by the image on the screen. A finger on the remote and the bruised girl vanishes" (2). It is only now, when we hear the maid's voice and follow her transfixed gaze to the screen, that we notice that we have actually been watching the victim Whitney in a film that the perpetrator Landman is watching on his screen. On the one hand, we are thus rendered as complicit spectators. On the other, the gaze that we have just been adopting is not merely exploitative, but empathic and empowering in its attendance to the victim's sufferings and her retributive agency. Orford here at once reproduces and contests the female victim's sacrifice. Bronfen's concluding remarks on the female dead bodies written by the women writers she examined can be applied to this third type of representational practice: "These narratives by women writers self-consciously install the cultural paradigm that links femininity with death in the same gesture that they critique it" (Bronfen 1992, 432).

Overall, reading Orford's Clare Hart series through the lens of the female victims, whose advocate Orford seeks to be, epitomises the complexities inherent in writing women's traumas, particularly if they ensue from sexual violence. Orford convincingly conceives of the investigative process as a form of addressing and working through the ongoing trauma caused by South Africa's pervasive culture of sexual violence. By turning her detective heroine Clare into a temporary victim who has the crimes that she investigates replayed on herself, Orford is able to change the outcome of this repetition. She repeats with a difference, in LaCapra's sense, and this difference opens up a political space. It is a space for female agency that variously resists, subverts or – as detective agency – restores the patriarchal order.

The same can be said of Orford's representational strategies, which reflect a similarly contradictory gender politics. Although at times she exposes and resists the practice of sacrificing the damaged female body anew in representation – a tactic that has long been employed to ward off both the horrors of death and the threats associated with femininity – on other occasions Orford reiterates and perpetuates it. This has the effect of undermining her feminist agenda and effacing the very pain of women to which she is intent on drawing attention. The serial nature of her crime fiction both calls for and enables varying, even experimenting with, ways of writing female pain and ethically engaging the reader/spectator in the atrocities playing out on the page. However, not all of these strategies do justice to the female victim or can be reconciled with the author's best intentions.

5   The Female Victim: Conclusion

The female victim, unlike the female detective or the female perpetrator, is a gender stereotype, so rewriting her and revising the ways in which she has been represented constitutes resistance from *within* the stereotype. This resistance strategy is fundamentally different from contesting the patriarchal script by "re-gendering" the protagonist as female, as it has as its starting point the reproduction and repetition of what it seeks to subvert and, possibly, transcend. In this respect, the process bears a striking structural resemblance to trauma work. Just as working through trauma may retain elements of acting out, when "working through" the stereotype of the female victim, writers can easily lapse back into "acting it out" and thus reinforce the status quo. None of the writers discussed here is entirely immune to acting out. Nonetheless, the female victims in Lorimer's, Nunn's and many of Orford's crime novels are a far cry from the stereotype of the passive, objectified and invisible female victim who caters to male desire and anxiety concerning femininity and death. This lends support to Priscilla Walton's claim that, whereas the media often obscure or distort the female victim, crime fiction provides a site where victims' stories can be told and issues of gender violence and victimisation explored (2013, 22). By engaging with female victims, the three South African crime writers examined here succeed in writing their stories. What is more, to a large extent they reframe and complicate rigid conceptions of female victimhood. This can be understood as a reaction to the perceived inadequacies of the TRC with regard to gender, a kind of "counter-narrative," as Kate Every puts it (2016, 35). The writers continue and complement the work of the TRC by retrieving the voices of women not just as secondary, but as primary victims, by emphasising the systemic nature and gender-specific effects of many of the violations that South African women have had to endure, and by highlighting not only women's victimhood, but their agency and ability to recover from trauma and to transcend the boundaries of the patriarchal laws that have so often have been enforced with violence against them. If violence against women, particularly sexual violence, is a message directed at men in order to produce male dominance, as Du Toit claims in her fourth frame (2014, 118), recovering the female victim brings her back into the conversation. This is an act of feminist resistance on the part of the authors that exposes the patriarchal nature of the colonial and apartheid projects in South Africa and their legacies for women.

Because these crime novels retrieve women's traumatic experiences in the South African past and present, while also rewriting the perception of them, I have read them as trauma novels that take a stance against real violence. Pitting the novels' overt political agendas against the more latent politics of their aesthetics, particularly the ways in which they represent the violated/dead female body – White and of colour – has revealed that, to varying degrees, the conflicting pressures within the genre persist. And yet, the novels offer a number of successful strategies to counter those pressures. Lorimer is able to preserve the voice of her murder victim Boniswa via her emails. In this way, she renders femininity and women's traumas present, "audibly" but also visibly, by averting the potentially predatory gaze from Boniswa's violated dead body. Nunn does not avert the male detective's hegemonic gaze from her female victim Amahle's dead body, but she undermines and transforms it into an empathic one. By writing a heavily traumatised male detective who is also traumatically implied in the cases that he investigates, Nunn makes her detective see and point to, rather than divert from, women's sufferings and numerous survival strategies. Although Orford sacrifices some of her female victims anew in representation, limiting the political thrust of her novels, even she finds methods of contesting this practice. Notably, she allows some of her victims to speak for themselves, through, but also beyond, Clare Hart's documentary camera. She also self-reflexively stages practices of seeing the female body and their compromising effects, thereby creating awareness of the reader's potential complicity and space for the reader to reflect on his/her own response to violence against women. This array of techniques allows for a writing of the female victim that does her justice. Not only does it save her from being effaced in representation, but it enables a sustained focus on, rather than a diversion from, her trauma. Thus, it potentially contributes to a breaking of the cycle of violence in crime fiction.

In the first part of this study, I have shown what can be achieved both culturally and in terms of race and gender politics by rewriting the female victim in crime fiction – a task made more difficult by the genre's commercial nature – and why it is important for scholars to widen their focus to include the female victim as well as the female detective. Although so far I have examined the female victim in isolation from the female perpetrator, to some extent this distinction is artificial: both Nunn's and Orford's novels testify to the proximity of the two roles, showing how in certain circumstances female victimhood can lead to female vigilantism and perpetration. The figure of the female perpetrator and her function within the genre will be explored more fully in the following part.

CHAPTER 2

The Female Perpetrator

Doing and Undoing Masculinity Through Crime—Exploring the Meanings and Politics of Female Counter-Violence

1   The Female Perpetrator: Introduction

At the end of Lauretta Ngcobo's *And They Didn't Die*, her Black protagonist Jezile murders a White policeman for trying to rape her daughter. In her discussion of the novel, Anne McClintock maintains that "the book asks what happens when women take the weapons of revenge into their own hands" (1995, 388). Even though Ngcobo's novel is not crime fiction and Jezile's transgressive act does not take centre stage in the work, this "what if" question is one that the female perpetrators in South African crime fiction continue to explore.[1] The question points to the threat posed by a woman's act of violence, by her assumption of the masculine role of the killer, by her radical transgression against gender norms. However, it also points to the empowerment that can result for a woman. It marks a shift from victimisation – be it her own or somebody else's – to acts of retaliation, to vigilantism, possibly even to finding satisfaction in killing. By owning her anger and expressing it in acts of violent crime to achieve her goals, the female perpetrator also interrogates and explores female agency and engages in a liberating counter-discourse.

In crime fiction, as in reality, female killers in the role of the protagonist are usually outnumbered by their male counterparts. Nevertheless, contemporary South African crime writers have created instantly memorable female killers who commit multiple acts of violence and murder. The three that stand out are Sheemina February, the female perpetrator in Mike Nicol's Revenge Trilogy, Jade de Jong, the protagonist of Jassy Mackenzie's crime series of the same name, and Angela Makholwa's murderous collective in *Black Widow Society* (2013). Drawing on Judith Halberstam's notion of female masculinity and Serena Dankwa's work on what she terms situational masculinity, I will read these perpetrators' violent actions as masculine gender performance. This is a resistant gender performance, for it not only runs counter to socially

---

1   Such imaginings are invoked beyond the fictional in South Africa. With regard to rape, Pumla Gqola muses, "But there are times when I wonder what would happen if women fought back in defence of ourselves, in numbers and unapologetically" (2015, 10).

constructed norms of femininity, but expands the scope of female agency. Because assertions of power have long been connected to assertions of masculinity, performing the male role of the killer is a way in which these female figures can move to a place of power. By doing so, they not only contest the dominant power, but expose gender norms as constructs and potentially transform the way in which readers of crime fiction view women. Furthermore, they permit the authors to probe questions of retribution and alternative notions of justice from a female perspective. As figures of unease, if not dissatisfaction, with the patriarchal order, fictional female perpetrators are often resistant to a definite reading, a single interpretation. They occupy shifting positions and challenge dichotomies: male – female, victim – perpetrator, perpetrator – detective. Although the female perpetrator appears to occupy a secure position between the female victim and the female detective – hence her placement at the centre of this study – she is a figure who eludes interpretative containment, who always exceeds control.

1.1 *The Female Perpetrator in Crime Genres: Genealogies and Feminist Readings*

Within the crime genre, the figure of the female perpetrator is generally associated first and foremost with the femme fatale of noir film and fiction. However, the femme fatale's roots reach far beyond the noir, even beyond the crime genre as a whole. Carola Hilmes finds in the femme fatale reminiscences not only of cruel female rulers such as Cleopatra or Messalina, but of mythological figures such as Circe, the sirens or the Sphinx. However, she maintains that the Christian dichotomy of witch and saint remains constitutive of the femme fatale (2003, 172). According to Helen Hanson and Catherine O'Rawe "the idea of the femme fatale is 'as old as Eve', or indeed as old as Lilith, Adam's first wife, turned demon and succubus" (2010, 3). One celebrated early example of a female perpetrator in popular fiction is Lady Audley, the protagonist of Mary Braddon's 1862 sensationalist novel *Lady Audley's Secret* (Gavin 2010). Once established as a "type" in the late 19th century (Hanson and O'Rawe 2010, 3), the femme fatale continues to appear in noir and neo-noir fiction and film. Of the three female perpetrators discussed here, Mike Nicol's Sheemina February bears the closest resemblance to the noir/neo-noir femme fatale, a figure who has been described as a "perennial site of uncertainty" (Hanson and O'Rawe 2010, 1).

Another, more recent, type of female perpetrator is the figure of the victim-avenger in rape-revenge fiction and film. According to Claire Henry, the victim-avenger has affinities with the femme fatale figure, but should be viewed as a figure in her own right (2014, 21). Rape-revenge narratives are defined by the female protagonist's "inevitable act of violent revenge against her rapist" (Henry 2014, 1). Based on the tenet that "retribution restores order following rape," this is a potentially feminist genre in so far as it "provides its spectators with a cathartic sense of justice through retributive violence" (1). Not all the female perpetrators discussed here fall into the category of victim-avengers, but they resonate with the victim-avenger in their concern with redress and justice and in their efforts to hold male perpetrators of crime accountable outside the formal criminal justice system. I will refer to the rape-revenge genre when and where it becomes relevant in my discussion.

Apart from the types of the femme fatale and the victim-avenger, the female perpetrator figure in crime fiction has attracted little critical attention. My study seeks to remedy this deficit My approach has been influenced by two critics in particular, Tiina Mäntymäki and Brigitte Frizzoni. Mäntymäki has written on the subject of female perpetrators in Nordic, British and North American crime fiction. She argues that moving away from an exclusive focus on female detective agency to include "morally and socially deviant women is particularly revealing regarding the construction of gender and power" (2012, 199). "Deviance," she claims, "always makes visible the norm, how the women murderers are represented makes visible the ideologies, values and practices that govern the inherently male discourse of power and violence in society" (199). What I have taken from Mäntymäki, besides curiosity and encouragement to consider the perpetrator angle in crime fiction, is a view of the female perpetrator's criminal actions as resistant gender performance. Mäntymäki bases her approach on Judith Butler, who famously perceives gendered identities as not given, but performatively produced. As performance, a reiteration of gender norms always entails a never quite identical repetition and therefore has the potential to subvert the existing order (Butler 1990, 1993). Violating traditional conceptions of femininity constructed as nurturing, compliant and vulnerable, the agency of a woman as murderer is not only disturbing, but extremely subversive. A woman who appropriates the traditionally male space of the killer "'does' gender against the grain" (Mäntymäki 2013, 444) – what I describe as "doing violent female masculinity".

Equally important for me has been Frizzoni's study on female-authored British and North American crime novels and their reception by publishers, reviewers, scholars and readers. The fourth chapter of Frizzoni's book focuses on the controversial debates around fictional female counter-violence, alerting us to the effects that representations of female violence can have on female readers and how this process is affected by the ways in which an author navigates ethical concerns. Drawing on the work of the media scholar Jutta Röser (2000), Frizzoni maintains that depictions of gender-based violence with the woman in the traditional victim role and the man as perpetrator can function to show the watching/reading woman "her place" and are therefore powerful reinforcements of gender hierarchies (2009, 88). As a consequence, fictional reversals, with the woman in the powerful position of the perpetrator – called "non-hegemonic scenes of violence (nichthegemoniale Gewaltszenen)" – by Frizzoni, have an empowering effect on the female audience (89). The female readers and spectators whom Frizzoni questioned reported not only a sense of gratification, but a sense of encouragement, as possibilities of female self-defence were opened up imaginatively. When a *male audience*, by contrast, is confronted by scenes of female violence, the effect produced is one of *terror*, as Judith Halberstam notes (1993). Frizzoni argues that in order to achieve an effect of female empowerment through identification with the female perpetrator, an author must ethically legitimate acts of violence. She emphasises that forms of violence that go beyond immediate self-defence, such as revenge, require particular ethical legitimation in order to offer female readers the potential for identification (2009, 89). Frizzoni's work is especially relevant to the more explicit feminist endeavours of Mackenzie and Makholwa.

1.2 *The Female Perpetrator in the (South African) Real: Interpretations and Cultural Significance*

Women who resort to violence and even murder are not just fictional phenomena in South Africa and elsewhere, although they account for a minority of perpetrators. Of particular interest for my purposes are the ways in which these women and their actions are perceived and interpreted. The most prominent female perpetrator in South Africa is without doubt Winnie Madikizela-Mandela, who as "'mother' of the struggle" and "mother of the nation" fell from grace and, as Brenna Munro puts it, has come to embody "a monstrous motherhood and the unruly, unfaithful wife" (2014, 92, 96, 101). Besides applying the classic good mother/bad mother dichotomy to Madikizela-Mandela, Munro speculates that her implosion as an icon of virtue may have opened up the possibility of less confining scripts for women, "allowing them to create other narratives for themselves" (108). This again points to the liberating potential that the female perpetrator offers for women, as reported by Frizzoni's readers in relation to fictional figures. Nevertheless, Munro regards Madikizela-Mandela's legacy for South African gender politics as "complex and contradictory" (108). Quoting Desiree Lewis, she maintains that Madikizela-Mandela is an "anarchic symbol" and stands as much for disrespect as for impatience and subversion (108).

Also playing into the notion of anarchy, but in different ways, is another aspect of female perpetration in South Africa. The female vigilantes described by the Comaroffs are a product of the anarchy of a failed state, as they contest that anarchy, taking it upon themselves to uphold justice and restore order. Describing her "as unambivalently heroic, even to the cops," the Comaroffs introduce us to Jasmine Harris, a 56-year-old woman from the Cape Flats. Called "the auntie who is scared by nothing," she uses violence to make even hardcore gangsters run and is said to be proud of ensuring safety and security in the neighbourhood (2016, 195). Apparently, women also organise in groups in order to apprehend or kill perpetrators of sexual violence towards elderly women. The Comaroffs mention two examples from different townships in Johannesburg, Westbury and Soweto, to illustrate this. The group in Soweto finds that "it [feels] good to strike back" and seems to agree that its "rituals of violent justice" function as "the ultimate deterrent" (200). What is highly interesting about these cases is that neither the women themselves nor the police perceive these women as having no agency. On the contrary: Jasmine Harris is seen as a hero, even by senior police, for her fearlessness and the effectiveness of her actions. The actions of the Soweto sisterhood also appear to be welcomed by the police (195, 200).

The local interpretation of and reactions to these female advocates of informal justice stand in stark contrast to international sociological, criminological and medical research on female violence. Adelene Africa has looked at how the phenomenon of violent women has been constructed. She identifies three prevailing discourses: violent women are labelled "as pathological (mad), victimised (sad) or deviant (bad)" (2010, 80). What these discourses all share is a conception of the female perpetrator as being devoid of agency. Within medical discourse, violence in women has been explained as a result of biological or psychological dysfunction, as mad (80). Female violence is thus pathologised and not recognised as a form of agency (81). Constructing female perpetrators as sad, as "battered women" who are victimised, can be equally problematic. Africa observes, "While on one hand [sic] these early feminist attempts were laudable, this construction has entrenched stereotypical notions of women as helpless, weak and passive" (81–82). The last type of discourse ("bad") regards women's deviancy as linked to "factors such as race, class, and regional location" (83). Not only does this way of accounting for female perpetration carry a strong risk of stigmatisation, especially of poor Black women, it also ignores women's agency, constructing them as "products of their environments" (84).

In their study on female prisoners in South Africa's Gauteng province, Sadiyya Haffejee, Lisa Vetten and Mike Greyling confirm the substantial victimisation of female offenders. However, like Africa, they caution that "[a]cknowledging this fact need not and should not be done in a manner that encourages the pathologisation of such women, nor deny [sic] them their agency and responsibility" (2005, 46).[2] Studies of this kind on real female perpetrators confirm what Mäntymäki argues for crime fiction: namely, that female perpetrators make gender norms visible. Moreover, framing real female perpetrators in ways that rob them of agency points to an enormous endeavour to socially contain the disturbance that their actions cause. As I shall demonstrate, the fictional female perpetrators examined here contest scholarly conceptions of such women as mad, bad or sad. Although Sheemina February and the Black Widows act from the place of victimhood, they also transcend this position. The Black Widows and Jade de Jong, in particular, echo the notions of "sovereign violence" that the Comaroffs see exemplified in South Africa's vigilantes (2016, 217). Informal justice is neither an entirely new occurrence in South Africa nor a phenomenon unique to that country. However, the Comaroffs see it as taking on a new acuteness in contemporary South Africa, an acuteness that it does not (yet) have elsewhere in the world (216–217). As the Comaroffs perceive them, the advocates of informal justice in South Africa, whether male or female, ultimately fill a space left by a weak state: "With lethal certainty, s/he appropriates the awful, awesome violence on which the sovereignty of the liberal state has always depended, the authorized violence that underwrites the social contract" (217). According to the Comaroffs, so-called "sovereign violence" not only assumes a role that the state should be performing, but seeks to address the very injustices and inequalities created by the state and its proponents: "The promise of that sovereign violence is not merely to harness rogue lawlessness or to lay to rest the threat of criminal disorder. It is also to redress the effects wrought by an amoral economy, one that, in fostering savage appetites and unfulfilled desires, undermines the very possibility of a legible, habitable, and socially viable world" (217). The fictional female perpetrators examined here certainly echo the concerns, addressed by vigilantism, but they do so from a distinctly female perspective. This creates an important difference. State sovereignty in itself is not a gender-neutral concept, as I will demonstrate in my analysis of the female detective. Even if functional, it tends to act in the

---

2   Two studies on female perpetrators in war reach similar conclusions. In their work on female perpetrators in conflicts throughout the world (Abu Ghraib, Bosnia, the Middle East, Rwanda etc.), Laura Sjoberg and Caron Gentry argue that the depiction of these women, too, relies on stereotypes that render them as having no agency (2007). In his study on the representation and judgement of women as perpetrators in the Holocaust, Adam Brown notes that the more than 3,000 women who served in the camps during the war have been mostly excluded from scholarly debates on perpetrator motivation and behaviour (2013, 72–73). Brown argues for "a nuanced approach to representing the complexities of women's complicity in the Holocaust" (86), to show them as human beings "to be judged but not to be demonised" (85) or (perversely) sexualised/eroticised.

interest of White, hegemonic masculinity. For those excluded by it, the redress to which the Comaroffs refer acquires a much broader and altogether more complicated meaning. What is more, because several of the fictional female perpetrators I discuss react to crimes committed by both the apartheid state and those contesting it, I read their retribution in conversation with notions of justice advocated by the TRC. Arguably, these women function to contest or at least complicate, each in their own specific ways, the TRC's concept of restoring justice through reparation and reconciliation.

1.3 Theoretical Preliminaries: Violent Female Masculinity

The fictional female perpetrator's gender political actions can best be understood with reference to Judith Halberstam's work on the performance of masculinity and violence and Serena Dankwa's notion of "situational masculinity". On this basis, I will propose that they constitute a specific type of gender performance that I term "violent female masculinity".

In her 1998 book *Female Masculinity*, Halberstam explores masculinity without men – that is, masculinity in and for women. For this purpose, she coins the term "female masculinity", which denotes masculinities that are produced not by men but by women. This term contests the idea that masculinity can be reduced to the male body (1, 15). Halberstam criticises the norm that "[m]asculinity [...] has been reserved for people with male bodies and has been actively denied to people with female bodies" (269). Such indifference to female masculinity, if not its rejection or pathologising, is ideologically motivated and serves to sustain dominant masculinity, which is wedded "to maleness and to power and domination" (2). In this society, Halberstam argues, dominant masculinity "inevitably conjures up notions of power and legitimacy and privilege" and "often symbolically refers to the power of the state and to uneven distributions of wealth" (2). For Halberstam, female masculinity is not an imitation of maleness; rather, it questions the conflation of maleness with masculinity and thereby renders masculinity visible and legible as a construct (1–2). "[T]he cultivation of female masculinity," she believes, entails political potential and is a "major step toward gender parity [...]" (272). Halberstam argues that her concept favours multiple gender options and serves to transcend the binary gender system that perceives masculinity and femininity as mutually exclusive and distinctive binary oppositions (20). Halberstam ascribes to female masculinity the potential for social rebellion based on an affirmation of different gender taxonomies (9). She concedes that female masculinity can occasionally mark heterosexual variation (9) and, in such instances, menace gender conformity (28); however, she finds that female masculinity is "at its most threatening when coupled with lesbian desire" as it is in the butch (28).

Given that the female perpetrators examined here are predominantly heterosexual and of feminine appearance, we need to extend female masculinity as theorised by Halberstam. This has been done by the social anthropologist Serena Dankwa, who has developed the notion of "situational masculinity". Based on her research on women who desire women in present-day Ghana,[3] Dankwa takes Halberstam's ideas a step further. Situational masculinity in Dankwa's understanding signifies a shift away from visible masculinity, away from a masculine appearance, to the masculinity conferred by a certain status or position of authority/social position. In a Ghanaian context, this can be socioeconomic power or seniority. Such situational masculinity, Dankwa explains, is both relationally and situationally produced; it is associated with masculinity, but not restricted to it (2009, 163–164, 176). The Ghanaian women with whom Dankwa is concerned become masculine (and call themselves "man" or "husband" or "king"), not necessarily because they look, dress and feel like a man, but because they take on a certain social role and/or position of authority.

In the case of the female perpetrator, a woman is able to produce masculinity and assume the power position not by looking butch or by desiring women, but through violent, criminal behaviour – hence my coinage "violent female masculinity". A brief look at masculinity studies reveals that violence is an effective way to produce masculinity. James Messerschmidt confirms that "force and threat of force may be used to help maintain hegemonic masculinity (for example, violence against women and homosexuals)" (2009, 791). Narrowing down violence to crime, he maintains that "[t]he two most significant and tenacious features associated with crime are age and gender. For example, young men account for a disproportionate amount of crime in all Western industrialised societies" (792).[4] Messerschmidt claims that, for men, crime is a way of doing masculinity in an intensified, distinct way, especially when they feel that their masculinity is contested or threatened (2014, 35).[5] For South Africa, as Robert Morell argues, the link between masculinity and violence is even more pronounced. Depicting the specific ways in which the nexus between masculinity and crime manifests itself in the country, he

---

3   Dankwa consciously refrains from using the terms "lesbian" and "homosexual" because they are inadequate in this particular cultural sphere (2009, 164–165).
4   According to Jonny Steinberg, the same is true for South Africa (2008, 30).
5   Messerschmidt, like Du Toit, views crime as a way of producing dominant masculinity. What Du Toit finds problematic, however, from a feminist perspective, is the notion of threatened masculinity as an explanation (or even justification) for crime (2014, 114, 117).

claims that – across the range of different South African masculinities and for different reasons – "[m]asculinity and violence have been yoked together in South African history" (Morrell 2001, 12).[6] Given the significant role that violent and criminal behaviour plays in constructing masculinity (and, by extension, power), it lends itself to an appropriation by women who aim for the power position. An article by Judith Halberstam on imagined violence (1993), written prior to her work on female masculinity, offers some useful insights in this regard. For Halberstam, imagined or fictional violence realised by subordinate groups – for example, women of any sexual orientation – is a "powerful rhetorical strateg[y]" because it opens up "a place of rage" on the part of subordinate groups (1993, 187).[7] In her understanding, a place of rage is a political space, "ground for resistance" (188), made powerful because the boundary between real and imagined violence is "unstable, and radically unpredictable" (187). Imagined violence need not be actualised, but the threat that it could be realised is always there.

This brings us back to the "what if" question raised earlier. Female perpetrators in crime fiction who are spurred by rage resonate powerfully with a real threat of actualisation of female (counter-)violence. Halberstam stresses that the political impact of fictional female violence goes beyond mere role reversal: "The depiction of women committing acts of violence against men does not simply use 'male' tactics of aggression for other ends; in fact, female violence transforms the symbolic function of the feminine within popular narratives and it simultaneously challenges the hegemonic insistence upon the linking of might and right under the sign of masculinity" (1993, 191). Once again, a violent masculine gender performance is much more than an act of imitation. It can be desirable for women not because it is associated with men, but because it confers authority and power that happens to have been associated with men. With regard to detective fiction, this point has been emphasised by Teresa L. Ebert, who insists that the female killer's power is a resistant power that tackles patriarchy (1992, 15–16). Doing violent female masculinity is about power. Likewise, it is important to note that violent female masculinity can assume negative connotations for women of colour. This point is of particular relevance to the female perpetrators depicted in the novels of Nicol, Mackenzie and Makholwa.

---

6 For details of his argument, see Morrell (2001, 12–37, 2005, 282–283).
7 Halberstam borrows the expression "a place of rage" from Prathiba Parma's film of the same name (187).

2 Mike Nicol's Femme Fatale Sheemina February: Empowered Female Agent or Symptom of Male Fears?

> Ever the black widow under the eaves, waiting for the fly, Mace Bishop.
>
> about SHEEMINA in *Black Heart* (16)

Black widow Sheemina February is a "striking woman with a presence" (Nicol 2010b) to her female reader, her male author and her male adversary Mace Bishop alike. She is also striking in deeply ambiguous ways. The lawyer with blood red fingernails on her right hand and a black glove on her left is an incredibly powerful, manipulative woman of racially mixed origins – Coloured in South African nomenclature. Intent on revenge, she takes the law into her own hands and strikes back at Mace, almost bringing about his downfall and shaking the very foundations of the state in the process. As De Kock remarks in his review of Nicol's Revenge Trilogy, which comprises *Payback* (first published in 2009),[8] *Killer Country* (2010) and *Black Heart* (2011), the action plays out in "a Mother City where the dark mother, femme fatale Sheemina February, spins a web of political machination with appalling effect" (2011, par. 3). As a garment that signals "man"ipulation, agency as well as its effacement, that draws attention to and hides what is underneath, and that is the attire of both the lady and the criminal, Sheemina's emblematic black gloved hand serves as the starting point for my discussion of her gender performance and its implications. Three different, largely irreconcilable sets of meanings will be unpacked. Unlike that of the classical noir femme fatale, Sheemina's disruptive impact is not the result of her sexual charms, so my first line of investigation is into the agency that empowers her, into her violent female masculinity. Next, I inquire into the injuries that are hidden beneath her fashionable glove and the ways in which the glove is a signifier associated with violations of Coloured women effected by the socio-political. Lastly, I read the glove as a screen for White and Black male anxieties about disempowerment post-apartheid, exposing the ways in which Nicol activates racist and misogynist myths long associated with the femme fatale in order to control, if not efface, female subjectivity and to deny Sheemina the recognition that she has demanded as a Coloured woman.[9]

The author of the Revenge Trilogy that features Sheemina is Mike Nicol, a Cape Town-born and bred poet, journalist and novelist. Throughout his long

---

8   My analysis is based on the slightly revised 2010 edition of *Payback*.
9   Parts of this chapter were first presented as papers in South Africa and Switzerland in 2014.

writing career, South African politics as well as the country's colonial and apartheid history have been the subject of Nicol's literary and non-literary explorations. Michael Titlestad and Ashlee Polatinsky note that "his oeuvre represents one of the most impressive and sustained literary engagements with the nation's agonized history" (2010, 260).[10] Nicol turned to the crime genre quite late in his career, having formerly written his novels mostly in the mode of magic realism.[11] At the onset of the new millennium, however, Nicol felt that a change was warranted in South African fiction writing. This was not so much about subject matter, as about style: "a change in how the stories are told" (Breysse 2001, 200). Nicol perceived a need for "a hard-hitting, sharper kind of book." As he puts it in one interview: "I think we need to switch back to less magic, more realism in order to come to terms with the current country. I think that's what literature does. But also to try and tell the stories, I just think it should be more immediate. [...] Stories have to be more entertaining. And the reader has to be considered more" (Breysse 2001, 207–208). With hindsight, it is possible to see that writing in the crime fiction genre answered Nicol's need for a fictional method more in keeping with local pressures and possibilities. His first novel in the new millennium, *Out to Score* (2006), co-authored with Joanne Hichens, was the first of eight thrillers that he has published so far.[12] It was followed by the Revenge Trilogy, which is the focus of the present chapter, *Of Cops & Robbers* (2013a), *Power Play* (2015b), *Agents of the State* (2017) and *Sleeper* (2018). In addition to being a prolific writer, Nicol has been an active, significant promoter and documenter of South African crime fiction in his popular, much-quoted blog *CrimeBeat*, set up in 2007, a platform that he publicises via other social media.[13]

Nicol's Revenge Trilogy straddles political commentary and the popular thriller noir form. It revolves around the antagonism between the White Mace and his Coloured nemesis Sheemina, which reaches back to the days of the anti-apartheid struggle. A freedom fighter and arms dealer in those days, Mace now runs a security company with his Black long-time business partner Pylon Buso. Sheemina is now a wealthy, successful lawyer in Cape Town, where their paths cross again over a conflict between their respective clients. However,

---

10 See Ian-Malcom Rijsdijk for more on Nicol's deployment of history and the transformation of his novelistic style (2011). Serge Breysse's interview with Nicol details how the notion of the past informing the present pervades Nicol's writing (2001).
11 Nicol's novels published before the turn of the millennium are *The Powers That Be* (1989), *This Day and Age* (1992), *Horseman* (1994) and *The Ibis Tapestry* (1998). His oeuvre also includes two poetry collections and a substantial body of non-fiction. For details see http://mikenicol.bookslive.co.za/about/.
12 In the USA, *Out to Score* was published as *Cape Greed* under the name of Sam Cole.
13 http://crimebeat.bookslive.co.za/.

recognition is not mutual: Sheemina instantly recognises Mace and Pylon, but the two do not recognise her. For much of the first novel, *Payback*, Sheemina operates in the background. In the second novel, *Killer Country*, Sheemina has firmly established her central position as the – mostly invisible – woman who plots and engineers every single hit, including the murder of Mace's wife Oumou at the end of the novel. It is only now that Mace begins to take Sheemina seriously. So the scene is set for the final showdown between Mace and Sheemina in the last and bleakest of the three novels, *Black Heart*, at the end of which she is murdered by an NIA agent.

Scholars working on Nicol's trilogy have highlighted its socially critical potential. For De Kock, Nicol's is "a devastating commentary on the beloved country" (2010, 17). Drawing on Deleuze and Guattari, De Kock reads the trilogy as a reflection on a diseased social body that is "stricken by the schizophrenia of late capitalism and the orgy of spectacular consumerism" (2011, par. 12). Crime is "the cancer that routs the healthy order of things" (2011, par. 14). Similarly, although Titlestad and Polatinsky are critical of what they perceive as Nicol's sell-out as a writer to a facile popular form, they acknowledge *Payback*'s resonance with the political (2010, 269). In a 2016 article, De Kock offers " 'more' and 'less sympathetic' readings" of Sheemina (104) and asks about the implications of all this "political 'evil' " being projected on to a female character of colour (99). I will return to his answer to this question later, but first we need to establish where Sheemina derives her power from and just why she constitutes such a threat to Mace and to the patriarchal state at large.

2.1 *Sheemina's Black-Gloved Hand: Epitome of Violent Female Masculinity*

Sheemina never leaves her elegant flat without the emblematic black glove on her left hand. Putting on her black glove becomes synonymous with the performance of her public persona; it is her trade mark and stands for her agency as a perpetrator, which is realised through her violent female masculinity. The black glove functions to blur gender boundaries. It is a device that connotes both female and male. It is a feminine fashion accessory that aptly signs Sheemina's stylish credentials (Nicol 2010b, 388, 407), but it also implies by association the sheath that conceals a dagger (2010a, 129), thus suggesting the prospect of violence. The male encoding comes into play as the glove is signed as a masculine criminal accessory, conventionally worn by the male perpetrator to avoid fingerprints contaminating the crime scene (2010a, 83). Sheemina's black-gloved hand can thus be viewed as a signifier for her violent female masculinity.

Sheemina's modus operandi could hardly be more violent: bomb blasts (66–67), kidnappings (2010b, 104, 415, 2011, 56), torture (2011, 86) and shootings, which more often than not result in death (2010a, 156, 165, 245, 247, 370, 2010b, 129, 351, 2011, 321). For Sheemina, violent masculinity and a female body are by no means mutually exclusive. When her stylist finds the way she wants her hair cut "'[a] bit butch ...,'" Sheemina replies, "'Butch's working,' [...]. 'It's a man's world, so we're told'" (2011, 96). In the man's world in which she operates, Sheemina is able to beat men at their own game, always remaining a step ahead of her (mostly violent) male antagonists. Sheemina's violent masculine gender performance constitutes a significant departure from both the classic femme fatale and her neo-noir successor. The classic femme fatale derives her power from her sexuality (Place 1980, 36). The neo-noir femme fatale, too, uses her now liberated sexuality to exercise substantial power over men (Bronfen 2004b, 106). Lee Horsley describes the new femme fatale as "ever more confidently putting on display the power of her sexuality" (2010, 263); she is "erotically empowered" and "unashamedly sexual" (264). Certainly, Sheemina's sex appeal is not lost on men: serial killer Spitz is clearly drawn to her (Nicol 2010a, 194) and NIA agent Mart leers at her (2011, 242), while Mace eyes her breasts and registers her Penelope Cruz lips (2010b, 55, 208, 396). But this says more about normative codes of masculinity in relation to femaleness than about Sheemina's seductive powers per se. As much as she works with the code of sexual seduction, her destructive power lies in her masculine gender performance. One of the signatures that she uses throughout the trilogy is the long-stemmed rose, deep purple, exactly the colour of her lipstick. She sends these roses to Mace, his wife, and his lover and leaves them at murder scenes (2010a, 354). However, as Mace comes to understand, her roses are not to be read as substitutes for her flirtatious kiss, but are meant to convey a different, threatening message: to make herself felt as a constant presence, a reminder to be taken seriously. The rose is meant "to anger him" (2010a, 267), "to put a chill in his blood" (2010a, 267) and, eventually, to communicate to Mace that he will be her next murder victim.

Although the trilogy is furnished with the iconography of the sexually enticing femme fatale, Sheemina does not seduce her victims. Instead, her strategy is a violent masculine one. However, masculinity is not only something that she performs through her acts of violence – it is also her target, especially as personified by her nemesis Mace. As an arms dealer during the anti-apartheid struggle, Mace is a legend of the past (2011, 161) to whom the post-apartheid present holds out only limited possibilities as a man. Mace and his partner Pylon are now working in the security business, a form of private army that allows them to perform a quasi-militarised function, replete with weapons and hyper-aggressive codes of conduct. In this way, they attempt to recreate the exaggerated, violent, heroic masculinity of the struggle, for which they are nostalgic. Despite their tough-guy names and identities, however, they have been reduced to mere goons, chauffeurs for scared people, babysitters for the paranoid, caretakers for rich clients on surgical safaris (2010a, 17, 2010b, 44, 173). The masculine roles that the struggle offered to Mace and Pylon resemble the warrior-inflected masculinities of a war. As Samuelson contends, such "[f]igurations of war delineate masculine and feminine positions, both depending on and exaggerating constructions of gender difference: men are presented as warriors and protectors whereas women, cast in turn as the protected, embody hearth and home and are thus rendered passive and inactive" (2007b, 839). By her unconventional behaviour, Sheemina not only significantly blurs such clear-cut boundaries, she also refuses to take the feminine position. What is more, with her successful assaults on Mace, she actively targets this masculinity that is stuck in the iconography of war. She engineers attacks on several of Mace's clients (Nicol 2010a, 165, 2011, 46) and thereby demonstrates his ineptitude as a post-apartheid "warrior" in the security business, compromising his masculinity in the process. She also has Mace's daughter kidnapped and violated and his wife Oumou killed (2010a, 357, 2010b, 104). Besides causing him unspeakable grief, she seriously compromises his masculinity as a father/husband who is unable to protect his family. Sheemina thus effectively emasculates Mace.[14] Sheemina's masculine gender performance, aimed at subverting Mace's masculinity, functions to expose what Halberstam calls the "fantasies about masculinity that have ensured that masculinity and maleness are profoundly difficult to pry apart" (1998, 2). The sheer scale of the threat that Sheemina poses not only to Mace, but even to government (Nicol 2011, 335), and the vehemence with which dominant masculinity fights back, in the figure of the Black NIA agent Mart Velaze, make clear that women doing crime

---

14   The tactics of Isabella, Nicol's other femme fatale, who appears only in *Payback*, differ markedly from Sheemina's, but they, too, expose Mace's weakness as a man. Whereas Sheemina emasculates Mace, Isabella promises to restore his wartime masculinity. She offers him a revival of the past, both sexually and professionally. She manages to seduce him because "sex with Isabella smelt of guns. Always had done. A brush of linseed when her body heat came up. [...] That excitement that possessed you" (Nicol 2010b, 227). Sex with Isabella allows Mace to evoke the armed struggle, and she reassures him: "Mace, you're still a good screw" (229). Isabella also allows Mace to assert his manhood professionally by offering him a shady deal that requires his skills as an arms dealer. The way in which he totally succumbs to Isabella, failing to see that she is manipulating him while also jeopardising his treasured marriage to Oumou (32), testifies to his desperate need for confirmation of his masculinity.

is more than a simple role reversal. As Halberstam emphasises, it "challenges the hegemonic insistence upon the linking of might and right under the sign of masculinity" (1993, 191).

The racial implications of female masculinity matter, since violent Black female masculinity resonates with racist stereotypes of the criminal Black woman. Talking about Black butches in an American context, Halberstam notes that "black women face far more damning accusations of masculinity than white women in our society" (1998, 271). Bell Hooks criticises the prevalence of the devaluing stereotype called "Sapphire", which entails "images of black female bitchiness, evil temper, and treachery" (1994, 209). While American constructions of blackness do not apply unreservedly to South Africa, what Halberstam says about Black female masculinity that works *against* racial stereotyping is still useful. Halberstam finds that Black female masculinity subverts racist stereotypes when "it is infused with racial and class dynamics that render the masculinity part and parcel of a particular form of abjected female identity" (1998, 229). This is realised, at least in part, in the figure of Sheemina due to the fact that her violent actions are motivated by an anger that originates in her racial abjection, thus countering potential racist stereotyping. She acts from a place of rage, and Nicol's narrative exposes the racist and misogynist practices that form the basis of that rage.

2.2 Underneath the Black Glove: Violations of the Coloured Woman Demanding Recognition

It is only in the privacy of her apartment, which she never allows anyone else to enter, that Sheemina takes off her black glove. During these scenes, we as readers become privy to the fact that her black glove hides a lasting "disfigurement" (Nicol 2010b, 431), the result of having been subjected to torture and rape. In this context, the black glove becomes a symbol of repression, a refusal to see and to acknowledge pain. Because Sheemina's injuries are not seen and not recognised by Mace, arguably they acquire a haunting, uncanny quality for him. They also point to stories of violations inflicted on Coloured women, particularly Coloured women activists, that are being repressed by the wider socio-political consciousness. Sheemina's black glove becomes so emblematic of her that, by the beginning of the third novel, it suffices to introduce the woman herself (2011, 1). It works to represent, through metonymy – the part standing for the whole – the damaged bodies of apartheid's others' extreme other, the Coloured female activists.

This is the story of Sheemina's disfigured hand, as we first hear it in the last scene of *Payback*: During the days of apartheid, 18-year-old Sheemina hitched her way from Cape Town to a training camp for freedom fighters in

Lusaka (Zambia). There, she wanted to learn to shoot so that she could join the guerrilla army. However, when she arrived at the camp, nobody believed her story and she was considered an apartheid spy. It was Mace and Pylon who tortured her in order to extract what they believed was the "truth". Mace smashed her left hand with a mallet, inflicting such pain that "death would've been a mercy" (2011, 322) and a lasting "disfigurement" (2010a, 131–132, 2010b, 431). Besides being tortured, "[t]he young girl was raped by the leaders. Not once. Not twice. Every day for months" (2010b, 431). Sheemina's is a story of violation that has both a gendered and a racial aspect. As a Coloured woman, she was subjected to the brutal violence of both Black and White men during the struggle. While seeking to take an actively resistant role in the struggle, she was objectified by rape, rendered powerless by the men on her own political side. The violations that Sheemina suffered have a real referent that has not been acknowledged by official South Africa to the present day. As Goldblatt and Meintjes make clear, "gender violence within the South African liberation movements has not been fully aired and remains an unwritten chapter of our history" (1997, 13). To a large extent, this continues to be the case (Gqola 2007, 120, Samuelson 2007b, 842, Tlhabi 2017). Not only did men not apply for amnesty for sexual violence committed before the TRC, but women, too, remained silent about it, "[e]specially in relation to having been raped by men in the liberation movement" (Borer 2009, 1176). As a consequence, these perpetrators were not held accountable. Tristan Anne Borer speculates that women did not speak out about sexual violence in the liberation movement for fear of undermining their comrades – some of whom were public figures – or jeopardizing their own careers (1176). Sheemina's maimed hand, hidden underneath the black glove, is testament to these silences.

The fact that Sheemina is objectified and rendered powerless as a Coloured woman in the guerilla camp also points to the long-standing marginalisation of Coloured people in South Africa. Coloured subjectivity has been characterised not only as "in-between" (Erasmus 2001, 15), but sometimes simply as "non-existent" (16). It was conceptualised as mixed or residual – as neither White nor Black – during apartheid and, consequently, has never been seen in its own right (17). The 1950 Population Registration Act defines Coloured subjectivity negatively, as "[n]ot a White person or a Black" (Wicomb 1998, 101). Thus, Mohamed Adhikari identifies marginality as the defining characteristic of Coloured subjectivity (2009, viii). As a result of their in-between position, of not being recognised as White or Black, Coloured people have also had a difficult, even compromised, position in South Africa's struggle for freedom. Heidi Grunebaum and Steven Robins illustrate the way in which the complex, in-between position of Coloured subjectivity resulted in "expulsion from political community" (2001, 163–167) during the anti-apartheid struggle by reference to the Coloured ANC activist and MK combatant Zahrah Narkadien. Narkadien recounts, "So even my comrades used the fact that I was not really in their eyes an African. It was painful for them to also deny me that right to be an African woman" (quoted in Grunebaum and Robins 2001, 167). More than anything, what Sheemina seeks is recognition, as we see from her reaction to her first accidental meeting with Mace: "To recognise but not be recognised. To be seen yet remain hidden. The thought angered her that in the life of Mace Bishop her life had barely registered" (Nicol 2010b, 54). "Recognise" must be understood in this context not simply as "to perceive to be the same as something or someone previously known or encountered", but also as comprising the meanings "to accept the authority, validity, or legitimacy" of, "to acknowledge, consider, or accept (a person or thing) *as* or *to be* something", "to show official appreciation of" and "to perceive clearly; to realize, understand, or apprehend" (*Oxford English Dictionary* 2017, original emphasis). Sheemina demands recognition in the full sense of the word.

In *Killer Country*, Sheemina's anger at still being denied recognition becomes more intense:

> The memory [of Mace and Pylon's torture] jolted her upright. "Bastards." The agony on her face. "Bastards." In a sweep of her arm, Sheemina February hurled her wine glass through the open door into the night. Sat staring at her crab hand. Flexed her fingers, stiff as claws. Could have cried for that young woman. That young woman still a girl really.
>
> NICOL 2010a, 132

Sheemina's anger gives way to revenge that is a "blood feud" (2011, 298) in the very city that her slave ancestors once built (2010b, 423): Cape Town. By giving Sheemina the surname February, Nicol makes a direct link to Cape Town's slave history. Slaves in the Cape Colony customarily took a new surname on their emancipation, which in the case of Sheemina's ancestors must have happened in the month of February.[15] The significance of Sheemina's insistent claiming of the White space, as exemplified in the trilogy by her prominently located, expensive apartment, becomes understandable in view of the

---

15 Cape Town's slave history and the controversies surrounding the treatment of excavated slave bones feature prominently in *Payback*, where Sheemina's clients fight for a memorial for the bones (Nicol 2010b, 394). The real events behind this fictional account are also referred to by Margie Orford in *Gallows Hill*.

marginalisation of the Cape Coloured population. She treasures her upmarket Bantry Bay apartment in Cape Town, which she refers to as her white "lair and sanctuary" (2010a, 9, Nicol 2011, 16). This space is not to be tainted by anyone's presence: it is "[h]ers and hers alone. Never had she invited anyone into it. Never would she" (2010a, 195). Significantly, it is again Sheemina's black-gloved hand that incessantly presses Mace to recognise her as a rightful inhabitant of the Cape and as the woman whom he tortured and raped in the struggle camps. In her interactions with Mace, Sheemina never allows him to overlook her gloved hand. She frequently draws attention to it by holding it up or touching it (2010b, 46, 84, 393, 2011, 321). Mace remains blind to this for a long time, despite perceiving a certain familiarity from the beginning. Following their second meeting, Mace is "irked by a detail he couldn't get to. 'There's more,' he said. 'Only I don't know what. She's familiar'" (2010b, 47). Mace dwells on this strange, but for him inexplicable, familiarity for two full novels.[16] Only after his wife Oumou is murdered at the end of *Killer Country* does he finally recognise Sheemina in a picture of him and his daughter taken on Table Mountain, the moment of recognition freeing him to relate her to his misfortunes:

> He looked at the photograph: the two of them locked tight. Christa pulled in against his chest. [...] Could anyone tell his wife had been murdered? Could anyone say her mother was dead? The lies photographs told. [...] He looked closer at their faces [...]. Then took in the background: above, a sky of wide and dying crimson. Behind them a terrace and a parapet wall. Standing at the wall, a woman in a long coat. A woman with a black glove. Sheemina February.
>
> 2010a, 373

Mace's protracted inability to recognise Sheemina for who she is becomes a sign of how successfully he represses any connection between the uncanny Sheemina and himself until she almost destroys him.[17] Sheemina occupies a place of "forgotten" absence in Mace's memories of his compromised past. She

---

16   Mace constantly muses on "ironies", "coincidences", "coincidence [...]. Sans irony" (2010a, 306, 333) with regard to Sheemina's associations with him.

17   Another poignant illustration of the return of the repressed and Mace's inability to shed the past is given in *Payback*. By having Christa shot in Mace's Victorian home, Sheemina turns it into an unhomely/uncanny place that Mace subsequently tries to cast off by selling it. Sheemina then buys the house, via an agent. Later she incarcerates Mace in the house's cellar, thus forcing him to return to it and to its very foundations (129, 180, 282–283, 424).

is portrayed as a spooky figure with a haunting, ghost-like presence,[18] prompting us to read her as an embodiment of the Freudian "uncanny". In his famous essay on the subject, Freud contends that what appears to us as uncanny and now induces anxiety is in fact the familiar, the already known, rendered uncanny through the process of repression. Hence, "uncanny" refers to what should have remained "secret, hidden away, and has come into the open" (Freud 2003 (1919), 132). Sheemina's Colouredness adds to an impression of her as uncanny. As a racial category, Coloured identity reveals the limits of racial categorisation. Lewis explains, "The semiotic coding of 'race' surfaces explicitly in definitions of racial hybridity or, in the South African frame of reference, coloured identity" (2001, 133), adding that in racial discourse "the term 'coloured' has been linked to a fixation with maintaining racial boundaries" (133). Coloured as a racial category is thus the uncanny, ever-resurfacing reminder not only of race as a construct, but of the futility of its attempt to draw boundaries. Overall, a reading of Sheemina as embodying repressed gender and racial truths of marginality, exclusion and boundary blurring allows female subjectivity to surface and to find expression in Nicol's novels. This is true to only some extent, however, as at the same time female subjectivity is also effaced in the Revenge Trilogy.

2.3 The Black Widow's Sexy Glove: a Screen for Black and White Male Anxieties

Even though Sheemina uses violent masculine ways, not sexual seduction, she nevertheless fantasises about taking revenge on Mace in explicitly sexual terms. For this reason, the black glove can also be read as what Sheemina herself calls a "sexy" glove (Nicol 2011, 312): namely, in its noir figuration as a signifier for the femme fatale's sexual allure, and thus as a screen on to which men project their anxieties. This facet of the glove, I will argue, not only loses sight of Coloured female subjectivity and Sheemina's agency as a woman, but effectively effaces her by reinscribing racist and misogynist myths.

In the soliloquy-like scenes that picture Sheemina alone in the privacy of her apartment – which increase in frequency with every new novel – we learn of her sexual attraction to Mace. She finds her opponent erotic and repeatedly imagines murdering him in a fatal sexual encounter, with Sheemina playing the role of the female black widow spider who devours her mate during sexual

---

18 Sheemina shadows and spooks Mace's every movement and "accidentally" bumps into him in the most unlikely places (Nicol 2010a, 63, 267, 286, 373, 2010b, 79, 2011, 1–6). She leaves a presence behind and makes her presence in Mace's life felt and known (2010a, 100, 2010b, 45, 271).

intercourse. In her fantasies, she turns into an actual spider woman (Nicol 2011, 16) who stages the final battle with her sexy adversary as a date, a candlelight dinner, complete with a cooked meal, a long black dress, high heels and a revolver (306). She anticipates squeezing him to death with her hands while he is thrusting into her (2010a, 268, see also 2011, 4). However, Sheemina's final encounter with Mace at the end of *Black Heart* turns out very differently from her fantasies. As soon as Mace arrives at her apartment, "Sheemina February unstrapped her high heels, left them lying beneath the table. High heels were not the shoes for a gunfight. She picked up the revolver, padded through to her bedroom" (2011, 311). Instead of seducing Mace, she ends up shooting him in his upper arm and thigh (318). If we read Sheemina as a rape avenger, her fantasies can be said to mirror Mace's rape of her in the struggle camp, but this time with Sheemina in the power position. Henry points out that this is a common practice in the rape-revenge genre: "In many contemporary rape-revenge films, [the] revenge is constructed to mirror the rape scene [...]" (2014, 93). In a similar vein, we can read her obsessive photographing of Mace as an oppositional gaze that reverses the dominant voyeur position. Again, this is not an uncommon feature of rape-revenge films (Henry 2014, 93). Sheemina habitually loses herself in her ever-increasing collection of photographs of Mace, often depicting him in his wet black Speedo, or even naked. The last novel opens with her watching footage of him through the eye of her private CCTV camera (Nicol 2011, 1–6). By showing the female gaze as engaging in surveillance and voyeurism of the male body, Nicol tempers the traditionally male gaze of the noir world and creates a potentially transgressive reader identification – or "alignment", as Henry terms it, based on Murray Smith (Henry 2014, 12).

However, such a revisionist reading of Nicol's representational practice is undercut by the way in which it activates demeaning myths about women in general, and about women of colour in particular, that are indicative of male anxieties about women and their power. The case of the famous southern African (Khoisan) woman Sarah Baartman serves to interrogate these myths. In her discussion of Baartman, who was put on public display in France and Britain in the 19th century as the "Hottentot Venus", Lewis reveals how "[b]oth African men and women have been defined in terms of sexual excess, bestiality and bodily deviance" (2011, 205). Depicting Sheemina as endlessly lost in sexual fantasies about the man who tortured her reiterates conceptualisations of the excessively sexual African woman. Such inscriptions mask a patriarchal and colonial desire for control and mastery (Lewis 2011, 202–203). On the other side of the Atlantic, Patricia Hill Collins exposes the explicit links between the stereotype of the sexually aggressive woman of colour, there called "Jezebel", and slavery, and unmasks this as an image of White male control: "The image of Jezebel originated under slavery [...]. Jezebel's function was to relegate all Black women to the category of sexually aggressive women, thus providing a powerful rationale for the widespread sexual assaults by White men [...]" (2000, 81).

Also problematic is the way in which Sheemina differentiates Mace's rape from the other rapes that she had to endure in the struggle camps and effectively eroticises it. In their final encounter, she recounts Mace's rape of her, calling him "my white angel" and telling him: "Troubling thing is, Mace, your gentleness. That's what I remember. How gentle you were for a rapist. Afterwards, the others, they wanted something different" (Nicol 2011, 322). Mace calls this "crap" and "your fantasy" (322). It is not clear whether his denial refers to the rape as such or to Sheemina's recollection of it as gentle and erotic. Either way, the effect is to marginalise the rape victim. Depicting rape as sex functions to mask the fact that rape is about power and about power in a very fundamental way. When discussing her fourth interpretative frame, Du Toit describes rape as an expression of ontological violence:

> [W]hat I call ontological violence aims to redescribe or redraw the very limits of the real, of the truth, of the world itself. What I thus argue is that the thrill of raping another person lies precisely in the embodied, manifested power, indeed the sovereignty, that this act bestows on the perpetrator. The new world of the perpetrator is built on the ruins of the victim's world.
> 2014, 120

Sheemina's attempts to counter the "truth" established by her rapists fail. In the end, her "truth" about the violations that she suffered in the struggle camp remains unacknowledged by Mace and, through her depiction of rape as gentle, erotic play, the power of the rapist is reinstalled. What is more, the victim is rendered as untrustworthy. The notion that Sheemina is not to be trusted is reinforced by her own sudden disclosure to Mace of her "secret" – namely, that she was in fact an apartheid spy. In the next sentence, she casts doubt on even this "truth": "How about that? And nobody ever knew for sure [...]. I got information on all the big players. Both sides" (Nicol 2011, 322). Here, Nicol not only questions the truth value of the victim's story, but rehearses the South African stereotype of the untrustworthy Coloured. Coloureds have faced accusations of untrustworthiness as a result of their "hierarchical relation to both white and black African identities; they are experienced and constructed as less than white and better than black" (Erasmus 2001, 24). Thus, while being subjected to White domination, they have taken part in the racist discourse of creating Black Africans as the Other and in excluding and subordinating them (2001, 24). By presenting Sheemina as the epitome of untrustworthiness, Nicol causes her version of events and the truth value of the accounts of female violation that she has brought to light – indeed, her very independent subjectivity – to become effaced.

Because Sheemina's accounts expose truths about patriarchal power that undermine it, they constitute a threat, suggesting that she is perhaps to be read as a mere symptom of male anxieties. This is a long-standing feminist reading of the femme fatale, initiated by Mary Ann Doane. Given the femme fatale's fundamental, dangerous instability and the fact that she is seen as evil personified and hence to be punished, often killed, Doane views her as a "desperate reassertion of control on the part of the threatened male subject" (1991, 2). In Doane's understanding, she is therefore not an independent, modern heroine, but a "symptom of male fears about feminism" (2–3). Sheemina, as an attractive, inscrutable, steely and ice-cold woman, has the traits of the classic femme fatale (Hanson 2010, 217–221, Hilmes 2003). She is described as "evil" (Nicol 2010b, 181, 396), as exuding "ruthlessness" (2010a, 100) and a "lingering malevolence" (101). What is more, she is "connected," as Mart Velaze warns, "'[l]ike you wouldn't believe. Government, business. A mover and a shaker. Not a pie she hasn't fingered in this city. Not a woman you want to mess with, buta'" (2011, 272). She is the mysterious woman lurking in the shadows who is "seen yet remain[s] hidden" (Nicol 2010a, 267–268, 373, 2010b, 54). Clearly, the generic script of the alluring, evil, manipulative and ultimately unknowable woman is activated. In his "less sympathetic reading" of Sheemina, De Kock follows an interpretation of the femme fatale as a symptom of male fears – in Sheemina's case, of post-apartheid White male "displacement anxieties" (2016b, 107). He finds "Nicol's creation of a 'bad' black woman [...] a tad too convenient," providing an outlet for "all those repressed anxieties consequent upon male marginalisation" (104). De Kock hints at the possibility that these fears include those of the White writer himself. For him, the gesture of "locat[ing] such a pronounced sense of political 'evil' in a *Black* female character" raises the question whether Nicol might "be seeking a sacrificial object for the perceived ills of post-apartheid" (98, my emphasis). As many White oppressive mechanisms have been applied to *both* Coloured and Black people, conflating Coloured and Black, as De Kock does, can sometimes be justified. However, the unsettling, menacing effect Sheemina has on both Black and White men suggests that her characterisation as a Coloured (not a Black) woman is of importance.[19] As I have shown, Sheemina's uncanny, destabilising quality derives both from her being figured as a femme fatale and from the fact that she is *Coloured* (not Black). Moreover, Nicol's text suggests that this is not an exclusively White

---

19 De Kock does mention the fact that Sheemina is specifically a Coloured woman, however (see 98, footnotes 1 and 3).

male perspective. Obed Chocho, one of Sheemina's Black clients, claims, "You couldn't trust a coloured" (Nicol 2010a, 59). The two hired killers, Manga and Spitz, both Black men, comment on Coloured ambiguity in a way that conflates racial with gender ambiguity in significant ways. In one of the novel's more comical episodes, Manga and Spitz are being satisfied by someone they think is a Coloured female prostitute at the Cape Town waterfront. When Manga realises that he is actually having sex with a man he is exasperated: "'Shit, captain, shit, man she's not a prossie. That's a guy. With a cock and balls squeezed between her legs.' Spitz stared at Manga. Stared at the prossie Cherildeen in her short skirt hurrying away in the distance, forced a laugh. 'Sometimes,' he said, *'with coloureds you cannot tell'* " (210, my emphasis). Interestingly, Spitz explicitly links Cherildeen to Sheemina, as a moment earlier he had observed that to him Cherildeen "looked the image of Sheemina February. Only younger" (208). Indeed, given her violent female masculinity, "you cannot tell" with Sheemina with regard to gender either. She blurs the boundaries between male and female just as she does between Black and White, to destabilising, uncanny and fear-inducing effect for both Black *and* White males.

The trilogy's ending provides further evidence of this shared weight of male anxiety that demands Black and White curtailment of the Coloured Sheemina. The trilogy ends with the elimination of its driving force, Sheemina, in what is suspected to be "a State hit" (2011, 339). Sheemina is murdered by the Black NIA agent Mart Velaze seconds before she can shoot Mace. The White Mace, though severely injured, is thus saved by Mart's last-minute intervention. In a world where all the major players, be they from the new or the old elite, male or female, are presented as flawed, it is Sheemina the Coloured woman who, as the biggest threat, is punished by both South Africa's "old White" and "new Black" male elite, relegated to objectification and inexistence. Unlike De Kock, I do not read Mart and Sheemina as being on the same side. Mart knows about the impending final confrontation between her and Mace from Sheemina herself, so when he appears in the midst of their battle Sheemina does not doubt that he has come to help her to kill Mace, as indeed he pretends (2011, 324). Angry at his intervention, she repeatedly tells Mart to "back off" (325), as this is *her* "play" (324), *her* "gig" (325). De Kock views "Velaze killing Shemina [sic]" as "death at the betraying hands of someone on her own side" (2016b, 110). Importantly, though, Mart betrays the Coloured femme fatale Sheemina (and saves Mace) not just as a man, but as a Black man who must not be conflated racially with her. Mart's intervention on the side of hegemonic patriarchy (Black and White in complicity) adds the finishing touch to Sheemina as male symptom. Her death is first and foremost about male anxieties over loss of control. Reading her as Coloured, rather than Black, reveals the threat not only of her femaleness, but of her Colouredness, to both Black and male hegemonic masculinity. I am reminded of Griselda Pollock's claim that one of the consequences of using the eroticised female body as a screen for male projections is to distract from female trauma. Although Nicol's intention may have been to draw attention to stories of Coloured women's trauma, by rendering Sheemina as a Coloured femme fatale and foregrounding the sexiness of her glove, he succeeds only in repeating them. In the end, Sheemina is denied recognition as a Coloured guerrilla woman while her comrades get away with their violations, which remain hidden.

Nicol has described Sheemina as manipulating not only his male characters, but curiously, to some extent, himself as the author. Looking back on the writing process, he says that "[t]o a degree there was a question mark over whether I was creating her or she was creating herself" (Binder 2015, 268). Elsewhere he suggests that she appeared "fully formed out of nowhere. All I was required to do was take dictation" (Nicol 2012b, par. 11), and describes her as walking in and taking over (Nicol 2012a). By "creating herself," Sheemina seems to have dominated the narrative drive, perhaps giving rise to authorial fears in the process. At the same time, it was her arrival that enabled Nicol to finish *Payback* (Nicol 2012a). In this context, his taking "dictation" from her, the domineering one, takes on another meaning – namely, that of the author as medium, with Sheemina speaking through him about Coloured female subjectivity and its repression. As a Coloured femme fatale, Sheemina both precedes and exceeds Nicol's texts (and his fears). The instability of Sheemina for her author as well as for the noir hero also extends to her meaning within the interpretative process, as is evident from my three different readings of her black-gloved hand. Bronfen maintains that "the meaning [the femme fatale] assumes in any given text refuses to be fixed" and that therefore "no single interpretation can be imposed on the disturbance posed by her resilient feminine power" (2004a, 115). The meaning of Nicol's femme fatale, too, remains full of contradictions. In her violent female masculinity, Sheemina is unlike the classic femme fatale, who relies instead on her sexual charms. This serves to bring out her independent, complex female subjectivity. Sheemina also surfaces as a woman with her own agenda and story when we examine what is hidden underneath her glove. The emerging narrative is that of the unrecognised, mutilated Coloured female guerrilla; at least in parts, this is a narrative of victimisation. Suppressed by her antagonist and by socio-political conscience as a whole, but returning with a vengeance, it adds to Sheemina's uncanniness. Undercutting Sheemina's power and thereby also repeating the suppression of her story, continuing the denial and refusing recognition of Coloured female subjectivity – possibly despite the author's best intentions – is the representation of Sheemina as evil, sexually aggressive, man-devouring woman. What is being actualised through Sheemina's black widow fantasies are racist and misogynist myths that have long served as controlling mechanisms. This yields a reading of Sheemina as an embodiment of male fears. It is not my intention to reconcile these different interpretations. All are valid, but on their own they each provide an incomplete picture. Sheemina cannot be read merely as a symptom of male anxieties, as this is to negate the agency that she undoubtedly possesses. In her reading of the prototypical femme fatale, Phyllis Dietrichson in Billy Wilder's *Double Indemnity*, Bronfen argues against an "avoidance of seeing" the femme fatale, which she finds exemplified in interpretations of the figure as a symptom (2004a, 115). Instead, she advocates ascribing the femme fatale feminine agency as a subject:

> To acknowledge her as a subject of her actions means no longer being blind to the way she is anything but a victim, and, in her conscious choice for death, gives voice to the way suffering, loss and fragility are inescapable. It also means overcoming a critical prejudice which, by treating her as a symptom of masculine anxieties and not as a subject of feminine desire, allows us as critics to avoid the tragic message she relentlessly embodies.
> 115

While the figure of Sheemina allows for different – and conflicting – interpretations, it is clear that she is no mere symptom. Neither is she – unlike the other female perpetrators I will discuss – a figure for reader identification. We can certainly "put ourselves in her presence," as Bronfen invites us to do with Dietrichson (115), but we cannot identify with her. As much as Sheemina evokes the reader's sympathy as a serial rape victim and someone marginalised by history, reader identification is jeopardised, if not severed, by her excessive violence against innocent people, even children. No ethical mitigation whatsoever, in Frizzoni's sense, is provided by the author. This is what differentiates Sheemina from Jassy Mackenzie's perpetrator, the murderous detective Jade de Jong.

3   Jassy Mackenzie's Renegade Detective Jade de Jong: Exploring Femininity and Justice

> " [...] Remember. We were going to open the first ever multi-racial, bisexual detective agency in South Africa."
> DAVID

> "Not bisexual. Multi-gender. There's an important difference," [...].
> JADE correcting DAVID in *Random Violence* (46)

The Johannesburg-based detective and serial murderer Jade de Jong counters her investigative partner and sometime lover Superintendent David Patel just as confidently as she challenges gender norms, the law and established notions of reconciliation and justice. In her double role as detective and killer, Jade, a White woman, retains some of the instability of the femme fatale as exemplified by Sheemina February. Like Sheemina, she is motivated in part by personal revenge. At the same time, Mackenzie takes the genre in new directions, crafting Jade in ways that allow female readers to identify with and, as women, to feel empowered by her. Partly, her heroine is inspired by the female assassins who feature in Quentin Tarantino's *Kill Bill* series, as the author explains (Mackenzie 2010a, par. 15). Elsewhere Mackenzie states, "When I developed Jade, I wanted to make her into somebody different and I wanted to make her a renegade. And in creating her I realized that if she is taking the idea of being independent and going against society to its limits, she has to be a killer. If she shies away from killing, she cannot live with integrity by her idea of justice" (Binder 2015, 266–267). Killing is a defining characteristic of Jade. For that reason – despite the fact that she is also an investigator, often in collaboration with the police – she will be discussed within the theoretical frame of the female perpetrator. Jade is as concerned with justice as the female detectives I will examine in part three, but her means to achieve it are of a decidedly different nature. Given the violence with which she acts, Jade is a more transgressive female figure than the female detective can be. Her gender performance is more pronounced in its masculinity and assertion of power and is best captured as violent female masculinity. What is more, Jade's mission for justice moves beyond personal revenge and is not exclusively about violence against women. She also fights against social injustice more generally and damage to the environment. As violent as it is, her female masculinity is not curtailed. Unlike Sheemina, Jade gets away with killing. "If she sticks to killing the bad guys, I keep her out of jail," Mackenzie assures us (Binder 2015, 269). In the South African context, Jade serves to highlight the fact that, in order to fully own their status as citizens, women require alternatives to the kind of justice that the TRC and the neo-liberal state at large can offer them. Although the angry retributive justice that Jade embodies requires careful navigation of ethical issues on the part of the author in the final part of the chapter, I will argue that her role as killer-detective is successful as a feminist intervention.[20]

---

20   This chapter is derived in part from a chapter published in *Cities in Flux: Metropolitan Spaces in South African Literary and Visual Texts* 2017, edited by Olivier Moreillon, Alan Muller and Lindy Stiebel, copyright LIT Verlag, Münster.

Jassy Mackenzie was born in Zimbabwe and moved to South Africa at the age of eight. A journalist, editor and internationally successful writer, she currently lives and works in Johannesburg. Mackenzie, who is White, has written two short stories and six crime novels: the standalone crime novel *My Brother's Keeper* (2009) and the Jade de Jong crime series, which so far includes *Random Violence* (2008a), *Stolen Lives* (2008b), *Worst Case* (2011b), *Pale Horses* (2012b) and *Bad Seeds* (2017). She also collaborated with James Patterson on the thriller *Private Gold* (Patterson 2017).[21] As a crime writer, Mackenzie enjoys exploiting all kinds of *multi*plicities when dreaming up a character. When writing evil characters, who have always fascinated her, she says that "it's good to have such a wide field of races, cultures, personalities and backgrounds to choose from" in South Africa (Mackenzie 2010b, 14). What is more, she argues that the end of apartheid in South Africa "has done one very important thing for crime fiction characters. It's levelled the playing field, giving everyone equal licence to be good or evil [...]. Interestingly, South Africa's apartheid history has allowed us to create more complex characters that combine elements of good and evil in a way that everybody can now understand better" (14). As will become evident, Mackenzie exploits this multiplicity as a resource when crafting her heroine, Jade, and the world around her.

Jade starts her chequered career on both sides of the law in *Random Violence*, which is set in Johannesburg. In this novel, Jade is on a double mission. While helping Superintendent David Patel to investigate a murder case, she secretly avenges her policeman father's murder, teaming up with her partner in crime, Robbie, for the purpose. The novel – and, indeed, the series as a whole – is thus a blend of two sub-genres, the detective novel and the thriller. *Stolen Lives* centres around human trafficking and features Jade in collaboration with David and Scotland Yard. Together, they track down the head of the trafficking network and his South African henchman, whom Jade executes herself. Jade also discovers an uncomfortable personal "truth": one of the serial killers whom she encounters tells her that he used to work with her late mother, a professional killer. *Worst Case*[22] sees David hospitalised early on, so Jade single-handedly investigates a murder case, discovers and frees some missing workers and prevents largescale environmental sabotage in iSimangaliso Wetland Park, a South African world heritage site in KwaZulu-Natal. In *Pale Horses*, Jade interrupts a chain of murders that started with the erasure of an entire

---

21 In addition, Mackenzie is a successful writer of erotic romances. These include *Folly* (2013), *Switch* (2014), *Drowning* (2014) and *Soaring* (2016).
22 In the USA, *Worst Case* is published under the title *The Fallen*.

community due to cancer-inducing, genetically engineered maize. *Bad Seeds*, Mackenzie's fifth and latest novel in the Jade de Jong series, shows Jade forging new alliances while continuing to rely on existing ones. As always, both Jade and her allies criss-cross legal boundaries. Together with David and her new White acquaintance, Carlos Botha, Jade prevents the sale of weapons-grade uranium by the director of Inkomfe nuclear research station to a terrorist in Iraq. At the end of the novel, Jade's long-time partner in crime, Robbie, pressurises her into the next "job": killing the would-be uranium buyer Rashid Hamdan, a terrorist who is still at large. Knowing that she owes Robbie for his help in *Bad Seeds* and *Worst Case*, Jade will find it hard to refuse. At this moment, Jade appears to be moving further away from the police and from law enforcement by legal means. Her renewed alignment with Robbie, as well as the fact that she distances herself from David and develops a new love interest in Carlos, who works in the security business, all point in the direction of the extralegal, if not the illegal. In terms of gender, however, Jade has been an outlaw from the beginning. As the daughter of a widowed policeman, who raised her alone, Jade was socialised into a masculine world, a space that she has always considered to be hers.

3.1   *Looking Like a Woman While Acting like a Man*

Jade is a White, good-looking woman of slim, wiry build, in her mid-thirties. While the jade-green "killer" eyes (2008b, 241) from which she derives her name tend to be judged somewhat unusual for a woman, her behaviour transcends the frame of conventional femininity even more clearly. From an early age, Jade trained and excelled in shooting guns and investigative work, rather than in needlework. Pulling the trigger comes naturally to her, and she delights in killing (2008a, 39–44, 2008b, 305, 2011b, 11, 24). Her non-stereotypical occupational choices in the realm of crime include work as a private investigator, operating as a professional killer and the occasional bodyguarding and surveillance job (2008b, 19, 2011b, 22). Jade herself draws attention to an understanding of gender as a construct that allows for flexibility and opens up the possibility of performance in various ways by questioning the notion of the "bisexual" as raised by David. " 'Not bisexual. Multi-gender. There's an important difference,' " she corrects him (2008a, 46). Her appropriation, as a woman, of the traditionally male space of the detective and killer constitutes a particular performance of gender as violent female masculinity. Violent female masculinity is rooted in Halberstam's notion of female masculinity, which does not perceive masculinity and femininity as mutually exclusive (1998, 20). Jade's extension of David's term from "*bi*-sexual" to "*multi*-gender" (Mackenzie 2008a, 46, emphasis mine) implies both a view of gender as performance and a rejection of mutually exclusive binary oppositions in favour of a multiplicity of gender options. Halberstam attributes to female masculinity the potential for social rebellion based on an affirmation of different gender taxonomies: "Such affirmations begin not by subverting masculine power or taking up a position against masculine power but by turning a blind eye to conventional masculinities and refusing to engage" (Halberstam 1998, 9). This aptly describes both Jade's preference for the masculine space, and her obliviousness to the fact that she does not quite fit in spaces that are marked as feminine, such as hair salons (Mackenzie 2008b, 183). Thanks to her upbringing, she has always inhabited the male space that grants her an extended scope of agency. She considers it as hers and is not bothered by its being marked as masculine. This illustrates another benefit of Halberstam's concept: namely, its power to act as a shield against othering, abjecting or pathologising those parts of Jade that are marked as masculine (see Halberstam (1998, 1–2)). It is a means of containing the parts of Jade that social norms have marked as irreconcilable. Jade is not a Dr Jekyll/Mr Hyde figure with a split personality. Her various parts are well integrated: she is a rounded character. Even her killer side, unacceptable as it may be from an ethical and legal view point, is "part of who she [is]" (Mackenzie 2008a, 324), and she is not prepared to lie about it (2008b, 74, 2012b, 292).

Jade's feminine appearance and heterosexual orientation – note that in rejecting the adjective "bi-sexual" Jade also rejects the application of this particular sexual orientation to her – mean that she does not produce masculinity by being and/or looking butch, but by assuming the masculine position of power, often violently so. Hers is a situational and relational way of producing masculinity, in the vein of Dankwa's situational masculinity (2009, 163–164, 176). The following exchange in *Stolen Lives* between Jade and Naude, a ruthless criminal who is in the business of trafficking women, illustrates how she assumes the male position despite her looks. During her first surprise encounter with Naude, she unhesitatingly takes the power position:

> "Who are you?" he said. His voice deep and grainy, and he sounded surprisingly calm. [...] "You're Naude," she said. His gaze darted left and right before fixing, sharp-eyed, on her again. "You're not a policewoman." – "No, I'm not." Jade moved around the couch and took another step towards him. Naude took a step back. [...] He turned and ran.
> 100

Even though Jade does not wear a police uniform that confers authority on her, and even though she is about two heads shorter than Naude and of much more fragile build, by being able to name and identify him – and through her drawn gun – she constructs herself as the one in power. As this position has traditionally been associated with masculinity, she thereby produces masculinity situationally. We see this again when she literally disarms men (2012b, 162), or when in *Pale Horses* she taunts the killer Victor on his lack of courage to kill with his own hands, a quality that was established as disgusting in a man earlier in the novel (164, 166, 292, see also 2017, 331). At other times, Jade protects men in dangerous situations. Chased by their enemies, she is the one who gives Harris a leg up to climb the wall (114), in the hope that if they are tackled she, the fitter of the two, will be their target, rather than him (153). She effectively saves not only Harris's life more than once, but also David's and Carlos's (2008a, 320, 2017, 118). Thus, time and again, Jade becomes a man situationally, a fact recognised by her male opponents and partners in crime alike (2008a, 164, 2008b, 244).

The most obvious way in which Jade performs masculinity, however, is through violent crime, particularly highly skilled shooting. Jade's perfection with guns – she even masters accurate left-hand shots (2017, 339) – in a South African context acquires heightened significance because gun ownership has been linked to citizenship. Jacklyn Cock emphasises that guns are a key feature of South African masculinity. Cock explains that the "ownership and use [of guns] vary across racial lines and between institutions, but nevertheless [are] central to the way many men act out their masculinity" (2001, 43). What is more, in post-apartheid South Africa, gun ownership has come to be seen as a sign not only of manliness, but of full citizenship (2001, 53). During apartheid, military service was compulsory for White male citizens. They had access to and were allowed to own guns, whereas Black men were denied not only citizenship, but ownership of firearms. According to Cock, post-apartheid, this legacy of "a militarised citizenship and a militarised masculinism" (2001, 53) has led many Black South African men to view access to the army and access to guns as markers of both masculinity and full citizenship. By assuming the role of the violent gun man, Jade also claims this male space of the citizen – a space that South African women have not been granted fully despite the fact that, de jure, their right to citizenship is constitutionally secured. In the realm of crime fiction, Teresa L. Ebert underscores the significance of women's unhesitating use of the gun as an assertion of power. Since assertions of power have long been connected to assertions of masculinity, for her the use of (gun) power is a necessary oppositional strategy: "contesting the dominant power requires the counter-use of power" (1992, 23). Through the frequent use of her gun, Jade produces masculinity, which confers agency, authority, full citizenship and power on her. Her success is heightened precisely because she becomes a man without looking like one. This allows her to strategically deceive her opponents and to catch them by surprise, thereby taking the masculine position even more efficiently. People mistake her as a supposedly harmless female because they are blinded by the binarity of the gender system and the association of violence with men. For this reason, Jade is subject to much less scrutiny and policing. In fights, for example, she deliberately starts with a weak punch, "a move that only tricked people because she was a woman" (Mackenzie 2008b, 256), before she "let rip with the double whammy. Her right knee hammered into his groin, and her right fingers straight into his eyes, as stiff as prongs" (2008b, 256). Time and again, Jade deploys the stereotype of the fragile woman in order to then surprise her targets by acting against their gendered expectations (2008a, 316–319, 2008b, 246, 2011b, 121, 2012b, 153). Jade proves that violent female masculinity serves to complicate constraining gender binaries.

As a White, middle-class woman, Jade acts from a power position, but Mackenzie is careful not to reproduce racial subjugation. The baddies Jade fights and kills are almost exclusively powerful, wealthy White men, while a constant feature of the series so far has been the prominent presence of Jade's racially other male partners. Robbie, Jade's male partner in crime in two of the novels, has a "dark olive complexion" and "black peppercorn curls" (2008a, 15). David, her investigative partner in all the novels and lover in the first four, is of mixed racial origin. He has a White South African mother and an Indian father. In an interview, Mackenzie specifies her reasons for pairing Jade with David: "I thought it would [...] explain the attraction between [David and Jade] if he was also a little bit of a misfit. So I thought mixed race is always a little bit borderline, let's make him mixed race, let's make him also grow up in difficult circumstances where he was not embraced really by either society that he came from" (2014). Thus, David's multi-racial background is paralleled with Jade's multi-gender upbringing, neither of which sits easily with hegemonic social norms. Mackenzie's comparative strategy harks back to the quote in the epigraph, where she has Jade contrast multi-racial with multi-gender (2008a, 46). It can also be read as a way of drawing attention to the lack of recognition in South Africa of the need for gender equality, particularly when compared with the widely recognised need for racial equality. It functions as a reminder that in South African society, which is very conscious of the need for racial inclusivity, the same mechanisms must apply to gender. This point is underlined in another exchange between David and Jade. When David complains to Jade about her neighbours' supposedly racist dog, which keeps barking at him, Jade counters that the dog may actually be sexist (2008b, 67). Whereas for David both options are bad news, from Jade's perspective the difference matters. As a violent, White female figure, Jade stands for oppositional gender practices rather than oppositional racial practices. The centrality of Jade within the series also means that Mackenzie gives relatively little attention to Black violent female masculinity in her novels. The one exception is *Pale Horses*, in which the Black female character Ntombi Khumalo features prominently. For the first time in the series, we have a Black female character as one of the major voices and focalisers throughout the novel. Ntombi and her little son are the only survivors of a Black community that was erased in an accident of genetic engineering. Because Ntombi confided in the wrong man, she and her son are in acute danger of being killed by him. In the end, Ntombi takes on the role of perpetrator and kills her White male opponent in a fabricated car accident, thus combining the struggles against gender and racial inequality. *Bad Seeds* features the powerful Black female masculinity of Warrant Officer Thokoza Mweli, though not in a violent form. Thokoza is a very efficient, hard-working police woman who compliments Jade on her "good investigation work" and provides her with a brief case update (2017, 144). Apart from this, however, there is little direct interaction between the two women. Violent female masculinity in the Jade de Jong series so far is mainly White.

3.2 Seeking Alternative Justice—Opening Up a Place of Rage in Post-Apartheid South Africa

If Jade's violent female masculinity reveals and subverts the constraints that gender norms place on women, in her role as avenger and killer she also speaks to a need for alternative conceptions of justice for women. Acting as she does, from what Halberstam terms "a place of rage" (1993, 187), Jade challenges both a South African discourse of repair and reconciliation initiated by the TRC and the fading sovereignty of a weak, neo-liberal state. The "place of rage" that imagined female violence opens up is a powerful resistant strategy, not least because it evokes a sense of terror about a possible and entirely unpredictable actualisation of violence in the real (1993, 187–188). Women with guns, women who act from a place of rage, such as Jade, "resist the moral imperative to not fight violence with violence," as Halberstam puts it (191).

In South Africa, this moral imperative has been extended to a quasi-foundational imperative. In order to negotiate peace and realise a democratic state after apartheid, refraining from revenge was an imperative, as otherwise "this country would have gone up in flames," to quote former Archbishop Desmond Tutu (Hamber and Wilson 2002, 47). In this context, imagined female violence, depicting women who resort to retributive justice, is doubly transgressive. The dominant discourse underlying the South African TRC was a psychological one that emphasised reconciliation through trauma work and repair (Black 2011, 50). However, Brandon Hamber and Richard Wilson caution that "nations are not like individuals" (2002, 35), that individual psychological processes of healing diverge from "national processes of remembering such as truth commissions. […] which repress other forms of psychological closure motivated by less ennobled (although no less real) emotions of anger and vengeance" (36). This is particularly true of South African women, for whom the kind of closure offered by the TRC is contested in the first place. Hamber and Wilson state that, along with memory work and reparations, "revenge and punishment (and perhaps the fantasies thereof) can [...] be a way to lay the ghosts of the violently killed to rest and end the liminal status of the victim and survivor" (48). Therefore, they demand "an ongoing space [...] for survivors to express both their grief and their rage, as they struggle to come to terms with [...] their loss" (49). Crime fiction, particularly the imagined violence of women, is one such space. Jade and several other female characters in the series, such as Detective Constable Edmonds of Scotland Yard (2008b, 266) and Ntombi Khumalo (2012b, 286) clearly act from a place of rage and thus give voice to it.[23] Driving behind the supposed murderer of her father, "Jade wondered if he could feel her rage like heat, radiating through the tinted glass of the back window. He had killed her father" (2008a, 162). It is this rage, which she has nursed for ten years, that spurs her to carry out her systematic revenge in *Random Violence*. In this way, she propels herself out of the liminal space that she has inhabited with regard to her father's murder and, at the same time, feeds into the terror of the contested boundary between imagined and real female violence. Moreover, Jade's rage is directed at the state's sovereignty, particularly its ineffective and unjust criminal justice system and a system of law before which not everybody is equal, where people who can afford good lawyers stand a much better chance of walking free (2008b, 68–69). Jade knows that, even if the guilty are identified by the police, there is no guarantee that justice will be served by the state. For this reason, she considers vigilantism to be more effective than handing the culprits over to the state's criminal justice system. Given the choice, and after careful thought, she acts the vigilante, be it in the case of Naude (2008b, 312–313) or Elsabe (2011b, 253) or Theron (2012b, 292). Her fundamental distrust – even as the daughter of one policeman and the lover of another – of the state's power to administer justice for women is made impressively evident in a scene in *Pale Horses*. Despite being tempted to share a tape that she has found – an all-important piece of evidence – with David, and fully aware that she is thus "singlehandedly sabotag[ing] the investigation" (260), Jade decides to keep her discovery secret. David is her investigative partner, even her lover at the time, but he is a member of the police. As such,

---

23   Mackenzie also exploits Jade's rage to comic effect in a hilarious road scene in *Random Violence*. Siding with the slow and therefore vulnerable pedestrians on a busy road, Jade teaches the ruthless, aggressive, wealthy male driver behind her a lesson by deliberately reversing her car back into his (Mackenzie 2008a, 85–87).

he represents the state and stands for the patriarchal law. Keeping the tape enables Jade to reserve her right to retribution – which she redeems later on. At the same time, she preserves the right of Zelda (the tape's owner) to her own story and to "break[ing] it herself" (259). Aware of the limited justice that the patriarchal law has in store for women, Jade takes a clear stance for alternative forms of female justice.

3.3 Navigating Ethical Problems

The fact that Jade kills people – and mostly not in self-defence – inevitably gives rise to ethical questions. Because Mackenzie wants her readers to be able to identify with Jade as a figure of female empowerment it is especially important for her to navigate these questions carefully. As the author explains in an interview:

> It's a case of channelling the power we women would like to be embodied in ourselves into a character. From a reader's perspective it's good to read about strong women. There's a need to read about women who take power into their own hands and don't rely on a man, who can stand on their own and give men a hard time.
> BINDER 2015, 270–271

In what follows, I will scrutinise the strategies that Mackenzie employs to legitimise Jade's morally questionable acts, as well as the space for critical ethical thinking that she provides for the reader. The first and most important ethically mitigating factor is Jade's other role of detective and the dedication that she puts into solving crimes in the interest of the victims. Besides training his daughter in the technical and strategic aspects of investigative work, her police commissioner father imbued her with his own dedication, verve and strong sense of justice (2008a, 31–32, 39–40, 53, 2008b, 82). Embodying her father's legacy, Jade is committed to truth-finding, to tracking down criminals and to protecting people and nature in danger in a very unselfish manner, which facilitates reader identification (2008a, 264, 311, 2008b, 214, 2011b, 206, 222, 250). Secondly, Jade's murder victims are abominable creatures through and through. Mackenzie takes great care to vilify them enough, to ensure that we as readers come to empathise with Jade's rage and desire to kill them. They are ruthless, misogynist, inhuman, greedy characters engaging in the most appalling crimes. Thirdly, Jade herself is conscious of the ethical problems that her killer side raises (2008b, 74). She is repeatedly plagued by feelings of guilt (2008a, 107–108, 2012b, 167, 292) and resolves time and again to refrain from killing in the future (2011b, 24, 2012b, 27). Increasingly, she also feels the need to make up for her killings and invests both her knowledge and her blood-money to the benefit of victims (2012b, 297). Lastly, Mackenzie employs one highly problematic mitigating factor in the Jade de Jong series: the pervasive notion of the "killer gene". Jade's ability to kill, and the pleasure that she derives from it, is constructed as a hereditary trait handed down by her mother, who died shortly after Jade was born (2008b, 305, 2011b, 18, 2012b, 27). Jade refers to her mother as "the woman who had passed on her deadly talents, as well as her slim build, brown hair and green eyes" (2011b, 18), thus clearly emphasising an inevitability grounded in genetics. While criminologists such as Adrian Raine assume that there are genetic influences on aggressive and antisocial behaviour, they emphasise the added necessity of an interaction with psychological risk factors in order to increase an individual's inclination towards criminal behaviour (2009). This complex bio-social interplay is a far cry from the biological determinism that is supposed to justify Jade's killer disposition. The damage caused by the crimes against humanity committed in South Africa and throughout the world in the name of biological determinism and, in particular, scientific racism (harking back to eugenics) can hardly be underestimated. What is more, from an ethical viewpoint, an assumed inherited killer-trait frees Jade from responsibility as much as it precludes her own free will. This stands in stark contrast with Jade's habit of careful reasoning and decision-making before most of her killings. Such essentialising of criminal behaviour is also at odds with the anti-essentialist stance that the series takes with regard to gender. Jade is a figure readers can identify with, despite the fact that she is a murderer, yet the iterative insistence on the killer gene is a problematic way out of her ethical-moral dilemma and serves to alienate the reader.

There are, however, productive disturbances of our alignment with Jade that open up spaces for ethical reflection, what Michele Aaron terms "artful reminders". From the beginning, the series takes us into ethically murky waters. In *Random Violence*, Jade ends up intentionally killing a relatively innocent security guard, or so she thinks. This leads her to an intense moment of self-loathing and self-scrutiny: "She had stepped too far over the line now. She was a murderer, *no better than* [any other murderer]" (107, my emphasis). It turns out that she is wrong about her victim's identity and that she did in fact kill the "right" man, the drug lord whom she had intended to kill all along, so "relief slowly dilute[s] her terrible guilt" (108). But does this really let her off the hook? After all, she pulled the trigger convinced that she was killing an innocent man. So what exactly is it that makes her "better than" other murderers? Mackenzie prompts us to query Jade's ethical reasoning by repeatedly raising the issue of whether there is a fundamental difference between Jade the killer and the criminals she tracks down and/or kills. Jade usually resolves the question to her own advantage. In *Stolen Lives*, she differentiates between traffickers and other criminals (300) and dissociates herself from her killer mother. While she has so far killed only murderers, her mother killed whoever she was paid to kill (305). In *Worst Case*, Jade encounters another female killer, Elsabe. Troubled though Jade is, she reassures herself that, unlike Elsabe, she has never killed innocent people (248). And in *Pale Horses*, Jade takes the moral high ground by pointing out that she has the courage to kill with her own hands, whereas Victor has always paid others to do the dirty work for him (292).

While Mackenzie absolves Jade of culpability in her own eyes, she confronts us as readers with more obvious faultlines. For example, we, but not Jade, get to witness Xavier Soumare's cruel torture of Eunice, the woman who fails to supply him with faked passports (2008b, 139–141). We are thus less inclined to agree with Jade when she judges him to be a lesser criminal. We subsequently learn that Xavier has been on Interpol's radar as an internationally wanted serial murderer for years (304). Similarly, Mackenzie makes it a little more difficult for us as readers to dismiss Elsabe, the other White female perpetrator in *Worst Case*. Three times, Mackenzie breaks up the narrative framework with interludes giving Elsabe's unmediated view, in her own voice, on the events that led to her son's and husband's tragic deaths (37, 154, 251–252). This does not resolve the opaqueness of the ethical situation and of Elsabe as a character, but it qualifies Jade's perspective and, as Mackenzie herself confirms, creates for us as readers a somewhat uncomfortable complicity with Elsabe (2011a, par. 32–33). This discomfort serves as an artful reminder that, as consumers of crime fiction, we as readers are implicated in the crimes and their ethical dimensions. In *Pale Horses*, the subtle, temporary dissociation from Jade is continued. The novel is framed by the narrative of a complete outsider to the story, and we get to see Jade through her eyes.

When Mike Nicol asks her in an interview, "Is Jade de Jong immoral?" Mackenzie confirms that "[w]ithout a doubt she is, but she doesn't think so. She thinks she's fine and the rest of the world is wrong" (Mackenzie 2012a, par. 11). For us as readers, it is more difficult to overlook the moral cracks. We are invited to probe the distinction that Jade establishes between the various types of murderers, yet we are never forced to do so. In fact, one might criticise Mackenzie for triggering moral uncertainty while quickly foreclosing it again. Every so often, the imperative for popular literature to entertain wins out. Arguably, when a plot is moving at breakneck speed, the reader is spared having to venture further into uncomfortable ethical terrain. But is this really the case? The very seriality of Mackenzie's crime fiction deters us from a simply evading such concerns. The constant recurrence of the same ethical questions (Are all killers the same? Are there factors or circumstances that legitimise killing, especially for women?) is testament to Mackenzie's awareness of the need to keep returning to such problems, despite the fact they may be insoluble. Mackenzie refrains from giving – maybe all too easy – answers, but by regularly confronting us with the questions she draws attention to the precarious boundaries between investigator and criminal, between guarantors of and transgressors against the law. Moreover, the next novel in her series is never just more of the same in terms of ethical (non)resolution. Instead, subtle changes become manifest as the series progresses. The first two novels offer closure in the end. In the third novel, *Worst Case*, the moral issues surrounding Jade and Elsabe remain unresolved. Only in the next novel do we learn that Jade and Robbie indeed killed Elsabe, thereby saving Elsabe's target, Craig (Mackenzie 2012b, 14). Similarly, *Pale Horses* ends on a note of uncertainty. Although the newspapers report Viktor Theron's death as suicide, we as readers know that Jade had a hand in it. Yet conclusive evidence remains undisclosed. Ending with Robbie the hitman's request for collaboration in killing a terrorist, *Bad Seeds* taunts the reader to join in the ethical dilemma that Jade will have to resolve before the next novel. The terrorist's murder is a paid hit – Robbie knows of "a shitload of money coming our way once we do this job. Serious moolah. We'll split it fifty-fifty" (357). Jade will have to weigh up her potential profits, her complicity and the fact that she owes Robbie against the greater threat that the terrorist may pose. But then, who knows the "insider" who has commissioned the hit? Given the global threat currently posed by terrorism and complicity with it, Mackenzie could hardly be raising more pressing, more relevant ethical issues. In the case of Mackenzie's Jade de Jong series, at least, the allegation that crime fiction evades serious ethical concerns must be rejected.

Jade's powers as a perpetrator and detective are as multifaceted and ethically controversial as those of the femme fatale, the figure who provides the generic blueprint, with some modification, for Nicol's Sheemina February. However, where Jade's violent female masculinity differs significantly from Sheemina's is in the expanded imaginative space that it opens up for women. Because female readers are able to identify with Jade, she functions as a figure of female empowerment. In a South African context, this gains further nuance. Given the alarm at high levels of real crime, Marla Harris reads Jade's actions as a woman's refusal to be paralysed and silenced, as a refusal to reproduce the awareness of powerlessness (2013, 124). The fact that Jade's transgressive agency goes unpunished contributes to these feminist political effects. The Jade de Jong series also modifies the South African transitional narrative of disclosure and repair as the only way to lay the violent apartheid past to rest. It functions as a fictional platform where female rage finds expression and the desire for female retribution can be realised. The series's engagement with alternative justice is revisionary in advocating an understanding of law and justice from a woman's perspective. At the same time, it includes ongoing meditations on the ethical complexities and dilemmas of female vigilantism. Given the gender bias inherent in criminal justice[24] and the South African state's increasing failure to enforce it, these meditations are as relevant as they are necessary. Within the single body of her murderous detective, Mackenzie combines a multitude of facets. I have read them as illustrations of a liberating multiplicity of both gender options and ethical complexities that contest clear-cut boundaries between victims, perpetrators and detectives. The next novel that I will discuss, Angela Makholwa's *Black Widow Society*, imagines female perpetration as multi-racial concerted group action and targets the privacy of domestic violence.

4 Angela Makholwa's Black Widow Society: Collective Female Terror against Gender Norms

> [T]he black widow spider [is] a sexual cannibal known for eating her male partner after mating.
> TALLULAH in *Black Widow Society* (217)

Tallulah Ntuli evokes the black widow spider and her resonances with the femme fatale through the name of the murderous female collective that she heads. This time, the spider woman is back as a feminist appropriation: with reinforcement, operating as a sisterhood, eliminating abusive husbands and building a brighter future for women. Makholwa's provocative thriller *Black Widow Society* envisages women's violent liberation from oppressive situations of domestic violence. Again relying on the notion of violent female masculinity, I will begin by outlining the ways in which the Black Widows' gender performance varies this concept. Arguably, here violent female masculinity undergoes an extension as both concerted and future-oriented action, in an attempt to achieve a structural change in the gender order. In the second part of the chapter, I will view the Black Widows' actions in their South African context. I will argue that their society, as an alternative family headed by deadly mothers, exposes the deep-seated gender inequalities in the South African national family. Finally, I will look at how *Black Widow Society* addresses the issue of domestic violence in South Africa. I will show that the novel manages to foreground this hidden crime and the gender constructions that facilitate

---

24   For further detail, see my discussion of Michéle Rowe's female detective.

it, and to instil a sense of terror at female counter-violence, while at the same time taking an ethical position against killing.

Angela Makholwa is an acclaimed writer, journalist and PR consultant who lives and works in Johannesburg. *Black Widow Society* (2013) is her second thriller. Like her debut novel, *Red Ink* (2007), it is inspired by real South African criminals. Makholwa takes inspiration from Nompumelelo Manyaapelo, who organised the murder of her abusive and unfaithful husband (Buti 2013, par. 6).[25] Whereas in *Red Ink* a woman writes the life story of a male criminal, the murdering women in *Black Widow Society* "plot their own destinies" (Makholwa 2013, 161). The enhanced agency that comes with plotting their own destinies takes them not only beyond conventional gender roles, but beyond legality.[26] My analysis of *Black Widow Society* focuses on its main narrative strand, which follows the secret group of women called the Black Widow Society. Headed by the "Triumvirate", a group of businesswomen that includes two Black women, Tallulah Ntuli and Nkosazana Khumalo, as well as the White woman Edna Whithead (Makholwa 2013, 18), the society's aim is to free women from the coercion of abusive marriages by murdering their errant husbands. The financial benefits of such actions – the women are entitled to part of the inheritance – contribute towards their other, long-term project of female empowerment through education: the Young Women's Academy. The novel's highly complicated plot has rightly been criticised, as have its stylistic shortcomings (Amid 2014, par. 10). However, these drawbacks are outweighed by the novel's innovative, indeed provocative, exploration of transgressive female agency.

4.1 *Makholwa's New Breed of Woman and Their Gender Transgressions*

Makholwa calls her murderous Black Widows "a new breed of woman" (2013, 17). I will read her conception of the new woman first as violent female masculinity and, as such, a resistant practice. The Black Widows "do" violent masculinity from a variety of female subject positions, but it is a strategy that unites them. However, Makholwa's new breed of woman moves beyond resistant agency and embodies a kind of communal agency that resonates with the wider tradition of Black South African women writers who create a female version of the African concept of *ubuntu*.

---

[25] Jennifer Platt mentions three other real South African black widow cases that inspired *Black Widow Society* (2013, par. 1).
[26] Makholwa has written two other novels, but not in the crime genre: They are *The 30th Candle* (2009) and *The Blessed Girl* (2017).

The Black Widows' agency is first and foremost a resistant kind of agency aimed at liberation from oppressive power structures. They actively fashion themselves as perpetrators, rejecting their victim status. For most of the Black Widows, as married women, the existing gender order has entailed being subjugated, abused and coerced. Unlike Jade de Jong, who was socialised into doing masculinity by her father and who has always refused to engage with conventional gender roles, the Black Widows' subversive gender performance originates in situations of entrapment and is a matter of survival, of refusing to be victimised any longer. Be it physical abuse, as in the case of Tallulah (1–3), or philandering, extra-marital relationships with other women and extreme humiliation, as in the cases of Nokuthula, Thami, Edna (13–15, 39–40, 125, 128, 155, 160) and Salome, who is also infected with HIV and forced to abort her child (49–50) – the triggering factor for all of the Black Widows is victimhood. Having their abusive husbands killed is an existentially liberating act, an act of survival (139). For Edna, the alternative was suicide (40), and both Tallulah and Salome consider themselves survivors (137, 159). As Salome puts it, "So far, I've never chosen to be the victim. I don't think there's much stock in that" (159).

What the Black Widows resist above all is victimhood, but by adopting the violently masculine strategy of the killer they also contest the kind of femininity that leads to victimhood. Rachel Jewkes and Robert Morrell call this kind of femininity "acquiescent femininity" (2010, 6). In many African societies, acquiescent femininity is a cultural ideal that promotes respect, obedience and passivity towards hegemonic masculinity (4). According to Jewkes and Morrell, an integral part of acquiescent femininity is "excusing male behaviour" (6), which means "tolerance of violence," tolerance of other partners and unprotected sex (6), despite the high risks this involves. Evidence of such acquiescent femininity is to be found lurking in the background of all the Black Widow cases, and it is this that they decide to reject. On their way from victim to "victor" (159), they produce two different kinds of masculinities: that of the criminal and that of the business executive. On the one hand, they have their abusive husbands shot or killed by electrocution or in engineered accidents by their hit man Mzwakhe (15, 100, 168). On the other, as previously exploited objects, they now become exploiting subjects in economic terms, thus contesting the economic dependence that has often characterised traditional African femininity (Jewkes and Morrell 2010, 4). The Black Widows propel themselves into their husbands' executive chairs, meaning that they now wield considerable economic power; Edna, for example, becomes the head of her husband's mining group (17). Tallulah, too, has "made a name for herself in the business world" (38). As Dankwa points out, female masculinity may be situationally produced by assuming an authoritative position or a position of socio-economic power

(2009, 173–179). The Black Widows' situational masculinity is indicative of a wish to take agency beyond the disruption caused by the criminal, to bring about lasting structural change for women. Such far-reaching change requires the economic power of the business executive. In line with Dankwa's tenet that situational masculinity does not have to be reflected in a woman's physical appearance, most Black Widows outwardly appear very feminine. They wear feminine attire and spend considerable amounts of time in beauty salons. The "androgynous" (Makholwa 2013, 37), "tomboyish" (114) Nkosazana, who fancies women, is the notable exception. Both her sexual orientation and her looks place her closer to Halberstam's notion of female masculinity. She is also the only Black Widow who has never been married. Nkosazana does not react to victimhood at the hands of a husband, but instead has "a triple-edged sword against her [...]; she was black, female and lesbian" (116–117). Impressed by her butch masculinity and shared feminist commitment (38), Tallulah appoints Nkosazana as her attorney: "this little woman who had grown up right under her nose and proceeded to be a tough litigator taking on criminal and corporate cases and winning them with the deftness of a bullfighter" (38). All in all, the Black Widows are characterised by a great diversity of looks, skin shades, sexualities and personal histories. They are testament to the fact that doing masculinity is a performance of which anyone is capable. The fact that Makholwa depicts the violent female masculinity of women of all shades, not just Black, has the further advantage of defusing the demeaning Sapphire stereotype of the Black, evil-tempered, treacherous female criminal. Extending beyond a purely resistant quality, these new women's authority also entails communal female agency. With this, Makholwa adds further nuance to violent female masculinity.

In her opening speech at the Black Widows' annual meeting, which she delivers to her sisters – a "pride of lionesses acquiescing to a hunt" – Tallulah invokes a sense of community arising out of shared victimhood, but also a responsibility for mutual support.

> " [...] We are here purely because of the ties that bind us. We have a moral duty to ourselves and each other to protect what we've lost, that innocence we recognise whenever we glimpse those who have not had to endure our baptism of fire," she continued. "We must guard this jealously; that which links us together ... and yet when we meet another in the same situation we come from, it is again our moral duty to be the rock for that sister. Be there for a sister who bears that dark, sad and haunted look that you used to wear. When you're out taking a walk or in a boardroom meeting, be aware of that woman whose smile does not reach the eyes.

Whose burst lip, and clumsy explanation of countless 'accidents' rings untrue. You remember those excuses. They sound just like you ... before you found your anchor."

MAKHOLWA 2013, 19

Emphasising the ties that bind the women and linking the moral duty to oneself with that to others, is evocative of the African notion of *ubuntu* and, beyond Africa, with the collective agency advocated by Marxist feminism. The notion of a fundamental relatedness of all human beings, the view that "the individual's existence and well-being are relative to that of the group" (Mokgoro 2012, 317), is central to African philosophy in general.[27] In South Africa, this communal worldview is captured by the Zulu/Xhosa term *ubuntu*, which is commonly defined as the idea that "a person is a person because of and through other people" (Driver 2005, 219).[28] However, because it encompasses only the female part of the community, the Black Widows' communalism both invokes and subverts the traditional understanding of *ubuntu*. Makholwa's all-female community grants its members a kind of support that neither Sheemina nor Jade receive. The latter act on an individual basis and their murderous actions render them isolated from other women. The Black Widows, by contrast, are tied to one another in manifold ways. Their society is founded on shared victimhood and the ensuing obligation of mutual support. Since this support entails the illegal action of killing, a further "tie" emerges, that of shared perpetration and hence the need for secrecy. As they violently and irrevocably cut their marital ties, they forge alternative "unbreakable ties" (Makholwa 2013, 18) with their fellow Black Widows, of which their gold bracelets are only the outward signs. This has various implications. In the first place, it enables them to retain the support and protection that human relations offer. Tallulah's metaphor of "finding one's anchor" implies that the Black Widows offer to members of their sisterhood the security they were previously deprived of by their abusive husbands. In an interview, Makholwa underscores the importance of female friendship as a support structure and likens the Black Widow Society to the traditional *stokvels* (Binder 2015, 275). A *stokvel* is an informal savings scheme, sometimes also called a burial society, and provides female support

---

27 I would like to acknowledge Azille Coetzee's unpublished paper entitled "Partiality, Plurality and Embodiment: A Philosophical Exploration of Certain Themes from African Womanism" as a source of inspiration here.

28 As Dorothy Driver outlines, *ubuntu* gained prominence in the political discourse of the Black Consciousness Movement in the 1970s and 1980s. The word entered the (South African) English language at this time (119).

when someone in the family passes away.[29] This comes with "the moral duty," as Tallulah calls it, "to be the rock" for another woman in the same situation. The Black Widows' agency is thus collective: it extends beyond resistance and perpetration and has the further advantage of enhanced power.

The significance of the enhanced power that lies in women's communal political actions has been noted in a very different context. Marxist feminist Ellen Riordan reminds us that it is important that feminists think as social agents. She maintains that women must act collectively in order to make a difference for all women and for structural change to occur (2001, 282–283). This link between collective response and structural change has been taken up and emphasised with regard to a different popular genre: rape-revenge cinema. In her examination of rape-revenge film, Henry claims that representations of multiple victims on the one hand and collective avengers on the other function to explore collective trauma and to draw attention to the systemic nature of sexual violence (2014, 143). Such representations propose a view of gender violence as a social, not just an individual, problem that must be addressed collectively (147).[30] As a matter of fact, aiming at structural change for women beyond the members of their society and their own generation is part and parcel of the Black Widow Society. Their Young Women's Academy, which Tallulah and Edna realise in the end, is designed precisely to bring forth "a new breed of woman who would be given the type of education that would empower her to avoid the kind of decisions that had led most of the black widows to their ill-fated marriages and partnerships" (Makholwa 2013, 16–17). In her analysis of constructions of gender in both of Makholwa's thrillers, Jessica Murray claims that Makholwa does not radically deconstruct existing gender relations (2016, 23). In her view, "[b]y placing the onus on women to make better choices, [*Black Widow Society*] fails to explore the extent to which a much more radical reconstruction of both femininity and masculinity is needed to achieve substantive gender justice" (21). However, this fails to take into account sufficiently the Black Widows' collective violent female masculinity as killers and as businesswomen and the ways in which they dispute traditional notions of acquiescent, economically dependent femininity, all in order to counter structural violence. In my view, *Black Widow Society* displays a radicalism with regard to challenges to the gender order that we find in no other South African crime novel. Jewkes and Morrell provide further evidence of women's capacity to bring about significant change. With regard to preventing the spread of HIV

---

29   For more details, see South African History Online (2012).
30   South African feminists share this view, insisting on the importance of tackling social complicity when it comes to gender-based violence (see "Introduction").

and thereby reducing the risk that it presents to Black women, in particular, they demonstrate how much dominant conceptions of masculinity depend on acquiescent femininity. In their research, they highlight a form of social complicity that is rarely mentioned: namely, women's own complicity in sustaining the kind of hegemonic masculinity that puts them at risk. According to Jewkes and Morrell, this is "interpreted by many women as sexually and socially desirable, and [...] men who practice more gender-equitable masculinities are often marginalized by women" (2010, 7).[31] By withdrawing their support from hegemonic masculinity, the Black Widows can make a difference. Even so, the collective violent female agency that Makholwa imagines for her Black Widows has its disadvantages. For one thing, the society is coercive. Its members are "forever bound to its codes. There [is] no way out" (Makholwa 2013, 16). In that respect, the society is potentially even more coercive than a marriage, which leaves at least the theoretical possibility of a divorce. Given the nature of their terrible secret, guarding it "jealously" becomes vital, as Tallulah emphasises in her speech. The group's heterogeneity and the different interests beyond the immediacy of victimhood (philanthropic, feminist, financial) add to the danger of betrayal. Betrayal by a single woman jeopardises all the Black Widows, as we witness towards the end of the thriller.

However, it would be wrong to say that the Black Widows advocate collective female agency only, or that they prioritise collective agency over individual female agency. The opening of Tallulah's speech illustrates the value that she places on individual agency: " 'Sisters,' [...]. 'For many years, [...] unappreciative dogs [...] [p]elted us with vitriolic words, and violent beatings until one day, we finally stopped and listened. We listened to what our souls told us. Yes. Yes. We listened to what our souls told us' " (Makholwa 2013, 19). The female collective agency that Tallulah advocates is paired with, if not preceded by, a need for individual action. A close look at Tallulah's speech reveals that each woman has to make the first step herself. To stop and listen, and thus to acknowledge her individuality, is a necessary condition for her liberation and connection to the community that guarantees her survival. Communal and individual agency are seen as mutually dependent in the novel. This constitutes an important – and, from a female perspective – necessary modification of the notion of *ubuntu*. Criticising the TRC's conception of *ubuntu*, Dorothy Driver notes that it one-sidedly conceived of women as communal selves only (or as "women-in-community"). She sees this as exemplified in the fact that women mostly

---

31   Bell Hooks makes a similar argument (see my discussion of Michéle Rowe's female detective Persy Jonas).

spoke for others, as secondary victims. "In their speaking for themselves, as women-in-themselves, women were excluded," she observes (2005, 224). It follows that "in the social performance of *ubuntu*, *ubuntu* is to be bestowed by women, but not *on* women as well. The TRC thus constructed a realm of limited reciprocity [...]" (225, original emphasis). Black South African women's writing, by contrast, has long redefined womanhood "as *both* individual and communal" (222, original emphasis). Modifying the concept of *ubuntu*, it has achieved what Driver terms a bridging between "women-in-community" and "women-in-themselves" (223). By emphasising the importance of "women-in-themselves", Tallulah's words can be read not only in relation to earlier, Black South African female modifications of *ubuntu*, but as opposing the TRC's one-sided conception of *ubuntu* for women. However, the act of bridging between the woman-in-community and the woman-in-herself is not romanticised in Makholwa's novel. Nkosazana personifies the fact that often the two can pull in opposite directions. Many years back, Nkosazana's legal assistance enabled Tallulah to kill her own husband. This first killing laid the foundation for the Black Widow Society and for Nkosazana's professional and financial success (Makholwa 2013, 38). What is more, the Black Widows have provided a safe haven for Nkosazana, "the lost young lesbian who wanted to belong" (246). And yet, after all those years, Nkosazana starts to distance herself from the Black Widows in order to save herself as an individual (141). She tries to liberate herself and to break the unbreakable ties with the society (181, 183) – with fatal consequences for herself and most of her sisters (274).

4.2 *Exposing the Cracks within the (National) Family*

The collective female agency epitomised by the Black Widows has profound implications for the notions of family and motherhood – and, by extension, for the South African national project. I argue that *Black Widow Society* deconstructs the mythologies of family and mothering that have been deployed to support colonialist and nationalist agendas, thereby exposing the tensions at the heart of the patriarchal nation.

Makholwa's thriller depicts families as little more than a façade that can be kept up only as long as the women play along and remain silent about their husbands' abusive behaviour. In other words, the family's very existence depends on acquiescent femininity that bolsters hegemonic masculinity. In Tallulah's family, for example, the "perfect family car" is in reality the perfect place for her husband to have extra-marital sex (Makholwa 2013, 2). As wives, the Black Widows grapple with cultural expectations that come with motherhood and are punished for failing to conform. Once Tallulah is pregnant, her husband starts to cheat on her with women he considers more physically attractive (2). Edna, who is unable to bear her husband an heir, is expected to accept that he now feels entitled to replace her with other women as sexual partners (39). None of the three members of the Triumvirate conform to the stereotype of the "good mother" that figures women primarily as caregivers and nurturers of their own biological children, thereby restricting them to the domestic space (Spencer 2013, 54–55). Tallulah has weak emotional ties to her children; she is "an atypical mother" (Makholwa 2013, 36). Edna is barren (39), and the lesbian Nkosazana plans to "make a few babies" (37), thus embodying exploratory femaleness that subverts social/biological norms. Once the women break free from dominant conceptions of family and mothering – once they become Black Widows – they make visible the gendered identities that sustain such conceptions and expose notions of family and mothering as cultural constructs. They also counter this construct with their own alternative, the Black Widow Society. Tallulah openly states that "the Black Widow Society provided her with the exact sort of familial ties that she so clearly lacked in her personal life" (36). The society provides a space for women to connect to a community that is based neither on kinship nor on marital bonds. Alternative notions of family and mothering are invoked when Tallulah "the godmother of this sect, an equal to any Italian-style Mafioso" (17) addresses her Black Widow sisters as "earth mothers" (19). This is not only illustrative of a power shift from the godfather to the godmother, but also parodic, given the fact that these earth mothers take lives rather than give them. In the end, the Black Widow Society is an utterly dysfunctional model and fails as a vision for an alternative family. However, alternative mothering does find realisation there. Edna and Tallulah succeed in mothering the girls of the school that they eventually set up in Malawi (276).

Despite its dysfunctionality, the Black Widow Society as an alternative family succinctly points to the ways in which dominant ideals of family and mothering severely compromise women, both within the nuclear family and within the South African national family. African feminists have highlighted the links between the ideal of the patriarchal family and the patriarchal projects of colonialism and nationalism. On the basis of McClintock's work on both Afrikaner and African nationalism (1995, 352–389), Desiree Lewis demonstrates that "the family in South Africa has functioned as a culturally-charged metaphor for ethnic or racial communities" (1999, 40). For women, this has several negative consequences. Once the family becomes the nation writ small, mythologies of mothering are never far away (40). Idealised versions of motherhood ennoble women, but at the same time depoliticise and dehumanise them. Eulogised as mothers, women are turned into icons and, as such, are "denied any verbal or executive substance" (39). They are valued purely in their symbolic roles as reproducers or protectors. Lewis also shows how women's dignity is sacrificed in the context of the South African national project, which was born out of racial oppression. So as not to jeopardise racial solidarity, many Black South African women remain silent about abusive marriages and sexual violence within the family. Airing these stories "seems to betray the spirit of communal or racial unity, especially when metaphorically represented as familial" (42–43). This is precisely reflected in Tallulah's dilemma. As the wife of a political activist under apartheid, she is regarded as a pillar of the community (Makholwa 2013, 2). It is therefore no wonder that she compares the Black Widows Society with a project on the national level, the South African government's BEE project: "Tallulah went as far as to draw parallels between the government's calls for Black Economic Empowerment and her own brainchild, the BWS, which addressed the very core of emancipation for women" by providing them "with empowerment and freedom in their own homes" (40).[32] For a woman, identifying with the national project, comes at the cost of her personal dignity, especially when race is given priority over gender. By depicting atypical mothers and dismantling the family, Makholwa refuses to sustain the patriarchal national narrative that is based on the subjugation of women. Just how problematic it is for women to belong in the South African nation is epitomised by the novel's ending, which sees the two surviving Black Widows leave the country and settle abroad.

4.3 *Motive, Means and Ethics: Women Entrapped by Domestic Violence Seek Change*

Given that Makholwa sets her novel in the higher echelons of society and in a relatively wealthy, urban environment, there is reason to ask why she has her female protagonists resort to such extreme measures and "cloak and dagger antics" (Makholwa 2013, 80). Although the storytelling impulse cannot be limited by social and economic factors or even by political correctness, it is hard to explain why married women, protected by a progressive constitution, do not choose a legal way to liberate themselves, such as reporting their abusive husbands to the police, laying criminal charges and, eventually, divorcing them. If called to the scene, Jade de Jong would probably support the abused women's murderous impulses, pointing to the inability of the South African legal system to do justice to women's rights. However, her resolution would translate into

---

[32] BEE (Black Economic Empowerment) or B-BBEE (Broad-Based Black Economic Empowerment) as it has been redefined, is a South African government policy aimed at redressing past economic inequalities by fostering the economic participation of Black people (Department of Trade and Industry 2014).

her drawing the gun: she would single-handedly resolve the problem, because hiring a man with a gun to do the dirty work, as the widows do, would be synonymous with undermining her own ethical stance. Here, it is important to stress that we are dealing with cases of *domestic* violence, a crime that differs in nature from the crimes Jade is involved with and that implicates the woman (and the children who all too often depend on her) in particular ways. This may explain, if not always justify, why, as victims of domestic violence, the Black Widows choose illegal actions and covert eliminations over literally or metaphorically drawing the gun themselves. In this section, I will look first at the key terms of entrapment and complicity. Next, I will return to the issue of the power of representation and Halberstam's discussion of the relationship between imagined and real female violence. Finally, I will consider the ethical implications of the methods employed by the Black Widows.

My discussion of the figure of the female victim showed how a number of South African crime writers are using crime fiction to address the issue of violence against women. Makholwa's *Black Widow Society* is informed by a similar impulse. Taking the skeleton of domestic violence out of its closet is Makholwa's main objective in *Black Widow Society*. In an interview, she emphasises the need to talk about this widespread form of violence and states that her intention is to show that it "is a very paralysing form of entrapment and a lot of women stay in those relationships because they are made to feel that there is no way out" (Binder 2015, 267). The statistics indicate that she is right. Jewkes and Morrell report, "Research has found that between 25% and 55% of women [in South Africa] have experienced physical intimate partner violence, and the rate of female homicide by an intimate partner is six times the global average" (2010, 2). The link that Makholwa establishes between domestic violence and HIV in the figure of the Black Widow Salome also has a real referent. Research in various countries, including South Africa, confirms that women who are violated by their intimate partners are more likely to be infected with HIV (Jewkes and Morrell 2010, 2). When Tallulah describes her marriage as tightening "its noose around her neck with each passing year" (Makholwa 2013, 2), she conveys something of the paralysing quality of intimate partner violence. A woman's entrapment is made even more paralysing by her real and felt complicity, which compromises both her liberation as such, and the means that are open to her to achieve it.

The constraints that the soon-to-become Black Widows face are of both a legal and a psychological nature. Thami originally comes from a wealthy family. However, because she agreed to marry in community of property, she would forfeit a substantial amount of her money if she divorced her husband Lloyd (80). Besides exploiting her family's wealth and political network, Lloyd has been having an affair with her cousin, yet he feels no obligation even to talk to Thami about their marital relationship. The couple's celebrity status compounds Thami's suffering, as does the fact that everybody but Thami seems to have seen through Lloyd all along. As a consequence, "Thami felt so violated and humiliated that all she wanted was to be vindicated" (160). While for Edna and Nokuthula divorce is made impossible by their husbands' refusal to accept the financial loss that this would entail for them as men (13, 40), for Salome, a mother of two whose philandering, denialist husband has infected her with HIV, divorce would mean financial disaster. Having signed a prenuptial agreement, she would leave the marriage empty-handed (50). Thus, these women are trapped in their marriages for legal reasons – an example of the law's inherent gender and racial bias, which I will explore further in my discussion of female detectives. Moreover, as Jewkes and Morrell note, divorce, as the "ultimate act of noncompliance," leaves Black South African women, in particular, highly stigmatised and is therefore rarely sought as a way out (2010, 6).[33]

What unites Black Widows of all skin colours, and adds to their sense of paralysis, are feelings of shame, humiliation and worthlessness (3, 29, 160). Murray argues that in *Black Widow Society* shame functions as gendered disciplinary power and inhibits women from seeking help (2016, 22). I argue that the women feel doubly humiliated, first by their husbands' abuse, and secondly by their own complicity in the situation. The Black Widows Thami and Salome, for example, blame themselves for the wrong decisions that they took out of love for their husbands, out of naivety or due to low self-esteem at an earlier, happier stage of their relationships. Such emotional reactions seem typical for victims of domestic violence. Julie Stubbs maintains that victims "[...] may be ashamed or humiliated by what occurred and they may fear the consequences of full disclosure for themselves, their children or supporters. Moreover, victims of violence often express guilt or take some responsibility for their victimization [...]" (2012 (2007), 344). Traditional gender roles expect women to maintain relationships, so women take responsibility for failures, according to Stubbs (344). The work of Jewkes and Morrell confirms this for South Africa, albeit in a more pronounced manner. For women, tolerating violence "is an integral part of dominant [i.e. acquiescent] femininity." Women are expected "to endure and accept their physical punishment," which includes tolerance of infidelity and the provision of good – that is, unprotected – sex on demand (Jewkes and Morrell 2010, 6). This cultural ideal of femininity is guaranteed

---

33 "In 2007, more white South Africans divorced than Africans (9935 versus 9055), despite the fact that the former represent only 9% of the population compared to the latter group's 80%" (Jewkes and Morrell 2010, 6).

by "a system of sanctions and rewards" (6). This explains why Tallulah feels that she has an ever-tightening "noose around her neck" – a noose that women themselves keep in place through acquiescence – but also why it is so difficult for women if they decide no longer to comply. Precisely because full disclosure comes with so many risks, women who are abused by their intimate partners may not opt for legal recourse. Even if instruments of the law happen to be accessible to them, a police report or a divorce requires open confrontation. This involves exposing themselves and their real and/or felt guilt, as well as implicating other family members. The Black Widows' covert, non-spectacular murders by proxy allow them to negotiate the paradoxical situation of remaining silent in public even while they effect their desired ends. In this way, they protect themselves from public humiliation and blame – at least, as long as their crimes are not uncovered.

The Black Widows' approach also makes sense in the context of Halberstam's work on representations of female violence. Makholwa wants her Black Widows to be read symbolically as well as literally. For her, they offer an opportunity to "view women differently" (Binder 2015, 271). Moreover, she wants to issue a threat to men: "[W]hen you do this to women, this is how desperate you make them. It could lead them to do something this ridiculous" (5). And something this dangerous, we might add. Makholwa's use of the term "ridiculous" here reminds us that her crime fiction does not simply mirror existing violence, but pushes beyond the bounds of credulity, in a projective, speculative manner. Because the violent acts of the Black Widows represent a threat, they produce an effect that is akin to Halberstam's notion of "post-modern terror" (1993, 190). What such terror reminds us, according to Halberstam, is that the boundaries between real and imagined female violence are unstable (187). The terror of fictional female violence always carries with it the threat of being realised. In the case of the Black Widows, the effect of terror is enhanced by the fact that the women's violence is not openly confrontational. Implicit in their stealthy "surprise elimination[s]" (Makholwa 2013, 16), which are carried out with unemotional efficiency and business-like precision, is the threat of actualisation. Potential targets' sense of control is further unsettled because men are unable to perceive the threat as such. Not only is it kept secret, but it comes in male disguise, rather than from the openly perceived other. This is epitomised by China Gumede's killing, the very first murder that we witness. The Black Widows' hired gun Mzwakhe approaches the target undisguised and addresses him by his name: "'China? *Unjani broer?*' China was in shock. '*Hhayi*! Where do you know me from *wena*?' The tall man took out a gun. 'This one is not from me *baba*. This one is from Nokuthula,' said the man as he fired four shots into China's short muscled body" (15). The terror of this deadly message is compounded by the ordinary, friendly greeting, man-to-man, which asks, as is customary, "How are you, brother?" Here, the phatic exceeds its remit, becoming actionable. The action also has reverberations at the level of plot. With two surviving *female* killers on the loose at the end, female violence is by no means contained by the narrative. Instead, the idea is that women have begun to own and to action their anger, so that the implications of terror persist beyond the ending. There is also a sense that female violence may take new directions in the future. Thus, when Tallulah, Edna and Salome kill the disloyal hit man Mzwakhe, they do so with their own hands for the first time (2013, 278, 272).

Although the Black Widows' killings gain plausibility and a degree of justification as a means for the author to induce a sense of terror and to expose the crippling reality of domestic violence, they nevertheless remain ethically questionable acts. For this reason, ethical questions must be taken seriously if the author does not want to undermine the novel's feminist political message. The existentially stifling quality of domestic violence and the straitjacket of gender norms that prevent women from speaking out serve to mitigate the Black Widows' actions and offer support for the claim that they acted in self-defence, but Makholwa also seeks to address the ethical concerns raised by her novel in other ways, notably by introducing characters who take a critical stance vis-à-vis the Black Widows and by attempting to resolve (or mitigate) ethical issues on a narrative level.

Because the group setting in *Black Widow Society* allows for a multiplicity of ethical viewpoints and possibilities for reader identification, as well as artful reminders, it lends itself to complex, nuanced ethical meditations. What Sally-Ann Murray has noted with regard to self-narration can be fruitfully applied and extended here. For Murray, "an author's questing engagement with female subjectivity through personae and voices" allows for an exploration of " 'I' as conflicted and multiple, socially embedded rather than solipsistic" (2014, 77). The same can be said for a writer's enquiries in the moral-ethical realm through the "personae" of a social entity. While conflicting moral stances in crime fiction can be incorporated into a single character, as Jassy Mackenzie does with Jade de Jong, there is a limit to how far plausibility can be stretched. A group configuration, as in *Black Widow Society*, allows for further ethical conflict and diversity, as well as more options for narrative resolution. While a single female perpetrator can only either die or survive in the end, when an author is dealing with a group of perpetrators, she can eliminate (even punish via death) some characters while letting others survive. Among the many women who "must" die at the end of *Black Widow Society* are Thami and Nkosazana, two members who have taken a critical position towards the group. Rather than feeling liberated or elated by her payback, Thami finds herself plagued by panic attacks and regret (171). As a consequence, she comes to view the Black Widows as evil and arrogant and dismisses their philanthropic project as mere posturing. "[T]hey were killers, plain and simple. And she, Thami Mthembu was one of them" (170). However, her one-dimensional reflections on the ethics of the widows' actions cease when she finds consolation in the arms of a new man, unconsciously initiating a new cycle of exploitation at his hands and unwittingly, through an indiscretion, contributing to the collapse of the society. The other critical character is the lawyer Nkosazana, one of the society's founding members, although her critique of the Black Widows is of a purely financial nature – a fact that leads to frequent arguments with and reproaches from Tallulah (38, 52–54). Nkosazana, too, is instrumental in bringing about the society's downfall. Behind the back of the other Black Widows, she persuades Mzwakhe to carry out a secret mission – a murder – that should earn them both enough money to disappear from the Black Widows' radar (183). Although this murder never takes place, Mzwakhe is so derailed by the episode that he resolves to turn against the Black Widows.

At the end of the novel, Makholwa punishes Thami, Nkosazana and Mzwakhe with death, silencing these critical voices – even though, in Thami's case at least, their criticisms are not entirely unjustified. At the same time, however, she is enabling the survival of Edna and Tallulah, and thus of the society's most valuable legacy from an ethical and feminist perspective: the school for girls. It is therefore also consistent that Makholwa renders Tallulah as a woman with a conscience. Tallulah feels the ethical responsibility that comes with the killings. She is presented as a complex but flawed woman who uses her charisma and theatricality to intimidate and manipulate others (17, 246, 258). However, she is a staunch defender of and fighter for the school for girls and unfailingly prioritises the well-being of women and children: "The reason I sleep well at night is because of my confidence in the righteousness of our actions. Once we start putting money before people, then I fear what will become of us" (53). Tallulah can be criticised for remaining untroubled by the killings that she engineers, but she cannot be accused of eschewing responsibility. When the Black Widows collectively face being killed by Mzwakhe, she steps in for her sisters and, as the society's founder, offers to die to protect them (265). This is a sign of her moral integrity. In stark contrast to Sheemina February, Tallulah has an integrity and humanity that precludes easy, misogynist stereotyping of her as a monster. Makholwa's legitimising strategies allow the reader to keep faith with Tallulah, despite her acts of murder.

The novel is less successful in providing space for complex ethical reflections, as the Black Widows' final meeting illustrates. Tallulah calls this meeting in order to identify the woman who broke the code of confidentiality by leaking classified information. However, the meeting room is hijacked by Mzwakhe, who turns it into a court room and execution hall (259–268). While such a setting could function as a space for ethical reflection, the scenario that Makholwa creates in *Black Widow Society* borders on the ridiculous. Amid's critique that "the story doesn't quite seem to know whether it wants to be taken seriously or make a play for dark satire" (2014, par. 12) seems apt, at least with regard to this particular scene. Mzwakhe's simplistic yes/no questions, assessed by a lie-detector under threat of death, serve as a pretext for his random revenge killings, but yield nothing in terms of ethical complexity. In an almost parodic take on the TRC, they revolve around whether or not the women loved their husbands and whether or not they killed them for money. Such closed-ended interrogations cannot shed any light on the emotional and moral dilemmas faced by an abused woman, so they do not allow for any serious evaluation of the actions of the Black Widow Society. It also strikes an awkward note that Makholwa first uses Mzwakhe's male agency in the service of the women as a hired gun, and then, disloyally, in the service of hegemonic masculinity.

The women in the meeting room eventually regain control of the situation; Salome delivers the final, fatal blow to Mzwakhe, and Edna and Tallulah decide that it is time to put their exit plan into action. They must get out of the country (269) and survive on the society's funds, which have been placed in overseas accounts (270). Their exit plan turns out to be fundamentally flawed in that it fails to provide all of the sisters with an opportunity to escape. As a mother and grandmother of small children, Salome and Mrs Nkosi are not free simply to walk away, and are "trapped by the choices" (271). At this point, we are faced with the dilemma of the woman-in-herself and the woman-in-community. We are made aware that the kind of justice administered by the Black Widow Society does not work for all women, and that it does not necessarily help to navigate the tensions between individual and communal agency. This critical view is supported by Edna and Tallulah in their stock-taking before they leave: "They looked at all the dead bodies, all the widows with their shining bracelets – the Black Widow Society. It had managed to eat them alive, just like all black widow spiders do" (273). In the end, with two exceptions, the Black Widows either die or are brought to court. Edna and Tallulah manage to get away to set up a school for girls in Malawi. Commenting on the way in which she resolved the narrative, Makholwa notes that she did not think it morally justifiable to let the Black Widow Society survive, but she wanted to preserve their supportive mission (Binder 2015, 269–270). For this reason, she let Tallulah and Edna live on as Mrs Phiri and Mrs Baker, so that the novel ends on a hopeful note: " 'This is it Mrs Phiri. This is the dream.'

Tallulah, for the first time in many years, had tears in her eyes, 'So true, Mrs Baker. So true' she said, taking hold of Edna's hand and squeezing it tightly" (Makholwa 2013, 278). Despite the lack of nuanced ethical reflection in *Black Widow Society*, ultimately the novel takes an ethical stance against its protagonists' murderous actions by having the society perish. Moreover, by allowing the school initiative to be realised, it acknowledges the pressing need for structural change in light of the failure of South Africa's education system, especially for women.

With *Black Widow Society*, Makholwa has created a powerful fantasy of terror. The terror arises out of the question of what can happen if women who are violated and humiliated in their own homes strike back by stealthily violent means. In this way, the Black Widows, as female perpetrators, are able to reconceptualise female victimhood. The Black Widows are a far cry from evil women who may be read as symptoms of male fear. Rather, their violent female masculinity functions as a feminist political strategy to expose and radically attack unfair gender norms: gender norms that sanction the violence of hegemonic masculinity within heterosexual partnerships and demand women's tolerance of it. If replicated in the larger family, in the larger home that is the nation, these gender dynamics cannot but result in national failure, a point underlined by the surviving Black Widows' decision to seek a future in exile. Above all, Makholwa's novel shows that long-term structural change for women demands a collective effort. Drawing on the African philosophy of *ubuntu*, yet balancing its emphasis on communal agency with individual agency, *Black Widow Society* speaks to a need for female empowerment that extends beyond the individual and can be secured as a legacy for future generations.

5   The Female Perpetrator: Conclusion

The female perpetrators in the South African thrillers examined here all assume a kind of agency and position of power that is usually associated with men. By doing so, they become radical transgressors of the law in at least two ways. First, as people who kill and commit other criminal acts, they go against the law as the code that regulates the social body that is the South African nation state. Even though the state has the right and the duty to enforce this set of codes and impose punishment on transgressors, it is telling that, with the exception of some of the surviving Black Widows, none of the female perpetrators in the novels are subjected to this formal, legal procedure. Sheemina is shot by a secret agent, and some of the Black Widows are killed by Mzwakhe – both killers representing a male hegemony that exceeds formal state justice as such. Jade, Edna and Tallulah are not apprehended at all. While any rule becomes most obviously real and visible the moment it is broken, these female perpetrators also point to the shortcomings, if not the fallibility, of the state and its laws for women of any skin colour. Inside the law, they seem to imply, there can be no justice for women.

Taken together, the novels display a fundamental distrust of the state and its laws, and offer a shattering critique of their capacity to deliver justice for women. Each of the female figures examined here points to such failures in her own way. Mike Nicol's Sheemina February brings to light the taboo subject of gender violence within the South African liberation movement. Sheemina's violence is an expression of her demand for recognition as a Coloured, activist woman in South Africa. Jassy Mackenzie's Jade, as a White woman, claims citizenship through her expert use of the gun. What is more, she enforces justice where the state will not or cannot do so. In cases of police corruption, human trafficking, environmental sabotage and genetic engineering or in the face of nuclear threats, she becomes the self-appointed advocate not only of justice and order, but of the disenfranchised, be they trafficked women, exploited labourers or the natural environment. Angela Makholwa's Black Widow Society uses violence to counter the rotten core, hidden by privacy, of the (national) family that is domestic violence and the gender constructions that sustain it. As avengers, who resort to *lex talionis* – to retribution – as a means of restoring a violated/flawed order, they challenge not only the national legal system, but the national imperative that formed the basis for South Africa's peaceful transition from apartheid to democracy: the principle of producing order through reconciliation and reparation. By doing so, they expose the shortcomings of the TRC, notably its failure to enable women to speak of the violations they endured as women, to acknowledge women as individual as well as communal beings, to hold male perpetrators of sexual violence accountable and to allow for the expression of rage.

Despite their brutality, Jade and the Black Widows – in contrast to Sheemina – are not rendered as monsters without a conscience. As much as they advocate retribution, Mackenzie's and Makholwa's novels do not shy away from the ethical repercussions that come with this form of justice. They do not deny the shortcomings of retributive justice. The solution envisaged by the Black Widows does not work for all women, Jade fails in her attempts to differentiate between "good" and "bad" killers, and the novels show how difficult it is to judge which crimes legitimise a counter-crime. Especially in its serial form, crime fiction has the capacity to navigate ethical complexity. It can provoke ethical reflection by repeatedly confronting its protagonists with similar but subtly different scenarios, while displaying the awareness that some ethical questions must remain unresolved. This is exemplified by Mackenzie's Jade de Jong series, in particular.

As *women* who kill, Sheemina, Jade and the Black Widows transgress against a second kind of law: namely, the rules that govern gender norms. It is clear that they radically subvert traditional femininity, but do they also subvert traditional, hegemonic masculinity? In other words, are their acts of counter-violence successful in undermining the gender system as a whole? And what is their feminist political significance? Relating the HIV epidemic to socially constructed and sanctioned gender norms among the South African population of colour, Jewkes and Morrell emphasise the importance of resisting the gender order as such. They maintain that occupying a dissident gender position alone does not constitute a fundamental challenge to the gender order (2010, 6–7). It is important to note that in my interviews with Nicol, Mackenzie and Makholwa, all three authors emphasised the need for a change to male *and* female gender roles, especially when it comes to fighting gender-based violence (Binder 2015, 275). The notion of violent female masculinity as applied here to the female perpetrator figure also pre-supposes structural change. Halberstam attributes to her model of female masculinity, which underpins my concept of violent female masculinity, the potential to function as "an active matrix of exchange" that transforms the gender order as such. She maintains,

> Indeed, male and female masculinities are constantly involved in an ever-shifting pattern of influences. We tend to identify the pattern as moving only in one direction, however, rather than seeing the possibilities of an active matrix of exchange between male and female masculinities. Exchanges between male and female masculinity, I suggest, have the potential to go both ways.
>
> 1998, 276

By borrowing from violent masculinity, how exactly do the female perpetrators examined here affect the gender order? And to what extent can their acts be called feminist political acts? If we define feminism as a conscious, political *strategy* aimed at achieving equality for women as a group, neither Sheemina nor Jade is a feminist figure.[34] Sheemina's actions are motivated by her

---

34   I am using the definition of feminist strategy offered by Joan Scott during the workshop that she held at the Interdisciplinary Centre for Gender Studies at the University of Berne on 18 October 2016. Scott differentiated between feminist strategy and feminist effect that may result from a transgression of gender stereotypes.

personal wish to avenge herself on Mace. Even though the violations that she suffered are reflective of wider female concerns in South Africa, she does not understand herself to be acting on behalf of other women. Quite the contrary: achieving her end of destabilising Mace entails killing other women. Like Sheemina, Jade is a relatively isolated figure and prefers solo missions. While she is generally guided by a concern for social justice and sometimes acts on behalf of disadvantaged groups, including women, her concern is not a solely feminist one. However, judging Sheemina and Jade by their *effects* alters the picture. No matter how we read Sheemina, it is clear that her actions expose, ridicule and explicitly target the militarised masculinities embodied by Mace and other male protagonists. Insofar as she reveals the weaknesses and inappropriateness of such a traditional masculinity, she has a feminist effect with regard to the overall gender system. Like Jade, she contests the link between masculinity and power, even if she remains ultimately contained by masculine power. For Jade, doing violent masculinity and gaining power from her expertly drawn gun is second nature and is not contained in any way whatsoever. It was her own mother who – problematically – passed this ability on to her and her father who nurtured and cherished it. The South African police, personified by David, are not enthusiastic about Jade's violence, but rely on her skills and therefore tolerate it.

All the female perpetrators discussed here allow us to view women differently and, to that extent, they all have a symbolic feminist effect. However, the partly racist and misogynist stereotypes applied to Sheemina significantly weaken her feminist effect. Jade's feminist effect, on the other hand, is heightened by her potential for reader identification. She is a successful figure of female empowerment. Likewise, the system of female counter-terror that the Black Widows manage to establish has a strong feminist effect. It symbolically undermines real women's terror of violence and evokes real men's terror of female counter-violence. Moreover, the Black Widows' feminism goes beyond feminist effects. Edna's and Tallulah's performance of violent masculinity is a conscious feminist strategy designed to empower women collectively. The variant of violent female masculinity that they advocate emphasises the importance of community, female solidarity and economic power. Also, they do not stop at the violent act: they move beyond resistance. Their long-term educational project aims to secure structural change, while the stand that they take against domestic violence equates to a rejection of both acquiescent femininity and hegemonic masculinity, signalling a transformation of the gender order as such.

The female perpetrator figure in South African crime fiction blurs the boundaries between imagined and real female counter-violence, between what is masculine and what is feminine and between the legal and the illegal – a powerful feminist effect. Jade and the Black Widows, in particular, speak directly to South African state justice, as do the real female vigilantes discussed by the Comaroffs. The last figure I will examine, the female detective, is also concerned with securing justice, albeit by different means.

CHAPTER 3

The Female Detective

Agent of (Gender) Justice? Exploring Female Detective Agency and Investigating

1   The Female Detective: Introduction

Female detectives or investigators occupy a lawful and visible position within the hegemonic patriarchal system.[1] As professionals, the detectives discussed here are employed by either the police or the media and are given authority to work on behalf of these still mostly male-dominated institutions. Female detection thus constitutes a claim to power and equality *within* these institutions. Licensed and empowered as these women are, they are also compromised to varying degrees as agents of the very institution, of the very law that marginalises them. In this context, the detective's quest for justice must necessarily include her own subject position and agency, as well as the gender and racial implications of the criminal cases that she solves. The female detective's scope for resistant agency will influence what truths she establishes and what kind of justice she is thereby able to serve.

The female detectives discussed here are all serial heroines of women writers, in series that are all still in their early stages. They are police detective Persy Jonas, who features in Michéle Rowe's novels *What Hidden Lies* (2013) and *Hour of Darkness* (2015); Vee Johnson, who is Hawa Jande Golakai's journalist protagonist in *The Lazarus Effect* (2011) and *The Score* (2015); and Maggie Cloete, Charlotte Otter's crime reporter in *Balthasar's Gift* (2014) and *Karkloof Blue* (2016). My aim is to explore the gender performances of these female investigators, who come from diverse social and ethnic backgrounds. How do they navigate the tensions they are subjected to as female professionals in male-dominated institutions? Do they enact or subvert the detective agency that they are granted? How do they, as gendered and raced agents of the law, resist and negotiate the law's construction of gender and race? These questions touch on what has been at the heart of the feminist scholarly debate surrounding this figure: her political effectiveness as a feminist resistant agent.

---

1   The terms "detective" and "investigator" are used interchangeably and regardless of institutional affiliation here.

I will argue that Persy, Vee and Maggie are not free of conflicting pressures, but that they negotiate them in creative and often successful ways.

Racial and gender politics is also a factor in determining the crimes and victims the detectives attend to, the truths they uncover and the kind of justice they thereby administer. This gives rise to a second set of questions. What aspects of the South African real are subject to female investigation? What kinds of violations do female detectives stumble upon, and where does the site of interrogation lie? What spaces for justice do they open up? What notions of justice do they enforce and restore? What alternatives do they envisage? Twenty years into democracy, these questions are still relevant in South Africa. The formal equality granted to South African women under the constitution remains incomplete in the lived reality of many women, especially economically disadvantaged women of colour. South African feminist legal scholars argue that, to some extent, the gendered nature of the law itself is to blame for this discrepancy. They therefore aim to highlight "the problems which the ostensible neutrality and objectivity of the law hold for women" (Albertyn and Bonthuys 2007, 2). Catherine Albertyn maintains that actual, substantive equality "encompasses some notion of remedial or redistributive justice [...]" (2007, 94). Arguably, the fictional detectives examined here not only operate as agents of the established criminal justice system, but adhere to forms of so-called "restorative justice", which is victim based and relies on remedial measures. By working for more equality and striving to remedy the law's masculine discourse, they are able to find different versions of "truth" and justice.

1.1 The Female Detective in British and American Crime Fiction: Legacies and Scholarly Debates

The fictional female sleuth has always been part of the history of crime writing (Gavin 2010, 258, Worthington 2011, 111). And yet, "[w]hether the detective is male or female, straight or gay, she or he always exists in negotiation with a series of long-established masculine codes" (Plain 2001, 11). For Kathleen Gregory Klein, the female detective is "a contradiction in terms" (1988, 225). She views fictional women detectives as compromised on the grounds that the genre portrays them either as inadequate women or as inadequate detectives (225). What is at stake here is the potential and efficacy of the female detective as a feminist resistant agent. There is disagreement about whether her position within the system allows her to resist that system or, as Gill Plain puts it, "whether changes in the subjectivity of the detective can effect a more fundamental challenge to wider socio-political structures" (2001, 88). The masculine codes to which Plain refers are reflected in the genre's preference for individualism – as embodied in the lone detective hero – and its emphasis on knowledge, logic, rationality and, more recently, forensic science (Worthington 2011, 109). It is thus not obvious at first why female writers would strategically adopt the genre for feminist ends. And yet they have done so – and with verve – especially in the context of women's demands for access to male-dominated areas. The late 1970s and early 1980s saw the advent of politicised feminist crime fiction, with pioneering writers such as Marcia Muller, Sara Paretsky, Sue Grafton and Liza Cody (Gavin 2010, 264–265, see also Munt 1994, 27, Kinsman 2010, 153, Knight 2010, 167). Adrienne Gavin considers "[t]aking detection in new overtly feminist directions" to be as much "a feminist response to male hard-boiled writing" as a continuation of "previous female detection" (2010, 265). In any case, it marked a significant change in crime writing. Stephen Knight maintains that "feminist crime writers have changed the face of the genre enormously" (2010, 165) and finds that Marcia Muller created "an authoritative new model of the detective," thus making "an impact like Doyle and Hammett" (168). As Heather Worthington puts it: "In the wake of the feminist movement, the fully formed modern female, or even feminist, detective comes into being" (2011, 48). It is important to note that the genre's feminist impetus has been channelled mainly through the figure of the female detective or private eye. The impulse behind feminist detective narratives, the "desire to translate passivity into action" (Plain 2001, 159) and to explore "the thorny issue of the relationship between woman's victimization and woman's agency" (Walton 2013, 23), has been realised in the female detective figure.

Crime fiction does not lend itself to feminist engagement for writers and their detective heroines alone: feminist scholars, too, have taken an avid interest in the genre. As Plain highlights, "the genre's profound investment in dynamics of power," which has inevitably resulted in the incorporation of "discourses of gender and sexuality," makes it a "prime site for the development of feminist readings" (2001, 8). Indeed, the suitability and effectiveness of the figure of the female detective for political, revisionist purposes has become a subject of heated debate. Prominent among those who accord the genre feminist potential are Priscilla Walton and Manina Jones. Their seminal work *Detective Agency: Women Rewriting the Hard-Boiled Tradition* (1999) follows in the footsteps of earlier critics such as Maureen Reddy (1988) and Sally Munt (1994). According to Walton and Jones, writing the detective figure as female allows for an alternative positioning of female characters. This equates to a recasting of the traditional role of woman as the generic outlaw (for example, in the figure of the femme fatale) and functions to destabilise the masculine codes of the genre:

> While the traditional hard-boiled novel demonized and punished the female character who contravened conventional ideas about feminine submissiveness by desiring and acting, the feminist hard-boiled novel makes that role a heroic one [...]. Working through the conventions of the genre to subvert some of its most powerful traditions, both authors and characters of the "tough gal" novels make a kind of feminist "outlaw agency" possible.
> 1999, 195

In Walton's and Jones's view, this act of rewriting and empowering the formerly outlawed female constitutes a "reverse discourse" in the Foucauldian sense; it explores "positions of resistance and agency that were offered by previous practices but that were inaccessible to women" (93). They contend that "these texts can both inscribe an empowered female subject and rework the conventions of subjectivity that make that position problematic" (113). What they also find is that novels premised on the female detective counter "the utopian notion that one can work outside the patriarchal structure of Western society [...]" (102–103). In other words, if the female detective is necessarily implicated in the socio-political status quo, the novels enable a playing out of possibilities and limits with regard to her resistant agency without naively assuming that gendered action can occur beyond normative constraints.

However, other critics do not regard detective agency as feminist agency. Teresa L. Ebert, for example, calls the female detective an agent of the phallus, a "surrogate agent of patriarchy" (1992, 16). The female detective may achieve equality and thus enjoy improved conditions within patriarchy, but she does not challenge it (14). Ebert rejects the notion that reform can be brought about from within the system.

> Detecting, in short, is a disciplinary practice that enlists individuals – regardless of their "gender" (anatomy) – as agents of phallic authority who act to restore patriarchal order and hegemony. Thus, women who engage in the ideologically encoded practice of detecting (whether as "detectives" or readers) do not indicate a significant alteration of the sexual politics of the genre but rather an expansion of the patriarchal agency and authority – often in spite of the women's own intentions.
> 13

Kathleen Gregory Klein takes a similar view. She describes the female detective as "a contradiction in terms" (1988, 225) and sees the authors of crime fiction as reinforcing patriarchal ideology (223). For Klein, the term "woman detective" is an oxymoron: "[i]f female, then not detective; if detective, then not really female" (1995, 174). Nevertheless, she identifies a possible way out of this impasse. In Klein's view, it is the *lesbian* detective who has truly feminist-disruptive potential, for as a sexual "deviant" her position "approaches the positionality of a criminal" (177). This line of argument is developed by Plain, who rereads male and female-authored crime fiction of the twentieth century through the critical lens of gender. She contends that the feminist project of the heterosexual female detective is a failure due to the inevitable complicity of heterosexual desire with patriarchy (2001, 163, 206). True subversion, according to Plain, lies in the lesbian detective and in the female detective's conflation with the serial killer. The latter she finds exemplified in Thomas Harris's *The Silence of the Lambs*, with Clarice Starling as a detective who "identifies the killer through proximity and similarity, rather than from a comfortable analytic or moral distance" (226–227). Yet, such subversion, for Plain, comes at the cost of generic dissolution: "What began as a mode of restoring order – a series of fictional fantasies that envisaged agency and order even in the midst of chaos – has evolved into a narrative mode that embraces exactly that which it initially sought to exclude. This attempt to contain the other through incorporation and inclusion has led, however, to dilution" (247). When the detective becomes "criminal" – be it through her sexuality or through her proximity to the serial killer – she constitutes not only a rupture of the system, but a crisis of the genre (221–222). As Plain points out, it is "impossible to resolve the competing claims for the [female] detective's agency or impotence" (89) in generalised terms. For this reason, it is important to consider not just the detective's subject position, but her mission in the specific context of South Africa.

1.2 *Female Investigating As Truth-Finding in South Africa*

Any detective's main duty is truth-finding. It is what he or she is both authorised and required to do in the interest of securing justice for the victim. However, this ostensibly simple directive is complicated by its entanglement in contexts where "truth" has been hijacked to preferred social ends. In reaction to the biases and prejudices that shaped "truth" under apartheid, in the early years of South African democracy truth-finding and truth-telling were instrumental in the country's transition to a more just dispensation. This was reflected in the very name of the institution mandated to facilitate it: the Truth and Reconciliation Commission. Pertinent here is the observation by Walton and Jones that, since the beginning of the American hard-boiled tradition, the detective's task has shifted from merely identifying the individual criminal to shedding light on the reasons behind the crime. Quoting Raymond Chandler, they emphasise that the detective's quest for "truth" involves "what the hell went on rather than who done it" (1999, 209). They argue that women writers of detective fiction have extended Chandler's tenet from locating the reasons "'in character and relationship' to the ideological raison d'être of systemic crimes," on the basis that " 'who done it' often turns out to be a societal entity" (209). The mandate of the TRC reveals a similar multifaceted understanding of the truth-finding process. In the first volume of its report, the TRC declared that its aim was to establish

> as complete a picture as possible of the causes, nature and extent of the gross violations of human rights which were committed during the period from 1 March 1960 to the cut-off date [10 May 1994], including the antecedents, circumstances, factors and context of such violations, as well as the perspectives of the victims and the motives and perspectives of the persons responsible for the commission of the violations.
> POSEL 2002, 147

As Deborah Posel notes, "The TRC's truth-telling mandate was partly descriptive (what had happened, when, who had done it), partly explanatory (why, with regard to structural, institutional causes as well as motives and perspectives of relevant historical actors)" (153). Given that the fictional detectives examined in this study display a strong concern with past crimes, their quest for the "truth" needs to be viewed not only against the background of traditions within the crime genre more generally, but in the light of the TRC's work in South Africa itself. In part one, I discussed the many reservations that have been expressed by South African women about the "truth" uncovered by the TRC. Their critique of the TRC's practices will also inform my reading of the female detective figure. In addition, I will draw on Posel's analysis of the kinds of truth (and their power) that the TRC revealed, and constructed, as well as South African and international feminist research into the law, the criminal justice process and inclusive models of justice.

In South African crime fiction, there is a long tradition of female investigators that goes back as far as June Drummond and her elderly amateur sleuth Nan. Nan, the protagonist of Drummond's 1959 novel *The Black Unicorn*, can be regarded as an influential precursor of contemporary South African fictional female detectives and investigators (Pretorius 2014). Another figure worth mentioning is Gillian Slovo's detective heroine Kate Baeier, who first appears in the 1984 thriller *Morbid Symptoms*. Although Slovo's detective is based in London, the Kate Baeier series has a distinctly South African ring and provides a means for Slovo to explore past secrets and silences in an attempt to produce a new history (Braude 1996, 43–52). These concerns persist in the post-transitional crime fiction boom that has brought forth an ever-increasing number of female detectives, notably Margie Orford's Clare Hart, Angela Makholwa's Lucy Khambule, Jassy Mackenzie's Jade de Jong, Tracy Gilpin's Dunai Marks, Joanne

Hichens's Rae Valentine, Penny Lorimer's Nix Mniki, Wessel Ebersohn's Abigail Bukula and Sally Andrew's Tannie Maria.[2] Many of these characters are rooted in the genre tradition of the feisty, tough, hard-boiled heroine. The three detectives I will discuss are among the most recent additions to the list. They were chosen because, together with their authors, they represent a range of new and different perspectives – domestic, immigrant and diasporic – as well as diverse, even conflicting, female subject positions. Around twenty years into democracy, they continue the South African tradition of female investigators while adding decidedly new twists and drawing attention to issues of crime, truth and justice in South Africa in new ways.

2 Not That Kind of Cop: Michéle Rowe's Detective Constable Persy Jonas

> All these years I felt like a rookie, looked up to Tucker and old-school career cops, and tried to follow in their hardass footsteps. But I'm not that kind of cop.
> PERSY in *Hour of Darkness* (338)

This chapter sets out to investigate precisely what kind of cop Persy Jonas, the protagonist in Michéle Rowe's detective novels *What Hidden Lies* (2013b) and *Hour of Darkness* (2015), is. Persy's difference is made obvious to the reader in several ways long before Persy herself becomes aware of it at the end of the second novel. As a young, bespectacled woman of slight build, she is at odds with the sexist macho mentality of the South African Police Service. Representing and enforcing state power as well as the law, Persy, the policewoman, occupies an uneasy position not only in relation to her corrupt colleagues in the police, but within her own Cape Coloured community, which has been criminalised by both the racist politics of the apartheid regime in the past and the precarious economic circumstances of the present. As I will show, Persy's impossible professional position both compromises her detective agency *and* requires her to navigate and to subvert the system in creative and alternative ways. By doing so, she is able to open up a space for agonistic solidarity, a significant form of agency, in her collaboration with her investigative partner Marge Labuschagne. I will explore the implications of this both for Persy's criminal

---

2 For a comprehensive list that includes female sidekicks as well as female detectives in fiction by South African authors writing in languages other than English, see Mike Nicol's Crime Beat blog (http://crimebeat.bookslive.co.za/whos-who-of-south-african-crime-writing/).

investigations and for the kind of justice that she is able to serve. Critical work on the TRC as well as South African and international feminist legal scholarship will undergird my reading and assessment of Persy's endeavours to find the "truth" and restore justice.

A graphic artist, production designer for films and TV commercials and award-winning scriptwriter, Michéle Rowe came to crime fiction relatively late in her career.[3] She arrived on the scene with fanfare by immediately winning the much coveted Crime Writers' Association Debut Dagger Award in 2011 for the opening chapters of *What Hidden Lies* (Rowe 2017, par. 7). *Hour of Darkness* is her second Persy Jonas novel in what is planned as a trilogy, to be rounded off with *Before His Time* (Rowe 2016, par. 18).[4] Her fiction has also been translated into French and German. Rowe lives in South Africa, where she was born and educated (Rowe 2013a, par. 1, 5, Fourie 2013, par. 1). From Nicol we learn that "[s]he has great-grandparents who came from Mauritius and whose children crossed over to the White side during the time of the pencil test," i.e. during the height of apartheid, when a pencil inserted into especially curly hair was often used to determine racial categorisation (2015a, 18).

The woman who will become Detective Constable Persy Jonas makes her first appearance as a girl of around seven in the opening scene of *What Hidden Lies*, which is set on the Cape Peninsula. In that haunting scene, we accompany Persy and her childhood friend Sean Dollery into the woods on the slopes of Chapman's Peak, where they manage to shake off Persy's younger brother Clyde, who has run after them. However, what was intended as a childish ploy by Persy to elude her annoying sibling leads directly to a tragic death, for moments later Clyde is buried alive when the nearby open kaolin mine is filled in. Twenty years later, Persy's first case inadvertently takes her back to this repressed childhood trauma as she investigates the murder of Andrew Sherwood, a local school teacher and alleged paedophile. The same past events have a bearing not only on Persy, but on her fellow investigator, retired criminal psychologist Marge Labuschagne. Persy and Marge first relate with great reluctance and hostility, but eventually they begin to bond. Their friendship deepens in the course of the second novel, *Hour of Darkness*, which is set

---

3   As detailed on her personal website, Rowe's projects have won her an Oscar documentary and International Emmy nomination, a Mail & Guardian Short Films Prize, a Special Jury Award at Skip City International (Japan), a Banff World TV Award (Canada), a SAFTA (South African Film and Television Award) and the Andrew Murray – Desmond Tutu Prize (Rowe 2017, par. 4).
4   In an earlier interview, Rowe gives the title of her third novel as *Before Her Time* (Rowe 2013a, par. 16).

in the southern suburbs of Cape Town and features a case of three missing women: Severine, teenage daughter of the affluent but emotionally damaged Hamilton-Langford family, Annette Petroussis, their neighbour, and Mandisa, teenage daughter of Nosapho Dasheka, the domestic worker for Severine's family. Land claims, some reaching far back in time, form the backdrop of the novel. As so often in South African crime fiction, the criminal investigation involves a review of the past and the grip that it has on the present. Later I will examine these pressures, together with Persy's dual mission to establish "truth" and justice respectively. First, however, I will explore the difficulties of Persy's position as an agent working for and in a social and professional system that restrains and subjugates her, and identify the possibilities for resistant political agency sketched out in the novels.

2.1 *Persy Jonas: Female Detective Agency Compromised*

Persy's full name, Persephone, was chosen for her by her grandfather – her Poppa (Rowe 2013b, 59, 176). Like her namesake in Greek mythology, she inhabits different worlds with conflicting pressures and is associated with dilemma and compromise.[5] Because the dilemmas that Persy faces fall into three categories – gender, sexuality and race – I will discuss them from a gender-race intersectional perspective.

The first of these dilemmas relates to gender. It is the typical predicament of the female detective in crime fiction, as well as of real women working in the South African Police Service (SAPS). As a junior member of the SAPS, Persy presents as the enterprising, tough, determined cop and has full detective agency. She is the equal, if not the superior, of her male colleagues in any situation. She boasts impeccable credentials and is very smart (2013b, 264, 2015, 120). Not only is she highly ambitious (2013b, 38, 56, 2015, 73), she is also admired for her guts (2013b, 288). Persy asserts her authority as a police officer despite the fact that she does not look the part. Marge "could hardly imagine a less likely detective": Persy reminded her of her "bookish, lesbian" Trotskyite university students from the 1980s (2013b, 34). Persy's dreadlocks and "God Bless Africa" T-shirt variously evoke admiration, humour and ridicule (2013b, 213–214,

---

5 In Greek mythology, Persephone is the daughter of Zeus and Demeter. When Persephone is kidnapped by Hades to become his wife and queen of the underworld, her enraged mother Demeter demands that she be returned. Mediating between Demeter and Hades, Zeus finally decides that Persephone should live with her mother for eight months a year and with her husband for four months. Demeter responds by allowing no crops to grow in the four months during which she is deprived of her daughter, thus creating the winter season (De Crescenzo 1998, 109–114, Morford 2016).

2015, 75, 203). Still, Persy functions as the cop. She bangs on suspects' doors, shouting "'SAPS! Open up!'" (2013b, 7); she forcefully and effectively stops an illegal dog fight and rescues Marge's dog Bongo (2013b, 186); she orders criminals to drop their weapons and shoots them when they fail to comply (2013b, 286). When questioning suspects, whether it be in their mansions, at the crime scene or in the police interrogation room, Persy is unfazed by their social class or skin colour (2013b, 184, 304–305, 2015, 175, 180–185, 207–208). In cases where she sees her investigation being stalled or hindered, she repeatedly disregards police hierarchies (2013b, 27, 91, 98, 2015, 216, 247, 290), spurns control by authority and becomes the maverick cop (2013b, 6, 106–107, 2015, 238–243). What is more, she refuses to be blackmailed by criminals and is not corrupt, nor is she prepared to turn a blind eye to corruption among her fellow police officers (2015, e.g. 278–279). In other words, she emulates and equals the personality and agency of the genre-typical male detective: heroic, autonomous, individually non-conformist and relatively violent. She thereby claims and fills the traditionally masculine space of the detective.

And yet this space, the institution of the police, also vehemently opposes her. She is repeatedly reined in by her superiors and colleagues alike. She gets reprimanded for insubordination (2013b, 146, 2015, 290), is criticised for turning down male protection (2013b, 189, 219, 287) and is allocated typically female jobs such as looking after the young sons of the missing Annette (2015, 36–37). Persy is quick to notice and criticise the gender bias inherent in this treatment, as when she indignantly reminds her superior Ren Tucker, "'I'm a detective, not a fucking babysitter'" (2015, 37). However, because she seldom does so openly, her criticisms remain ineffective. Another female officer, Dina Martinez, although much further up the police hierarchy, is subjected to the same gender bias as Persy. As Persy notes, "You did not make Captain heading up a detective unit unless you were tough, and Dina was tough. If Dina were a man, it would be cause for admiration. As it was, she was very unpopular among the male cops" (2015, 118). Time and again Persy also has to deal with misogyny and sexual harassment from her male colleagues and with insinuations that she has advanced this far in the force only because she is a woman (2013b, 43, 143, 150, 2015, 73, 180–181). As combative as Persy is, she does not challenge these manifestations of the fact that the police service remains a male institution. Mostly, she is silent, and thus appears to be silenced. When Tucker mocks her saying, "'[f]emales don't last in this job'," Persy does not rise to the bait, recognising that "there was no point. At least he'd said to her face what most of her male colleagues only thought. His dismissal of her only strengthened her resolve to prove him wrong" (2015, 70). Similarly, while she retaliates verbally when her colleague Mhlabeni issues sexual threats, she resolves that "[i]t was no use complaining about intimidation. Her life would not be worth living if she ran crying to Titus." Instead, "she had to control herself. That's all she had, her ability to appear impervious, no matter what" (2013b, 43). In Persy, Rowe gives us a familiar female figure uneasily emplaced within male-oriented, patriarchal professional structures. As Hans Bertens and Theo D'haen note in relation to female professionals in American crime fiction, "[b]ringing women into the police departments almost invariably made the institution show its true, thoroughly masculinist colors and thereby undermined its supposed neutrality" (2001, 14). Rowe must be credited for making this bias visible in her crime fiction.

It is a bias that extends beyond the fictional: Rowe is reflecting the experiences of actual policewomen in South Africa. As Theresa Ulicki's recent work on gender equity and sexual harassment in the South African Police Service in Gauteng province demonstrates, female police officers routinely face a dilemma similar to Persy's. For example, even though in 2008 the SAPS prided itself on the fact that nearly 21 percent of its officer complement were female (Ulicki 2011, 97) – a figure higher than that for most police services across the world – and even though the SAPS drafted a sexual harassment policy as far back as 1998, in 2011 the service was still rife with *systemic* gender discrimination. According to Ulicki, this discrimination manifests itself mainly in the form of sexual harassment and factors that deter policewomen from reporting such behaviour:

> They have insider knowledge of how civilian women who report rape, sexual assault and domestic violence are treated by police. They fear a backlash, particularly by male colleagues, who make up the vast majority of their co-workers. There are few women in leadership positions to whom they can report abuse. The grievance process itself is flawed: the chance of disciplinary action against an abuser is low, the process lacks confidentiality and is very lengthy. Finally, as some women have discovered by reporting sexual harassment, standing up for your rights can result in other forms of harassment and a negative work environment.
> 110–111

Policewomen adopt protective strategies of acceptance and denial (109), while the systematically ingrained resistance of the male institution persists. Ulicki concludes that a focus on formal equality issues has a limited impact, as "the underlying systemic causes of gender inequity" remain untouched (114). In Rowe's crime writing, the gender bias of the South African Police Service is brought to light through Persy. Rowe exposes, yet at the same time fictionally perpetuates, the discrimination against policewomen. Persy's male colleagues are not held accountable for their abusive behaviour. By letting her protagonist seem to be subdued by the displays of male power, it can be argued that the female author not only proves them to be efficient at silencing women, but becomes complicit in the very practice of female effacement herself. In the long run, Persy's resolutions to work harder, to disprove the men, to appear unaffected, emerge as ineffective strategies. Indeed, at the end of the second novel, the policing institution seems to have successfully evicted her, since Persy is put on indefinite leave (Rowe 2015, 340). According to the masculine logic of the police, she is defeated, her detective agency is thwarted. For the police to become more gender inclusive, they would have to punish gender discrimination on a systemic level, as Ulicki's work shows. While in theory crime fiction could be one of the places to imagine this, Rowe's detective novels refrain from doing so.

Sexuality (and sexual orientation) comprises another arena for dilemma. Persy is androgynous in appearance (Rowe 2013b, 27), but clearly heterosexual. These factors awkwardly intersect, such that she appears to blur boundaries while at the same time conforming. In *Hour of Darkness*, she has an intense, disastrous sexual relationship with her immediate superior, Ren Tucker:

> Persy had found him utterly compelling from the first moment she'd fixed eyes on him. Now [...] Persy thought about how sleeping with Tucker was about the worst idea she could have come up with – considering that he was white, head of the four squads of detectives at the station, and in the middle of a messy separation from his wife – and Persy's boss – Captain Dina Martinez, with whom he had three kids.
>
> 2015, 28–29

In *Hour of Darkness*, there is a heavy emphasis on Persy's sexuality (71, 83, 141, 187, 260–261). Insofar as her sexuality is portrayed as autonomous, with her desiring Tucker as much as he desires her, their relationship seems to be a successful, democratic rewriting of the racist South African script that heavily criminalised interracial relationships in the past.[6] Yet Persy's desire and sexual agency are also represented as debilitating, which is problematic from a racially critical perspective. The disastrous implications of her relationship with Tucker can be intuited from the beginning (and are even expressly articulated

---

6 In Rowe's novels, equal interracial relationships – which are still far from being the norm in South Africa – are also tentatively imagined, though not (yet) realised between Persy and her Black colleague Dizu (2013b, 60), and between Persy and Marge's White son Will (2015, 129–130).

by Persy), and it soon becomes clear that Persy will be the one to pay the price. Not only does she depend on Tucker in their unequal professional relationship, but there is an increasing difference in their emotional goals, with Persy (as in the habituated gender economies of conventional romance) longing for more intimate affective attachment than does the male partner (190). What she has sensed all along then proceeds to happen: Tucker gives in to outside pressure and lets her down (242, 274, 333). The novel hints at the fact that it will take a different kind of masculinity from the hegemonic machismo that Tucker embodies for an interracial relationship to work and to be truly equal. However, this suggestion is undermined by the way in which Persy's relationship with Tucker and her sexuality as such corner her on several levels. Far from being positive, liberating or even empowering, Persy's sexuality is portrayed as anomalous, even slightly pathological, as no more than a dubious coping strategy in moments of psychic distress. Sex, for Persy, is part of her "breakouts" (2013b, 182), serving to blunt her panic and temporarily drive out her demons (2015, 142). Without fail, sex leaves her full of remorse and self-loathing, feeling sick, confused, unsettled and wound up, even guilty (2013b, 182, 2015, 139, 142, 164, 187, 263). Apart from this, whenever she gives in to her desire, she feels that "[t]he acorn does not fall far from the tree" (2015, 140, see also 2013b, 182–183), fearing that she is following in her mother's footsteps. Sexual libertinism, paired with alcohol addiction, have been painted by Persy's Poppa as the source of her mother's problems. He invariably describes her to Persy as debauching in shebeens, drinking and sleeping around (2013b, 178, 182–183, 2015, 140), so that Persy thinks of her as "a slut and a drinker and a bad mother" (2015, 334).

Rowe's depiction of sexuality as the source of much trouble for both Persy and her mother must be understood in the context of how the sexuality of women of colour has been demonised. A wealth of research has explored the ways in which conceptualisations of the sexuality of women of colour as pathological and degenerate have been deployed in the service of the patriarchal, imperial project, masking a desire for control and power (Lewis 2011, 202–203). The famous case of Sarah Baartman is just one example of this. Drawing on the work of Pumla Gqola, Lewis points out that control is "anchored in discursive representations of the sexualised and degenerate female body, a body that threatens to pollute or weaken the 'healthy' national body politic" (206). Rowe's depiction of Persy's and her mother's sexuality serves to reinscribe rather than to expose this racial and gendered script.[7]

---

[7] For a much more positive depiction of Black female sexuality, see Hawa Jande Golakai's detective protagonist Vee.

In *What Hidden Lies*, Persy's sexual encounter with a random man whom she meets in a bar is also problematic for its celebration of male dominance. Persy is on the lookout for a sexual partner, but, once she has identified the object of her desire, she actively encourages him to play the game of conquest: "The male animal. Trawling the water holes looking for prey. Fine, let him think he was the predator. [...] He was a crap [pool] player but she let him beat her. [...] Raoul leaned over her, pressing into her back ..." (Rowe 2013b, 180). Here, Persy asserts her sexual agency as she activates and then complies with the masculine code, both doing and undoing it. Moreover, she appears to celebrate and thus condone not only phallocentrism, but rape culture. Bell Hooks argues provocatively that

> one major obstacle preventing us from transforming rape culture is that heterosexual women have not unlearned a heterosexist-based "eroticism" that constructs desire in such a way that many of us can only respond erotically to male behaviour that has already been coded as masculine within the sexist framework.
>
> 1994, 131

According to Hooks, if we want to oppose rape culture, we need to shape "our eroticism in ways that repudiate phallocentrism" (133).[8] In this vein, one could read Persy's sexual behaviour as potentially complicit with male violence. In addition, Persy's sexuality and sexual agency place her in a professional quandary, thereby echoing Gill Plain's contention about the heterosexual female detective. For Plain, the feminist potential of the heterosexual female detective is flawed due to the complicity of heterosexual desire with patriarchy (2001, 163, 206). At the end of *Hour of Darkness*, Persy finds her career and future detective agency severely compromised by her sexuality. When Ren tries to reconnect with her, she retorts angrily, "Don't confuse fucking me in bed with fucking me over at work" (Rowe 2015, 163), yet this is precisely what happens, albeit indirectly. Their affair is abruptly curtailed when Persy and Tucker receive contract killer Fred Splinters's email with an attachment that shows them having sex in a car (276). Splinters's blackmail (commissioned by Ricardo Heinrich) works its effect on Tucker: he is afraid and wants to drop the Petroussis case. However, it has the contrary effect on Persy, who is determined to find out who is behind it and will not be intimidated. She asks Tucker to hand the case over to her (278–279). When he refuses, Persy not only starts to suspect Tucker – a

---

8 For a similar argument by Jewkes and Morrell (2010), see my discussion of *Black Widow Society*.

man she has always adored as a straight cop – of being corruptible, but decides to continue the investigation on her own, unauthorised. With the support of her colleague Dizu and the psychologist Marge, she manages to link and solve the mysteries of the three missing women, but promptly faces Tucker's disapproval. He accuses Persy of insubordination on the Petroussis case (338) and asks Martinez to send her on indefinite leave (333) while the matter is under investigation. Although Persy retains the moral high ground and, in more ways than one, outgrows Tucker, she is compromised professionally. Her career now depends on whether or not Tucker takes the case against her further (340). All is not lost, but for the time being Persy is banished from the detective scene.

On race, too, Persy faces a series of predicaments. Like Sheemina February, as a Coloured person she occupies position that has been both empowered and marginalised in the historical South African racial hierarchy. As outlined previously, the position of Coloureds in between the powerful and the powerless has resulted in negative stereotyping of the community as untrustworthy by Black people and as manipulative by White. This is reflected in Rowe's novels when Persy's Black colleague Mhlabeni views her "as a betrayer, a snitch" (2013b, 25), as well as when the White Tucker calls his Coloured wife "a manipulative bitch" (2015, 163). Persy's own view as a Coloured person is that she is "torn between white and black interests," with nobody really representing Coloureds' interests (2013b, 134). Consider also her rage at being painted "as some kind of reactionary coconut enslaved to the witbaas" (2015, 150) by Heinrich. What Rowe does not unpack, however, are the links between Coloured subjectivity and shame. Persy recounts how much she envied her cousin's straight hair as a child. "It was shameful to have kroeshare,[9] proof of your African blood" (2015, 106). Contract killer Fred Splinters taps into this by making sure that Natasha, his partner and probably Persy's mother, has "her hair blow-dried dead straight" as well as highlighted, since he "hated that natural bushy look she'd had when he met her. Now she looked classy, to go along with her new life – no more hiked-up skirts and low-cut tops" (2015, 67). What is being reinscribed here is the association between so-called Coloured hair, shame and female sexuality. Erasmus calls this a mechanism for "creating a stigma of shame around those of 'mixed' descent" (2001, 18). Zoë Wicomb identifies the colonial roots of "coloured shame" as "shame for our origins of slavery, shame for the miscegenation, and shame, as colonial racism became institutionalized, for being black" (1998, 100). As she points out, Coloured people attempted to erase their "shameful" origins by assuming European names. As a consequence, they

---

9 "Kroeshare" is Afrikaans for curly hair.

"have lost all knowledge of [their] Xhosa, Indonesian, East African, or Khoi origins" (1998, 100). Constructing the colonial encounters that formed Coloured identities as unilaterally shameful was thus a complex mechanism of sociohistorical control.[10] Persy's quasi orphan status, the loss of her father, mother and brother and, eventually, also of Poppa (2015, 143), could be said to re-enact the loss of origins associated with Coloured subjectivity. Insofar as her curly hair as a child and the fact that she is having a sexual relationship with her White boss Tucker in the present evoke feelings of shame in Persy (2015, 34), these old colonial controlling mechanisms continue to operate. They are internalised by Persy and remain unchecked by the narrative arc of the novel.

In contrast, Rowe's portrait of Persy is highly successful in exposing the direct and lingering effects on her life, especially as a woman, of the apartheid policy of forced removals. Persy muses on how forced removals back then created "[d]ormitory towns filled with labour that travelled to the white areas to work, and then back to the hellholes at night. Not much had changed even though the act had been abolished more than twenty years ago" (2013b, 89). This lack of change is exemplified by her own long, laborious and dangerous journey to work and back every day. Being able to afford neither a car nor a flat of her own, in *What Hidden Lies* Persy depends on getting rides across the peninsula from colleagues and her violent cousin Donny, who is also her landlord. This exposes her to the latter's drug-induced violence and drunk driving – and on two occasions nearly gets her killed (43–44, 84, 201–204, 283–285). Here, Rowe must be given credit for showing an awareness of the ways in which a woman's racial and class background can leave her vulnerable to structural violence.

Persy's position as a Coloured woman in South Africa is already ambiguous, but as a Coloured female *police officer* she moves into another collision zone. In this role, she qualifies for the label of "ethnic" or "postcolonial detective". Using Homi Bhabha's notion of liminality, Ed Christian argues that "the postcolonial detective *is* this space, this area of overlap, this space of meeting. In the detective the colonizer and the colonized collide, the oppressor and the resistor struggle for space" (2001, 11, original emphasis). For Persy, this struggle for space has two aspects. First, as a woman, she faces opposition from the masculinist police force. Secondly, as a Coloured person, she occupies a position *in between* Black and White, and thus finds herself at odds with both the old White elite and the new Black one. As a postcolonial detective, Persy is also

---

10 Historically, "[c]oloured identities were formed in the colonial encounter between colonists (Dutch and British), slaves from South and East India and from East Africa, and conquered indigenous peoples, the Khoi and San" (Erasmus 2001, 21).

drawn into conflict with her own Coloured community. Applying Bhabha's concept of mimicry, Christine Matzke and Susanne Mühleisen view the postcolonial detective as "simultaneously a colonised subject and a postcolonial agent, a veritable 'contact zone'" (2006b, 11–12). Persy's conflicted status as a postcolonial detective, at once insider and outsider to the Coloured community, is exemplified by her relationship to Sean Dollery in *What Hidden Lies*. As her closest childhood friend, Sean not only shares Persy's racial background, but is privy to her childhood trauma – the fact that she was partly responsible for her brother's death in the kaolin mine. In *What Hidden Lies*, Persy expends a substantial amount of her detective energy hunting down Sean. Despite their common background, Persy managed to go to police college – thanks to Poppa's support – but Sean "succumbed to the thug life, like so many of their peers" (7). Persy's hatred of Sean transcends past loyalties, and she knows that their former intimacy will help her to get him behind bars (2013b, 6). Her feelings are reciprocated by Sean, who sees his own failure thrown into even sharper relief by Persy's relative success and resents the fact that she is frustrating his criminal activities. He calls her a "sell-out bitch [who] thought she was so high and mighty now that she was a detective, shaking the township dust off her feet, above him in some way" (10), and does everything he can to thwart her as a detective. He tries to ambush her (108–109) and sets fire to her caravan in an attempt to murder her (283–284). Persy narrowly escapes and immediately goes after Sean. She manages to shoot him, but he eludes her (286–287). Only by literally retracing their childhood steps up to the mine is she able to track him down. However, this means facing her long-suppressed trauma and guilt, which leaves her momentarily defenceless. Sean manages to overwhelm her and, at gunpoint, forces her to look out of the window of the house in which they hid from her brother twenty years previously. Once again, she witnesses her brother's death:

> The giant metal claw rears up with its burden of dripping black earth. Persy can't move, can't think. The claw tips over. The black earth rains down and Clyde is gone.
>
> Persy's knees buckled and gave way. She sagged heavily, and Sean's arm loosened on her neck. In that split second she brought his gun hand down on the jagged glass in the window with all her strength. He cried out. She heard the gun clatter to the floor. She pulled free.
>
> 2013b, 326

The moment she faces the tragedy, including her own perpetrating agency, she also regains her detective agency. She can overpower Sean and thus pull free not only from the past, but from her captor. However, she no longer manages to cut herself off from him emotionally, and the fact that she has finally arrested him does not leave her feeling triumphant. The search that she carries out on Sean is not the jubilant action of a winner, but a fraught tracing of his body, a poignant gesture towards the loving intimacy that might have developed between them had their paths not diverged:[11]

> "Turn around."
> He turned around with his back to her, arms spread on either side of the window for support, his legs splayed. Keeping him covered, she searched him: her left hand moving up his thighs, patting the pockets of his jeans, around his buttocks and up under his jacket, feeling the crisscross ridges of the childhood scars on his bare skin. Beneath her hand she felt his ribs heave, as the wrenching sobs came without a sound.
> 2013b, 326

From this point onwards, Persy is no longer able to view Sean as the abject criminal he has been for her so long. In front of the court building in which he is sentenced, she acknowledges their sameness: "She and Sean, the dispossessed. She had got away; he hadn't" (2013b, 346). She takes in the fact that, if she had not had Poppa to stand up for her, she could easily have ended up like Sean, even with Sean. When he is driven away to Pollsmoor Prison, for a last time "she recognised the boy she had known," resolves to visit him and lifts her hand in a final greeting (2013b, 346–347). This may seem sentimental, but as an authorial tactic the gesture is very deliberate: at the end of *What Hidden Lies*, the supposedly clear-cut divisions between detective, perpetrator and victim no longer hold. The ending of *Hour of Darkness* similarly dissolves the boundaries between Persy's roles as detective and as victim and exposes her indirect links to one of the perpetrators. Fred Splinters, the contract killer, finally manages to get the upper hand because his partner Natasha is probably Persy's long-vanished mother. This possibility gives Splinters a hold over Persy. On the pretext of enabling her to see her mother, he lures Persy into his trap. She escapes death only narrowly, and her mental breakdown as a result of her encounter with Natasha leaves her more victim than detective.

As an agent of the state, Persy has a substantial amount of legitimate agency as a detective, which allows her to solve her criminal cases and to unsettle gender norms. At the same time, as a Coloured, heterosexual woman, she sees her professional agency thwarted by the patriarchal frame to the point of

---

11 A romantic relationship between Sean and Persy was in the air for a while until Sean's dad was imprisoned and he moved away with his mother (2013b, 138–139).

indefinite suspension from the police service. Having emulated the ideal of the masculine detective script and having striven for nearly two full novels to become a detective modelled on the masculine code of practice, as embodied by men such as her Black colleague Dizu and her Coloured and White superiors Titus and Tucker, Persy has become disillusioned. Her gradual and painful disaffection with regard to her male detective hero Tucker is indicative of this. Initially, she considers Tucker to be "by far the best detective she'd ever worked with. Disciplined, effective, driven, disdainful of the higher-ups, and full of a righteous rage he channelled into hunting criminals and, more importantly, convicting them" (2015, 70). Yet more and more she comes to disapprove of his decidedly masculine ways. She is bored by his "habit of always trying to out-dick the other" and by his pit bull strategy when interrogating suspects (108, see also 109–110). The final straw for her is the moment she realises that he is intimidated by their criminal blackmailers, when his moral integrity is at stake: "She could hardly believe it was Ren Tucker speaking. One of the most fearless, determined detectives on the force. Someone she had looked up to, admired and emulated" (279). By the end, she understands that aspiring to be like "old-school career cops" and following in "their hardass footsteps" (338) is not for her. She wonders "why she'd ever imagined that she and Tucker were soulmates. She was nothing like him" (339). The script of masculine, especially White masculine, detection and law enforcement proves to be inadequate: she definitely is "not that kind of cop."

2.2   *Persy Jonas: Female Detective Agency Reshaped*

Where does this leave the female detective's resistant agency? Is she ultimately powerless, her position ineffective from a feminist political viewpoint? I suggest that we look for Persy's resistant agency in different, unexpected places. Bonnie Honig offers a radically new take on the figures of Antigone and Ismene in Sophocles' tragedy *Antigone*. Whereas for centuries Antigone's martyrdom has been assumed to be for her dead brother, Honig opens up the possibility that it may have been just as much for her living sister Ismene. She shows how both sisters are faced with forced or impossible choices, but refuse to yield to such limitations by creating new possibilities. Insofar as these new possibilities are acts of conspiracy beyond the radar of hegemonic patriarchy and acts of sororal loyalty and solidarity, Honig views them as political as well as ethical (2013, 151–189). The notion that it is possible to counter the framework of forced choices favoured by patriarchy with creativity, and thus acting ethically and politically, can also be applied to the forced choices, or dilemmas, that Persy faces. Via Alenka Zupančič's elaboration of the Lacanian "forced choice," Honig explains that the classic forced choice "Your money or your life" is an impossible choice, because "the two terms are asymmetrical." Life is more than an oppositional alternative – it is the essential condition of the choice (172). If we compare this to the forced choices of Persy, our detective heroine – "Your heterosexual, Coloured, female life or your detective agency" – we can see that they are equally asymmetrical, equally impossible. Honig maintains that "[i]t is essential to an ethics of forced choice that the tested subject does more than simply yield to the force of the choice" (173). What is more, the passive resistance or civil disobedience of simply refusing to choose is not enough, since it is still a submission to the force of the choice. What is needed – and here Honig agrees with Zupančič – is a move "into the position of creator" (274), which entails generating a third possibility. Honig takes Zupančič further by specifying that this new possibility in Sophocles' tragedy "refers to sororal solidarity" (173). This solidarity makes the act not only ethical but political. What is important for Honig is the creativity of the new possibility that allows the subject to resist the force of the choice, paired with the fact that this is done as a concerted action by partners (180). She calls this the "*twinned* negotiations of [two sisters'] forced choices" (182, my emphasis).

The cooperation (and non-cooperation) between Persy and Marge can be read as precisely such "twinned negotiations of their forced choices" (Honig 2013, 182). This reading allows us to grasp the nature of the women's resistant agency. Persy and Marge negotiate their situational constraints as female investigators in a concerted, twinned action that requires both women to extend themselves and to make sacrifices. Persy and the White, elderly Marge meet over the dead body of the White Andrew Sherwood, which Marge finds during her morning walk on the beach. She is not only a key witness, but also a retired, renowned criminal psychologist, an advisor to the TRC and a former investigative partner of Persy's current boss Paul Titus. Persy is the first detective called to the crime scene. The two women feel an instant dislike for each other. At first, Marge mistakes Persy for a mere "sidekick", "an undersized coloured youth with short dreads and glasses," and is "momentarily taken aback by the effrontery of the boy, whose voice, by the sound of it, had not even broken" (Rowe 2013b, 26). Marge is soon made to realise that Detective Jonas is a woman, that she is in charge (or puts herself in charge) and that she does not welcome Marge's help. When Marge says that this looks like murder to her, Persy retorts, " 'It's our job to decide that, ma'am' " (27), and asks a protesting Marge to move away from the crime scene. Marge deems Persy a patronising, "[o]fficious little cow!" (27). Persy, on the other hand, finds Marge's arrogance "breathtaking" (66) and experiences an allergic reaction to her cigarette smoke and the cat hair in Marge's home when she is subsequently sent to interview her (65).

Despite their mutual aversion, Marge and Persy share a strong compulsion to work the Sherwood murder case. This is motivated partly by professional ambition: Persy needs a first murder case to further her career, whereas Marge needs new professional challenges now that both of her sons have left home. In addition to this, however, both women are drawn to the case by a semi-conscious force that neither of them is quite able to articulate. Both women also encounter obstacles. To Persy's dismay, the case is initially assigned to her corrupt colleague Mhlabeni, with little chance of justice being done (59). Marge is an outsider to begin with, is retired and is forbidden to disclose confidential information about the patients whom she treats as a psychotherapist. And yet, thanks to coordinated action in Honig's sense, the two women manage to obtain and exert intersecting forms of agentive detective power in the Sherwood case. Marge gets the wheel turning when she realises that she needs a "proxy" in the police service in order to bring her wealth of background knowledge to the case. The only suitable proxy is Persy, so Marge asks Persy's superior to let her assist the detective (125–126). Knowing how much Persy wants the case, he offers to put her in charge on condition that she work alongside Marge. Persy grudgingly agrees to this "poisoned chalice" (147). In this way, both women achieve together what neither could achieve on her own. Still, the mutual resentment does not simply abate (152). The reader sees Marge's professional experience, arrogance and sense of racial entitlement pitted against Persy's competence, obstructionism and irritation at "being treated like a *meid* at the white madam's beck and call" (165). Their mutual distrust is heightened by the fact that each woman (rightly) suspects the other of having some hidden agenda, of hiding something. Only when Persy rescues Marge's beloved stolen dog Bongo from an illegal dog-fighting den does the tension between the two women begin to ease (187). A slightly humiliated Marge is aware that Bongo survived only thanks to Persy and shows gratitude: "There was an awkward silence. A shift had happened and neither knew what position to adopt" (208). This enables Persy to let Marge in on the fact that she was evicted from her home by her violent cousin. In return, Marge tells Persy about a friend who is looking for someone to caravan-sit. At first, Persy displays her "in-built aversion to any favours, especially one that came from Marge" (208), but eventually she gives in with relief at "having the older woman take charge" (209).

The picture that is being drawn here is one of a subtle, gradual alignment, through give and take. Each woman's moves are portrayed as mutually dependent on those of her colleague, the step of one triggering the step of the other. Their common point of reference in creating what Honig calls a new or third possibility is a desire for empowerment through detective work and an interest in solving the murder case. A further valuable benefit, as yet still undeveloped, will be the mutual support structure that reaches beyond detecting. At this point, however, not only is their solidarity reluctant, but they both have to concede the need to substantially extend themselves beyond their own received categories and experiences. What is required of them is to face and acknowledge past wrongdoings and guilt; we might as well call it a personal TRC move. Marge is plagued by guilt for mishandling Theo Kruger, the suspect in the Clyde Cupido case twenty years earlier, and thus driving him to suicide. She also finds it hard to accept that Clyde has never been found (236). Under increasing pressure from these "[r]eal-life ghosts crowding her, crying out for justice" (236), she comes to admit that she has a personal stake in the case and that "if she could find out what happened to Andrew Sherwood, she might feel in some way absolved" (236) – particularly as she senses a connection between the two cases (263–264). Again, Marge realises how dependent on Persy she is. "What would it take for them to overcome their mutual antipathy and neurotic projections? And if they weren't able to, how would they ever untangle the 'truth' of the Sherwood case, and bring the killer to justice?" she ponders (265).

For a positive change in their relationship to happen, however, Marge's past connection with Persy needs to be brought to light. This connection, of which neither of the women is conscious, reaches back far into the past. Twenty years ago, Marge, then a young criminal psychologist, and Persy's current boss Titus worked the investigation into the sudden disappearance of Persy's brother Clyde (28–29). When the two women interview Ivor Reitz, Marge's close friend and Andrew's landlord, Persy finds out that he is the White man who "bought" the land on which Persy's Poppa's smallholding was located (306–307). This convoluted happenstance both brings the connection between Persy and Marge to light and reveals that Ivor is partly responsible for the injustice done to Poppa, who was moved to a township and lost his source of income. Both women feel the effects of apartheid looming large over their relationship – "the racial divide yawned between them" (307). Marge begins to see Ivor – this admired friend, a man to whom she had also been attracted – in a more dubious light; In new-found humility, she eventually renounces her loyalty to him and sacrifices their friendship (343–344). In the plot development, it is now Persy's turn to admit her guilty role in her brother's disappearance, and thus facilitate the next turn of the screw that is her connection with Marge. Persy needs to sacrifice her innocence, too. After their visit to Ivor, she can no longer keep the floodgates to her long-suppressed trauma closed. She is finally able to articulate her own hidden agenda in the case. Realising that "[c]hasing down Sherwood's killer was like chasing down some lost part of herself, going deeper into that darkness" (313), she suddenly knows what she has to do: namely, to find her childhood friend and nemesis Sean up at the mountain, by the kaolin mine at Bellevue, in the house they were hiding in all those years back when they watched her brother being buried alive (315). Reliving that fateful moment, Persy sacrifices the blameless innocence she has long tried to preserve; to some extent, she sacrifices Sean, too, handing him over to the police. What she gains is a deep bond with Marge. She asks Marge to listen to her traumatic experience, certain now that "Marge would bear witness to her story without judgement or comment" (328). Marge agrees, and "Persy began slowly, haltingly, to speak, not sure if what she said made sense, or where the words were coming from, only knowing that she had to let them out before she shattered into a million pieces" (328). In this voicing, filling what had previously been the gap of silence and ignorance, the narrative ties the factual workings of empirical detection to the affective emotional-psychological knowledge of coming-to-consciousness. For with Persy's account, Marge's own guilt becomes a fact. Theo Kruger, whom she suspected of being responsible for Clyde's disappearance, was innocent; she was indeed to blame for driving him to suicide. So the previously undisclosed secret personal agendas that have stood between Marge and Persy manifest as the bonds that have always tied them together, a deep entanglement through tragedy. Persy was right when she felt that she and Marge "were talking code. On the surface it appeared to be about Sherwood, but underneath it was about something else" (170–171).

Clearly, Persy and Marge make ethical choices. That they are political, too, as Honig claims they must be, becomes evident in the ways in which they defy the systemic obstacles to their detective agency. They negotiate the constrained choices of a racialised patriarchy and at the same time manage to engineer their own process of "truth and reconciliation" – beyond the immediate ambit of paternal law. This is clarified for us via Honig's contention that viewing heroic autonomy as the only form of political agency is limited, for it blinds us to "sororal and other solidaristic forms of agency and their powers" (2013, 155). Thus, while Persy's endeavour to claim the male space of the detective and his autonomous, heroic agency fails, her uneasy, troubled collaboration with Marge Rowe opens up another space for political agency: one that is resistant, but not simplistically so.

In a post-apartheid South African setting, the intricate entanglement of Persy's history with that of Marge in Rowe's novels can be read as a stand-in for interracial relationships on a national scale and as a model for future cohabitation and collaboration. And yet, from a racially critical viewpoint, reservations remain. Consider, for example, Marge's tendency to view Persy as a child. From one perspective, this is not problematic, as it can be attributed to their difference in age. However, given the racial hierarchies that inflect Marge's view, it can smack of the patronising, especially since the more their relationship develops, the more Marge sees the needy, vulnerable child in Persy (Rowe 2013b, 295, 301, 328). This persistent inequality in their relationship is at odds with the equality of their working relationship. As McClintock observes, infantilising the racially other long served as an alibi for imperial intervention (1995, 45). If the colony is fashioned "as a 'family of black children ruled over by a white father'" (1993, 64), the colonised is the immature child in need of paternal control. Subjugation is thus both naturalised and legitimised. When the White Marge views the Coloured Persy as a child, she is reactivating and reinforcing this controlling mechanism, a vestigial trace of power hierarchies that operated between coloniser and colonised. On the other hand, in the novel childhood is presented as a psychological protective mechanism, a form of "magical thinking" used in order to handle difficult situations, as Marge explains to Titus (Rowe 2013b, 329). Childhood is also a mitigating factor in judging Persy's culpability in her brother's death and in the fatal silence that characterises her afterwards. This makes the guilt that Marge, the adult, must shoulder all the more pronounced as she herself acknowledges: "Persy was a child. She wasn't responsible for what happened. I *knew* what I was doing" (329). Marge holds herself accountable, whereas she absolves Persy of guilt. Moreover, she fashions Persy not merely as a child, but increasingly as her daughter. Persy's rescue of her dog reminds Marge of the daughterly support that she has been denied because her own daughter was stillborn (209). The extent to which she allows Persy the position of a daughter and feels both protective and proud of her becomes evident when she asks herself whether her own daughter, who would now be exactly Persy's age, would be as "[b]rave, self-sufficient, vulnerable" (295) as Persy is.

Conversely, in *Hour of Darkness*, which depicts Persy grappling with the loss of her mother, Persy shows an increasing tendency to give Marge the maternal position. Thoughts of her mother often surface alongside thoughts of Marge, whom Persy describes as the person who was there when her whole world collapsed in the course of the Sherwood case. Persy longs to see and speak to Marge as a mother, yet is sometimes reluctant to do so because of their racial difference (2015, 39, 196). It is Marge she confides in about her disastrous affair with Tucker (273), as well as Fred Splinters's attack and her mother's possible involvement, which left her so distressed (334). It is also Marge who looks after and comforts Persy after this incident, making it possible, finally for Persy to ask Marge about her mother, whom Marge met during the Clyde Cupido case. In a very motherly way, Marge protects Persy from the brutal truth that her mother displayed complete indifference towards her then seven-year-old daughter, telling Persy instead about their physical likeness, her hair and her eyes (334–335). At the end of the novel, Persy does not know for sure whether

Splinters's partner is indeed her mother or whether she will ever see her again. Meeting the now motherless boys of Annette Petroussis for the last time, "Persy recognised her own lonely childhood. No one could take the place of a mother. Especially a good one. For some reason, Marge Labuschagne sprang into her mind" (342). With Marge allowing Persy to take her daughter's place and Persy allowing Marge to take her mother's, the bond between them becomes mutual and empowering on an emotional level, too. With Persy as an adult daughter and Marge as an aging mother, this is a move towards equality and solidarity where mutual need weighs up mutual benefit. It could pave the way for further, much needed female professional agency and collaboration in the third novel. Persy's move beyond the patriarchal frame of the police may give her and Marge the opportunity, when solving their next case, to continue exploring what Honig terms "a female agency that is agonistically and solidaristically sororal and not merely subject to male exchange" (2013, 170). By pairing Persy with Marge as an investigative partner and proxy mother, Rowe achieves a kind of genre bending. She modifies the conception of the detective figure as an autonomously heroic one – a conception not limited to the stereotypical male lone wolf, but found in female detectives, too. As Frizzoni notes, while many female investigators since the 1990s operate in a social and professional network, they still adhere to an ideal of autonomous agency (2009, 104–105). By creating a mutually dependent investigative pair with effective solidaristic agency, Rowe changes the generic blueprint. Honig herself cautions that, in making sororal agency visible, she does not seek to normatively "promote sorority as a privileged site of agency" (2013, 183). What she foregrounds is "the politics of agonism, in which not only struggle and rivalry but also mutual respect and equality – even care – are characteristic elements" (183). This is exemplified in the contentious yet caring and empowering relationship between Persy and Marge.

2.3 Truth-Finding: Persy Jonas's Detective Gaze and the Criminal Cases under Its Scrutiny

A detective's truth-finding cannot be separated from the kind of gaze that he or she adopts. In her analysis of African American female detectives at the turn of the 1990s, Munt perceives a movement from "Black Woman as a sight, towards a new generation of investigatory visions, controlled by the shifting gaze of Black women themselves" (117–118). This insight can be applied to Persy. According to Ebert, the detective gaze is by default a Foucauldian panoptic instrument, "a means of power constituting reality and constraining subjectivities" in the service of the dominant patriarchal order (1992, 18). However, even though Persy is a detective and thus empowered, I would argue that her gaze differs fundamentally from the obliterating, sexualised and hence violent gaze on the female body discussed by Bronfen and Pollock, which aims to deflect from the threats posed by femininity, death and trauma.

Persy's first dead body is that of a White man, Andrew Sherwood. Her gaze on him bears no traces of patriarchal control, makes no attempt to classify, judge or fix him in place (Ebert 1992, 19). Persy's direct view of the dead body remains undisclosed to the reader, but we get her memories of it when he is being carried away in a body bag by the morgue attendants: "She kept seeing the corpse's pallid face in close-up." As she remembers the details of Sherwood's face, her own emotional response to and rapport with the victim are foregrounded. She records "her anger, and deep sense of grievance at the indignity of his death. What malice or passion or fear would cause someone to do this to another human being?" (Rowe 2013b, 37). Her gaze is anything but the objectifying, detached gaze of the detective. "Having never heard the timbre of his voice, his laugh, or seen him walk or eat or smile, she should be unmoved by his death" (37), Percy thinks to herself, but clearly she is not: she is shaken. Later, when she goes through the autopsy report and the photographs, her gaze is more objectifying and voyeuristic. She calls the photographs the "pornography of violent death" (147), but notices that she herself is partly depicted there, too. She also qualifies the pathologist's scientific, violent gaze by pointing to what he has in common with Andrew: drug abuse (151). In this way, she prevents easy distancing between male onlooker and male victim.

Persy's second case involves the dead body of a White woman, Annette. It is with great reluctance that she brings herself to look at Annette, "redirect[ing] her gaze" and "finding it hard to focus on the job" while the pathologist examines the body and Tucker searches the ground (Rowe 2015, 173). Having hoped against all the odds to find Annette alive, Persy again offers an emotional response to the discovery of Annette's body. Her gaze is empathic, intimate, even domesticated, despite the prosaic necessities demanded by her professional role at the crime scene: "Persy pulled on some gloves and forced herself to kneel beside the dead woman. Thank God Kai and Alexi would never see their mother like this. The image of the smiling woman in the photograph on their refrigerator door would be what they would remember" (173–174). Only now does Persy do what is required of her. She takes detailed notes on Annette's clothes and the drag marks on her skin, while picturing her last moments and thoughts. This leaves her shaky and aching: "[s]he had to put Kai and Alexi out of her mind or she would be no use to this investigation" [174]. Again, Persy is aware of the difference between an objectifying and a compassionate gaze. The latter is more difficult to handle emotionally, but it allows her to be touched, to see the victim's trauma and the traumatic ramifications of her death for her young family. Persy's empathic gaze prevents her from sacrificing the victim and deflecting from her trauma, from exerting power. Through Persy, Rowe successfully shifts the site of interrogation away from the dominant White phallic position to the female detective of colour, who is able to see *women*, not *woman*. It is this empathic gaze, coupled with her different subject position, that also allows her to bring specific crimes to light.

The crime that sends Persy on her first truth-finding mission is the murder of Andrew in *What Hidden Lies*. Quite unexpectedly, his murderer turns out to be his ex-partner, a White woman called Colette McKillian. The parameters of this crime remain firmly grounded in the individual characters and their relationships. Colette kills Andrew in what she believes is self-defence during an argument fuelled by a fatal mix of alcohol, medication, Colette's long-standing suspicion that Andrew has sexually molested her son Jasper and Andrew's equally long-standing view that Colette is an unfit parent due to her mental illness (340). In a way, they are both victims of Jasper's real abuser, Gregory Crane, who also is White, and who spreads rumours about Andrew and manipulates Colette in order to deflect attention from himself. The novel does not explore possible structural reasons behind child abuse – it is only hinted at that Crane grew up in a care home and was himself a victim of sexual molestation (290) – mental illness or single parenthood. However, the Sherwood case leads Persy and Marge to the "truth" about the cold Clyde Cupido case and their reciprocal personal involvement. Their individual journeys of trauma and recovery have significant ethical and political reverberations, as I have already discussed, but the apartheid structures that rendered Persy vulnerable as a child in the first place, that failed to protect her, are not investigated further. This is despite the fact that we learn that it was more than curiosity that regularly drove Persy and her friend Sean out of their homes to the forest near the kaolin mines. The forest was a place of refuge, sheltering Sean from his father's violence and Persy from her mother's indifference (2013b, 29, 264, 277, 297, 2015, 334). However, the interplay between the constraints of the apartheid system, and the debilitating family structures that it produced, and Persy's mother's choice to be a single parent and to seek solace in alcohol is not part of the novel's truth-finding process. Here Rowe's narrative repeats the TRC's shortcomings by depicting trauma as event based and by failing to shed light on the interaction between the system and individual actors. For Posel, this complex and elusive dynamic must be considered if truth-finding processes are to be meaningful, but the TRC did not sufficiently establish the links between individual agency and broader structures (2002, 168), preferring to highlight epiphanic or cathartic moments of individuated, often spectacular, confession, confrontation and appeal.

In Rowe's other novel, by contrast, Persy's investigation into the murder of Annette Petroussis brings to light a more complex "truth" that links systemic crimes with individuals' lives. Like Andrew's, Annette's murderer is a woman. The seventeen-year-old Xhosa teenager Mandisa Dasheka kills the affluent White Annette in a robbery gone wrong and rescues Annette's baby (287–289, 291–293). It is made clear that the criminal here is not Mandisa alone. Equal blame is put on criminal socioeconomic and political systems such as Mandisa's precarious living conditions, an apartheid legacy that makes her vulnerable to post-apartheid criminal Ricardo Heinrich in a gender-specific way. Mandisa's mother has worked as a domestic servant for the wealthy, White Hamilton-Langford household for a long time, a fact that leaves Mandisa humiliated, jealous and full of hatred. Not only does she detest that "[e]verything [her] family owned was 'rubbish' the Hamiltons had thrown out" – "the hand-me-down clothing" particularly disgusts and humiliates her (232) – but she feels deprived of a mother, fearing that the Hamiltons mean more to her mother than her own family: "She especially hated Severine. [...] It was as if her mother had a white daughter in the suburbs, a white daughter whom she looked after and took care of in a way she never had for Mandisa" (232). Her mother's work-related absence also means that the housework and care of her siblings are left to Mandisa: "Sometimes she felt like the family slave" (232). It is easy to see how this drives her into the arms of a boyfriend. Axolile Sama lures her with his attention and material possessions: his car and expensive gifts. Thus, when he asks her for her mother's keys to the Hamilton-Langfords' house, suggesting that she accompany him on a robbery "to teach [grandfather Langford] a lesson" (287) – a robbery commissioned by Heinrich – she readily consents, unable to imagine the consequences. The consequences of Mandisa's actions are fatal for Annette, whose house they mistakenly break into, for Axolile, who is killed by the kingpin, and for the future of Mandisa and her family.

This layered attribution of the "truth" behind Annette's murder deftly eschews more typical crime patterns of spectacular revelation and is successful in several respects. First, through Mandisa we are given the perspective of the young, Black, normally invisible daughter who has to share her mother with a White family. Although this situation is extremely common in South Africa, the divided attention of mothers of colour is hardly seen as an issue; it is still more unusual for the perspective of their own daughters to be highlighted. Turning unthinkingly to a clichéd trope of South African life, Severine naturally introduces her family's domestic servant as "my second mom" (282). She does so in Mandisa's presence, blithely unaware of the implications for Mandisa. Severine's friend Jos does notice and observes, "Severine hadn't seen, but if looks could kill, the glare Mandisa gave her would have" (282). What is more, it is not only employment as such that keeps Mandisa's mother away from her own daughter. The fact that her journey to work takes several hours – another direct effect of the segregated geography imposed by apartheid – aggravates the situation (98). Here, Rowe interrogates dominant perceptions of interracial relations and draws attention to blind spots. Such complex truths have the potential to create the basis for a new kind of understanding. Her truth-finding process moves beyond the "who done it" and sheds light on the reasons behind the crime. She does so in a way that Posel deems crucial in processes of truth-finding: she tries to understand "*why* individuals act the way they do by inserting their actions into a broader causal context" (2002, 159). Mandisa is undoubtedly rendered as an agent, too. While she is constrained by larger structures, she also takes decisions that shape and even extinguish others' lives. Individual guilt is not glossed over. Reflecting on the fateful night, she keeps asking herself "why she hadn't told the white woman to drive away while [her gangster-boyfriend] Axe was in the tavern" (291). Posel and Simpson emphasise the importance in the truth-telling process of moving beyond "simple moral binaries of 'victim' and 'perpetrator' associated with unambiguous judgements of right and wrong" (2002, 10). Mandisa exemplifies this complexity.

Secondly, the novel draws attention to how race interacts with other categories such as gender and class. Mandisa's brother suffers less, for example, because as a boy he is not expected to do housework (Rowe 2015, 232). For the individual criminal masterminds, money has superseded race as a motive, as Persy points out (88). Democratically elected politicians of colour such as Heinrich use their political and material power to collaborate with privileged Whites such as Gray Langford and become complicit in the exploitation of those marginalised by gender and skin colour. And even though their criminal machinations are exposed, they experience no repercussions. A political system that is characterised by widespread corruption exonerates individuals, especially if they hold positions of social influence.

Thirdly, both the Sherwood and the Petroussis murder cases expose the issue of land ownership in South Africa and the ways in which past structural inequalities in ownership based on race both persist and have become more complex in the post-apartheid present.[12] Both novels highlight land issues in their historical dimensions. In *What Hidden Lies*, this happens through Persy's family history. Up until the late 1980s, Persy's grandfather had a lease on a smallholding on the

---

12   In *What Hidden Lies*, land issues indirectly facilitate the novel's murder case. Sherwood is an obstacle to Crane's plans to develop Bellevue, so Crane spreads rumours about him that feed Colette's suspicions and thus indirectly contribute to his murder. In *Hour of Darkness*, Annette's murder is a direct result of land issues.

coast in Noordhoek. When the White owner of the big house nearby wanted more land, he pressed Poppa for the title deeds. Poppa could not produce them and was forced to sell his smallholding for a pittance. There was nothing that Poppa could do since, according to the Group Areas Act, "coloureds were not meant to be living in this area anyway. It had been zoned for whites long ago" (313). With the law against them, Persy's family was moved inland to the township of Ocean View, which was designated for Coloureds (11, 89, 306–307). The history of Poppa's smallholding in Noordhoek mirrors that of the Coloured flower farmer Moses Petersen and his Summerley farm in affluent Constantia, which features in *Hour of Darkness*. These are "[p]atterns repeating in Cape Town's history" (2015, 79), as Persy points out. We hear that Constantia was first claimed by the governor of the Dutch East India Company, Simon van der Stel, in the 17th century as part of his Groot Constantia farm. He brought "slaves from Java, Madagascar, Mauritius, Zanzibar" (201) with him. When they were eventually freed, they were sometimes given subdivisions of the farm as owners or tenants. However, when the area was declared "Whites only" by apartheid law in the mid-20th century, White people bought the land cheaply from the Coloured community, which was evicted to the townships on the Cape Flats (133–134, 201–202). Through Persy's murder investigation, *Hour of Darkness*, which in parts reads like a history book, remembers and attests to the historical intricacies of land use, ownership and tenancy. Land restitution is a sore point for South Africa's historically dispossessed, as Persy tries to make clear to Tucker when they argue:

> "And where will it all end? Must we sommer now give the land back to the bloody Bushmen, or Hottentots or whoever?" Tucker was off, riding a favourite hobby horse. "The blacks would have to fuck off back north and the whiteys can trek back to Europe and we can all go back to the fucking Stone Age."
>
> "En die bruinmense? Where are we supposed to go?" [Persy] asked with a bite in her voice. He shook his head. "Now you are insulting my intelligence."
>
> "Don't we have legitimate claim to the land you stole from our forefathers?"
>
> 188

Tucker's insults and Persy's insistence on the complicated position of the "bruinmense" (the "brown" i.e. Coloured people) are illustrative of the various conflicting discourses that arise from the many ethnic groups that have laid claim to the land over time. This complicates any "simple" notions of "racism" as an explanation (Posel 2002, 168). Both novels also depict how, in contemporary South Africa, land issues have begun to cut not just along but across racial lines, through expedient alliances between wealthy White property owners and corrupt politicians of colour. Analysing aspects of South Africa's present economic situation and its underpinnings of race, class and gender, Achille Mbembe notes that the end of apartheid has accelerated the country's transition from a "society of control to a society of consumption," thereby aggravating old structural contradictions tied to property ownership. "At least since the wars of dispossession of the 19th century, citizenship and rights of personhood have been constructed in relation to a particular regime of ownership. Whites owned property and blacks sold their labour at a cheap price on a captive market" (2014, par. 9). In the present, Mbembe claims, "processes of accumulation are happening, once again, through dispossession – except that this time round dispossession is conducted by an increasingly predatory black ruling class in alliance with private capital[13] and in the name of custom and tradition" (par. 13), the latter being fashioned in explicitly patriarchal terms (par. 26). While neither novel explores the gender dimensions of land issues, both of them expose the crimes of this new alliance and show who suffers as a result: namely, the expropriated owners, the landless and the natural world of plants and animals. Marge is quick to identify the mechanisms of "self-enrichment posing as social conscience" in both politicians and property owners (Rowe 2013b, 77). Commenting on the impending Bellevue property deal, she foresees that "'[g]overnment cronies will get their kickbacks while passing it off as a local-housing initiative; the developers will make a killing, and the rich buyers will feel safe in their electrified shoeboxes. It's a win-win situation'" (77). In *Hour of Darkness*, Persy's investigation reveals the same dynamic at work. The Coloured politician Heinrich pretends to represent the interests of the original inhabitants of Constantia, when in fact he is instrumentalising them in order to fill his own pockets (2015, 148–150, 131). Here again, the interaction between the system and its actors is revealed. However, despite exposure, many of these systems stay in place and many criminal individuals go free, rendering justice incomplete.

2.4 *Criminal Justice and Alternatives*

In the last section of this chapter, I will discuss Rowe's novels as reflections on state-administered, formal criminal justice, examining the ways in which the female detective and her investigations not only serve the criminal justice system, but resonate with the more inclusive, restorative notions of justice put forward by feminist legal scholars. Persy has her doubts as to the kind of justice

---

13 According to Mbembe, "[t]o a large extent, South African capitalism still depends on the institution of migrant labour, a highly unequal and racialised partition of land and a thoroughly extractive economy" (2014, par. 18).

that is achieved by her arrests of Sean and Mandisa. Even though she is instrumental in arresting Sean at the end of the first novel, increasingly she comes to regard his imprisonment as an inadequate solution. If anything, she feels that his time in prison is likely to criminalise him further (Rowe 2013b, 347). Mandisa's arrest leaves Persy even more frustrated. She feels deflated when Annette's killer turns out to be Mandisa, who got caught up in murder almost inadvertently. "'I so wanted to find Annette's killer. Now I just feel sick,'" she remarks (2015, 297). In the end, the kingpins behind Mandisa's crime, the likes of Langford and Heinrich, walk free.

Persy's physical discomfort at discovering Mandisa's guilt against the background of larger injustices is symptomatic of a tension typically experienced by female detectives in feminist detective novels. According to Walton and Jones, the individual crime is solved and individual criminals have been identified, but the criminal systems persist (1999, 208–213). They observe:

> at the same time as the narrative forecloses on the enigmatic aspect of individual crimes in a traditional way, it is also structured according to the disclosure of less easily resolved endemic injustices and oppressions, making possible a level of social or psychological inconclusiveness and thus critique.
> 211

It is in displaying a "consciousness about such conflicts" that the crime narrative's political thrust lies, in the "unsettling disruption of established norms" (212). With Persy, Rowe goes a step further. As Persy comes to recognise the inherent violence in the work of the police ("Could a detective be an instrument of peace? Cops were required to maintain some kind of harmony in society. With brute force if necessary" (Rowe 2015, 267))[14] and has to acknowledge that she is "not that kind of cop," her reservations increasingly point to the concept and system of justice itself. The discrepancy between the crimes exposed by Persy and what happens in practice in the criminal justice system, where the true culprits are not held accountable, renders the system and its ineffectual legal foundation criminal. Feminist legal scholars and feminist criminologists have long challenged the seeming neutrality of the law and the criminal justice process. They have established that "law in western societies reflects the subjectivity of the dominant, white, affluent, adult male" (Hudson

---

14 See also Walter Benjamin, who in his "Critique of Violence" elucidates the violence inherent in the law and in the institution of the police. He sees the role of the police as ignominious, since "in this authority the separation of lawmaking and law-preserving violence is suspended" (62).

2012, 385). This liberal notion of subjectivity as governed by reason privileges behaviour denoted as male (Büchler and Cottier 2012, 252–253). Karin van Marle and Elsje Bonthuys criticise the fact that "[p]atriarchal interpretations of justice and equality exclude qualities like emotion, relationships and care, which characterise the lives of women, while valorising abstraction and independence, which are associated with male behaviour in the public sphere" (2007, 21). As a result, social situatedness and social relations are removed from legal perception (Büchler and Cottier 2012, 254), and the law's ability to perceive and respond to the problems of those who fall outside its narrow frame, such as women, is impaired (Van Marle and Bonthuys 2007, 29). Thus, the law both protects and produces White, hegemonic, male subjectivity and behaviour: "The law not only accepts male life experiences as the basis for the formulation of universally applicable rules, but the very structure of legal reasoning replicates the ways in which men of particular racial, class and social status are socialised to think and behave" (45).

In order to "move beyond the closures and exclusions of *white man's justice*" (2012, 384, original emphasis), Barbara Hudson suggests an alternative, more inclusive notion of justice that is based on the three principles of discursiveness, relationalism and reflectiveness (2012, 388). Her principles are closely related to, though not identical with, what is termed "restorative justice" in legal discourse, the tenets of which underlie the "transitional justice" that the TRC was seeking to achieve. "Restorative justice" denotes a form of justice that is victim based and espouses values such as "truth, accountability, reparation, reconciliation, conflict resolution and democratic participation" (Doak and O'Mahony 2012, 305). Facilitating meaningful dialogue and "restoring relationships to community as well as between victim and offender" are central to restorative justice (Hudson 2012, 394). Restorative justice is generally perceived as opposed to conventional criminal justice, the kind of formal justice dispensed by the state, which focuses on the perpetrator by ascertaining his/her guilt and delivering punishment. The three principles of discursiveness, relationalism and reflectiveness suggested by Hudson are realised to a higher degree in restorative justice than in established criminal justice. At the same time, Hudson criticises restorative justice for its tendency to revert to "the closures of male, white justice" (395) when confronted by practical and ethical dilemmas. It is these closures that her three principles seek to transcend. First, they give "free rein" (395) to a proposition of *discursiveness*, which demands that everyone has equally privileged access to discourse (389). Those "outside the discursive circle of justice must be brought inside" and "the outsider must be able to put her claims in her own terms, not have to accommodate to the dominant modes of legal/political discourse" (389). This includes ensuring that there is space for any topic; in particular, "behaviour in the private sphere must not be off-limits" (390). By investigating crimes from the perspective of a young woman of colour, Rowe allows such outside positions to become heard and visible, as I have already shown. Private issues such as the pain and jealousy of a Black teenage daughter who must share her domestic worker mother with a White girl who by implication styles herself a "sister" can be disclosed. Secondly, Hudson argues that inclusive notions of justice must adhere to the principle of *relationality*. Relationality, as she understands it, "recognizes individuals as embodied in a network of relationships, which include relationships with community and with the state" (392). Crucially, Hudson views not only identities and rights but responsibility and culpability as relational (392). Rowe takes the principle of relationality in account both by valuing the collaborative cooperation of Persy and Marge over male, liberal conceptions of individual, heroic agency and by highlighting the role of systemic violence and the way in which it interrelates with individual culpability. Finally, *reflective* justice requires reconceptualisation of the very (male, White, bourgeois etc.) legal categories that delimit what is relevant or irrelevant in legal judgement, what is admissible and what is not (393). Reflective justice works against a "restricted range of legal categories of crimes, aggravations and mitigations which [...] abstract individuals from wider inequalities and oppressions" (394). Instead, it aims at "situating particular circumstances in their wider social context" (394). This principle is clearly operative in Rowe's fiction. Whenever Persy draws attention to the frame of structural inequality, by implication she prises open the constricting determinism that underpins the received legal categories of crimes. Moreover, Rowe calls into question the "abstract generality of the law" (Hudson 2012, 393) – and the rationality that underlies traditional detection, too – by including and valuing supernatural powers in her crime novels. In *What Hidden Lies*, justice is dealt out to one of the culprits (Gregory Crane) by supernatural circumstances outside the criminal justice system. They lead him to what the latter would frame as a suicide (318). In the second novel, Severine's visitations by the Virgin Mary help to save her and many others when she gets caught up in a pharmacy robbery (312). Even though later her "religious hallucinations" are scientifically explained by her mother as the effects of a benign brain tumour, a mere "brain malfunction due to neurobiological reasons" (336), Marge feels "a whisper of a doubt" stir in her and considers the possibility that there may have been more to Severine's visions (336). The novels hint at such alternative realms of power on those occasions when Persy's life is saved by animals – for example, when a cat alerts her to the existence of a cat flap and thus provides her with an escape route from the burning caravan (2013b, 284), or when she escapes Splinters' attack thanks to the sudden materialisation of

Houdini the hippo, which causes her attacker to flee (2015, 330). In such instances, the achievement of justice cannot be objectively measured. The episodes have a quirky, playful and serendipitous quality, which, while provoking scepticism in some readers, can be read as a deliberate attempt by the author to trouble the foundations of more rationalist legal solutions that all too often fail to effect change, to extend empathy or to credit underlying causes. While these episodes do not destroy the novels' rational underpinnings – Rowe does not, after all, write magical realism – they hint at the limitations of justice as conventionally conceived, teasing open the realm of imaginative possibility so that other, as-yet-unforeseen and perhaps more culturally inclusive forms of justice can be considered.

In the first two novels of the Persy Jonas trilogy, Rowe successfully unsettles both crime genre conventions and the gendered and raced social and legal norms that form the basis for the South African post-transitional real. Her in many ways unconventional detective heroine Persy has her detective agency triply compromised on the grounds of her gender, sexuality and race, yet she counters the constrained choices into which the various constricting frames would coerce her. Rather than bartering her female, heterosexual subjectivity of colour for her agency as a detective, Rowe creates a third space of agentive intervention for her heroine through concerted, if agonistic, collaboration with Marge. Together, they trouble the patriarchal criminal justice system and resist its exclusionary mechanisms at the same time as they are compromised by it. While the occasional sexist or racist controlling mechanism is at work in Rowe's representation of her detective protagonist, Persy nevertheless constitutes an exploratory revisioning of the gendered and raced script of autonomous, heroic detective agency. Persy's multifaceted outsider-within position allows her to ascertain complex truths about land rights and White employment of female domestic servants of colour in South Africa that not only move far beyond a simple "who done it", but highlight the ways in which power, responsibility and culpability oscillate between systems (patriarchy, colonialism, apartheid, capitalism) and individuals. She thereby continues to establish the kinds of truths that the TRC was mandated to uncover. Recognising the relationality between systems and individuals is in itself a means of serving justice so as to counter the bias inherent in the formal criminal justice system. Allowing access to non-dominant positions and voices that speak in non-dominant ways about otherwise hidden (e.g. domestic) issues, thereby bringing them into the realm of the political, further works towards establishing more inclusive notions of justice, while resisting and negotiating the formal justice system's deceptively liberal constructions of race and gender.

3 Not What South Africans Expect: Hawa Jande Golakai's Investigator Vee Johnson

> "You're not what I expected." […]. "How come your name's Johnson?" […].
> "In a nutshell, I'm related to the president of my country. We're all royalty, so we get to rule." […]. "Oh, you're messing with me. 'Course you're not related to a *president*" […]. "That's what I mean by you're not what I expected."
>
> MARIEKE and VEE in *The Lazarus Effect* (169)

Hawa Jande Golakai's heroine Vee Johnson hardly conforms to South African's expectations of immigrants from other African countries as she roams the streets of Cape Town. She confounds expectations in multiple respects. Vee (Voinjama) is a stylishly dressed, female investigative journalist who works with Chloë Bishop, her White, lesbian sidekick. The almost 6-foot-tall Vee is a Liberian refugee and holds a "top-class degree in journalism and media from Columbia University" (Golakai 2011, 39). She is generally hard to place for South Africans, both racially and linguistically. Given her black skin, in the Western Cape Black people react with incredulity when they realise that she does not speak Xhosa (2015, 47). Her surname evokes puzzlement, as she is "obviously not coloured" (2011, 46), and people struggle to pronounce her first name: " 'Miss Va …um, Viona … Voiaja … uh, Miss Johnson' " (2011, 25). Her English accent gets noted as "very different" (45) or, less diplomatically, as sounding "like a Jamaican reading a dictionary" (2015, 67). In short, Vee resists easy accommodation within South Africa's racial and linguistic grid, and this is where her power for renegotiation of generic and social scripts lies. With Rowe's protagonist Persy, Vee joins the ranks of the feisty, tough, hard-boiled investigator heroines of the crime genre as a woman of colour. While the two are subjected to similar tensions and dilemmas as female agents in a male-dominated professional environment, with Vee, Golakai adds several decidedly new twists to the female investigator in local crime fiction: an outsider's view on South African society, an unprecedented combination in a female detective duo and the opening up of the crime genre to include elements of chick lit.

My discussion of Golakai's budding Vee Johnson Mystery series follows three main avenues. The first is concerned with the revisionary potential of Vee's agency as an outsider detective and her collaboration with Chloë. Vee and Chloë as a detective duo represent an impressive revision of racial relations that can hardly be overestimated in the South African imaginary. The second part of the chapter critically engages with Golakai's genre blending.

I argue that her infusion of crime fiction with chick lit gives rise to certain tensions, but that, overall, it is a successful feminist intervention. Finally, I look at the kind of truths that Vee is able to establish in her investigative work and the fictional justice that she thereby serves. Here my arguments are again underpinned by the feminist scholarship in legal studies and criminology cited in my discussion of Persy Jonas. I suggest that Vee's endeavours in this area display contradictory effects, simultaneously opening up and closing down opportunities for more inclusive modes of justice.

Hawa Jande Golakai's debut detective novel *The Lazarus Effect* (2011) was an instant hit, receiving nominations for three prestigious literary prizes. The novel was long-listed for the Wole Soyinka Prize for Literature in Africa and short-listed for the Sunday Times Fiction Prize, as well as for the University of Johannesburg Debut Prize for Creative Writing (Steiner 2017, 1). *The Score* (2015) is the second novel in Golakai's Vee Johnson Mystery series. A trained immunologist and a newcomer to the crime writing scene, Golakai says, "I want to reclaim crime writing as an African woman" (McCracken 2014, par. 19). In her biographical note in *The Score*, she calls herself "a modern-day nomad and cultural sponge." Born in Frankfurt, Germany, she spent her childhood in her family's country of origin, Liberia, but in 1990 was compelled to leave due to the Liberian Civil War. After moving around several African countries, she came to South Africa in 2003, where she lived for almost a decade before returning to Liberia (Akinwotu 2016, par. 6, 17).

The Lazarus Effect is set in Cape Town in 2009 and features investigative journalist Vee Johnson's first case, the disappearance of the teenage girl Jacqueline (Jacqui) Paulsen, who had gone missing two years earlier. While Vee is unable to raise Jacqui from the dead (as implied by the title), she certainly saves her from oblivion by reviving a cold case. Troubling hallucinations featuring the teenager kindle Vee's interest. She manages to establish not only the "truth" about the emotionally crippling life of Jacqui's family, but that Jacqui was murdered by her half-sister Rosie. In *The Score*, Golakai's second detective novel, "the score" has nothing to do with football, but refers to settling an old score in the business world in post-World Cup 2010 South Africa. Vee's investigation into the murders of Gavin Berman and Rhonda Greenwood in a lodge in Oudtshoorn, in South Africa's Western Cape province, reveals the exploitative business practices that motivated the murderer, IT specialist Xoliswa Gaba.

3.1   *The Politics of Vee Johnson's Detective Agency and Her Collaboration with Chloë Bishop*

Vee is not on an explicit mission for feminist and racial equality, but her visibility as a successful female migrant investigator with detective agency and the confidence and naturalness with which she claims and manages to secure her own space as a Liberian woman within the male-dominated media work towards these ends. Vee's very *choice* to become an investigator is informed by political concerns. The investigative journalist attracts crime like a magnet (Golakai 2015, 79) and her motivation to fight it is strongly personal, yet in Vee's case the personal is also political. Shedding light on Jacqui's mysterious disappearance in *The Lazarus Effect* is an act of self-preservation for Vee, as is finding Gavin's murderer in *The Score*. Vee suffers from panic attacks and repeatedly experiences disconcerting visions of a teenage girl in a red woollen hat. Rightly suspecting that this "ghost" that keeps bothering her is Jacqui's, Vee knows that "her own health and sanity depended more than her livelihood on finding the 'truth' behind Jacqueline Paulsen's disappearance" (2011, 47). Living at the intersection of at least two cultural spheres, Vee has various interpretative models available to account for her "anxiety attacks" and concomitant "hallucinations". According to a Western scientific belief system, she is suffering from post-traumatic stress disorder (157), whereas from an African traditional viewpoint she is being visited by a spirit (150). Neither system is a feasible choice for Vee, however, as both are undergirded – more or less overtly – by patriarchy. She feels uncomfortable about seeing a psychotherapist, and the Nigerian spirit consultant she once saw turned out to be a violent lecher (37, 150). By rejecting these alternatives, Vee implicitly refuses to allow herself to be pathologised and thus controlled by patriarchal structures. Instead, she herself takes the traditionally male space – that of the detective – thereby opting for an actively resistant strategy. In the second novel, Vee's personal motives for investigating Gavin's killing are likewise political: her detective work is a refusal to be criminalised. Shortly before Gavin is found murdered, she has to fight off his sexual advances. In the course of this struggle, she loses her scarf and leaves the marks of her fingers around his neck (2015, 72). She does not kill him, but the evidence of her scarf and the strangulation marks around his neck lead the police immediately to regard her as a prime suspect. Vee knows that, given her vulnerable foreigner status – a "kwerekwere with [an] unpronounceable name" (88) – she is liable to be criminalised by a xenophobic South African society. Xoliswa drives this point home when she tries to blackmail Vee later on, detailing how Vee's version of events would not be believed by the police (289) precisely because of her foreignness. Vee's gender and race are also factors in her decision to investigate Gavin's murder. By choosing to exert her agency as a detective in *The Score*, Vee is resisting the stereotype of the criminal Black woman, a controlling mechanism that dates back to colonialism. Lewis maintains that "colonial definitions of [black] women's urban work as peripheral and unlawful, together with the stereotypes surrounding their presence in towns, frequently persist in the post-colonial period" (2011, 206). Occupying the position of the investigator and exercising detective agency as a Black immigrant woman in South Africa gives Vee a legal status in the public sphere, a kind of visible social authority on the street that is on the right side of the law. Her choice to investigate becomes an act of inventive recasting of received social categories.

The question remains as to whether this choice actually allows Vee extended scope of action. Vee's agency as a detective repeats the male blueprint; it is that of the lone, heroic, tough, authority-defying male noir hero (2011, 241, 247, 274–276, 2015, 233ff., 257–258). Vee loves and frequently embarks on "solo missions" (2011, 38), and, with her excellent combat skills, she is generally happy to engage in physical fights. Her heroism is rewarded in the media world: both Rosie's and Xoliswa's attacks and the way in which Vee resists them enhance her credibility with her superiors and substantially boost her career as an investigative journalist (2011, 237, 2015, 184). Unlike Persy, Vee is rewarded for her performance of the male detective model. It works to secure her the visibility and the place in the male-dominated media world that she covets.

In addition to her gender and race, Vee's migrant status has an important bearing on the political implications of her agency as a detective. In her discussion of *The Lazarus Effect*, Rebecca Fasselt emphasises the significance of the migrant detective in a South African context, where more often than not immigrants from other African countries are perceived as a threat to local livelihoods and are frequently subjected to violent assault and murder (2016, 1111–1112). Reading Golakai's first novel alongside other South African crime novels that address similar concerns, Fasselt points to the uniqueness of Golakai's perspective (1113). She views *The Lazarus Effect* as "a powerful vehicle for an enquiry into constructions of 'foreignness' and a means to allot a space to African migrants in the 'new' South African imaginary" (1109). Not only does Vee move beyond the space of stereotypical female migrant victimhood, as Fasselt argues (1122), but, as a female investigator, she fights to secure a space within the male-dominated institutional framework of the media. Vee's career trajectory as an investigative journalist takes her from Cape Town's *Urban* magazine, which is presented by Golakai as having strong female connotations, to inhabiting her very own office space in the "male" *Chronicle*. Vee starts off at the *Urban*, which "makes most of its revenue from fashion. [...] by appealing to urban women with a fashion sense" (Golakai 2011, 82). Here Golakai is somewhat simplistically reinforcing existing assumptions about female fashion media as limited, so it comes as no surprise to the reader that the power of Vee's female boss, the editor Portia Kruger, is constrained. Rumour has it that she is "no more than a seat-warmer" put in place by her father (39), who owns the media group made up of the *Urban* and the more prestigious *City Chronicle*

(41). The *Chronicle*, headed by the White managing editor Nico van Wyk, is the larger and "more respectable newspaper," where the "serious material" is published and where the decisions are made (41). Following Vee's success in the Jacqui Paulsen case, this is where we find Vee and Chloë at the beginning of *The Score*. However, her posting to the *Chronicle* is an uncomfortable space for Vee. She is reined in by Nico, "a racist dick" (2015, 20) whose office is described as "a man's space" (14). She finds herself jammed into "a cubicle next to a sealed-off window" (14) and being sent on a fatuous travel and tourism assignment to the Grotto Lodge in Oudtshoorn (19). Once there, Vee decides to do the forbidden and steps outside the confines of her narrow job description to investigate two murders at the lodge. Her transgressions are met with opposition for a long time, but eventually she wins Nico over with her investigative success and the financial gains that accrue to his paper as a result. Somewhat defying Vee's simple labelling of him as misogynist and racist, he rewards her with a promotion to the online team (348). While she still has a way to go to reach the coveted crime desk, which for now remains occupied by two men who swing "their dicks around" and "muscle out" women (134), she has made inroads into the management sector of the male-dominated *Chronicle* (359). What is more, inside this structure, she has secured her own office space, a room of her own, her "place to think" (17), her refuge from the noisy, "old guard" newsroom where her personal space was constantly interfered with (17). This office stands for her own gendered and cultured space in which she, the African female migrant detective, further negotiates the terms and conditions of her job with her White South African boss Nico (351–352).

Finally, there is political significance in the professional pairing of Vee and Chloë, who is both White and lesbian. This strategic authorial pairing implies a provocative contestation of various established power relations in South Africa and jars with the traditional feminist notion of "sisterhood (in crime)". The dynamics of Vee's relationship with Chloë are characterised by clear hierarchies. Vee is in the superior position to Chloë, which constitutes a radical reversal of power hierarchies that generally place the Black migrant woman beneath the White South African woman. Vee's seniority is established from the beginning through the power of the gaze. When she sees Chloë for the first time in *The Lazarus Effect*, Vee looks at her through the blinds between two offices without Chloë's knowledge and without Chloë being able to look back (81). In a detective novel, such a scene is immediately evocative of the one-way mirrors in police interrogation rooms. Through Vee's one-way gaze, Chloë becomes the suspicious object of investigative enquiry; she is being scrutinised and exposed without knowing the source, number and nature of those who have her under surveillance. In this case, Vee holds the singular (and presently concealed) position of power. She assesses Chloë using the characteristic physical itemisation of the male gaze applied to female embodiment. She notices her "red hair," her "[c]lear skin of whipped cream," her fashionable outfit and "a body to be envied," and immediately judges her to be "too fashionable" and unsuitable for the job (81–82). From an historical racial perspective, Chloë as a representative figure of White South African female privilege is indeed liable to be considered "guilty". By implication, she is complicit in the racist state's collective subjugation of people of colour, even though the novel later revokes such easy assumptions. It is this racial privilege that Vee immediately addresses when her boss Portia informs her that Chloë badly needs a job and that she is therefore going to be her new assistant: " 'I'm fine with chances. But lots of people really need jobs. Plus they *look* like they actually need the money. Did you have to hire the whitest girl in the universe?' " (83, original emphasis). Portia rebukes Vee for her racism, but then immediately invokes race herself by reminding Vee that she, as a "half-white" person, has "the power to fire" Vee. Portia thus tries to mask the fact that she was forced by her superior to employ Chloë by playing the (reverse) equal chances card. When challenged by Vee, the Black migrant, who reminds her that in the new South Africa privilege still mostly runs along colour lines, Portia, the South African of racially mixed origins, is quick to assert her racial superiority.

Vee remains insistent and changes tactics by doubting that Chloë has ever worked a day in her life, as it "[l]ooks like the last heavy thing she lifted was a Barbie" (83). To her surprise, Chloë, once hired, disproves the Barbie image. She throws herself into the Paulsen investigation at once and proves highly efficient. Both Portia's and Vee's racial prejudices are exposed, their easy presumptions complicated. Despite Vee's initial misgivings about what she fears will be an "extensive baby-[sitting]" job (85), she soon comes to like and appreciate her young White assistant. When Chloë starts calling her mentor "bosslady", Vee is secretly pleased: "*Bosslady*. It conjured an image of a buxom authority figure swathed in the colourful lappa cloth of home, multitasking like an octopus and beating off with wooden spoons the ears of anyone who dared to be idle in her presence. She liked that. She ought to act more like it, now that she had her own personal slave" (137, original emphasis). As her fondness for Chloë grows, Vee responds by calling her "finegeh", which is Liberian pidgin for "finegirl". Chloë guesses it is an affectionate term "like 'meisie' in Afrikaans" (2015, 79), although the diminutive label "girl" also serves as a casually reminder of her inferior social position.[15] As age is a common social marker that confers

---

15   In the beginning, Vee even calls Chloë "*Baby* Gingernut" (Golakai 2011, 85, emphasis mine).

authority in African societies, here Vee superimposes on the White Chloë her own cultural way of organising the social fabric. The "bosslady – finegeh" trope poignantly captures Vee's understanding of her hierarchical relationship with Chloë. It firmly establishes Vee's superior power position and her authority – which is further underlined by the fact that Vee is a knowledgeable professional journalist and Chloë is not. Golakai's cunning recalibration of power relations is further exemplified by the way in which Vee takes on the role of protector for Chloë, whom she feels is in need of care. Being in the superior position for Vee not only confers privilege, but also, crucially, the obligation to act as a guardian. Vee takes this obligation very seriously. After their success with the Paulsen case, Vee uses her leverage with Portia to get Chloë a permanent job (Golakai 2011, 298). When they both move to the *Chronicle*, Vee makes one condition clear to her new boss Nico: " 'Where there's room for me, there's room for her' " (2015, 15). She remains committed to providing this support (350). However, the serious argument that Vee and Chloë have towards the end of *The Score* reveals that Vee experiences her obligation to fight for and protect Chloë as a heavy burden and that she thinks that Chloë fails to see and appreciate how much work Vee is doing to save her in their competitive, even vicious, professional environment (279). Chloë, for her part, questions whether she can ever learn to fight her own battles when all she does is trail after Vee (278–279). Their argument revolves around the balance between dependence and autonomy, between control and protection, and testifies to the challenges of shifting power relations. At the same time, it shows that recasting character relations among female protagonists offers a productive space in which to test possibilities of new forms of social relationship.

Despite her own powerful position, Vee feels driven to contest Chloë's power of looking and knowing. The friendship between the two women almost reaches breaking point when Chloë reveals that she has been secretly investigating a sensitive issue in Vee's family history. Vee is enraged that Chloë has meddled in personal family matters that she has so far refused to share. Chloë recognises that she has overstepped the line, but complains that she feels excluded: she does not know where she stands with Vee and needs to understand "what kinda partnership" this is (2015, 281; see also 280–282). Chloë perceives being allowed to look at the other, knowing the other, being let "in" (281), as an essential basis for trust-building in a relationship, but Vee does everything to thwart Chloë's inquisitive gaze. She goes on solo missions during their investigations and refuses to talk about her family with Chloë. While this behaviour is amenable to various interpretations, I would argue that Vee is contesting the power of the gaze, a power that defines who has the right to look at whom and who has the right to know whom. Vee's secrecy here functions like the Du

Boisian veil that "deflects and refracts the gaze of domination from knowing 'the truth' of the submitted," as Munt reads it (1994, 117). As a Black foreign woman, Vee is sensitive to the gaze as a mechanism of control and domination. By being secretive and an individualist, she seems to be adhering to the archetypal isolated loner detective blueprint, but with Vee this acquires more complex nuance, for it works as a protective shield against the potential violence of the mastering, objectifying White gaze of the local. Vee's use of Liberian pidgin serves the same goal, obscuring herself and excluding Chloë. As Tina Steiner argues in her analysis of the use of Liberian pidgin in Golakai's novels, "The use of pidgin is a powerful device to assert cultural specificity and to withdraw linguistic transparency [...]. It also points to a convivial sociality from which locals are excluded due to their linguistic limitations [...]" (2017, 12). While it is not entirely clear why Vee, given her powerful position in relation to Chloë, would have to shield and defend herself, the use of pidgin asserts her difference and is aimed at distancing her from Chloë. Secrecy, not disclosing "the important stuff" (Golakai 2015, 103), for Vee is a distancing device. Overall, what we see in the relationship between Vee and Chloë is a powerful recalibration of received social positions. The relationship addresses key questions of where care ends and control starts, highlighting the thin line between protection and disenfranchisement, as well as issues of tolerance, naturalisation and assimilation. These concerns are at the heart of the power struggles not only in the arenas of race and gender, but in relation to foreignness. That such a reworking of social relationships in a South African context is imagined as initiated by an outsider calls attention to the hitherto unnoticed potential of African immigrants as agents for social change. Foreignness here is presented not merely as a question of being taken in by South Africa, but as prompting a realignment of power. For all its benefits, however, Golakai's focus on recasting power relations between Vee and Chloë forecloses the possibility of sisterhood. Even though at the end of *The Score* Vee decides to overlook the fact that Chloë has again failed to respect her privacy boundaries and starts to share some of her personal history with Chloë (354–358), they do not become "sistas". This becomes even more obvious when we look at another aspect of genre disruption in Golakai's detective novels: her inclusion of elements of chick lit.

3.2 *Crime Fiction cum Chick Lit: Strengthening Feminist Detective Agency and Disrupting Misogynist Generic Blueprints*

Like Makholwa, Golakai merges elements of chick lit into her crime fiction. The popular genres of crime fiction and chick lit share an engagement with gender issues, and both genres' potential for gender politics has been discussed along similarly controversial lines.[16] My aim at this point is to examine how blending the two genres, as Golakai does, has the capacity to prompt interventions in the fields of race and gender. Specifically, I want to probe for tensions and synergies that may arise from combining the genres.

Pamela Butler and Jigna Desai describe chick lit novels as telling "clever, fast-paced stories about young, predominantly white women's messy journeys of personal and professional growth – heroines gain self-knowledge and self-acceptance, and are thus empowered to take control of their intimate relationships and professional lives" (2008, 2). When such novels are written by women of colour, "the characters' engagements with femininity and gender are often articulated through questions of race, nation, ethnicity, and socioeconomic class" (2008, 4). Demarcating chick lit from the romance genre, with the primacy that it accords to the male-female couple, Suzanne Ferris and Mallory Young maintain that "chick lit jettisons the heterosexual hero to offer a more realistic portrait of single life, dating, and the dissolution of romantic ideals" (2006, 3). Raymond Chandler, for his part, advises that a crime author jettison not so much the hero per se, but any romantic interests that he may pursue. He warns that "[l]ove interest nearly always weakens a mystery because it introduces a type of suspense that is antagonistic to the detective's struggle to solve the problem" (1962 (1949), 70). However, female crime writers usually disregard this and allow their heroines romantic attachments and a sex life, albeit that these may prove problematic. Rowe confirms Chandler's tenet in so far as her heroine's sexual agency seriously undermines her agency as a detective. By contrast, Golakai's turn to the conventions of chick lit works to complicate the assumption that love interests negatively influence the labours of detective agency. Vee's romantic liaison with Joshua Allen clearly furthers her investigations. She frequently discusses her cases with him, takes his advice and occasionally elevates his status from lover to sidekick (Golakai 2011, 282, 2015, 160). Often this comes at some cost to him, as, for example, when Vee spoils their love-making with a sudden flash of investigative inspiration that needs to be followed up instantly (2011, 159). Rather than competing with the tension created by the investigation, such scenes add a delightfully humorous touch for the reader.

Besides assigning women a central role, authors of chick lit "present women as sexual agents" (Ferriss and Young 2006, 10). In her analysis of Ugandan and South African chick lit, Spencer demonstrates that "chick lit provides the space

---

16 Ferris and Young provide a brief overview of the controversy surrounding the feminist potential of chick lit (2006, 9–10).

to reflect on and articulate women's desires" and allows them to assert the power of sexual negotiation (2014, 106). The crime genre, on the other hand, has a long tradition of criminalising female sexuality – for example, through the figure of the femme fatale. What is more, Black women's sexuality has been criminalised way beyond the crime genre. Hooks notes, "Traditionally, Hollywood's sexual black women are whores or prostitutes [...]" (1994, 65). White supremacist patriarchy has constructed them as "licentious" (66), as "she-devil[s]" (67) who lure and enthral men and are therefore in need of (White) male restraint. Against this background, blending crime fiction with chick lit opens up a space for rewriting female sexuality, especially Black female sexuality, and works to subvert both the generic frame of crime fiction and demeaning practices of representation more generally.[17]

This is the approach that Golakai pursues consistently in her depiction of her heroine Vee. At the beginning of *The Lazarus Effect*, we encounter a sexually frustrated Vee, following a lengthy period of emotional turmoil while she recovered from an ectopic pregnancy, an ovarian cyst and the messy break-up of her engagement to Titus Wreh (66–67). "Since re-entering singlehood" she sees sexy men everywhere and finds their "obliviousness with respect to their sexual appeal [...] practically malicious. Striding around displaying V-shaped torsos misted with sweat and bare, muscled legs ... it had to stop" (43). Vee's arch remarks here straightforwardly invert the traditionally male gaze on the Black female body, sexualising the men's embodiment for her own delicious pleasure. Soon afterwards, numerous opportunities arise for Vee, but despite her longing for intimacy, she carefully negotiates men's sexual advances. She says no to men many times, regardless of her previous history with them, and always finds her decisions respected (2011, 70, 228, 308, 2015, 145, 213). Being able to choose is a source of liberation for her: "It was strange and a little funny. For the first time, she had two men in her life that she cared for fiercely, and yet, at her own choosing, her arms were empty. She didn't enjoy being alone, and saw no reason to be [...]. But at times it was necessary. The situation needed to breathe" (2011, 228). When she is ready, however, Vee does not hesitate to take the initiative – and she thoroughly enjoys her erotic encounters, which are always focalised from her female perspective (2011, 205, 304, 2015, 154, 365). Unlike Persy, she experiences her sexuality as empowering and as a source of joy.

---

17 In a recent article, Rebecca Fasselt reads Golakai's novels as "chick-lit mysteries" (2019, 189). Fasselt claims they recast both the crime and the chick lit genre insofar as they subvert the quest structure that is inherent in both genres: the quest for a resolution of the crime and the restoration of order in the case of crime fiction, and the quest for romantic love in chick lit (189–190).

Drawing on Audre Lorde, African feminist Patricia McFadden boldly calls for the foregrounding of female sexual pleasure and choice and encourages women to embrace their "erotic power as a political resource" (2003, par. 7). Moving beyond postcolonial criticism, McFadden takes issue with the contemporary policing and surveillance of female sexuality in Africa by both women and men (par. 15, 17). The current discourses on female sexuality in Africa revolve around reproduction and the avoidance of disease and violation, and are a means to silence and delimit women (par. 15, 18). A redefinition of female sexuality that goes beyond these discourses is thus required (par. 23) in order to reimagine female subjectivity and to transform the social space at large (par. 7). Against the background of McFadden's argument, celebrating Black female sexual agency and eroticism through elements of chick lit becomes a feminist resistant act and disrupts the generic frame of crime fiction. Thus, Plain's claim about "criminal" White lesbian sexuality in crime fiction, where "the pleasures enjoyed by the detective herself will have repercussions far beyond the bedroom" (2001, 207), can also be applied to equally "criminal" Black female heterosexual sexuality in the genre.

Although Plain takes these repercussions to be positive from a feminist point of view, in the case of the White lesbian Chloë they are somewhat more ambiguous. Even though we first meet Chloë having sex with a certain Mr Cohen, her sexual orientation is made immediately obvious to us as readers. Promised a job by Mr Cohen, but horrified at now having to face his erect penis, she tells us that she is glad that she has no prior knowledge of heterosexual encounters: "Her feelings about [men] had been cemented early on in life and weren't likely to ever change" (Golakai 2011, 81). Vee never learns about Chloë's "carpet interview" (81), but Chloë openly displays her interest in women. Nevertheless, Vee remains blind to Chloë's sexual preferences until the end of the first novel, when she asks her assistant whether the tech guy who has helped them is her boyfriend. In response, Chloë tells her that the question is ridiculous because she is gay (265). Vee is taken aback, even though "[i]n hindsight it was so obvious" (266). Unfortunately for Chloë, who would have liked to impart more to Vee, the moment of revelation happens when they are both in mortal danger, locked in the darkness of a tool shed by a murderer. Vee is busy trying to find a way out for them and only listens to Chloë's story with one ear. They soon manage to escape, and the moment is gone (269).

This is worth dwelling on, for the crime conventions here conflict with and override the chick lit generic features. Chick lit's emphasis on female friendship and female bonding (Spencer 2014, 92) gets marginalised by the plot requirements of the crime novel. Where chick lit would in all likelihood elaborate on Chloë's intimate revelation through female conversation, crime fiction, driven towards final resolution, has no space to develop and deepen such details, which are pushed to the side. All that Vee offers at this moment lies within the limits of her obligations as bosslady; she promises to protect Chloë at work (Golakai 2011, 266). The only other time Vee makes a reference to Chloë's sexual orientation is in *The Score*, when she warns her not to sleep with one of the female suspects (147–148). It seems that Vee is strangely reluctant to talk about female same-sex sexuality. When she does, Chloë's lesbianism is defined as a problem that must be kept from Portia, and that must also be kept in check. Vee occupies the hegemonic phallic position here, which is anomalous given the heterosexual liberties that she herself enjoys. The genre of chick lit would allow her to take a more straightforward and a more sisterly approach here; after all, she and Chloë find time to discuss Vee's own amorous adventures and relationship issues in the midst of their busy detective lives (2015, 67–69; 148). Vee's reticence with regard to Chloë's transgressive sexuality may be another distancing strategy aimed at maintaining the superior position that she occupies in her relationship with Chloë, which would be undermined by an invocation of chick lit's political potential for nurturing female friendships. Alternatively, there is a possibility that Vee is distancing herself from the potential threat of Chloë's lesbian sexuality per se. Does Vee have to abject Chloë so as to avoid confronting her own suppressed lesbian desire? At this early point in Golakai's series, the question remains unresolved. There is no textual evidence to suggest that Vee's inability to decide between her two male lovers Joshua and Titus is testament to a frustration with heterosexual desire. Likewise, even though Chloë is very fond of Vee and is aware of her attractiveness – at one point, she notes that Vee has a "dirty beauty" and a face that makes "men look, and look again. At certain angles it spelled trouble, and could suck you into wanting to find out how much" (2015, 69) – there is no indication so far that she is sexually interested in Vee. In any case, this is a space to watch as the Vee Johnson Mystery series continues.

What is disturbing in the light of Golakai's otherwise progressive gender politics, however, is the fact that at times Chloë herself seems to take the hetero-patriarchal position. In a bout of relationship frustration, she calls women "evil, twisted sirens" who can "crush you like a cockroach" (2011, 180). Later on, she displays self-hatred and reinforces the trope of the monstrous woman by applying it to herself. She suspects her sexual orientation to be the reason that her circle of caring female friends is dwindling. She muses that "perhaps women were right to be antsy, seeing as her sexual preferences made her a monster to be feared" (232). Chloë's internalisation of patriarchal sexism and homophobia jars with Golakai's otherwise very successful strategy of mixing crime fiction with elements of chick lit, which not only serves feminist political ends but disrupts the generic blueprint for crime fiction. The effect of this goes far beyond simply "jazz[ing] up the entertainment value" of her novels (Naidu 2013b, 734). Chick lit puts women into the limelight, depicting a cast of predominantly female protagonists, and is largely written by and for women. Golakai transfers this centrality of women to her detective novels. Not only does she populate them with an abundance of professional women, but she assigns to women all three pivotal roles in the crime genre. Golakai writes female detectives, but women also feature prominently as perpetrators and victims, as we shall see when we look at the kind of "truth" and justice that Vee establishes as a detective agent.

3.3 *The Outsider's Detective Gaze: Finding Conflicting Truths, Achieving Limited Justice*

Prior to studying Vee's cases and the kind of justice that she administers by solving them, we need to consider the justice that comes from having a migrant detective per se. In my view, imagining the detective gaze as that of a foreigner is in itself a source of alternative justice in Barbara Hudson's sense. In the South African real, Vee *herself*, as an African immigrant, would normally be the one facing interrogation and scrutiny. What Golakai does in her crime fiction is turn the tables: she has her detective heroine subject South African society to her gaze and her questions. In this way, she integrates the one who is normally outside the constituency of justice; fulfilling the requirement that justice be discursive (2012, 388). According to Hudson, "[a] major theme of feminist and post-structural, post-colonial critiques [...] is that established liberal justice suppresses the voice of the outsider" (389).

By integrating the outsider's voice – and gaze – Golakai also achieves what Steiner, with reference to Viktor Shklovsky, terms a "defamiliarization" (2017, 3) that "exposes reified structures of relation" (1). This extends to gender, too. When in *The Lazarus Effect* Vee is watched and later pursued and run down one night by an unidentified driver in a Mercedes, readers automatically assume that the culprit is male; Vee herself fleetingly thinks of Lucas Fourie (221, 228–230). But the driver turns out to be Rosie Fourie, the very woman who killed Jacqui. In the end, Vee admits, "I made the biggest mistake by assuming this had to be a man's crime" (279). When Vee's home is broken into at night and she is brutally attacked in *The Score*, the reader is likely to picture the assailant's "hefty" human body (174) as that of a man. When Vee's boss Nico is told about the attack, he, too, worries that the "man" could have killed her (180). Given her physical contact with the attacker, however, this time Vee is sure it was a woman. We later find out that it was Xoliswa, the murderer of both Gavin and Rhonda. By defamiliarising the attacker's gender, here Golakai deliberately plays with and renders tangible the gender bias that tends to govern how we respond to criminal acts.

Race also undergoes defamiliarisation. Steiner provides a detailed discussion of the defamiliarising effect of Golakai's use of humour and irony that functions to "probe racial categorization" in South Africa and to debunk racial bias on all sides in inter-cultural encounters (2017, 14–17). An outsider's gaze is needed for the disarming directness and humorous audacity with which Golakai alludes to and remoulds apartheid categorisations. Take, for example, Vee's comments on her boss Portia's curly, cinnamon-hued hair. According to Portia, "her hair guaranteed she was coloured" (Golakai 2011, 39). Vee, however, is sure that the "real lesson" is a different one: namely, that "her hair and dress code gave vital clues as to her mood. Curly and up was bad […]" (39). When Portia, despite these portents, likes Vee's proposal for an article, Vee notes with relief, "Luckily, Portia's coiffed hair signalled a playfully combative, but not spiteful, mood" (42). Her own reinterpretation of the hair as signifier is thus modified, its meaning unmasked as notoriously arbitrary and unstable. There are other ways in which Golakai defamiliarises the gaze. The following scene, just prior to Chloë's interview with Tamara, a former friend of the missing Jacqui, is a case in point: "Tamara finally wandered back with a cup of Mugg&Bean coffee and a box of confectionery. Chloë pasted on a polite smile as the leggy, cookie-coloured girl, her height boosted by a pair of weapon-toed boots, eyed her up and down. For the second time that day, Chloë Bishop felt too short and too white" (110). Despite the fact that Chloë is the focaliser, the power of the gaze here lies with the woman of colour, Tamara, who eyes Chloë "up and down." Tamara renders Chloë the object of her gaze and thus changes the power relations. From her position of power, Tamara is the one who defines what is "normal", prompting a feeling of inadequacy in Chloë, who suddenly feels "too short and too white." Besides recasting power, Tamara's gaze makes Chloë's generally "invisible" white skin a visible colour. The same can be said of Vee's gaze on Chloë, as we have seen. In his study on the representation of Whiteness in film, Richard Dyer argues that "white is no colour because it is all colours" (1988, 45), and that it is precisely this characteristic of being everything and nothing that allows White people to "colonise the definition of normal" (45). According to Dyer, "The colourless multi-colouredness of whiteness secures white power by making it hard, especially for white people and their media, to 'see' whiteness. This, of course, also makes it hard to analyse" (46). Whiteness requires a comparative element so that it can be studied – a colour is required to make it visible (47). Thus, making White visible and open to enquiry is a means of securing justice. It is as significant an achievement of Vee's detective gaze as her exposure of racial and gender stereotypes.

When it comes to the dead bodies of the victims whose murders she is investigating, however, Vee's detective gaze is severely limited. In the first novel, Vee never actually gets to see Jacqui's dead body. The only way she "perceives" her is as the effervescent "Air Girl" in her visions (Golakai 2011, 26). During these visions, it is more a case of the Air Girl looking at Vee than the other way around: "[W]ith head cocked to one side, for a few moments she regarded Vee's prostrate form as if it were some pathetic animal. Then she looked over her shoulder several times, beckoning with a hand" (13). In an authorial move that throws into sharp contrast the limits of the detective's gaze, *readers* are granted exclusive access to Jacqui, both dead and alive. At the beginning of the novel, and again later on, our attention is directed to the location of the teenager's "corpse" (9) in a dry storm drain, and to the ways in which it has been vulnerable to the elements and subjected to a process of mummification (9–10, 143). At the end of the novel, we return to the body in the dream of a dying street child, who dreams of his encounter with the Jacqui on the night she was dumped in a drainage canal. Through the street child's empathic gaze, we see the terror in Jacqui's eyes: "It looked like a human being. […] a girl, or a boy with a pretty face and lots of hair" (302). In addition, at regular intervals readers are privy to a number of flashbacks featuring what turns out to be Jacqui's last day alive.

In *The Score*, it is not so much Vee's gaze as her *right* to see that is questioned. She looks hard at the bodies, closely, though it is in no way a sensationalising or eroticising interest. Instantly recognising Gavin, she screens his clothes for traces of mud and – as he is dangling from a coat hook – for signs of strangulation (1, 3–4). Hers is a tentatively objectifying detective gaze, but it is dominated by her own fears of being incriminated. The look that she takes at Rhonda's dead body in the same novel is not predatory either, but it is a "forbidden" look, in the sense that she knows that she is not supposed to interfere with the police investigation. For this reason, she urges the servant who showed her the body not to tell anybody that she has seen, let alone photographed, Rhonda's corpse (48–54). As in *The Lazarus Effect*, readers are given an extra look at the body in question. The novel's final scene reveals the existence of a secret, so-called nanny camera that was hidden inside a glass figurine in Rhonda's room. Through the camera's eye, we witness Rhonda's last moments alive, how Xoliswa chokes her with a pillow and then rearranges the scene to give Rhonda's death the appearance of a suicide. Finally, we see the maid who discovers Rhonda and Vee who examines and photographs the body (371–376). Besides creating suspense in the crime narrative, the extra information in both novels is evidence of Vee's detective skills and functions to confirm her agency as a detective. As such, it does justice to the dead victims. The existence of Jacqui's physical remains and the flashbacks to her last day alive provide the (material) evidence for Vee's visions, which might otherwise be dismissed as the hallucinations of a deranged person. They also support Vee's intuition that Jacqui has not simply run away. Likewise, the nanny camera footage confirms Vee's findings and proves the official police version of events wrong: Rhonda did not commit suicide. At the same time, the extra information renders visible the limited frame of the detective's gaze and limits it further. The right of the outsider detective to look at the dead body is denied (Jacqui) or her actions are portrayed as illegitimate (Gavin and Rhonda). What is more, the detective herself comes under scrutiny, as she is subjected to both the Air Girl's counter gaze and the eye of the nanny camera. The camera's hidden eye incriminates and frames both the real murderer, the Black woman Xoliswa, and the Black detective's forbidden act of looking at Rhonda's dead White body. Golakai's critique of race and gender relations is also compromised, as the nanny camera footage is in the hands of Trevor Davis, the Coloured male concierge at Grotto Lodge. His threat to keep it as potential leverage for "a rainy day" is disturbingly left dangling over the Black women at the end of the novel, potentially framing them (376).

The question remains as to what kind of justice is served by Vee's investigative work and the truths that she uncovers. Vee's first case, investigating the disappearance of the teenager Jacqui Paulsen, taps into the sadly common phenomenon of missing children in South Africa,[18] which Vee uses as a pretext to secure her boss's permission to write an article. It turns out that Jacqui was murdered by her half-sister Rosie, who then disposed of the body with the help of her older sister Serena. What Vee uncovers in the course of her investigation does nothing to illuminate the real plight of missing children or the conditions that facilitate their disappearance in South Africa, but it put the spotlight on children as both victims and perpetrators in conflicts or wars that are only partly their own – if at all. However, although the novel debates the question of the responsibility and moral accountability of teenage children for their actions by portraying them as both victims and perpetrators in a crime story, it presents us with discordant answers. According to Vee, the detective, Rosie ran over her half-sister Jacqui with her parents' car in "a moment of madness," because she felt let down by Jacqui and believed that she was going to wreck their family (Golakai 2011, 287). Rosie, had come to view Jacqui as the ally she badly needed, as the rest of the family made her feel that she did not really

---

18   Orford has her detective heroine Clare Hart investigate this phenomenon in *Daddy's Girl* and *Water Music*.

count (280). However, she felt betrayed (281) because Jacqui started bonding with Serena and because she wrongly suspected that Jacqui was pregnant by her brother Lucas (286). In Vee's opinion, Rosie was motivated not just by anger, but by the fear that Jacqui would destroy her already fractured family "all over again" (286).

What Vee construes as an argument between two half-sisters and as an attempt to protect the family happens against the following background. Dr Ian Fourie, a famous Cape Town cardiologist, has four children with his German wife Carina, a paediatrician: Sean, Serena, Lucas and Rosie. At the same time, he has a daughter with Adele Paulsen: Jacqui, who is the same age as Serena. Adele was Ian's girlfriend before he went to study abroad. When they met again many years later, they had an affair and Adele fell pregnant. Ian, now a husband and father-to-be, asserted his patriarchal authority (52) and coerced Adele into complying with his "grand plan concerning his two families [...]: he had two families and they would stay separate. I'm sure you're aware this kind of thing happens all the time" (53). When Adele tells Vee about this arrangement, she is not surprised. "Big house, small house. Vee was very familiar with it, having grown up in a similar set-up. It was as old as the hills and a virtually indestructible pillar of the African family structure" (53), she informs us, thus anchoring the South African Ian Fourie's actions and decisions within the larger African practice of polygamy. Ian's plan to keep his two families apart fails because his oldest son, Sean, develops leukaemia and the only one who is a match for a life-saving bone marrow transplant is his half-sister Jacqui. Ian demands the secret collaboration of Adele and Jacqui (now 12 years old). Adele agrees on condition that Ian finally tells his wife Carina about her and Jacqui, which he does (54–55). Sean and Jacqui are being prepared for the transplant when Adele loses her nerve and temporarily takes Jacqui home. By the time Adele gives her consent for Jacqui to resume the process, Sean has developed an infection, which he dies of (56). His death effectively breaks his mother Carina. She never forgives Ian for his affair with Adele and their marriage crumbles, even though they stay together. Jacqui, however, can no longer be forced to stay away from the Fouries: "she wanted to be part of them so much" (57).

In the light of this larger system comprising the family and the "big house – small house" model that undergirds it, Rosie's murder of Jacqui takes on a different dimension. What Vee uncovers about Ian Fourie and his two families reveals the sheer futility of either Rosie's attempt to protect the family or Jacqui's efforts to become part of it. Too many adults have failed on the way: Ian by enforcing his patriarchal "big house – small house" model, Adele by jeopardising the transplant process and Carina by absenting herself emotionally from her other children. By refusing to resolve their conflict or at least to address it openly, the adults harm their children and pave the way for the fateful sororicide. As Jacqui reflects to Rosie before she is run over, "'Nobody tells us anything, Rosie, not you and not me. Live with it'" (292). Even once Jacqui is dead, the sisters try to deal with the murder by themselves. Serena organises a car, and they secretly dispose of Jacqui's body. These complicated plot twists may cater to the generic need for spectacle and, at times, distract from the truth-finding process. Yet insofar as the novel draws into focus the bigger frame – that is, the failures of the adult world, including the patriarchal family structure as upheld by Ian, with the complicity of Carina and Adele,[19] it can be considered a successful attempt at truth-finding. Looked at closely, Rosie's actions as an individual are accounted for in interaction with broader structures, which Posel sees as a prerequisite for successful truth-telling (2002, 159). This is in keeping with the importance that she attributes to "understanding *why* individuals act the way they do by inserting their actions into a broader causal context [...]" (159, original emphasis). Moreover, Jacqui the victim is imbued with agency both through the role that she plays in provoking Rosie and, after her death, through her appearances to Vee as a spirit. Responsibility and culpability are presented as relational, a principle that Hudson identifies as crucial in her outline of an alternative, more inclusive notion of justice (2012, 392). Without excusing Rosie, the novel lifts a substantial part of the responsibility from the children's shoulders and shifts it to where it primarily belongs: namely, with the adults and the patriarchal family structures that they reproduce. In this way, the novel allows for an exposure as well as for a modification of the limits of formal justice.

These limits are exposed further by Golakai's integration into the novel of Vee's traumatic experience during the Liberian Civil War (Golakai 2011, 255–258). Locked up by Rosie in the darkness of a tool shed, Vee relives how she killed a child soldier who threatened to rape her when she was taken captive by the rebels (258). Back then, she was only a "little girl" (255), the soldier a "boy" who was "old, but not *old* old – maybe five years more, like her brother" (258, original emphasis); they were both caught up in a war that was not theirs. The two children both perpetrate crimes, yet they are also both victims of the larger crime that is war. Criminal justice fails to account for such moral

---

19   Both Carina and Adele become complicit as neither of them openly challenges Ian or the system as such. As financially independent professional women, both have the means to resist Ian, but instead they take out their anger and frustration on their children – Adele by refusing to collaborate fully in the transplant, Carina by emotionally abandoning her children after Sean's death and by allowing her bitterness towards her husband to poison her children's home (Golakai 2011, 146).

complexity and the concomitant questions of responsibility. Further outside the bounds of the formal justice system, if not society itself, is the street child, whose perspective and voice Golakai includes towards the end of her narrative. The "watcher" (10, 300) whom we met in the novel's opening scene, when he was waiting for Jacqui's remains to resurface from the storm drain after the rain, is now himself dying. He is dreaming of how he realised that Jacqui was still alive when Serena and Rosie dumped her, of how he stayed with her, making sure that she did not have to die alone, and of how he tried to alert the police, but was not believed, his account being rejected as storytelling "while high on tik" (303). By including him, the outsider who is discredited by the police, by acknowledging his existence and by giving him credibility – Jacqui's remains are indeed found, later on, in the place that he indicated – the novel fulfils the demands for a more inclusive kind of justice, in keeping with Hudson's principle of discursiveness (2012, 389). Yet at the same time as the novel opens up such spaces for alternative notions of justice, it forecloses them. Despite unveiling a larger picture during her investigation, Vee finally settles for a narrow interpretation of Rosie's motives. When Chloë concludes, after she and Vee have gone over Rosie's and Serena's statements, " 'That's so ... despicable and sad.' [...]. 'They were just two stupid kids having a typical stupid argument' " (Golakai 2011, 294), Vee does not contradict her. Nor does she question the kind of formal justice that will be administered to Rosie and Serena – justice that she was instrumental in bringing about. She states, " 'This will be the blow to destroy them forever: Serena and Rosie have practically screwed up their whole lives [...]' " (296). While their children are punished, either with death (Jacqui) or by the criminal justice system (Rosie and Serena), the adults all get away with their crimes (309–310). In terms of justice, the reader is thus left with a discomforting paradox. While the novel imagines an inclusive sort of narrative justice, in the end it nevertheless gives in to and reproduces the status quo of the real.

In *The Score*, Vee's investigation into the murders of Gavin and Rhonda, which happen at the Grotto Lodge in Oudtshoorn during a conference on government incentives for private entrepreneurs, almost instantly reveals the larger structures of corporate and state-corporate crimes that frame the two murders. Vee establishes that Gavin was murdered by Xoliswa Gaba, a highly talented software developer and former employee of Berman & Moloi Financials, a company owned by Gavin and his partner Akhona Moloi. Xoliswa had developed an evaluation software, which Gavin and Akhona monetised and promoted without crediting her, thus effectively stealing her intellectual property and its associated benefits (338). At first, Xoliswa pressures Gavin and Akhona for financial compensation. Later, she takes revenge by murdering Gavin, along with Rhonda, the lodge's deputy manager, who was in the wrong place at the wrong time. Crucially, Akhona, frustrated at having been sexually rejected by Gavin, manipulated Xoliswa's revenge by feeding her information, but did not think that Xoliswa would go so far as to kill Gavin (341–342). Once Vee arrives on the scene and starts probing, Akhona manipulates her into exposing Xoliswa in order to deflect attention away from her own illegal machinations. What moves on to Vee's radar in the course of her detective work is the way in which government corruption goes hand in hand with corporate crimes and the exploitation of low-ranking employees (Golakai, 239–240). Semi-legal and illegal business practices such as undercutting the minimum wage by commissioning "freelancers", inflating quotes and denying workers their salaries are facilitated by corrupt state officials (240). This revelation has a sobering effect on the Liberian Vee, who realises that business practices in South Africa, the place of dreams for so many other African nationals, are on a par with the "shenanigans from my corner of the continent" (247). Other than locating South Africa in the wider African context of corruption, Golakai's novel adds little that is new to the representation of state-corporate crimes, a problem addressed frequently both in South African crime and true crime fiction in the South African media.[20]

What the novel stages convincingly, however, is the blurring of any neat boundaries between victim, perpetrator and detective, thus allowing for the ethical complexity and questioning that is conducive to inclusive forms of justice. It does so mostly through the figures of Vee and Xoliswa. Xoliswa has much of the destructive agency of the perpetrator. She has a history of physically attacking people and, as Vee experiences first hand, she fights "[...] dirty. Ghetto kinda dirty" (180). She has killed two people, one of them innocent, and, if Vee had not managed to stop her, she might have killed a third, Vee's neighbour Tristan, a boy of 11. At the same time, she is also a victim of the criminal machinations of her employers, so that at times Vee feels sympathetic towards her (216). She also admires Xoliswa's skills, to some extent (276), and is shocked to hear of her suicide (323). Writing Xoliswa as both perpetrator and victim not only complicates questions of guilt, but works against freezing her in either the stereotype of the Black female criminal or that of the Black female victim. Recalling Adelene Africa's study on limiting conceptions of real female perpetrators as mad, sad or bad (2010, 80), we notice that Akhona taps into this discourse when she describes Xoliswa to Vee as a psychopath with drug issues

---

20   See, for example, Mike Nicol's Revenge Trilogy and Mandy Wiener's *Killing Kebble* (2012). State-corporate crimes such as the Arms Deal and "Guptagate" are regular features in the South African media.

(Golakai 2015, 294). Even though Vee recognises that Xoliswa has psychological challenges, she has reservations about dismissing her in this manner. After Xoliswa's suicide, Vee finally succeeds in exposing the extent of Gavin's and Akhona's fraud. This proves that Xoliswa had real cause for anger, as she was indeed deceived and robbed by her employers: " 'They left me nothing. *Nothing* do I have left, you understand?' [...]. 'I handed everything to them on a plate, my ideas, my creation, and they [...] played me for a fool. Right under my own nose [...]' " (311, original emphasis). The allegations that Xoliswa had made all along were not the ravings of a madwoman: "Now Vee understood the seat of Gaba's outrage, her inability to let sleeping dogs lie. They'd excised a piece of her soul and gone running" (338).

Yet in the end Xoliswa kills herself over the injustice done to her (334). Despite the fact that the novel allows for a differentiated view on Xoliswa and, by doing so, serves a kind of justice that is in keeping with Hudson's principles of relationality and reflectivity, it sacrifices Xoliswa while the larger criminal structures stay in place. Through her suicide, Xoliswa anticipates and reifies the punishment meted out by the state's criminal justice system. What is more, Vee is partially responsible for this sacrifice. As a detective-journalist, she is implicated in the crimes against Xoliswa. It dawns on Vee that she herself has been no more than another player in Akhona's scheme. Akhona had deliberately set her on Xoliswa's trail in order to further incriminate Xoliswa and deflect attention from herself. Intent on a news scoop as Vee was, she unwittingly became complicit in Xoliswa's death. She realises, "I should've connected the dots. Akhona strung me along, *strung me up*, yet I didn't see it. She made me before I made her, smelled the hungry journalist vibe and fed it' " (340, original emphasis). As the dispenser of the justice that she has served by shedding light on the "truth" behind Xoliswa's claims, Vee herself has to face scrutiny. She is forced to admit, " 'We are all the bad guy! Me, you, Gavin, Moloi. Even Xoli ... if she'd just gotten out of her own goddam way and asked for help' " (343–344). Here Vee is confronted with the effects of her work and with the kind of justice that it achieves. She has to acknowledge that, as a journalist, she is prone to being instrumentalised by the wrong party. Investigative journalism can work as a means of alternative justice, but it can just as easily become criminal, reinforcing a conventional form of criminal justice that has been hijacked by a criminal society. There are also questions as to its effectiveness. Vee's colleague Darren offers a scathing judgement. According to Darren, journalists can "dig all this [crime] up" and trigger "an avalanche of articles," but eventually people will be "desensitised and it will die" (249). The novel acknowledges the complicated position that the investigative journalist occupies vis-à-vis questions of justice and the justice system – as does Vee herself. When reminded by her boss, "'You're a journalist, Johnson, not a crime fighter. You chase stories to boost circulation. You don't save lives'" (346), she is unable to draw such clear lines and is not comforted. Studies on the real impact of investigative journalism suggest that her discomfort is justified. For example, Roxana Galusca finds that investigative journalism in the US with regard to sex trafficking forms a questionable "regime of truth" (2012, 1). Since it excludes the migrant women concerned, it is not in a position to address the complex realities of their lives (16). Galusca's analysis reveals that the anti-trafficking discourses employed by US investigative journalists are "not simply humanitarian"; rather, they are "always already imbricated with institutional and noninstitutional forms of power, as well as wielding and producing new effects of power" (16). Golakai's novel serves to raise awareness of such potential imbrications in South Africa.

With her Liberian investigative journalist Vee Johnson, Golakai has successfully written herself into the South African crime fiction scene. As she has established Vee in both the global generic and the local South African frame, she has significantly revised the perception of those frames. Her empowered, gutsy, stylish female African migrant detective in Cape Town signifies a radical recasting on various levels. She is the Black woman who secures herself a place inside the institution of the "serious" media, which is still cast as predominantly White and male. She is also the Black foreign "bosslady" of the White local "finegeh" sidekick. Rather than allowing others to have her under their surveillance and to render her a visual object, she reserves to herself the power of the gaze and scrutinises patriarchal family structures as well as the corporate world. As one who embodies the traditionally invisible and marginalised, she makes visible criminal structures, as well as the dominance of Whiteness. She rewrites the stereotype of the female migrant victim as a more empowered script that involves gender mobility and moving towards more appropriate and complex forms of lived justice that are not accommodated by the current system. Instead of writing about sexual violence wrought upon women, Golakai writes a sexually empowered detective. Rather than having the generic frame contain crime, she disrupts the frame with both a criminal detective and elements of chick lit. However, although Golakai's interventions with regard to race and gender are generally successful, some inconsistencies remain. While Vee's agency as a detective serves to rework the stereotype of the Black female criminal, the sacrifice of Xoliswa in *The Score* reifies it. For Xoliswa, victimhood prevails: her disruptive criminal energy is contained through her suicide. In a similar vein, chick lit functions to strengthen the gender politics of the crime novel, but its emphasis on empowering sisterhood is subordinated to the project of rewriting established power relations. Moreover, the subversive act of celebrating Vee's heterosexuality is compromised by the narrative repression of

Chloë's homosexuality. Finally, Vee's at times inhibited, criminalised detective gaze limits her empowerment and potential for administering more inclusive, restorative modes of justice. Justice is served by Vee, as her investigations reveal the effects of patriarchal family structures and female complicity in them (in *The Lazarus Effect*) and the ways in which criminal state-corporate structures violate lower-ranking staff (in *The Score*). At the same time, the novels allow for much narrower interpretations that blank out the larger structures and present the murders as the result of jealousy between individuals. Such ambiguities threaten to reproduce hegemonic structures, also with regard to justice. On the plus side, they at least militate against neat generic closure and allow for a narrative marked by moral complexities. Overall, the contradictions in the Vee Johnson Mystery series contribute to Vee's strong and refreshing presence as a character who introduces an innovative "pan"-African element into the writing of a South African imaginary. Hers is a unique perspective from both within and beyond South Africa's borders. *The Score*, in particular, initiates a meditation on the kind of justice dispensed by investigative journalism – a question that is also central to Charlotte Otter's Maggie Cloete Mystery series.

4   Renegade Contained: Charlotte Otter's Investigative Journalist Maggie Cloete

> This was exactly why she stayed in crime. She couldn't write about James Bond movies or ballet or diabetes when degenerates out there were preying on the smallest, weakest and most vulnerable members of society. She wanted them found and put away and left to rot.
>
> MAGGIE in *Balthasar's Gift* (121)

When Charlotte Otter's fearless heroine Maggie Cloete guns the engine of her "Chicken", a 1998 Yamaha XT 350, and roars down the streets of Pietermaritzburg, the signal she sends to wrongdoers is unmistakeable. Maggie, a White woman, leaves no stone unturned in her determination to find them and effectively uses her sharp journalist's pen to expose them, thus providing justice for their victims. Like Rowe's detective protagonist Persy, Maggie works on home turf in Pietermaritzburg, where she was born and bred. This town was also once home to the author, who now lives in Germany. In this chapter, I will investigate the nature and politics of Maggie's agency as a detective. I will argue that this tough, confrontational and openly resistant investigator differs from Persy and Vee in that her powerful rage is as much a strategic gender performance as it is the motivation behind her actions, coming to resemble the kind of masculinity performed by the female perpetrators.

Maggie's first case in *Balthasar's Gift* (2014a), set in Pietermaritzburg at the turn of the millennium, is the murder of AIDS activist Balthasar Meiring. It brings to light not only that Balthasar was murdered by his father Lourens Meiring, but also the dark chapter in South Africa's recent history commonly referred to as "AIDS denialism", which grew under Thabo Mbeki's presidency. Otter thus shares Lorimer's focus on non-spectacular, structural violence and the racist and misogynist frames that sanction it. *Karkloof Blue* (2016b), which is set in the same town fourteen years later, moves far beyond the endangered butterfly of the book's title. The narrative traces various crimes emanating from Sentinel, a local forestry company, and those associated with it. Some of these crimes go back to the 1980s and South Africa's apartheid past. Maggie's investigations are motivated by her strong and successful commitment to justice. With the journalist's pen as Maggie's weapon, Otter's detective novels, like Golakai's, offer reflections on investigative journalism as a means of achieving justice. While Maggie is able to provide a more inclusive kind of justice, especially with her renewed attention to cases that were prematurely closed by the formal justice system, ultimately her endeavours remain contained by the very same system.

Charlotte Otter was born in South Africa and grew up in Pietermaritzburg, near Durban. Like her heroine, she is White and has a background as a journalist, having worked as a crime and court reporter for various South African newspapers. In 1996 Otter emigrated to Germany. She now lives in Heidelberg (KZN Literary Tourism 2015, par. 1). *Balthasar's Gift* is her critically acclaimed first novel in the Maggie Cloete Mystery series. The novel was first published by Aufbau Verlag/Ariadne in German translation in 2013 as *Balthasars Vermächtnis*. The English edition was published in South Africa in 2014 by Modjaji. The second novel in the series, *Karkloof Blue*, was again published first in Germany (2015) and then in South Africa (2016). It, too, has received enthusiastic reviews. Currently Otter is working on her third Maggie Cloete Mystery, entitled *Durban Poison*. As the author details, she writes her novels in English and then reworks them in collaboration with her translator Else Laudan of Ariadne, who has been publishing crime fiction by women as a feminist project for over twenty years. At the end of this process, the changes are fed back into the English original (2016a, par. 12). The inter-cultural genesis of the Maggie Cloete Mystery novels, which involves cross-fertilisation between the English and German versions of the texts, is in itself a topic worthy of exploration, although it is beyond the scope of the present study. Otter is explicit about wanting to join the ranks of feminist crime writers. The label "feminist crime fiction" features prominently on both her website and her Twitter account, and Otter calls herself "an angry feminist" who embraces the label (2014b, par. 45). I read the creation of her heroine Maggie as part of her feminist impulse.

4.1 Doing Angry Female Masculinity as a Detective: a Feminist Resistant Act?

Maggie is introduced to us in a spectacular stunt in the opening scene of *Balthasar's Gift*. When she witnesses the robbery of a female market trader while waiting at the traffic lights on her way to work, Maggie immediately guns her motorbike and sets off in pursuit of the thieves, subsequently following them on foot through alleys and over rooftops until she manages to tackle one of the men, wrestles with him and gets hold of his knife. Just before she ties him to a lamp post with the laces of her steel-capped Docs, she receives a call from Zacharius Patel, her boss, who dispatches her to the scene of a shooting at HIV House (7–10). The episode effectively establishes Maggie's key characteristics: she is an intrepid, tough, determined, lone warrior hero, who does not hesitate to throw herself into a physical fight with men if necessary. Like Persy and Vee, she embodies the generic male detective script as a woman. Maggie is both an efficient crime fighter and a respected journalist who works in and is framed by a male-dominated environment, initially as a crime beat reporter and later as a news editor for the Pietermaritzburg *Gazette*. However, her performance of masculinity goes beyond her professional role and is more ostentatiously angry than that of the other female detectives examined so far. Arguably, her rage over injustices is as much the driving force behind her actions as it is a strategic masculine gender performance. "Doing rage", as well as "doing detection", is her way of "doing masculinity", which very nearly leads this detective to "doing crime". Since Maggie is reminiscent of the female perpetrator, my reading of her agency draws on Judith Halberstam's work on both female masculinity and the expression of rage as a resistant strategy, as a political response (Halberstam 1998, 1993).

The most obvious aspect of Maggie's masculine demeanour, her trademark, is her favourite ride, a motorbike nicknamed "Chicken". Chicken represents a visible means of the "cultivation of female masculinity" (Halberstam 1998, 272). What is more, it is a celebration of a particularly aggressive, rebellious kind of masculinity. Maggie enjoys nothing more than gunning her bike, be it in her free time or on professional missions. She regularly exercises Chicken on the plantations, her "off-road playground" (Otter 2014a, 201). "Screaming up the highway," doing "[s]ome good healthy lorry-dodging" (34), allows Maggie to let off steam and process emotional turmoil (2016b, 188). It is the kick she craves as an adrenaline junkie, the "rush of freedom, the thin line between life and death" (51). Even a potential lover's mettle is tested by taking him on a scary ride on the Chicken (201).

Maggie looks and acts the man in other ways. While she is heterosexual, the combative, short-haired journalist has the looks of a "butch" (109) and is treated "as one of the boys" as soon as she enters the Alpha Garage run by Piet (2016b, 46), who "like[s] to imagine her combating criminals at every turn" (2014a, 146). Her "uniform" consists of "black t-shirt, cut-off jeans and short Docs" in summer (2014a, 48) and an equally black long-sleeved/long-legged outfit, supplemented by a fleece and motorcycle leather jacket, in winter (2016b, 37–38). An expert on cars, she also has a reputation for abusing them during car chases with criminals (2014a, 113, 155). She is a drinker who likes her drinks strong (2014a, 62, 2016b, 99), tends to wolf down her food (2016b, 53) and fights pain with pain (2014a, 75). In an interview, Otter describes Maggie as "a crime reporter on steroids […]. It's just that she's a Maggie, not a Mark" (Otter 2014b, par. 23, 42). Maggie also acts the male part within the family. In the absence of their parents, she is the provider for her war-traumatised brother Christo, thus taking the traditionally masculine role. In between the two novels, Maggie becomes a mother, but for the duration of *Karkloof Blue* her 11-year-old son Leo conveniently stays with his father in Johannesburg. Clearly, Maggie's maternal side is not (yet) an issue that Otter wants to explore.

Maggie's resistant agency is infused with an anger that is not characteristic of all female detectives. Rage over injustice is what spurs her criminal investigations. Anger at being compromised by male criminals and bosses alike triggers the fight in her and leads her to attack verbally and physically – time and again (Otter 2014a, 9, 115, 173, 188, 225, 2016b, 43, 77, 84, 106, 206). When she narrowly escapes a kidnapping and is rescued from a crashed car in *Balthasar's Gift*, Maggie does not feel relief, but anger: "Her head was pounding and her body felt weak, but a new energy was coursing through her. It was her old friend, anger, icing her body so that her teeth chattered" (163). In this particular example, Maggie is incensed as much by the fact that the criminals managed to get away as by the fact that she was cheated of a story and that Ed, a male colleague, presumed that she was actually in need of rescuing. Ed had got in her way "by acting the hero. Bloody idiot" (163). Ed's faux pas here is applying normative standards of femininity as the interpretative frame for Maggie's situation "as a female;" despite all the cues that she evinces in her daily behaviour and personality, he is unable to concede – or even acknowledge – Maggie's identification with the powerful codes of masculinity. Maggie's rage is more than the motivation that drives her to investigate – it is also her way of performing masculinity. She does so by giving explicit expression to her outrage such that it becomes a form of political activism as delineated by Halberstam (1993, 189).

Maggie's anger reflects her author's and is part and parcel of Otter's feminist project. Otter's German reviewers, in particular, have emphasised the angry quality of her writing (Krekeler 2013, par. 16, König 2013, par. 4).[21] When asked by Jonathan Amid what being a feminist means to her, Otter mentions, among other things, her anger. Persistent gender-based injustice, gender-based violence and the slow progress to gender equality make her "furiously angry" (Otter 2014b, par. 45). Maggie is a way for Otter to channel her own rage. Unlike the female perpetrators I have examined, Maggie does not kill, yet the anger that she feels when she faces the perpetrators is within a hair's breadth of fuelling retaliatory murder. Having tracked down Vincent Ndlela, rapist of a baby girl, "[s]he felt the heft of the gun in her hand. Anger iced her veins and her finger hovered on the trigger" (2014a, 243). Similarly, in her confrontation with serial killer John Evans, aka Alex Field, Maggie is wild with rage; she knees him and, training the gun on his face, keeps on kicking him violently with her boots (2016b, 229). Both times, she is stopped by her male allies. In the second incident, it is the police captain Solomon Njima, an unmistakeable representative of the male law, who shouts, "'Enough Maggie!'" and handcuffs the criminal (229). Defeated as John already is, the act of handcuffing him is superfluous. Handcuffing in this case does not serve the practical purpose of containing a male criminal, but is rather a symbolic act aimed at containing the threat of *female* violence. After all, Maggie's violent outrage is hard to halt. Female violence, as Halberstam reminds us, contests the coupling of power with masculinity (1993, 191), and this is where its threat to hegemonic masculinity lies. The police captain's intervention is also a reminder that Maggie's weapon, as an investigative journalist, is not the gun, but the pen. Maggie's revenge has to stay within the confines of the law. What further distinguishes Maggie's masculine gender performance from that of the female perpetrators is that her rebellion does not lie in "indifference to the law," as Halberstam suggests for her model of female masculinity; hers is rather an open "opposition of the law" (1998, 9). Maggie's professional role obliges her first and foremost to engage with the representatives of the male law, be they police or media,[22] and this means a relentless tug of war. Her open resistance to her superiors causes her to be "called in front of the board and reprimanded" only two weeks into her new job as

---

21   "'Balthasars Vermächtnis' ist die wütende, schnelle, handkantenharte Ouvertüre für eine hoffentlich lange Serie" (Krekeler 2013, par. 16). "*Balthasars Vermächtnis* ist ein wütender Roman. Zu Recht" (König 2013, par. 4).
22   Maggie's direct superior in *Karkloof Blue* is a woman, Tina Naidoo, yet she is entirely compliant with and answerable to an all-male board of directors (93–94). Despite female middle management, *The Gazette* is still a male-dominated company.

news editor of *The Gazette* in *Karkloof Blue* (2016b, 99). Her bosses repeatedly threaten to take her off the case (Otter 2014a, 40–42, 2016b, 49, 71–72, 77, 82–84, 95). In *Balthasar's Gift*, she is suspended for two weeks (2014a, 246); in *Karkloof Blue*, she is explicitly forbidden from writing the case up in the media. In both instances, Maggie continues investigating anyway. However, as she is unable to flout the law, she must now operate covertly.

At this point, it is important to examine how Maggie's gender performance intersects with race. Two strategies are apparent in Otter's novels. First, Maggie's gender performance is characterised not only by an angry masculinity, but by a rejection of (White) femininity. This dis-alignment with White femininity is accompanied by a simultaneous affiliation with Black femininity, especially Black female masculinity. There are a number of ways in which Maggie distances herself from conventional femininity. Maggie is explicit about the fact that she does not have and does not need typically female skills such as arranging flowers and doing small talk at dinner parties (2014a, 113). "[W]omanly pursuits like having their nails done and drinking cappuccinos with their girlfriends at the mall" are outside the range of her interests (2014a, 149–150), and she does not frequent the "sort of restaurant[s] women liked" (2016b, 178). As important as her explicit rejection of the traditionally feminine is her rejection of Afrikaner culture and thus – as a woman – the stereotypical femininity that pertains to this ethnicity. Maggie is called a "renegade Afrikaner" by her boss (2014a, 41), and later on she recounts the very particular experience that turned her into one. The mother of Maggie's school friend Lynn "was too brassy, too blonde, too busty, too lipsticked to fit in with the other tannies" (133). The fact that she was a prostitute, and looked like one, made her and her daughter outcasts in the Afrikaner community (50) and also vulnerable to violence. When Lynn and her mother were murdered by one of her mother's regular clients and it later turned out that he was "one of the *dominees* from church" (204),[23] Maggie "turned her back on church, refus[ing] to return. She became a renegade" (204). With Lynn's death, Maggie loses her only ally, as well as all respect for the religion brought to South Africa by her Calvinist forefathers. Her contempt extends to the "self-important buffoons who ruled church and state for so many decades, who pretended that their cause was righteous and found justification for it in the Bible" (261).

Maggie's own mother, by contrast, embodies the ideal of the traditional Afrikaner woman. Unpacking the origins of that ideal, McClintock notes that "[t]he family household was seen as the last bastion beyond British control

---

23 "Dominee" is Afrikaans for a minister in the Dutch Reformed Church.

and the cultural power of Afrikaner motherhood was mobilised in the service of white nation-building" (1995, 379). All the while, however, women were "denied any formal political power" (379). As a dutiful housewife whose favourite place is the kitchen and who is forever cooking (2014a, 187), Maggie's mother fills the role assigned to her by Afrikaner patriarchy. When her son Christo goes AWOL from the army, she is shamed to the extent that she and her husband have to move away, as they can no longer show their faces in church in Pietermaritzburg (90). Maggie repudiates everything that her mother embodies and never forgives her for effectively abandoning her and Christo by giving in to the pressures of church. Maggie's female masculinity is thus also a contestation of the kind of religious Afrikaner femininity that her mother represents. By choosing such angry masculinity as a woman, Maggie resonates with and powerfully contests the icon of the *volksmoeder*, the mother of the Afrikaner people. McClintock discusses this culturally influential social category as manifested in the *Vrouemonument* (women's monument) that was erected in 1913 in memory of the female victims of the Anglo-Boer War. The monument takes "the form of a circular domestic enclosure, where women stand weeping with their children." In this way, according to McClintock, "women's martial role as fighters and farmers was purged of its indecorously militant potential [...] enshrin[ing] Afrikaner womanhood as neither militant nor political, but as suffering, stoical and self-sacrificing" (1995, 378). Maggie's rage, in particular, serves to expose this long-standing containment of women's more assertive and agentive roles.

And yet, while Maggie unambiguously rejects stereotypical Afrikaner femininity, the way in which she simultaneously differentiates herself from the White English-speaking population – this time by means of social class, rather than gender – gives rise to a certain paradox. In many ways, Maggie confirms the stereotype of the strained relationship between Whites of British extraction and White Afrikaners in South Africa, acting out the old enmity between Afrikaner colonialists and British imperialists. Maggie notes a sense of entitlement and self-importance in the comportment of the former pupils of an English-speaking private school (2014a, 71). She, by contrast, "felt no such ownership" (71). This is also the reason for her break-up with Spike. She does not fit in with his family: "She would always be the discordant note, the Afrikaans underclass piercing the bubble of his family's WASP privilege" (2016b, 22). More than once she criticises "the tiny world of the wealthy" into which Spike had briefly introduced her for the fact that even now, post apartheid, they "own everything" (39, 40). On the one hand, Maggie's opposition to the White, wealthy population of British descent has the advantage of making visible the differences within White South Africa. Accordingly, the invisibility of

Whiteness that Dyer criticises, along with its concomitant normative power, is challenged (1988, 3–4): White, too, becomes a colour. On the other hand, her self-differentiation from Whites of British heritage also positions her more clearly as one of the Afrikaner Whites whose values she contests so forcefully.

At the same time as Maggie distances herself from traditional White Afrikaner femininity, she seeks and finds allies in Black women, especially those of the angry, avenging type. In *Balthasar's gift*, the most remarkable case in point is Cora Ncube, sister of Pontius Ncube, who was killed by Balthasar's father because he was his son's lover. After Pontius's murder more than a decade earlier, Cora was taken on by the Meiring family "as part of the reparations" to enable her to sustain the Ncube family after Pontius's death (2014a, 217). Cold, tall Cora is silent for most of the novel, until Maggie approaches her and she offers to help the journalist (250). As an invisible insider in the Meiring household, and having waited for her moment all these years, Cora now takes charge over her employer and metes out justice. She rescues Maggie from Lourens's clutches. Knowing that he is about to be exposed, Lourens has set fire to the farm in an attempt to annihilate himself, his wife Sanet and the 11-year-old girl Mbali whom he has been holding captive, as well as Maggie and Cora. " 'Stop!' said a voice. In the doorway, holding Meiring's gun [...] was Cora" (264). Cora takes the commander's chair, confronts the Meirings with the facts behind Pontius's murder and identifies Lourens as the murderer of his own son (267). In an apocalyptic scene, she directs Maggie, with Lourens, Sanet and Mbali in their car, to drive through a wall of fire to safety (269–270). *Karkloof Blue* continues female interracial cooperation by featuring the grown-up Mbali as Maggie's intrepid Black female ally. Mbali now works in the PR department of Sentinel, where Maggie bumps into her: "Fourteen years ago, Mbali Sibanyoni had been a little girl in danger. Now she was a woman in a sleek corporate suit" (34). Initially loyal to her employer, Mbali later becomes instrumental in disclosing the company's criminal activities (233). In the novel's final scene, we learn that Mbali is to be Maggie's new business partner: "Sibanyoni and Cloete would soon be setting up shop in Durban as private investigators" (234). Another openly resistant Black woman in the same novel is Hope Phiri, a scientist and expert on the Karkloof Blue butterfly who speaks out about the ecological damage wrought by Sentinel (130). In an attempt to silence her, Hope is severely beaten up by Sentinel's henchmen, but her resilience and outrage triumph: "A fire burned in her eyes. 'Angry. So fucking angry. If someone gave me a knife and one of those guys, I would murder him with no compunction. [...] And I think I would enjoy it' " (160). In the end she resorts not to killing, but to reporting the crime to the police despite the criminals' threats (163).

The way in which Maggie joins forces with angry Black women is reminiscent of Mackenzie's heroine Jade, who similarly aligns herself with Ntombi in *Pale Horses*. As we have seen, both Jade and Ntombi take the extra step of killing the perpetrators (Mackenzie 2012b, 286). How are we to read this strategy of White female investigators seeking and forging ties with Black women in acts of female masculinity? Speaking about *Balthasar's Gift*, Otter explains that it was part of her "feminist agenda" to "give voice to the voiceless and agency to those who are usually in the background of other people's lives" (2014b, par. 41). Given the fact that, as women, White authors and White investigators share the plight of patriarchal hegemony with their Black sisters, but, as Whites, are also historically complicit in their subjugation, such an act of "giving voice" must be examined critically. At least potentially, it harbours the danger of reinforcing racial hierarchies. There is evidence for and against such neo-colonial tendencies in Otter's novels. As insistently as Maggie rejects White Afrikaner femininity, she does not explicitly acknowledge White women's complicity in the racist project. McClintock details how "[w]hite women are both colonized and colonizers, ambiguously complicit in the history of African dispossession" (1995, 379). While Maggie is insistent about her difference from the wealthy descendants of upper-class English South Africans, she does not recognise her own status as privileged in comparison to that of Black women. She likes to view herself as the saviour, as "the last person still asking questions, a lone light in the dark" (2014a, 215) – albeit with a certain irony at times, as when she calls herself a "self-appointed hero" who "had ridden in on her steel charger to sort things out" (137).[24] She is plagued by feelings of guilt on several occasions, but these are unrelated to race. Mostly, she feels guilt for not living up to the high moral aims that she sets herself as a saviour and advocate for the disenfranchised – for not having reacted to Balthasar's request for help when he was still alive (2014a, 16), for putting her brother at risk and being unable to protect him (2014a, 246, 2016b, 194), or for endangering Hope (2016b, 130–131). Maggie has a patronising side that is commented on by several characters, but is seldom reflected on by Maggie herself, let alone with regard to race.

Despite her lack of self-reflexivity as regards potential complicity in racism, Maggie's actions and results in both of her cases take a clear stance against White racism and – in *Karkloof Blue*, in particular – against the injustices committed by White people during apartheid. Importantly, too, Black female masculinity is acknowledged as positive and powerful, rather than erased and

---

24 She is also reproached for her "saviour complex" by both her brother and her boss, which functions as a qualifier (2016b, 41, 147).

punished, in both of Otter's novels. This is significant if we recall that Black female masculinity resonates with the racist stereotype of the Black criminal woman. However, Halberstam notes that "there is a difference between racist representations of supposedly failed femininity and a potentially queer or at least subcultural representation of a potent black butchness" (181). Maggie's alignment with Cora, Hope and Mbali is politically effective, but it remains to be seen whether it will develop into a true partnership between Black and White female masculinity that involves more than an occasional ceding of power on the part of the White investigator, as when Maggie hands over control to Cora during the rescue mission in *Balthasar's Gift*. The fact that the new agency established by Maggie and Mbali is to be called "Sibanyoni and Cloete" (2016b, 234), with Mbali's name featuring first, is a sign that the series may be moving in that direction.

4.2 Cases of Premature Burials of the Past: the Female Detective as (Contained) Agent of Justice

True to Otter's resolution, neither of the novels that she has published so far features female corpses. The author has repeatedly stated her discomfort with the sexy female corpse in crime novels, the problematics of which have been exposed by Bronfen (see my discussion of Penny Lorimer's female victims). Otter says that she is tired of this representational practice and finds it dull and disrespectful to women: "I took it as my personal challenge to step up imaginatively and not start a book with the dead, naked, mutilated corpse of a young woman" (2014b, par. 39). As a consequence, all her dead bodies are male, although some still pander to genre expectations. Balthasar, for example, offers a variation on the spectacular death. From a distance, we see his bleeding body through Maggie's eyes, lying on the veranda of Pietermaritzburg's HIV House (Otter 2014a, 11). Together with a group of other onlookers, she witnesses the paramedics' frantic but futile efforts to revive him, while she is simultaneously on the hunt for information to write her story. When she realises that Balthasar was the person who called her a few weeks earlier asking for help in exposing a fake AIDS cure, she asks herself whether "someone [had] to die nowadays to get her attention" (13). Thus, she self-reflexively recalls the media's problematic obsession with spectacular crime. The spectacular in *Karkloof Blue* lies in the surroundings of the corpse – Howick Falls form an impressive backdrop. What turns out to be Dave Bloom's dead body we see as a mere "slash of white" on the blackened rocks, through the eyes of a passer-by alerted by a pile of clothing at the edge of the falls (2016b, 9). Here again the body functions as a cipher, at least initially. In the case of the seven young freedom fighters, the Umlazi Seven, we witness the ghastly crime itself across time, mainly through the eyes of the perpetrators. We do not know who they are as they secretly poison the equally anonymous victims, then burn and bury them deep in the forest (68, 96–97). The mystery is for Maggie and for the police to solve. None of these male dead bodies is entirely without individuality, but they all exemplify Otter's main concern, which lies less with the individual victim than with the structures and systems that he represents – structures that the perpetrators are determined to deny or to conceal. Before we examine those structures, however, it is important to dwell for a moment on the particularities of Maggie's gaze and the kind of spectatorial position that she assumes.

It is striking how frequently Maggie's conflicts with her various superiors revolve around the nature of her, the journalist's, gaze on and relationship to the subject she is writing about. Both Maggie's news editor in *Balthasar's Gift*, Zacharius, and his predecessor remind her, " 'Jeez, Maggie [...] the verb is report. You are a reporter. It's not your job to get in there and get your hands dirty' " (2014a, 87). "We will report what [the police] say, and only what they say" (40). With this, they stand for "neutral observ[ance]" (174), "objectivity" (174), "professional distance" (95) and "professional indifference" (99), as well as for submission to the state's justice system. Maggie's stance, by contrast, is to relate to the victims, to care for them (87), to identify with them (41). Maggie decides against keeping herself distanced from what she sees; her gaze is an empathic one, and she cannot help but involve herself (91, 99, 174). Her radical refusal to remain objective in the face of injustice is also an ethical stance, in that she will not exempt herself from responsibility by way of distance and refuses to objectify the people she looks at and writes about. Moreover, her position opens up a path for alternative justice. In the light of feminist legal scholars' critique of the seeming neutrality and objectivity of the legal system as adhering to male standards (Van Marle and Bonthuys 2007, 29), as well as their claim that any alternatives to this model must acknowledge a person's relationality to other people – with regard to rights as well as responsibility and culpability (Hudson 2012, 392) – Maggie's decision to get involved appears not as unprofessional, but as principled. In fact, Maggie seems to represent a kind of journalism that takes seriously the affective dimension of communication. Lelia Green and Steven Maras maintain that impartial objectivity in journalism is an illusion (2002, 19). As the former BBC correspondent Martin Bell puts it, there is "nothing object-like about the relationship between the reporter and the event" (24). On this basis, Green and Maras advocate a journalism that acknowledges (both the journalist's and the reader's) affectivity in ethical ways, without neglecting the media's established "responsibilities concerning democracy, the provision of information, informed debate, and accuracy" (28).

In *Karkloof Blue*, in particular, Otter challenges the idea of journalistic objectivity and detachment and emphasises the need to adopt different principles. On the one hand, it is impossible for Maggie to remain an emotionally distanced onlooker when one of the murder victims in the novel is her own brother, Christo. On the other, the media's involvement in broader power structures is exposed, giving the lie to the notion of media impartiality. Formerly "snuggled up to the City Hall and the courts complex" (2014a, 202), the *Gazette*'s offices have been relocated to an office park on the outskirts of Pietermaritzburg (2016b, 14), close to Sentinel's corporate headquarters (33). Corporate interference is rife. As neighbours and paper suppliers, Sentinel are able to exert direct influence over the *Gazette*'s board members and journalists (77, 83). In addition, they secretly infiltrate the news team with a spy (204), all for the purpose of camouflaging their criminal activities and allies. Controlled by criminals, such journalism becomes complicit and devoid of justice. Even though Maggie battles against it, her own journalistic endeavours, too, endanger a life. In an attempt to raise public awareness of Sentinel's ecological crimes, she quotes Hope, the biologist, who is subsequently targeted by the criminals and nearly killed. Here journalism, even of the responsible kind, is depicted as a double-edged sword in the fight for justice. Maggie's final move out of journalism at the end of *Karkloof Blue*, when she decides to become a private investigator, is consistent with her determination to combat injustice, but even this does not render her entirely free of the media frame: the agency's first case, she tells us, will be paid for by a newspaper, the *Joburg Sun* (234).

In *Balthasar's Gift*, Maggie exposes the slow but devastating violence of South Africa's AIDS pandemic, highlighting its strongly gendered and racialised components. The homosexual Afrikaner AIDS activist Balthasar is killed by his own father, Lourens, who fears having to admit his own HIV positive status. Balthasar, rejected by his father for his sexual orientation, is the only person who knows that his father is HIV positive. He also knows that his father did not kill his lover Pontius in self-defence all those years ago. Using this leverage over his father to pressurise him into confessing his HIV status and his infidelity to his mother is what gets Balthasar killed. The underlying reason for his murder is thus HIV/AIDS denialism, as well as denialism in relation to homosexuality. While investigating Lourens's crime, Maggie also brings to light the larger crime of then South African president Thabo Mbeki's AIDS denialism. Mbeki and his Department of Health – both in the novel and in reality – denied that HIV actually causes AIDS. They also questioned antiretrovirals (ARVs) as an effective antidote, claiming they were toxic (Otter 2014a, 227, Decoteau 2013, 144). This attitude let the virus spread unabated and contributed to the deaths of almost half a million South Africans at the turn of the millennium

(Decoteau 2013, 144). With the help of key figures such as Lindiwe Dlamini, the head of the AIDS mission, who used to work with Balthasar, Nkosazana Mbanjwa, who looks after the children in Balthasar's private orphanage, and eleven-year-old Mbali, the eldest of the children in Balthasar's care, Maggie is able to document the multitudinous ways in which those affected with the virus and their families suffer. These include stigmatisation and grief (Otter 2014a, 92, 78, 135); children being raised by grandparents and siblings in the absence of parents (92, 94, 139–140, 188); baby rape (93); mother-to-child transfer of the virus and the concomitant diseases affecting everybody, including babies and small children, once they develop AIDS (99–102, 226); denialism on the part of men, who refuse to be tested (179, 192); exacerbation of poverty (60); and erosion of communities (124). Maggie's investigation renders visible the unspectacular, systemic forms of violence ensuing from the AIDS crisis and puts at the centre its victims, mostly marginalised people of colour, who are forgotten by the government (184). In Hudson's terms, Maggie's fictional justice consists of accommodating, of bringing in those who are "outside the constituency of justice" (Hudson 2012, 389): "Balthasar's constituency, the hundreds and thousands of people with AIDS and no recourse to life-saving drugs" (Otter 2014a, 202). What is more, Maggie serves reflective justice, insofar as she draws attention to structural forms of violence, normally inadmissible in the formal criminal justice system (Hudson 2012, 393). Besides portraying the effect of the government's denialism, the novel shows how it facilitates crimes such as the rape of babies and the fake AIDS cure industry. The government's claim that ARVs are toxic is depicted as playing into the hands of criminal business people and as furthering exploitation of the most vulnerable. Maggie attends a court session in the case against Dr Schloegel, a German selling a fake AIDS cure. When asked by the judge why she spent large sums of money on Schloegel's vitamins rather than on ARVs, the mother, whose son has since died, replies: " 'We were told they made people sick.' " Maggie fumes, "This rumour had gone from a whisper to a rumble. If the government didn't trust the medication enough to make it universally available, then people didn't trust it either" (Otter 2014a, 59). In the course of her investigation, Maggie uncovers a whole network of criminals behind this travesty: "[A]s a crime lord you fed AIDS victims a cure that potentially hastened their deaths, or at the very least did nothing to obviate it, then you lent the grieving families thousands of rands to hold a funeral. When they couldn't pay you back, you turned them into Schloegel's Herbals salespeople. And the money just kept on rolling in" (197). Moreover, the government's attitude fosters myths like "sex with a virgin will cure HIV" (228), and therefore "[r]ape of both women and children is part and parcel of the spreading of HIV" (229).

Alongside the South African government, Otter's novel features another, individual, AIDS denialist: the murderer Lourens. This staunchly religious Afrikaner patriarch hushes up the fact that he is HIV positive. His status, which is the result of extramarital sex, is incompatible with the religious beliefs that he purports to uphold: "It burnt his soul, this responsibility to tell his wife. It was admitting failure, a weakness. The crack in the dam" (170). This makes it easier for him to remain blind to his own role in contracting the disease and instead to put the blame on the women he had sex with (170) and to denounce the HIV virus as something "evil" brought to "the innocent" by homosexuals from overseas (104). Thabo Mbeki's reasoning behind his denialist stance – which is not touched on in the novel – reveals a similar distancing of Africa from the rest of the world. According to Posel, Mbeki insisted that "AIDS in Africa was different from AIDS in the West." In Mbeki's view, AIDS in Africa "was a primarily heterosexual epidemic [...] unlike the largely homosexual incidence of AIDS in the West" (Posel 2008, 16). Because Western experience cannot be superimposed on African reality (16), ARVs come to be seen as un-African (18).[25] Otter, who locates Balthasar's first homosexual relationship – with Pontius – in South Africa itself, and who has him travel to Europe, work there in a hospital, see his partner Stephen die and come back to South Africa healthy and with a mission to help those with AIDS (2014a, 27, 54, 265), contests Mbeki's and Lourens's trajectory of differentiating themselves from the evil and homosexuality in the "West".

As well as rejecting the claim that AIDS and sexuality are fundamentally different in Europe and Africa, Otter repudiates the notion of a radical break between the apartheid past and post-apartheid present, as invoked by Mbeki in his rhetoric portraying the new South Africa as a nation reborn from a wretched past (Posel 2008, 19). Repeatedly, Otter draws parallels between the horrors of the AIDS crisis and the horrors of apartheid: then and now, a high death toll among children and young people (2014a, 143, 145); then and now, children raised by their grandparents (188); then and now, rape as a tool of war (229). Otter's depiction of the crime of denialism in South Africa, "one of the

---

25 Posel explains the controversy surrounding the nature of HIV/AIDS during Mbeki's presidency with reference to the "symbolic politics of the 'new' South Africa in transition from the horrors of apartheid" (2008, 18), linking Mbeki's AIDS denialism with his promotion of an African Renaissance as the basis for his nation-building project. According to Posel, the imagery of sexuality that Mbeki associates with orthodox understandings of HIV/AIDS evokes "the spectre of the past: the colonial nightmare that imprisoned the black mind, enslaved the black body and degraded the pursuit of pleasure. It is exactly that which the African Renaissance has to vanquish: the demon within 'our African selves'" (Posel 2011, 142).

few developing countries with the resources to have made a significant dent in the epidemic if it had acted concertedly and unambiguously" (Posel 2008, 18), can also be considered a symbolic move towards doing justice to those directly or indirectly afflicted by the disease, especially Black women living in poverty. Given that those who suffer most from HIV/AIDS are Black women, the consequences of any form of denialism have a gender and race dimension (Otter 2014a, 179, 228–229). According to the AIDS Foundation South Africa, "South Africa has the highest prevalence of HIV/AIDS compared to any other country in the world with 5.6 million people living with HIV. [...] Women face a greater risk of HIV infection. [...] The difference is greatest in the 15 to 24 age group, where three young women for every one young man are infected" (2017, par. 1–5). Adding the category of race, Albertyn argues that HIV/AIDS has further entrenched inequality, especially for Black women: "Women bear the greatest social and financial burden of domestic and caring work, especially in the context of the AIDS pandemic. Gender inequalities mean that women are more vulnerable to HIV than men, infected in higher numbers, and at a younger age" (Albertyn 2007, 82). The fictional empowerment of Black women such as Cora, Nkosazana and, most significantly, young Mbali becomes all the more significant in the light of these depressing realities. By using and satisfying the crime genre's preference for spectacular, event-based violence in order to bring into focus the underlying structural violence of the AIDS pandemic and its gendered and racial aspects, Otter, much like Lorimer, successfully establishes the power of popular fiction as a form of "currency" for the dissemination of these truths.

Maggie's case in *Karkloof Blue* again highlights the impact of violent structures and the links between South Africa's past and present. The novel features various crimes against human beings and the natural world. All of them revolve around the Pietermaritzburg-based forestry company Sentinel. The murder of Dave Bloom, a long-time Sentinel employee, was instigated by Xolani Mpondo, the company's current CEO. When Dave realised that one of his colleagues was doing research into biological weapons, he threatened Xolani with exposure unless he stopped logging the Karkloof forest, natural habitat of the endangered Karkloof Blue butterfly (Otter 2016b, 233). Maggie's brother Christo also dies because he knows too much. He finds out that Xolani has been paying hush money to John Evans, aka Alex Field, so he is killed by John. John knows about Sentinel's secret laboratory, which goes back to the apartheid era, when he was a security policeman working for a unit that experimented in biological warfare. Moreover, in the 1980s, John was responsible for killing the Umlazi Seven, a group of young ANC freedom fighters who were believed to have blown up a power station. After they had been poisoned with anthrax-laced food, their bodies were burnt and buried in the Karkloof forest by John and his helpers (207, 227–228, 230). This secret killing in the past is the reason that John launches a militant campaign, supposedly fuelled by ecological concern, against Sentinel when they announce plans to log the Karkloof Forest – home to both the butterfly and the apartheid grave. Dave's murder thus simultaneously leads Maggie to present-day corporate and ecological crimes *and* returns her to apartheid crimes, as old bones are dug up in the Karkloof forest.

What are the implications of this explicit link between the violent apartheid days of the 1980s and the equally violent times in South Africa's young democracy 30 years later? What Otter is painting here is a picture of continuity that questions notions of radical change between the two different eras in the country's history. Sentinel's "lab within the lab" has always been used for research into biological weapons (168) and has always been a destructive tool of war. Sentinel's obsession with making profits and past and present governments' demand for weapons have led to a collaboration beneficial to both sides. Maggie learns that in the old days Sentinel's director "was offering certain high-up members of the government [their] research facilities in return for favours. [...] Access to land that Sentinel could turn into plantations, logging permits, fewer obstacles in buying up pristine grasslands" (168). The present government, too, is interested in Sentinel's research (233). However, to realise the immanent violence of structures, it takes people. Given the inherent power of the structures, the individual actors may change – both the government and Sentinel's CEO are new – but their interactions with the structures will lead to similar violent results. What is more, the agents of the old days are still alive, as is their knowledge and their interest in protecting themselves from exposure. John chose to conceal his actions and never asked for amnesty during the TRC hearings (231). His helpers, Chief Mjoli and Mandla Cele, also "want to bury the past" (157, see also 230). Both sides violently oppose Maggie's probing into this complex web of collaboration and complicity that crosses not only colour lines, but gender lines. The researcher who runs Sentinel's secret lab is Susannah Hynde, while Sentinel's main ally at *The Gazette* is the editor Tina Naidoo. The agency of these two women contributes significantly to the crimes that are committed.

Posel and Simpson argue that it is necessary for complex truths, "moral ambiguities born of the politics of complicity or collaboration," to emerge if we are to process and understand the past (2002, 10). Enfolding multiple layers of agency as it does, Otter's novel illustrates the value of crime fiction as a site where past and present complexities can be explored. Depicting the perpetrators' interaction with the structures is a further necessity in this process, according to Posel, as it allows insight into the causes of past violence and may help to transcend it (168). Otter's fictional version of the past reveals various causes for such interaction. Sentinel's former manager shared the racist ideology of the apartheid government, but he was also very keen to further his business. Falling paper prices forced him to find new land for more plantations, so good relations with the government were useful (2016b, 167). John, as a secret policeman and spymaster, was clearly a henchman of the apartheid government. We can infer that his motives were ideological. His Black accomplices opposed the government, but disliked the violent resistance of the Umlazi Seven. Instead, they chose "a middle route, a dangerous straddling of two worlds that pays now" (96). Although Otter's fictional apartheid crimes are motivated as much by racism as they are by opportunism and greed, it is the latter that fuel crime in the democratic era, supported by criminal structures that survived the end of apartheid. The persistent crimes to which corporate greed, in particular, leads are illustrated succinctly: destruction of natural forest, the country's natural heritage (10) – including trees, all the other plants that grow there, rich soil and animal life (33, 63) – erosion and water shortages (64), pollution of the environment and damage to the health of paper mill workers caused by the chemicals used in paper production (167), as well as retrenchment of workers without compensation (211).

It is interesting to note that Mackenzie's most recent novel, *Bad Seeds* (2017), follows a very similar course. The violent structure that Mackenzie's novel exposes is a nuclear research centre, used for nuclear warfare then and now. As in *Karkloof Blue*, the main agents have changed with the onset of democracy, but those formerly in power continue to exert influence. In this respect, both authors seem to agree with Anthony Butler that "[t]he institutional executors of apartheid – in business, the media, the judiciary, and the universities – avoided admission of (and so reflection upon) their own culpability" (2009, 53) before the TRC. While Mackenzie's novel frames the South African present in terms of the latent threat of present and future international terrorism, in *Karkloof Blue* Otter depicts the present as still heavily influenced by the past. She generates a strong impression that not enough justice has been done with regard to South Africa's apartheid past and explicitly refers to the work of the TRC. As Maggie reflects,

> South Africa had a history of secrets, buried under the weight of second chances. In their rush to reconcile under the rainbow banner, the government had given those who'd confessed to apartheid-era crimes their own walk to freedom. During the Truth and Reconciliation Commission, many of their secret crimes had been unearthed, but there were hundreds of families still living without knowing what the apartheid state had done to their loved ones. [...] Peace had been achieved, but not justice.
> OTTER 2016b, 91

By returning to these "secret crimes" in her crime fiction, Otter aims to provide an imaginary space to continue and complement the work of the TRC. When Maggie listens to Thandi Mshenge and seeks to establish the identity of the bodies in the mass grave in the forest, she caters to a perceived need to unearth more secrets than the TRC was able to uncover. Maggie works to restore the respect that is due to the families of the victims by providing knowledge about what happened, holding the perpetrators accountable and giving the relatives a body to bury. This allows for a reintegration of their losses into their lives and for closure. Given the necessarily incomplete achievements of any truth commission, crime fiction takes on a remedial role. In their reflections on the TRC, Hamber and Wilson touch on what Maggie calls the "rush to reconcile". They note that "[t]ruth commissions often operate on a time frame which is highly curtailed and limited, and which requires a premature process of dealing with the past from survivors of atrocities for whom the process of grieving often lasts a lifetime" (2002, 36). Literature can prolong and continue a truth commission's limited frame. This is particularly true for crime fiction, the genre that serially uncovers the past in order to account for the present.

For Otter, the key figure in this endeavour is not the victim, but her female detective, who, as a journalist, becomes the victim's advocate in the public space of the media and, thanks to this power, guides the police and can serve as their corrective. Maggie has close ties to the police throughout both novels. In *Balthasar's Gift*, she has the police liaison officer, Thandi Mathonsi, who briefs her daily, on speed dial (2014a, 9): "Tall and clever, she had an attitude as sharp as her designer spectacles and knew how to keep a journalist's appetite for more satiated without stepping outside her political boundaries" (2014a, 14). Maggie retains good relations with the police in *Karkloof Blue* through Solomon, the police captain, who develops a love interest in her. Yet all the while, Maggie is not uncritical of the police. She knows that they are insufficiently resourced and do not always have the best reputation (2016b, 149, 182) and she repeatedly questions the police's versions of the crimes she is faced with. For example, she can prove that Balthasar's death is not a "a robbery gone wrong," as the police claim (2014a, 14), and nor is Dave's a "suicide" (2016b, 55). At the end of both novels, she personally hands over the perpetrators to the police and to state justice (2014a, 254, 270, 2016b, 225–229), either by delivering them directly into the hands of the police (Lourens) or by leading the police to the place where they are hiding (John). In *Karkloof Blue*, the narrator describes how, with back-up stationed at the edge of the forest, "Njima, Rankin, Maggie and three constables walked the path to Karkloof Extension 7. [...] When they reached the chosen spot, Sol and his team stayed back and Maggie walked on *by herself*" (2016b, 225, my emphasis). Maggie confronts and defeats John the armed serial murderer single-handedly (2016b, 229). Only then does the police captain step in to arrest him. In a country where the criminal justice system is both inefficient and distrusted, resorting to investigative journalism as an alternative means to deliver justice seems reasonable. It is also actually practised in the contemporary South African real, as Antony Altbeker's true-crime account *Fruit of a Poisoned Tree* (2010) shows.

In line with her feminist mission, Otter substantially empowers her female detective to function as a necessary corrective to the police. However, there is an element of idealisation in her depiction of Maggie as acting without opposition from the police, while the absence of gender criticism of the institution itself elides the gender complexities inherent in this relationship. This contradiction in a feminist detective novel is further underlined by *Karkloof Blue*'s ending, which is basically a reinstatement of the patriarchal frame and an effacement of the female detective's work. The novel's last chapter features crime reporter Menzi Gumede's article in *The Gazette* entitled "Mass Graves – Apartheid-Era Deaths Explained" (2016b, 230–231), which publishes Maggie's findings and states that formal justice has been served. The media is given the last word, but Maggie has no voice. The epilogue also renders Maggie and her female "supporters in justice" invisible. Maggie is shown attending the funeral of the seven freedom fighters:

> Beautiful singing filled the tent. Women's and men's voices entwined in spirals rising up into the sky in sorrow and in thanks as guards of soldiers, dressed in Defence Force fatigues, carried in seven coffins and placed them, tenderly, respectfully, on seven tables. The guards moved to the sides of the tent, standing formally to attention. […] When the singing stopped, a man got up to speak.
>
> OTTER 2016b, 232

The man is the provincial premier, who delivers a speech in honour of the dead. The Umlazi Seven are given a belated but formal acknowledgement of their part in the struggle by a representative of the state. A certain kind of restorative justice is served, as they are finally returned by the state's soldiers to their families (2016b, 234) and are included in the nation's memory. What is surprising, however, is that the premier emphasises that it is "through the work of the police" that the families can now bury their sons (2016b, 232), while failing to mention the women who guided the police. The roles of both Thandi Mshenge, the sister of one of the dead teenagers, and Maggie go entirely unnoticed and unacknowledged by male, official South Africa. It was Thandi, distrustful of the police, who alerted Maggie to the possibility that one of the bodies found in Karkloof forest might be her brother's, and it was Maggie who pressured the police to follow up (2016b, 78–81) and who identified the web of perpetrators. In order to demonstrate the power and justice of the state, the female agency it depends on is elided completely. In the absence of any artful reminder, be it by Maggie or by the narrator, that qualifies such discursive violence towards women, the novel here effectively performs a patriarchal backlash against women, as Otter recasts her powerful, angry and effective female detective as a humble, invisible servant of the patriarchal law. One can only speculate as to whether the author is making a sardonic comment on the power of the status quo here. In any case, the episode is an illustration of the conflicting constraints to which the figure of the female detective finds herself subjected. The fact that Maggie gets Thandi's acknowledgement in the form of a "small smile and a nod" as she follows her brother's coffin does little to remedy this situation. The epilogue offers the closure required by the genre, as not only are the Umlazi Seven buried with dignity, but Sentinel gets a "new-style CEO" who closes down the company's secret lab and pledges to preserve Karkloof forest (233). At the same time, however, it also closes over the space previously opened up for Black and White female masculinity.

Otter's headstrong and fearless heroine speaks to a continued need for truth-finding beyond the confines of the present and the constituencies of the privileged. As an investigative journalist, she focuses on cases whose existence is denied or that are prematurely closed by official South Africa, leaving the victims without recognition and justice: AIDS denialism under Thabo Mbeki's presidency, as well as crimes committed under apartheid. Maggie's role vis-à-vis the state's justice system is corrective and remedial rather than radically resistant. The justice that she dispenses ultimately remains within the realm of the law, but by foregrounding structural violence that goes unnoticed by the law, by bringing to the centre those who are marginalised by the law, she shapes an understanding of the law as a more inclusive discursive space. As an angry, determined female journalist who looks like a butch, fights like a man, involves herself emotionally, exposes the media's potential for criminal complicity, repudiates traditional Afrikaner femininity and finds powerful allies in angry Black women, she herself changes the face of justice. And yet, neither the White woman Maggie nor the Black women Cora, Hope, Mbali and Thandi whom Otter invests with significant agency and envisages as agents of improved justice question or challenge the legal frame as such. While their powerful actions do not go entirely unnoticed and are validated by success, *Karkloof Blue* ends with the institutional frames firmly in place and firmly male. Justice is served as formerly disregarded or secret crimes and criminals are now identified and held accountable, but the female agency behind this act of justice is effaced. The ending of Otter's second novel functions to contain the female masculinity that she has been celebrating and blunts the force of what would otherwise be a powerful feminist intervention.

5   The Female Detective: Conclusion

A woman who investigates always reveals truths about her criminal cases, as well as about the institution from which she operates. With regard to the latter, Walton and Jones note that "feminist detective novels in general, explore – and exploit – the possibilities of individual agency even as they expose the limitations of that agency. In the process they convey to their audience, especially women readers, both a sense of potential empowerment and a consciousness of systemic oppression" (1999, 208). The three female detectives examined here confirm this observation. As a police detective, Persy Jonas brings out the gendered nature of the police and faces a patriarchal backlash as an empowered Coloured woman. In a similar vein, the investigative journalists Vee Johnson and Maggie Cloete leave no doubt about the – mostly White – male hegemony that dominates their newspapers. In the face of these stifling constraints, they all find remarkably effective spaces for resistance, and in this respect they are figures of female empowerment and agents of gender justice. Their resistant strategies include the solidaristic yet agonistic negotiation of forced choices between Persy and Marge, the recalibration of interracial power relations, as well as combining detective with sexual agency, in the case of Vee, and Maggie's angry female masculinity. Persy's and Maggie's tactics, in particular, also create possibilities for powerful female interracial cooperation and alignment. At the same time, however, the female detectives are undone as empowered agents. Although the patriarchal structures are exposed, they still contain, resist and sometimes even efface the women's agency as detectives. Overall, the institutional frame of the media seems to offer more leeway to women than that of the police. While Persy is not only denied institutional recognition at the end of the second novel, but expelled, Vee and Maggie see their investigative success acknowledged, albeit in attenuated ways. The police receive the credit for Maggie's work, while Vee's success is dampened by the realisation that she has been complicit in Xoliswa's suicide.

For Vee, the main obstacle is not so much the gendered nature of the media frame as the media's partiality and the fact that, as a journalist, she is prone to being instrumentalised. Maggie, too, finds that her newspaper, *The Gazette*, is increasingly being manipulated by criminal corporate interests. Golakai's and Otter's detective novels thus constitute reflections on the limits of investigative journalism within the justice process. This is noteworthy in light of the close relationship that exists between journalism and crime writing in South Africa. A number of the authors whose crime novels feature in this study – Nicol, Mackenzie, Orford and Otter – are or used to be journalists themselves. The same is true of many detective protagonists: Lorimer's Nix Mniki and Orford's Clare Hart are journalists, like Vee and Maggie. What is more, on the South African book market crime novels face serious competition from non-fictional, so-called "true-crime" books (also called "literary/creative non-fiction") based on investigative journalism. De Kock reads *both* crime fiction and non-fiction works of true crime as expressions of what he terms the "plot loss" that followed South Africa's transition to democracy (2016a, 3). For him, they have the same function: they are investigations "into the causes of the perceived inversion, or perversion, of the country's reimagined destiny, a derailing that has widely come to be regarded as criminal" (4).[26] I will return to crime fiction and non-fiction in the conclusion to this study. For now, it is sufficient to note how heavily invested in real crime the detectives discussed here are. The real referents are always present in the fictional crimes that they bring to the fore, and this is precisely what makes their investigations so valuable as social criticism.

What is striking about the female investigators is how they contest, critique, correct or remedy official truths established by the dominant order, be it represented by the police, the courts or the TRC. Both Maggie and Vee disprove police versions of the official record. Persy and Vee reopen cold cases, revealing new truths and revising existing ones. Maggie and Persy return to old cases that were disposed of too quickly or subjected to insufficient scrutiny at the time, thus correcting and complementing officially recognised truths. They warn against haste in transition, persuading us to look at the past again or to see the present differently. They act against forgetting, and their unrelenting insistence on truth functions as a constant reminder of the law's hegemonic tendencies and restricted ability to serve justice as a broad human good. It is true that Rowe, Golakai and Otter repeat some colonial, racist or misogynist practices and that, as agents of the justice system, their heroines become complicit with this system even as they expose its bias. Nevertheless, by exploring *alternatives* to "white man's justice" (Hudson 2012, 384), these novelists move beyond a mere critique of the established system. They adhere to the principle of discursiveness by allowing access to justice to those most vulnerable, forgotten or shunned by society – ungrievable lives, in Judith Butler's terminology

---

26   Earlier contributors to the debate include Hedley Twidle (2012), Mike Nicol (2013b) and Anneke Rautenbach (2013).

(2010): AIDS victims, isolated teenage daughters, orphans, street children, parents looking for their missing children, secretly buried freedom fighters. Exposing complex relations of dependency and complicity between individuals and the interaction between individuals and structures means taking into account the principle of relationality. Reflectiveness is involved when the categories that define what constitutes a crime, or what violations are susceptible to legal judgement, are amplified in order to include long-term structural violence. By having their protagonists strive for a more inclusive kind of justice – in terms of both gender and race – Rowe's, Golakai's and Otter's novels take a political stance and imagine a possible change to the face of justice.

Conclusion

As I was completing this study, the South African author and broadcast journalist Redi Tlhabi's biography of Fezekile Kuzwayo, the woman who laid rape charges against then president Jacob Zuma,[1] was being published to tremendous acclaim. Serendipity? Maybe. A testament to the pressing need to include the category of gender in any analysis of the South African present? Definitely.

What Tlhabi describes in her introduction as "neither an exhaustive nor an authoritative account of Fezekile's life" is in many ways a "true-crime" book, a creative non-fiction account that resonates not only with how I have approached post-transitional South African crime fiction, but with many of the concerns raised by the crime novels discussed here. The late Fezekile Ntsukela Kuzwayo, aka Khwezi, was an HIV-positive South African AIDS activist. As we learn from Tlhabi, Kuzwayo had close ties to Jacob Zuma that had their origins in the struggle.[2] Regarding him as an uncle, Kuzwayo frequently visited Zuma in his home, where in 2005 he is alleged to have raped her. According to Zuma, then ANC deputy president, it was consensual sex. When the case came to trial in 2006, Zuma was acquitted by the court. Kuzwayo was vilified, her home was burnt down and, together with her mother, she was "hounded out of the country in the trial's aftermath" (Tlhabi 2017, introduction). Zuma became South Africa's third democratically elected president in 2009. Tlhabi views the rape trial and Kuzwayo's journey as "an opportunity to interrogate concepts such as justice, equality and fairness, which the law may not always serve" (introduction). Not surprisingly, her interrogation reaches back into the past, to apartheid, the war against which "was fought on and across women's and children's bodies" (ch. 3). Kuzwayo's tale, as reported by Tlhabi, also makes apparent the opportunities offered by crime *fiction*, as opposed to creative *non-fiction* about crime. Comparative scholarship on these two related yet distinct modes of writing the post-transitional present is urgently needed, particularly with regard to the fields of gender and justice. Tlhabi believes "that the outcome of the Jacob Zuma rape trial was a triumph of law over justice" (introduction) and asks: "Could the court be a deeply patriarchal space too?" (ch. 5). Crime fiction of the sort that I have analysed has been asking very similar questions, and this

---

1 Jacob Zuma was South Africa's president from 2009 to 2018. At the time of the biography's publication he was still in office.
2 For example, Zuma led the unit named after Kuzwayo's father, who was a senior commander in Umkhonto we Sizwe (MK), the ANC's military wing. The two men also served a 10-year prison sentence together on Robben Island in the early 1960s (Tlhabi 2017, ch. 2).

© SABINE BINDER, 2021 | DOI:10.1163/9789004437449_006
This is an open access chapter distributed under the terms of the CC-BY-NC-ND 4.0 license.

calls for comparative work. In what follows, I will suggest some possible lines of comparison between crime fiction and non-fiction, while summarising the key insights to be gleaned from my own work.

Reading the three pivotal roles available in the crime genre – the female victim, perpetrator and detective – alongside one another, as I have done, is a novel approach to both South African crime fiction and crime fiction in general, where gender-critical scholarship has tended to focus either on the female detective or on the female perpetrator, mostly in her embodiments as femme fatale or rape avenger. What is more, although my reading has artificially separated the three figures, it has also revealed their close proximity, if not ultimate inseparability. For example, Nicol's Sheemina, repeatedly victimised as she is, chooses to become a perpetrator in order to strike back, placing the kind of masculinity that led to her being violated in the first place under her intense scrutiny. The three figures of the victim, the perpetrator and the detective are linked at a deeper level by the pervasive notion of silence/silencing. As this study has shown, each of them resists in different ways the silence about and silencing of women who suffer violence. Silence is further opposed, or rather overcome, when it is the result of trauma. Facing and narrating personal trauma is key in solving murder cases for Persy and Vee, as investigators, but also for Lilith, as one of Orford's victims.

Applying the gender lens is imperative when studying crime fiction, a genre that in South Africa is preoccupied with the quest for "truth" about and the origins of the violent real. In the post-transitional period, it has emerged as one of the principal literary means of social interrogation. If it is true, as De Kock notes about post-apartheid writing, that "the TRC inaugurated a quest for establishing the truth of 'what really happened' – and what continues to happen – in relation to a past that is itself subject to continual revision" (2016a, 10), gender as a category of analysis must necessarily be part of such truth-finding and truth-establishing, not only because much of the violence in South Africa is gender-based, but because, as Tlhabi's book reminds us, racial emancipation was given priority over gender emancipation both during and in the aftermath of the struggle. My intersectional analysis of female victims, perpetrators and detectives in South African crime fiction meets this need for gender-critical truth-finding and works to counter devaluating assumptions about women from the Global South, as called for by Mohanty (1984). What it reveals above all is the enormous variety of forms of non-conventional agency available to women. The book can be read as a way of rendering visible and taking stock of female agency in crime fiction, be it subversive, transgressive or simply of the kind that broadens the scope of action for a woman, and thus of countering hegemonic, limiting and potentially violating ways of *seeing* women.

Unidimensional representations of women facilitate their functioning as *woman*, with their bodies becoming a screen for fears and desires that are not their own, as Bronfen has demonstrated. One of the results of this in the South African imaginary has been a "dismembering" or "disremembering" of women, as diagnosed by Samuelson in the context of nation-building: a shaping of the female body into ideals that reflect the aspirations for the national body (2007a, 2). Making visible a wide array of forms of agency for women allows for an emergence of complex female subjectivities and complicates instrumentalising women as national symbols.

Moreover, endowing women with transgressive agency defamiliarises what Frizzoni calls hegemonic representations of violence (2009, 89), disrupting entrenched representations of gender-based violence that function to show women their (inferior) "place". Tlhabi's account of the Zuma rape trial illustrates just how pertinent the normalisation of sexual violence against women and children is in South Africa. Kuzwayo was raped several times as a child, the first time when she was five years old by a man she and her mother were close to. During the trial, her multiple victimhood was used against her to construct her as a sexually licentious woman. Tlhabi voices her confusion: "[T]he question that should be asked of us is, why can a little girl not get into bed with a close adult male and trust that she will be safe? Why is it a given that 'something will happen' or she is 'willing for something to happen'?" (2017, ch. 5). One of the merits of fiction over creative non-fiction is that it can reverse or recast, through its female characters' transgressive agency, such dangerously normalised concepts of girls and women. When Naude and Jade meet, alone, in the privacy of a house in Mackenzie's *Stolen Lives*, it is he who has to fear for his life, not her. It is he who comes under scrutiny for his crimes as a human trafficker and is held accountable (2008b, 313). Crime fiction offers a privileged space for experimenting with gender roles and forms of female empowerment, as well as for contesting hegemonic representations of violence. The effect of this is not to be underestimated, especially as regards the figure of the female victim. Reflecting on silence in violent conditions, Nthabiseng Motsemme acknowledges the importance of opposing silence with language, by giving voice to the voiceless, but she also makes a strong claim for silence as a tool in itself (2004, 917). Motsemme argues that withdrawal to an inner world can open up a powerful imaginative space, where "different validation processes are at play, which allow women to reimagine, refashion and thus accrue the necessary psychic resources to act in an openly unjust world" (925). Writing women who, despite being silenced into and by victimhood transcend their victim status, women who dare to imagine themselves otherwise in the midst of oppression, means mobilising this form of agency. This is where crime fiction can make a unique contribution that is not open to creative non-fiction about crime.

Besides tracing an imaginatively expanded scope of agency for women, the study has enabled me to elucidate and interrogate questions of gender justice and gender politics from various perspectives. By permitting the victim and her "truth" to come to the fore, South African crime writers successfully resist the genre's impetus towards effacement and invisibility of this figure, despite and amidst her spectacularly high visibility. Here the writers connect directly to the testimonial mode established by the TRC, which encourages the emergence of individual stories of suffering and acknowledges their truth value and importance in the healing process. However, crime fiction testimonies also substantially modify the TRC's template for retrieving victims' stories by having women voice their pain as primary victims, by broadening the scope of sufferings that are addressed, and by homing in on the slow, prolonged and therefore less spectacular types of suffering that result from structures like the education system, the apartheid laws, poverty and patriarchal family structures. Lorimer's characters Boniswa and Lulu, for example, testify to a wide range of forms of violence, structural and event-based, to their gendered and racialised effects and to the ways in which one type of violence can act as a breeding ground for others. By having their victims speak in the first person, the authors create an effect of immediacy. Orford embeds Clare's documentary film material in her fiction, while Lorimer has her survivor Lulu address the public and makes accessible the personal emails of the murdered Boniswa. This serves to enhance the truth value of the victims' stories and removes the safe distance between reader and victim, creating at times a bond that is reminiscent of the autobiographical pact. Lorimer's, Nunn's and Orford's victim-protagonists also highlight the fact that agency and victimhood do not exclude each other, thus giving expression to Butler's insistence that we "think vulnerability and agency together" (2015, 139). The authors' reconceptualisation of female victimhood transcends the generic impulse to obsessively and hauntingly "act out" the traumatic moment and enables culturally and politically effective ways of "working through", to quote LaCapra. This equates to both an exposure and a critique of real violence against women, and to its inclusion in the cultural memory and present reality.

South African crime novels that foreground the female victim function to deepen our understanding of women's suffering, both in the past and in the present. In this respect, crime fiction closely resembles non-fiction, as exemplified by Tlhabi's book. Tlhabi aims to tell *Kuzwayo*'s story, to give a voice to the woman who was effectively silenced by the accused, his supporters and the patriarchal state apparatus. This amounts to a revisiting, and also a reworking and processing, of the past very similar to that which we find in some crime novels. Silence as a result of trauma is overcome by giving previously inaccessible pain a narrative shape. Tlhabi's book reviews and supplements the official "truth" enshrined in the reports of the Johannesburg High Court – or the "legal truth", as she calls it in her introduction. In my exploration of crime fiction, however, the limitations, if not violations, inherent in the telling of the female victim's story have also become apparent. The gender-political effectiveness of documenting female pain and resilience largely depends on the representational practices employed by a writer, especially when it comes to the violated female body. Lorimer's, Nunn's and Orford's writing self-reflexively negotiates the violence of the writing itself. Given their preference for the aesthetics of the spectacular and the eroticised female body, however, Orford and Nicol at times deflect attention away from the stories of female victimhood that their characters tell. Since crime fiction is more pressurised by expectations of entertainment value than factual stories of female pain, this genre is possibly more prone to resacrificing the female victims. By and large, however, caution with regard to representational practices is warranted for true crime as well.

There are also parallels between the fictional and factual modes of writing crime when it comes to female detection. The true-crime author/investigator Tlhabi's concerns with restoring justice to Kuzwayo by truth-finding mirror those of the fictional detectives examined in this study. As advocates of the victims and their families, Lorimer's Nix, Orford's Clare, Mackenzie's Jade, Rowe's Persy, Golakai's Vee and Otter's Maggie all investigate both within *and* beyond official, patriarchal jurisdiction. By reopening "cold" cases or digging up "old bones," the fictional female detectives call for renewed attention not only to *what* actually happened, but also to *why* it happened. On the one hand, they bring to light the bigger frames of persistent systemic violence and injustices and the ways in which women are particularly vulnerable to them: patriarchal family models, land ownership, segregated living space, access to resources, organisation and conditions of labour, health and research institutions, education, the police and the state itself. On the other, they highlight how individuals interact with and perpetuate these structures. In doing so, they establish nuanced truths that often call into question received ones. Their ways of including the past, be it the distant past of colonialism or apartheid, in order to shed light on the present closely resemble Tlhabi's true-criminal investigations. In order to put into perspective not only Kuzwayo's behaviour, but also the reasoning underlying Zuma's defence during the trial and the "licence" so many men feel to sexually abuse women, Tlhabi re-examines the struggle to end apartheid (2017, ch. 2 and 3). She concludes, "Liberators and oppressors had something in common: their propensity for violence and demand for women's bodies. Two enemies, polarised by politics, yet in agreement that the female body was theirs to take" (ch. 3). Moreover, like that of the crime fiction detectives, Tlhabi's version of the "truth" exposes the gender bias of the law and the criminal justice system as "platforms of patriarchy". As an investigator of true crime, Tlhabi is an agent of gender justice, a function also performed by fictional female detectives. They serve more inclusive forms of justice premised on discursiveness, relationalism and reflectiveness, as proposed by Hudson's feminist legal scholarship. By advocating justice that seeks to move beyond the bias of gender, race and class of the criminal justice system, and through their visible presence in professional positions within the system that have long been associated with masculinity, female detectives change the very face of detection and justice. By not being "that kind of cop," Persy also alters what cops are. At least in fiction, the concept of a cop is subjected to revision, and this amounts to a subtle recalibration of the gender order itself.

Moreover, as women who occupy professional roles long associated with masculinity, female detectives symbolically act as role models for women. This is not an insignificant point and marks one of the ways in which fiction has a potential impact on the real social world. In her work on gender equality in the world of work, the Harvard behavioural economist Iris Bohnet emphasises the crucial importance of creating role models in achieving greater diversity in business and politics, since it affects how women are perceived by others and by themselves: "Seeing women leaders changed perceptions – making women more confident that they could run for public office and making men more accepting of women as leaders" (2016, 206). According to Bohnet, "Seeing is Believing" (210). If we extend her argument to investigators of crime, it is clear that fiction has a slight advantage over non-fiction. Crime fiction never leaves readers in any doubt as to the presence of the detective herself and she can become an effective role model, whereas investigators of true crime, such as Tlhabi, may assume less "visibility" for the reader. They may at times disappear behind the protagonists of their tales and thus be rather more implicit role models. This has a bearing on how the investigators themselves and the pressures they are subjected to can be critically reflected upon. Reading the female detective as a witness of violence, as I have suggested, necessitates critical scrutiny of her own subject position and of her "gaze" on the victim. That is not to say that it is impossible to make the investigator's position visible and/or open to reflection or that this does not occur in works of creative non-fiction, but, in the fiction under discussion here, exploring the position of the investigator herself, be she a police officer like Persy or a journalist like Vee and Maggie, has emerged as fundamental in assessing her gender-political impact. And it has given rise to a certain amount of disillusionment. The very fact that female detectives remain bound by and are agents of literally criminal and/or ineffective institutions renders them complicit, if not culpable. Persy, Vee and Maggie all have to acknowledge this in very painful ways, as they themselves contribute to injustice, and even to several deaths. Also, more often than not, the constraints of the real seem to catch up with South African fictional detectives. They fail to hold accountable the "true" culprits, the rapists, the kingpins, and can thus achieve only limited gender justice.

The female perpetrator, by contrast, has a far greater feminist political effect – at least in the realm of crime fiction. This, too, reveals the ways in which the three figures speak to one another, even challenge one another. Like the detective, the perpetrator renders visible the bias inherent in entrenched forms and institutions of justice, but she can do something about it. As radical transgressors of the law – in the sense of both gender norms and a country's legal code – perpetrators like Jade and the Black Widows ruthlessly expose its shortcomings for women. Refusing to be silenced and kept in place, the perpetrator cuts her ties with the female victim while also acting on her behalf. By assuming the violently masculine role of the killer, she deconstructs the link between masculinity and power and unapologetically claims the power position. Through her performance of violent female masculinity, she creates a regime of female counter-violence and terror. Hers is thus a direct attack on the gender order, as Sheemina, Jade and the Black Widows illustrate. Sheemina's bomb blasts, Jade's high-precision gun shots and the Black Widows' stealthy murders are also violent claims to full citizenship in the post-transitional moment. If the "war", the struggle for racial freedom, has been fought over and across women's bodies, as Tlhabi claims, the female perpetrators discussed here recast this war, turning it into their war, on their terms, against patriarchal power. What is at stake here is more than a simple role reversal, as gender-based violence in South Africa is less a weapon *against* women than *itself* a weapon in a war between men (see "Introduction"). According to Louise Du Toit, the "conversation" about the assertion of male power is not between men and women, but between men, with the violation of women serving as a weapon. The war that the female perpetrators written by Nicol, Mackenzie and Makholwa wage signifies a radical change in the game of war insofar as it features women as conversational partners, and equal ones at that.

In addition, if read in relation to the TRC, the female perpetrators give expression to feelings of rage and vengeance. They represent precisely the feelings and the kind of retributive justice that the TRC worked to placate in its effort to secure a peaceful transition. Unlike the female detective, the perpetrator can take the law into her own hands. South African feminists have repeatedly cited impunity for and social complicity with perpetrators of violence against women as major obstacles to gender justice (see "Introduction"). In crime fiction, this view is shared by both detectives and perpetrators. Persy and Vee, for example, both have to arrest teenagers, while the adults walk free. These teenagers, Mandisa, Rosie and Serena, are not without guilt, but making them the only ones to pay the price for their crimes is highly unjust and serves to deflect attention from criminal adults and criminal systems. By contrast, Jade the investigator-cum-perpetrator and the Black Widows can step in. They are able to hold wrongdoers accountable; by administering vigilante justice, they can achieve for women what the criminal justice system cannot. This turns the female perpetrator into a serious challenge to the female detective and her endeavours. She mercilessly reveals the dubious construction of the very norm within which the detective is working and that she is trying to keep in place. In a way, the perpetrator becomes the detective's uncanny double who haunts her time and again, reminding her of the limitations of her work and the porous boundaries between herself and the perpetrator. There is copious evidence of this in the novels: Clare's own sister is a rape avenger; Clare herself pushes Gilles to his death; twice Maggie is a hair's breadth away from killing perpetrators; Nix, Marge and Vee are responsible for driving people to suicide; Persy and Vee are both saddled with guilt at having killed at a young age. The female perpetrator constantly hints at the ways in which the detective, by keeping social norms in place, is working counter to women's interests. Hers is a brutal logic that rejects the more brutal logic of a biased, ineffective justice apparatus and other forms of systemic violence that insistently keep women in their place. She draws attention to the precarious ethics of investigative work for a woman and her precarious position as a servant of the patriarchal law, thereby allowing for a new, disturbing view of the female detective.

However, the monstrous, vile or pathological criminal woman, particularly the Black criminal woman, is a well-established gender stereotype, having been used to justify women's subjugation for millennia. Caution is thus required if this stereotype is not to be perpetuated and reinforced. The figure of the female perpetrator, like that of the female victim, affords authors an opportunity to rewrite debilitating stereotypes, but the risk of reifying them is still there, as my reading of Nicol's Sheemina and of Golakai's Xoliswa has demonstrated. If crime novels premised on female perpetrators are to make an effective feminist political gesture, it is important that they do not eschew critical ethical reflection. Mackenzie and Makholwa raise the problematics of female vigilante justice, showing that it can be as criminal as the criminal justice that it seeks to replace.

The female perpetrator crystallises one of the major advantages of crime fiction, especially in its thriller form, over non-fiction crime stories. Fiction's greater artistic licence guarantees more leeway in terms of gender politics. The female perpetrator figures in the thrillers examined here are as rooted in the failures of the present and as affected by the crimes of the past as the victims and detectives. They are also as grounded in the South African real as non-fiction crime stories are. Unlike non-fiction, crime fiction can, through its very transgressiveness, refashion the past-infected present, thus acquiring a future-oriented, utopian, visionary function. Such "imaginative future mapping" is typical of popular fiction (Spencer, Ligaga and Musila 2018, 3). Tlhabi quotes from gender activist Dawn Cavanagh's furious speech at Kuzwayo's funeral, which was addressed to Zuma's accomplices: " 'If you did not speak then, do not speak now. The feminists of South Africa are coming for you. Our rage cannot be stopped. Our rage is coming for you' " (2017, ch. 1). Tlhabi notes that the speech was greeted with wild applause, commenting, "Cavanagh's words had opened a gaping wound, one that many women in South Africa feel. It is the wound caused by sexism, violence, poverty and discrimination. South African women are, collectively, a pressure cooker waiting to explode" (ch. 1). The female perpetrators discussed in this study embody the release of that pressure. They are the pressure cookers in full explosion. Fiction is able to go the extra step of imagining the actualisation of female rage and its effects.

This brings me full circle, back to the rather disquieting question with which I began this study: Can a genre that depends on crime and violence be a platform for debate about those issues, if not a means of political opposition to them? The short version of the long answer that *Women and Crime* has provided is a qualified yes.

Works Cited

Aaron, Michele. 2007. *Spectatorship: The Power of Looking On.* London: Wallflower.

Adhikari, Mohamed. 2009. "Introduction: Predicaments of Marginality: Cultural Creativity and Political Adaptation in Southern Africa's Coloured Communities." In *Burdened by Race: Coloured Identities in Southern Africa*, edited by Mohamed Adhikari, viii–xxxii. Cape Town: University of Cape Town Press.

Africa, Adelene. 2010. "'Murderous Women'? Rethinking Gender and Theories of Violence." *Feminist Africa* 14: 79–92.

Aids Foundation South Africa. 2017. "HIV/AIDS in South Africa." Accessed May 11, 2017. https://www.aids.org.za/hivaids-in-south-africa.

Akinwotu, Emmanuel. 2016. "Hawa Golkai: The Liberian Scientist Turned Cult Crime Writer." *The Guardian*, June 9, 2016. https://www.theguardian.com/world/2016/jun/09/hawa-golakai-the-liberian-scientist-turned-cult-writer.

Albertyn, Catherine. 2007. "Equality." In *Gender, Law and Justice*, edited by Elsje Bonthuys and Catherine Albertyn, 82–119. Cape Town: Juta.

Albertyn, Catherine, and Elsje Bonthuys. 2007. "Introduction." In *Gender, Law and Justice*, edited by Elsje Bonthuys and Catherine Albertyn, 1–14. Cape Town: Juta.

Altbeker, Antony. 2010. *Fruit of a Poisoned Tree: A True Story of Murder and the Miscarriage of Justice.* Johannesburg: Jonathan Ball Publishers.

Amid, Jonathan. 2011. "Crime Fiction and the 'Metaphysics of Disorder'." Review of *Counting of the Coffins*, by Diale Tlholwe, and *The Lazarus Effect*, by Hawa Jande Golakai. *Stellenbosch Literary Project*, accessed May 30, 2014. http://slipnet.co.za/view/reviews/crime-fiction-and-the-%E2%80%98metaphysics-of-disorder%E2%80%99/.

Amid, Jonathan. 2014. "Reader's Review: *Black Widow Society*." Review of *Black Widow Society*, by Angela Makholwa. *Litnet,* January 3, 2014. http://www.litnet.co.za/Article/readers-review-black-widow-society.

Amid, Jonathan, and Leon de Kock. 2014. "The Crime Novel in Post-Apartheid South Africa: A Preliminary Investigation." *Scrutiny2: Issues in English Studies in Southern Africa* 19 (1): 52–68.

Andersson, Muff. 2004. "Dreaming of a New Kind of Freedom." *Mail & Guardian*, May 6, 2004.

Andrews, Chris, and Matt McGuire. 2016. "Introduction: Post-Conflict Literature?" In *Post-Conflict Literature: Human Rights, Peace, Justice*, edited by Chris Andrews and Matt McGuire, 1–15. Abingdon: Routledge.

Balaev, Michelle. 2014. "Literary Trauma Theory Reconsidered." In *Contemporary Approaches in Literary Trauma Theory*, edited by Michelle Balaev, 1–14. London: Palgrave Macmillan.

Barber, Karin. 1987. "Popular Arts in Africa." *African Studies Review* 30 (3): 1–78.

Barber, Karin. 2018. *A History of African Popular Culture*. Cambridge, UK: Cambridge University Press.

Benjamin, Walter. 1999. "Critique of Violence." In *Violence and Its Alternatives: An Interdisciplinary Reader*, edited by Manfred B. Steger and Nancy S. Lind, 57–69. New York: St. Martin's Press.

Bertens, Hans, and Theo D'haen. 2001. *Contemporary American Crime Fiction*. London: Palgrave MacMillan.

Biko, Hlumelo. 2013. *The Great African Society: A Plan for a Nation Gone Astray*. Johannesburg: Jonathan Ball Publishers.

Binder, Sabine. 2015. "Female Killers and Gender Politics in Contemporary South African Crime Fiction: Conversations with Crime Writers Jassy Mackenzie, Angela Makholwa and Mike Nicol." *The Journal of Commonwealth Literature* 52 (2): 263–280. DOI: 10.1177/0021989415619466.

Binder, Sabine. 2017a. "A Case of Transgression: Investigating the Gender Performance of Jassy Mackenzie's South African Renegade Detective Jade de Jong." In *Cities in Flux: Metropolitan Spaces in South African Literary and Visual Texts*, edited by Olivier Moreillon, Alan Muller and Lindy Stiebel, 37–56. Münster: LIT Verlag.

Binder, Sabine. 2017b. "Whose Story Is Written on Her Dead Body? Writing Gender Justice and Transformation by Re-Writing Female Victims in South African Crime Thrillers." *Current Writing: Text and Reception in Southern Africa* 29 (2): 100–110.

Black, Shameem. 2011. "Truth Commission Thrillers." *Social Text* 29 (2): 47–66.

Bohnet, Iris. 2016. *What Works: Gender Equality by Design*. Cambridge, MA: The Belknap Press of Harvard University Press.

Boonzaier, Floretta. 2017. "The Life and Death of Anene Booysen: Colonial Discourse, Gender-based Violence and Media Representations." *South African Journal of Psychology* 47 (4): 470–481.

Boraine, Alex. 2014. *What's Gone Wrong? On the Brink of a Failed State*. Johannesburg: Jonathan Ball Publishers.

Borer, Tristan Anne. 2009. "Gendered War and Gendered Peace: Truth Commissions and Postconflict Gender Violence: Lessons From South Africa." *Violence Against Women* 15 (10): 1169–1193.

Braude, Claudia. 1996. "The Archbishop, the Private Detective and the Angel of History: The Production of South African Public Memory and the Truth and Reconciliation Commission." *Current Writing: Text and Reception in Southern Africa* 8 (2): 39–65.

Breysse, Serge. 2001. "Interview with Mike Nicol: 31/07/2001." *Alizés* (21): 197–211.

Brink, André. 1998. "Stories of History: Reimagining the Past in Post-Apartheid Narrative." In *Negotiating the Past: The Making of Memory in South Africa*, edited by Sarah Nuttall and Carli Coetzee, 29–42. Cape Town: Oxford University Press.

Bronfen, Elisabeth. 1992. *Over Her Dead Body: Death, Femininity and the Aesthetic*. Manchester: Manchester University Press.

Bronfen, Elisabeth. 1995. "Weiblichkeit und Repräsentation – aus der Perspektive von Semiotik, Ästhetik und Psychoanalyse." In *Genus: Zur Geschlechterdifferenz in den Kulturwissenschaften*, edited by Hadumod Bussmann and Renate Hof, 408–445. Stuttgart: Alfred Kröner Verlag.

Bronfen, Elisabeth. 2004a. "Femme Fatale – Negotiations of Tragic Desire." *New Literary History* 35 (1): 103–116.

Bronfen, Elisabeth. 2004b. " 'You've Got a Great Big Dollar Sign Where Most Women Have a Heart': Refigurationen der Femme fatale im Film Noir der 80er- und 90er-Jahre." In *Hollywood hybrid: Genre und Gender im zeitgenössischen Mainstream-Film*, edited by Claudia Liebrand and Ines Steiner, 91–135. Marburg: Schüren Verlag.

Brown, Adam. 2013. "Screening Women's Complicity in the Holocaust: The Problems of Judgement and Representation." In *Representing Perpetrators in Holocaust Literature and Film*, edited by Jenni Adams and Sue Vice, 69–90. London: Vallentine Mitchell.

Büchler, Andrea, and Michelle Cottier. 2012. *Legal Gender Studies, Rechtliche Geschlechterstudien: Eine kommentierte Quellensammlung*. Zurich: Dike Verlag.

Buti, Thanduxolo. 2013. "The Black Widow Society Uncovered." *Destinyconnect*, October 8, 2013. http://www.destinyconnect.com/2013/10/08/the-black-widow-society-uncovered/2/.

Butler, Anthony. 2009. *Contemporary South Africa*. 2nd ed. London: Palgrave Macmillan.

Butler, Judith. 1990. *Gender Trouble: Feminism and the Subversion of Identity*. Abingdon: Routledge.

Butler, Judith. 1993. *Bodies That Matter: On the Discursive Limits of 'Sex'*. Abingdon: Routledge.

Butler, Judith. 2010. *Frames of War: When Is Life Grievable?* New York: Verso.

Butler, Judith. 2015. *Notes toward a Performative Theory of Assembly*. Cambridge, MA: Harvard University Press.

Butler, Pamela, and Jigna Desai. 2008. "Manolos, Marriage, and Mantras: Chick-Lit Criticism and Transnational Feminism." *Meridians: Feminism, Race, Transnationalism* 8 (2): 1–31.

Cawelti, John G. 1976. *Adventure, Mystery, and Romance: Formula Stories as Art and Popular Culture*. Chicago: The University of Chicago Press.

Chandler, Raymond. 1962 (1949). "Casual Notes on the Mystery Novel." In *Raymond Chandler Speaking*, edited by Dorothy Gardiner and Katherine Sorley Walker, 63–70. New York: Books for Libraries Press.

Christensen, Matthew J. 2015. "Managed Risk and the Lure of Transparency in Anglophone African Detective Noir." *Textual Practice* 29 (2): 315–333.

Christian, Ed. 2001. "Introducing the Post-Colonial Detective: Putting Marginality to Work." In *The Post-Colonial Detective*, edited by Ed Christian, 1–16. London: Palgrave Macmillan.

Cock, Jacklyn. 2001. "Gun Violence and Masculinity in Contemporary South Africa." In *Changing Men in Southern Africa*, edited by Robert Morrell, 43–55. Pietermaritzburg: University of Natal Press; London: Zed Books.

Cole, Sam. 2006. *Cape Greed*. New York: Minotaur Books.

Collins, Patricia Hill. 2000. *Black Feminist Thought*. Abingdon: Taylor & Francis.

Colvin, Christopher J. 2008. "Trauma." In *New South African Keywords*, edited by Nick Sheperd and Steven Robins, 223–234. Johannesburg: Jacana; Athens: Ohio University Press.

Comaroff, Jean, and John L. Comaroff. 2016. *The Truth about Crime: Sovereignty, Knowledge, Social Order*. Chicago: The University of Chicago Press.

Comaroff, John, and Jean Comaroff. 2004. "Criminal Obsessions after Foucault: Postcoloniality, Policing and the Metaphysics of Disorder." *Critical Inquiry* 30 (4): 800–824.

Comaroff, John, and Jean Comaroff. 2006. "Law and Disorder in the Postcolony: An Introduction." In *Law and Disorder in the Postcolony*, edited by Jean Comaroff and John Comaroff, 1–22. Chicago: The University of Chicago Press.

Crenshaw, Kimberlé. 1989. "Demarginalizing the Intersection of Race and Sex: A Black Feminist Critique of Antidiscrimination Doctrine, Feminist Theory and Antiracist Politics." *University of Chicago Legal Forum* 1989 (1): 139–167.

Dankwa, Serena. 2009. "Female Masculinity Revisited: Situatives Mannsein im Kontext südghanaischer Frauenbeziehungen." In *Gender Scripts: Widerspenstige Aneignungen von Geschlechternormen*, edited by Christa Binswanger, Margaret Bridges, Brigitte Schnegg and Doris Wastl-Walter, 161–182. Frankfurt: Campus Verlag.

Davis, Geoffrey. 2006. "Political Loyalties and the Intricacies of the Criminal Mind: The Detective Fiction of Wessel Ebersohn." In *Postcolonial Postmortems: Crime Fiction from a Transcultural Perspective*, edited by Christine Matzke and Susanne Mühleisen, 181–199. Amsterdam: Rodopi.

De Crescenzo, Luciano. 1998. *Kinder des Olymp: Antike Göttermythen neu erzählt*. München: BTB.

De Kock, Leon. 2010. "Hits Keep Coming But It Ain't Enough." *The Sunday Independent*, February 14, 2010.

De Kock, Leon. 2011. "High Noon in the Badlands." *Mail & Guardian*, May 6, 2011. http://mg.co.za/article/2011-05-06-high-noon-in-the-badlands.

De Kock, Leon. 2015. "From the Subject of Evil to the Evil Subject: 'Cultural Difference' in Postapartheid South African Crime Fiction." *Safundi: The Journal of South African and American Studies* 16 (1): 28–50.

De Kock, Leon. 2016a. *Losing the Plot: Crime, Reality and Fiction in Postapartheid Writing*. Johannesburg: Wits University Press.

De Kock, Leon. 2016b. "Off-Colour? Mike Nicol's Neo-Noir 'Revenge Trilogy' and the Post-Apartheid *Femme Fatale*." *African Studies* 75 (1): 98–113.

Decoteau, Claire Laurier. 2013. "The Crisis of Liberation: Masculinity, Neoliberalism, and HIV/AIDS in Postapartheid South Africa." *Men and Masculinities* 16 (2): 139–159.

Department of Trade and Industry, Republic of South Africa. 2014. "Broad Based Black Economic Empowerment." Accessed February 19, 2015. http://www.thedti.gov.za/economic_empowerment/bee.jsp.

Dietze, Gabriele. 2014. "Decolonizing Gender – Gendering Decolonial Theory: Crosscurrents and Archaeologies." In *Postcoloniality – Decoloniality – Black Critique: Joints and Fissures*, edited by Sabine Broeck and Carsten Junker, 253–276. Frankfurt: Campus Verlag.

Dlamini, Nhlanhla. 2007. "The Birth and Development of Coloured Identity in Swaziland, 1913–1941." Unpublished thesis, University of the Witwatersrand, Johannesburg. Accessed April 6, 2016. http://wiredspace.wits.ac.za/bitstream/handle/10539/5833/Thesis%20Four.pdf?sequence=7.

Dlamini, Nhlanhla. 2015. "Fighting a Losing Battle in a Racially Discriminating Colony in British Southern Africa: The Case of the Swaziland Coloured Welfare Association (SCWA) 1950–1963." Research paper, University of Swaziland. Accessed April 8, 2016. http://www.uct.ac.za/sites/default/files/image_tool/images/376/Events/Norm/Colouredness-HUMAUCTOCTOBER-final-draft-8-oct-2015.pdf.

Doak, Jonathan, and David O'Mahony. 2012. "Editorial: Transitional Justice and Restorative Justice." *International Criminal Law Review* 12: 305–311.

Doane, Mary Ann. 1991. *Femmes Fatales: Feminism, Film Theory, and Psychoanalysis*. Abingdon: Routledge.

Driver, Dorothy. 2005. "Truth, Reconciliation, Gender: The South African Truth and Reconciliation Commission and Black Women's Intellectual History 1." *Australian Feminist Studies* 20 (47): 219–229.

Du Toit, Louise. 2005. "A Phenomenology of Rape: Forging a New Vocabulary for Action." In *(Un)Thinking Citizenship: Feminist Debates in Contemporary South Africa*, edited by Amanda Gouws, 253–274. Aldershot: Ashgate.

Du Toit, Louise. 2014. "Shifting Meanings of Postconflict Sexual Violence in South Africa." *Signs: Journal of Women in Culture and Society* 40 (1): 101–123.

Dyer, Richard. 1988. "White." *Screen* 29 (4): 44–65.

Ebert, Teresa L. 1992. "Detecting the Phallus: Authority, Ideology, and the Production of Patriarchal Agents in Detective Fiction." *Rethinking Marxism* 5 (3): 6–28.

Edwards, Martin. 1999. "Victim." In *The Oxford Companion to Crime and Mystery Writing*, edited by Rosemary Herbert, 478–479. Oxford: Oxford University Press.

Erasmus, Zimitri. 2001. "Introduction: Re-Imagining Coloured Identities in Post-Apartheid South Africa." In *Coloured by History, Shaped by Place: New Perspectives on*

Coloured Identities in Cape Town, edited by Zimitri Erasmus, 13–28. Cape Town: Kwela Books; Maroelana: South African History Online.

Every, Kate. 2016. " 'Growing Scar Tissue around the Memory of That Day': Sites of Gendered Violence and Suffering in Contemporary South African Literature." *Journal of International Women's Studies* 17 (2): 30–42.

Fasselt, Rebecca. 2016. "Making and Unmaking 'African Foreignness': African Settings, African Migrants and the Migrant Detective in Contemporary South African Crime Fiction." *Journal of Southern African Studies* 42 (6): 1109–1124.

Fasselt, Rebecca. 2019. "Crossing genre boundaries: H. J. Golakai's Afropolitan chick-lit mysteries." *Feminist Theory* 20 (2): 185–200.

Ferriss, Suzanne, and Mallory Young. 2006. "Introduction." In *Chick Lit: The New Woman's Fiction*, edited by Suzanne Ferriss and Mallory Young, 1–13. Abingdon: Routledge.

Fletcher, Elizabeth. 2013. "Margie Orford's *Daddy's Girl* and the Possibilities of Feminist Crime Fiction." *Current Writing: Text and Reception in Southern Africa* 25 (2): 196–209.

Fourie, Liezel. 2013. "Book Review: *What Hidden Lies*." Review of *What Hidden Lies*, by Michelle Rowe. *9lives*. Accessed September 18, 2013. http://9lives.co.za/book-review-what-hidden-lies.

Frenkel, Ronit, and Craig MacKenzie. 2010. "Conceptualizing 'Post-Transitional' South African Literature in English." *English Studies in Africa* 53 (1): 1–10.

Freud, Sigmund. 2003 (1919). *The Uncanny*. Translated by David Mclintock. London: Penguin Books.

Frizzoni, Brigitte. 2009. *Verhandlungen mit Mordsfrauen: Geschlechterpositionierungen im 'Frauenkrimi'*. Zürich: Chronos Verlag.

Galusca, Roxana. 2012. "Slave Hunters, Brothel Busters, and Feminist Interventions: Investigative Journalists as Anti-Sex-Trafficking Humanitarians." *Feminist Formations* 24 (2): 1–24.

Gates, Henry Louis Jr. 1985. "Editor's Introduction: Writing 'Race' and the Difference It Makes." *Critical Inquiry* 12 (1): 1–20.

Gavin, Adrienne E. 2010. "Feminist Crime Fiction and Female Sleuths." In *A Companion to Crime Fiction*, edited by Charles J. Rzepka and Lee Horsley, 258–269. Chichester: Wiley-Blackwell.

Golakai, Hawa Jande. 2011. *The Lazarus Effect*. Cape Town: Kwela Books.

Golakai, Hawa Jande. 2015. *The Score*. Cape Town: Kwela Books.

Goldblatt, Beth, and Sheila Meintjes. 1997. "Dealing with the Aftermath: Sexual Violence and the Truth and Reconciliation Commission." *Agenda* 36: 7–18.

Goltermann, Svenja. 2015. "Der Markt der Leiden, das Menschenrecht auf Entschädigung und die Kategorie des Opfers: ein Problemaufriss." *Historische Anthropologie* 23 (1): 70–92.

WORKS CITED

Gqola, Pumla Dineo. 2007. "How the 'Cult of Femininity' and Violent Masculinities Support Endemic Gender Based Violence in Contemporary South Africa." *African Identities* 5 (1): 111–124.

Gqola, Pumla Dineo. 2015. *Rape: A South African Nightmare*. Johannesburg: MF Books, Jacana.

Graham, Shane. 2009. *South African Literature after the Truth Commission: Mapping Loss*. London: Palgrave Macmillan.

Green, Lelia, and Steven Maras. 2002. "From Impartial Objectivity to Responsible Affectivity: Some Ethical Implications of the 9/11 Attacks on America and the War on Terror." *Australian Journal of Communication* 29 (3): 17–30.

Green, Michael. 1994. "The Detective as Historian: A Case for Wessel Ebersohn." *Current Writing: Text and Reception in Southern Africa* 6 (2): 93–112.

Grunebaum, Heidi, and Steven Robins. 2001. "Crossing the Colour(ed) Line: Mediating the Ambiguities of Belonging and Identity." In *Coloured by History, Shaped by Place: New Perspectives on Coloured Identities in Cape Town*, edited by Zimitri Erasmus, 159–172. Cape Town: Kwela Books; Maroelana: South African History Online.

Haffejee, Sadiyya, Lisa Vetten, and Mike Greyling. 2005. "Exploring Violence in the Lives of Women and Girls Incarcerated at Three Prisons in Gauteng Province, South Africa." *Agenda* 19 (66): 40–47.

Halberstam, Judith. 1993. "Imagined Violence/Queer Violence." *Social Text* 37: 187–201.

Halberstam, Judith. 1998. *Female Masculinity*. Durham: Duke University Press.

Hamber, Brandon. 2007. "Masculinity and Transitional Justice: An Exploratory Essay." *The International Journal of Transitional Justice* 1: 375–390.

Hamber, Brandon, and Richard A. Wilson. 2002. "Symbolic Closure through Memory, Reparation and Revenge in Post-Conflict Societies." *Journal of Human Rights* 1 (1): 35–53.

Hanson, Helen. 2010. "The Big Seduction: Feminist Film Criticism and the *Femme Fatale*." In *The Femme Fatale: Images, Histories, Contexts*, edited by Helen Hanson and Catherine O'Rawe, 214–227. London: Palgrave Macmillan.

Hanson, Helen, and Catherine O'Rawe. 2010. "Introduction: 'Cherchez la *femme*'." In *The Femme Fatale: Images, Histories, Contexts*, edited by Helen Hanson and Catherine O'Rawe, 1–8. London: Palgrave Macmillan.

Harris, Marla. 2013. " 'You Think It's Possible to Fix Broken Things?': Terror in the South African Crime Fiction by Margie Orford and Jassy Mackenzie." *Clues: A Journal of Detection* 31(2): 122–131.

Hayner, Priscilla B. 2001. *Unspeakable Truths: Confronting State Terror and Atrocity*. Abingdon: Routledge.

Henry, Claire. 2014. *Revisionist Rape-Revenge*. London: Palgrave Macmillan.

Hilmes, Carola. 2003. "Femme Fatale." In *Handbuch Populäre Kultur: Begriffe, Theorien und Diskussionen*, edited by Hans-Otto Hügel, 172–177. Stuttgart: J.B. Metzler.

Honig, Bonnie. 2013. *Antigone, Interrupted*. Cambridge, UK: Cambridge University Press.

Hooks, Bell. 1994. *Outlaw Culture: Resisting Representations*. Abingdon: Routledge.

Horsley, Lee. 2010. *The Noir Thriller*. London: Palgrave Macmillan.

Hudson, Barbara. 2012. "Beyond White Man's Justice: Race, Gender and Justice in Late Modernity." In *Gender and Crime: Critical Concepts in Criminology. Volume III: Gendered Experiences of the Criminal Justice Process*, edited by Sandra Walklate, 384–401. Abingdon: Routledge.

Jewkes, Rachel, and Robert Morrell. 2010. "Gender and Sexuality: Emerging Perspectives from the Heterosexual Epidemic in South Africa and Implications for HIV Risk and Prevention." *Journal of the International AIDS Society* 13 (6): 1–11.

Key West Literary Seminar. 2014. "Authors: Malla Nunn." 32nd Annual Key West Literary Seminar: The Dark Side. Accessed March 14, 2016. http://www.kwls.org/authors/malla-nunn/.

Kinsman, Margaret. 2010. "Feminist Crime Fiction." In *The Cambridge Companion to American Crime Fiction*, edited by Catherine Ross Nickerson, 148–162. Cambridge, UK: Cambridge University Press.

Klein, Kathleen Gregory. 1988. *The Woman Detective: Gender & Genre*. Urbana: University of Illinois Press.

Klein, Kathleen Gregory. 1995. "*Habeas Corpus*: Feminism and Detective Fiction." In *Feminism in Women's Detective Fiction*, edited by Glenwood Irons, 171–189. Toronto: University of Toronto Press.

Knight, Stephen. 2010. *Crime Fiction Since 1800: Detection, Death, Diversity*. 2nd ed. London: Palgrave Macmillan.

König, Jochen. 2013. "Balthasars Vermaechtnis: Charlotte Otter." Review of *Balthasar's Gift*, by Charlotte Otter. *Krimi Couch*, July 2013. http://www.krimi-couch.de/krimis/charlotte-otter-balthasars-vermaechtnis.html.

Krekeler, Elmar. 2013. "Es sind zwei Viren los im kranken Haus von Afrika." *Die Welt*, August 30, 2017. https://www.welt.de/kultur/literarischewelt/article119563143/Es-sind-zwei-Viren-los-im-kranken-Haus-von-Afrika.html.

Krimi-Couch. 2016. "Malla Nunn." Accessed March 22, 2016. http://www.krimi-couch.de/krimis/malla-nunn.html.

Krüger, Gesine. 2007. "Vergangenheitsbewältigung? Zum Umgang mit Kolonialismus, Sklaverei und Apartheid." In *Afrika im Wandel*, edited by Thomas Bearth, Barbara Becker, Rolf Kappel, Gesine Krüger and Roger Pfister, 37–48. Zürich: vdf Hochschulverlag AG an der ETH Zürich.

KZN Literary Tourism. 2015. "Charlotte Otter." Accessed May 17, 2017. https://www.literarytourism.co.za/index.php?limitstart=81.

LaCapra, Dominick. 2001. *Writing History, Writing Trauma*. Baltimore: Johns Hopkins University Press.

Le Roux, Elizabeth. 2013. "South African Crime and Detective Fiction in English: A Bibliography and Publishing History." *Current Writing: Text and Reception in Southern Africa* 25 (2): 136–152.

Lewis, Desiree. 1999. "Gender Myths and Citizenship in Two Autobiographies by South African Women." *Agenda* 40: 38–44.

Lewis, Desiree. 2001. "Writing Hybrid Selves: Richard Rive and Zoë Wicomb." In *Coloured by History, Shaped by Place: New Perspectives on Coloured Identities in Cape Town*, edited by Zimitri Erasmus, 131–158. Cape Town: Kwela Books; Maroelana: South African History Online.

Lewis, Desiree. 2009. "Gendered Spectacle: New Terrains of Struggle in South Africa." In *Body Politics and Women Citizens*, edited by Ann Schlyter, 127–137. Stockholm: Sida.

Lewis, Desiree. 2011. "Representing African Sexualities." In *African Sexualities: A Reader*, edited by Sylvia Tamale, 199–216. Cape Town: Pambazuka Press.

Lorimer, Penny. 2014. *Finders Weepers*. Cape Town: Umuzi.

Lorimer, Penny. 2015. "Africa Scene: An Interview with Penny Lorimer." Interview by Michael Sears. *The Big Thrill*, April 30, 2015. http://www.thebigthrill.org/2015/04/africa-scene-an-interview-with-penny-lorimer-by-michael-sears.

Lugones, Maria. 2010. "Toward a Decolonial Feminism." *Hypatia* 25 (4): 742–759.

Mackenzie, Jassy. 2008a. *Random Violence*. New York: Soho Press.

Mackenzie, Jassy. 2008b. *Stolen Lives*. New York: Soho Press.

Mackenzie, Jassy. 2009. *My Brother's Keeper*. Cape Town: Umuzi.

Mackenzie, Jassy. 2010a. "Jassy Mackenzie and the Braai Factor." Interview by Crime Beat, edited by Mike Nicol. *Sunday Times*, October 4, 2010. http://crimebeat.bookslive.co.za/blog/2010/10/04/crime-beat-jassy-mackenzie-and-the-braai-factor/.

Mackenzie, Jassy. 2010b. "Of Heroes and Villains." *Wordsetc* no. 1 (First Quarter): 13–15.

Mackenzie, Jassy. 2011a. "An Interview with Jassy Mackenzie about *Worst Case*: A New Setting in KZN, Jade's Mother and Her Rocky Road with David Patel." Interview by Crime Beat, edited by Elizabeth Fletcher. *Sunday Times*, August 25, 2011. http://crimebeat.bookslive.co.za/blog/2011/08/25/crime-beat-an-interview-with-jassy-mackenzies-about-worst-case-a-new-setting-in-kzn-jades-mother-and-her-rocky-road-with-david-patel/.

Mackenzie, Jassy. 2011b. *Worst Case*. Cape Town: Umuzi.

Mackenzie, Jassy. 2012a. "Jassy Mackenzie and the Horses of the Apocalypse." Interview by Crime Beat, edited by Mike Nicol. *Sunday Times*, September 11, 2012. http://crimebeat.bookslive.co.za/blog/2012/09/11/crime-beat-jassy-mackenzie-and-the-horses-of-the-apocalypse/.

Mackenzie, Jassy. 2012b. *Pale Horses*. New York: Soho Press.

Mackenzie, Jassy. 2014. "Interview with Jassy Mackenzie." Personal unpublished interview by Sabine Binder. Johannesburg, South Africa, April 11, 2014.

Mackenzie, Jassy. 2016. *Soaring*. New York: Astor and Blue.

Mackenzie, Jassy. 2017. *Bad Seeds*. New York: Soho Press.

Makholwa, Angela. 2007. *Red Ink*. Johannesburg: Pan Macmillan.

Makholwa, Angela. 2009. *The 30th Candle*. Johannesburg: Pan Macmillan.

Makholwa, Angela. 2013. *Black Widow Society*. Johannesburg: Pan Macmillan.

Makholwa, Angela. 2017. *The Blessed Girl*. Johannesburg: Pan Macmillan.

Mäntymäki, Tiina. 2012. "Lover, Avenger or Deadly Delusionist? Women Murderers in Contemporary Crime Fiction." In *Kielet liikkeessä, Språk i rörelse, Languages in Motion, Sprachen in Bewegung*, edited by N. Nissilä and N. Siponkoski, 198–208. Vaasa: VAKKI Publications.

Mäntymäki, Tiina. 2013. "Women Who Kill Men: Gender, Agency and Subversion in Swedish Crime Novels." *European Journal of Women's Studies* 20 (4): 441–454.

Martin, Caitlin Lisa. 2013. "Profiling the Female Crime Writer: Margie Orford and Questions of (Gendered) Genre." Unpublished Master's thesis, University of KwaZulu-Natal, Durban.

Martin, Caitlin, and Sally-Ann Murray. 2014. "Crime Takes Place: Spatial Situation(s) in Margie Orford's Fiction." *Scrutiny2: Issues in English Studies in Southern Africa* 19 (1): 35–51.

Matzke, Christine, and Susanne Mühleisen. 2006a. *Postcolonial Postmortems: Crime Fiction from a Transcultural Perspective*. Amsterdam: Rodopoi.

Matzke, Christine, and Susanne Mühleisen. 2006b. "Postcolonial Postmortems: Issues and Perspectives." In *Postcolonial Postmortems: Crime Fiction from a Transcultural Perspective*, edited by Christine Matzke and Susanne Mühleisen, 1–16. Amsterdam: Rodopi.

Mbembe, Achille. 2014. "Class, Race and the New Native." *Mail & Guardian*, September 25, 2014. https://mg.co.za/article/2014-09-25-class-race-and-the-new-native.

McClintock, Anne. 1993. "Family Feuds: Gender, Nationalism and the Family." *Feminist Review* 44: 61–80.

McClintock, Anne. 1995. *Imperial Leather: Race, Gender and Sexuality in the Colonial Conquest*. Abingdon: Routledge.

McCracken, Patricia. 2014. "Book Review: *The Lazarus Effect*." Review of *The Lazarus Effect*, by Hawa Jande Golakai. *Business Day*, April 22, 2014. https://www.businesslive.co.za/bd/life/books/2014-04-22-book-review-the-lazarus-effect/.

McEwan, Cheryl. 2000. "Engendering Citizenship: Gendered Spaces of Democracy in South Africa." *Political Geography* 19: 627–651.

McFadden, Patricia. 2003. "Sexual Pleasure as Feminist Choice." *Feminist Africa* 2: 50–60. http://agi.ac.za/sites/agi.ac.za/files/fa_2_standpoint_1.pdf.

Meintjes, Sheila. 1998. "Political Violence and Gender: A Neglected Relation in South Africa's Struggle for Democracy." *Politikon: South African Journal of Political Studies* 25 (2): 95–109.

Meintjes, Sheila. 2001. "War and Post-War Shifts in Gender Relations." In *The Aftermath: Women in Post-Conflict Transformation*, edited by Sheila Meintjes, Anu Pillay and Meredith Turshen, 63–77. London: Zed Books.

Meintjes, Sheila. 2011. "The Women's Struggle for Equality During South Africa's Transition to Democracy." *Transformation* 75: 107–115.

Meintjes, Sheila, Anu Pillay, and Meredith Turshen. 2001. "There Is No Aftermath for Women." In *The Aftermath: Women in Post-Conflict Transformation*, edited by Sheila Meintjes, Pillay Anu and Meredith Turshen, 3–17. London: Zed Books.

Mengel, Ewald. 2009. "Truth and Reconciliation in the Contemporary South African Novel." In *Memory, Narrative and Forgiveness*, edited by Pumla Gobodo-Madikizela and Chris van der Merwe, 302–318. Newcastle, UK: Cambridge Scholars Publishing.

Mengel, Ewald. 2012. "Trauma and Genre in the Contemporary South African Novel." In *Trauma, Memory, and Narrative in the Contemporary South African Novel: Essays*, edited by Ewald Mengel and Michela Borzaga, 143–175. Amsterdam: Rodopi.

Mengel, Ewald, and Michela Borzaga. 2012a. "Introduction." In *Trauma, Memory, and Narrative in the Contemporary South African Novel: Essays*, edited by Ewald Mengel and Michela Borzaga, vii-xxix. Amsterdam: Rodopi.

Mengel, Ewald, and Michela Borzaga, eds. 2012b. *Trauma, Memory, and Narrative in the Contemporary South African Novel: Essays*. Amsterdam: Rodopi.

Messerschmidt, James W. 2009. "Hegemonic and Subordinated Masculinities." In *Key Readings in Criminology*, edited by Tim Newburn, 791–795. Cullompton: Willan Publishing.

Messerschmidt, James W. 2014. *Crime as Structured Action: Doing Masculinities, Race, Class, Sexuality, and Crime*. 2nd ed. Lanham: Rowman & Littlefield.

Moffett, Helen. 2006. "'These Women, They Force Us to Rape Them': Rape as Narrative of Social Control in Post-Apartheid South Africa." *Journal of Southern African Studies* 32 (1): 129–144.

Moffett, Helen. 2008. "Gender." In *New South African Keywords*, edited by Nick Sheperd and Steven Robins, 104–115. Johannesburg: Jacana; Athens: Ohio University Press.

Mohanty, Chandra Talpade. 1984. "Under Western Eyes: Feminist Scholarship and Colonial Discourses." *boundary 2* 12/13 (3/1): 333–358.

Mokgoro, Yvonne. 2012. "Ubuntu and the Law in South Africa." In *Ubuntu and the Law: African Ideals and Postapartheid Jurisprudence*, edited by Drucilla Cornell and Nyoko Muvangua, 317–323. New York: Fordham University Press.

Morford, Mark P.O. 2016. "Persephone." In *Classical Mythology*, 9th ed., edited by Mark P.O. Morford, Robert J. Lenardon and Michael Sham. Oxford: Oxford University Press. http://global.oup.com/us/companion.websites/9780195397703/student/glossaries/character/pq/.

Morrell, Robert. 2001. "The Times of Change: Men and Masculinity in South Africa." In *Changing Men in Southern Africa*, edited by Robert Morrell, 3–37. Pietermaritzburg: University of Natal Press; London: Zed Books.

Morrell, Robert. 2005. "Men, Movements, and Gender Transformations in South Africa." In *African Masculinities: Men in Africa from the Late Nineteenth Century to the Present*, edited by Lahoucine Ouzgane and Robert Morrell, 271–288. London: Palgrave Macmillan; Scottsville: University of KwaZulu-Natal Press.

Morris, Rosalind C. 2006. "The Mute and the Unspeakable: Political Subjectivity, Violent Crime, and 'the Sexual Thing' in a South African Mining Community." In *Law and Disorder in the Postcolony*, edited by Jean Comaroff and John Comaroff, 57–101. Chicago: The University of Chicago Press.

Morris, Rosalind C. 2011. "In the Name of Trauma: Notes on Testimony, Truth Telling and the Secret of Literature in South Africa." *Comparative Literature Studies* 48 (3): 388–416.

Motsemme, Nthabiseng. 2004. "The Mute Always Speak: On Women's Silences at the Truth and Reconciliation Commission." *Current Sociology* 52 (5): 909–932.

Munro, Brenna. 2014. "Nelson, Winnie, and the Politics of Gender." In *The Cambridge Companion to Nelson Mandela*, edited by Rita Barnard, 92–112. Cambridge, UK: Cambridge University Press.

Munt, Sally R. 1994. *Murder by the Book? Feminism and the Crime Novel*. Abingdon: Routledge.

Murray, Jessica. 2013. "'The Girl Was Stripped, Splayed and Penetrated': Representations of Gender and Violence in Margie Orford's Crime Fiction." *English Academy Review: Southern African Journal of English Studies* 30 (2): 67–78.

Murray, Jessica. 2016. "Constructions of Gender in Contemporary South African Crime Fiction: A Feminist Literary Analysis of the Novels of Angela Makholwa." *English Studies in Africa* 59 (2): 14–26.

Murray, Sally-Ann. 2014. "Writing like Life? 'Life-like' Relation, Femaleness and Generic Instability in *Small Moving Parts*." *Agenda* 28 (1): 72–84.

Naidu, Sam. 2013a. "Crime Fiction, South Africa: A Critical Introduction." *Current Writing: Text and Reception in Southern Africa* 25 (2): 124–135.

Naidu, Sam. 2013b. "Fears and Desires in South African Crime Fiction." *Journal of Southern African Studies* 39 (3): 727–738.

Naidu, Sam. 2014. "Writing the Violated Body: Representations of Violence against Women in Margie Orford's Crime Thriller Novels." *Scrutiny2: Issues in English Studies in Southern Africa* 19 (1): 69–79.

Naidu, Samantha, and Elizabeth Le Roux. 2017. *A Survey of South African Crime Fiction: Critical Analysis and Publishing History*. Pietermaritzburg: University of KwaZulu-Natal Press.

Nicol, Mike. 2010a. *Killer Country*. London: Old Street Publishing.

Nicol, Mike. 2010b. *Payback*. London: Old Street Publishing.

Nicol, Mike. 2011. *Black Heart*. London: Old Street Publishing.

Nicol, Mike. 2012a. "Interview with Mike Nicol." Personal unpublished interview by Sabine Binder. Zürich, Switzerland, December 7, 2012.

Nicol, Mike. 2012b. "News from South Africa." Interview by Michael Sears. *The Big Thrill*, July 31, 2012. http://www.thebigthrill.org/2012/07/news-from-south-africa-by-michael-sears-2/.

Nicol, Mike. 2013a. *Of Cops and Robbers*. Cape Town: Umuzi.

Nicol, Mike. 2013b. "Our Fascination with True Crime." *Sunday Times*. October 23, 2013. http://crimebeat.bookslive.co.za/blog/2013/10/23/our-fascination-with-true-crime/.

Nicol, Mike. 2014. "SA's Crime Movies." *Red Bulletin*, March 2014. http://crimebeat.bookslive.co.za/blog/2014/04/07/crime-beat-sas-crime-movies/.

Nicol, Mike. 2015a. "How Dark Was My Valley: Cape Town Is a Crime, Says This Acclaimed Writer." *Sunday Times*, September 20, 2015.

Nicol, Mike. 2015b. *Power Play*. London: Old Street Publishing.

Nicol, Mike. 2015c. "A Short History of South African Crime Fiction." Crime Beat, Sunday Times. Accessed July 28, 2017. http://crimebeat.bookslive.co.za/a-short-history-of-south-african-crime-fiction/.

Nicol, Mike. 2016. "Who's Who of South African Crime Fiction." Crime Beat, Sunday Times. Accessed July 28, 2017. http://crimebeat.bookslive.co.za/whos-who-of-south-african-crime-writing/.

Nicol, Mike. 2017. *Agents of the State*. London: Old Street Publishing.

Nicol, Mike. 2018. *Sleeper*. Cape Town: Umuzi.

Nunn, Malla. 2009. *A Beautiful Place to Die*. New York: Washington Square Press.

Nunn, Malla. 2010a. "Durban Noir – Malla Nunn on 'Let the Dead Lie'." Interview by Nick Terrell. *The Ember*, 2010. http://theember.com.au/durban-noir-malla-nunn-on-let-the-dead-lie/.

Nunn, Malla. 2010b. *Let the Dead Lie*. London: Picador.

Nunn, Malla. 2012a. "AWW Feature & Review: Chatting with Malla Nunn about *Silent Valley*." Interview by Shelleyrae. *Book'd Out*. May 15, 2012. Audio, 29:53. https://bookdout.files.wordpress.com/2012/05/malla-nunn.mp3.

Nunn, Malla. 2012b. *Blessed Are the Dead*. New York: Washington Square Press.

Nunn, Malla. 2014. *Present Darkness*. New York: Washington Square Press.

Nunn, Malla. 2019. *When the Ground is Hard*. New York: G. P. Putnam's Sons.

Nuttall, Sarah. 2009. *Entanglement: Literary and Cultural Reflections on Post-Apartheid South Africa*. Johannesburg: Wits University Press.

Orford, Margie. 2007. *Blood Rose*. London: Corvus.

Orford, Margie. 2010a. *Like Clockwork*. London: Atlantic Books.

Orford, Margie. 2010b. "Writing Crime." *Current Writing: Text and Reception in Southern Africa* 22 (2): 184–197.

Orford, Margie. 2011a. *Daddy's Girl*. London: Corvus. First published in 2009.

Orford, Margie. 2011b. *Gallows Hill*. Johannesburg: Jonathan Ball Publishers.

Orford, Margie. 2012. "Crime Beat: In the Shadow of Gallows Hill." Interview by Crime Beat, edited by Mike Nicol. *Sunday Times*, August 22, 2012. http://crimebeat.bookslive.co.za/blog/2012/08/22/crime-beat-in-the-shadow-of-gallows-hill/.

Orford, Margie. 2013a. "News from South Africa by Michael Sears." Interview by Michael Sears. *The Big Thrill*, October 31, 2013. http://www.thebigthrill.org/2013/10/news-from-south-africa-by-michael-sears-13/.

Orford, Margie. 2013b. "The Grammar of Violence, Writing Crime as Fiction." *Current Writing: Text and Reception in Southern Africa* 25 (2): 220–229.

Orford, Margie. 2013c. *Water Music*. Johannesburg: Jonathan Ball Publishers.

Otter, Charlotte. 2014a. *Balthasar's Gift: A Maggie Cloete Mystery*. Cape Town: Modjaji Books.

Otter, Charlotte. 2014b. "Interview: *Balthasar's Gift* by Charlotte Otter." Interview by Jonathan Amid. *Litnet*, September 5, 2014. http://www.litnet.co.za/interview-balthasars-gift-by-charlotte-otter/.

Otter, Charlotte. 2016a. " 'I Find Thinking about an Audience Distracting': An Interview with Charlotte Otter." Interview by Tiah Beautement. *Short Story Day Africa*, June 15, 2016. http://shortstorydayafrica.org/news/i-find-thinking-about-an-audience-distracting-an-interview-with-charlotte-otter/.

Otter, Charlotte. 2016b. *Karkloof Blue: A Maggie Cloete Mystery*. Cape Town: Modjaji Books.

Oxford English Dictionary, 2nd ed., s.v. "halal," accessed February 27, 2017. http://www.oed.com.ezproxy.uzh.ch/view/Entry/83362?result=2&rskey=i2nbzw&.

Oxford English Dictionary, 2nd ed., s.v. "kaffir," accessed October 28, 2017. http://www.oed.com.ezproxy.uzh.ch/view/Entry/102330?redirectedFrom=kaffir#eid.

Oxford English Dictionary, 2nd ed., s.v. "muti," accessed February 27, 2017. http://www.oed.com.ezproxy.uzh.ch/view/Entry/124321?redirectedFrom=muti#eid.

Oxford English Dictionary, 2nd ed., s.v."popular," accessed March 21, 2020. https://www-oed-com.ezproxy.uzh.ch/view/Entry/147908?redirectedFrom=popular#eid.

Oxford English Dictionary. 2nd ed., s.v. "recognize," accessed September 24, 2017. http://www.oed.com.ezproxy.uzh.ch/view/Entry/159656?rskey=7tmekm&result=1#eid.

Oxford English Dictionary. 2nd ed., s.v. "sjambok," accessed October 20, 2017. http://www.oed.com.ezproxy.uzh.ch/view/Entry/180611?rskey=fNQWuI&result=1#eid.

Pather, Ra'eesa. 2015. "Forgotten Bones Haunt Cape Town." *Mail & Guardian*, December 13, 2015. http://mg.co.za/article/2015-12-13-forgotten-bones-haunt-cape-town.

Patterson, James with Jassy Mackenzie. 2017. *Private Gold*. London: BookShots; London: Penguin Random House UK.

PEN South Africa. 2015. "Board Members." Accessed September 15, 2017. http://pensouthafrica.co.za/about-us-2/who-we-are/board-members/.

Place, Janey. 1980. "Women in Film Noir." In *Women in Film Noir*, edited by E. Ann Kaplan, 35–67. London: British Film Institute.

Plain, Gill. 2001. *Twentieth Century Crime Fiction: Gender, Sexuality and the Body*. Edinburgh: Edinburgh University Press.

Platt, Jennifer. 2013. "Love You to Death: Jennifer Platt Chats to Angela Makholwa about *Black Widow Society*." *Sunday Times*, September 9, 2013. http://bookslive.co.za/blog/2013/09/09/love-you-to-death-jennifer-platt-chats-to-angela-makholwa-about-black-widow-society/.

Pollock, Griselda. 2010. "Aesthetic Wit(h)nessing in the Era of Trauma." *Euramerica* 40 (4): 829–886.

Posel, Deborah. 2002. "The TRC Report: What Kind of History? What Kind of Truth?" In *Commissioning the Past: Understanding South Africa's Truth and Reconciliation Commission*, edited by Deborah Posel and Graeme Simpson, 147–172. Johannesburg: Witwatersrand University Press.

Posel, Deborah. 2008. "AIDS." In *New South African Keywords*, edited by Nick Sheperd and Steven Robins, 13–24. Johannesburg: Jacana; Athens: Ohio University Press.

Posel, Deborah. 2011. " 'Getting the Nation Talking about Sex': Reflections on the Politics of Sexuality and Nation-Building in Post-Apartheid South Africa." In *African Sexualities: A Reader*, edited by Sylvia Tamale, 130–144. Cape Town: Pambazuka Press.

Posel, Deborah, and Graeme Simpson. 2002. "Introduction: The Power of Truth – South Africa's Truth and Reconciliation Commission in Context." In *Commissioning the Past: Understanding South Africa's Truth and Reconciliation Commission*, edited by Deborah Posel and Graeme Simpson, 1–12. Johannesburg: Witwatersrand University Press.

Pretorius, Antoinette. 2014. "Sisters in Crime: Reading June Drummond and Margie Orford." *Scrutiny2: Issues in English Studies in Southern Africa* 19 (1): 5–17.

Raine, Adrian. 2009. "Biosocial Studies of Antisocial Behaviour in Children and Adults." In *Key Readings in Criminology*, edited by Tim Newburn, 119–126. Cullompton: Willan Publishing.

Rape Crisis South Africa. 2017. "Prevalence." Accessed July 30, 2017. http://rapecrisis.org.za/rape-in-south-africa/#prevalence.

Rautenbach, Anneke. 2013. " 'Every Technique Known to Prose': The Aesthetics of True-Crime in Contemporary South Africa." *Current Writing: Text and Reception in Southern Africa* 25 (2): 153–163.

Reddy, Maureen T. 1988. *Sisters in Crime: Feminism and the Crime Novel*. New York: Continuum.

Rijsdijk, Ian-Malcolm. 2011. "History and the 'Imagination of Men's Hearts' in Mike Nicol's *Horseman*." *Ilha do Desterro* (61): 109–135.

Riordan, Ellen. 2001. "Commodified Agents and Empowered Girls: Consuming and Producing Feminism." *Journal of Communication Inquiry* 25 (3): 279–297.

Röser, Jutta. 2000. *Fernsehgewalt im gesellschaftlichen Kontext: Eine Cultural Studies-Analyse über die Medienaneignung in Dominanzverhältnissen*. Wiesbaden: Westdeutscher Verlag.

Ross, Fiona. 2003a. *Bearing Witness: Women and the Truth and Reconciliation Commission in South Africa*. London: Pluto Press.

Ross, Fiona. 2003b. "The Construction of Voice and Identity in the South African Truth and Reconciliation Commission." In *Political Transition: Politics and Cultures*, edited by Paul Gready, 165–180. London: Pluto Press.

Ross, Fiona. 2008. "Truth and Reconciliation." In *New South African Keywords*, edited by Nick Sheperd and Steven Robins, 235–246. Johannesburg: Jacana; Athens: Ohio University Press.

Rowe, Michéle. 2013a. "Author Interview: Michéle Rowe." Interview by Shelag Parry. *The Word Fiend*, July 2013. http://www.thewordfiend.net/2013/07/author-interview-michele-rowe.html.

Rowe, Michéle. 2013b. *What Hidden Lies*. Johannesburg: Penguin Books (South Africa).

Rowe, Michéle. 2015. *Hour of Darkness*. Cape Town: Penguin Random House South Africa.

Rowe, Michéle. 2016. "Finding the Psychological Truths." Interview by Michael Sears. *The Big Thrill*, July 31, 2016. http://www.thebigthrill.org/2016/07/africa-scene-michele-rowe-by-michael-sears/.

Rowe, Michéle. 2017. "Home Page." Accessed 23 January 2017. http://www.michele-rowe.co.za/.

Rzepka, Charles J. 2010. "Introduction: What Is Crime Fiction?" In *A Companion to Crime Fiction*, edited by Charles J. Rzepka and Lee Horsley, 1–9. Chichester: Wiley-Blackwell.

Samuelson, Meg. 2007a. *Remembering the Nation, Dismembering Women? Stories of the South African Transition*. Scottsville: University of KwaZulu-Natal Press.

Samuelson, Meg. 2007b. "The Disfigured Body of the Female Guerrilla: (De)Militarization, Sexual Violence, and Redomestication in Zoë Wicomb's *David's Story*." *Signs* 32 (4): 833–856.

Samuelson, Meg. 2010. "Scripting Connections: Reflections on the 'Post-Transitional.'" *English Studies in Africa* 53 (1): 113–117.

Savage, Tyrone. 2011. "Closing the Books or Keeping them Open." In *Closing the Books or Keeping them Open? Contributions to the Bonn Conference on Adult Education and Development (BoCAED) 'Remember for the Future'*, edited by Vanya Ivanova and Matthias Klingenberg, 7–16. Bonn: DVV International.

Singh, Jaspal K., and Rajendra Chetty, eds. 2010. *Trauma, Resistance, Reconstruction in Post-1994 South African Writing*. New York: Peter Lang.

Sjoberg, Laura, and Caron E. Gentry. 2007. *Mothers, Monsters, Whores: Women's Violence in Global Politics*. London: Zed Books.

Snodgrass, Lyn. 2015. "South Africa: A Dangerous Place to Be Poor, Black and a Woman." *The Conversation*, September 11, 2015. http://theconversation.com/south-africa-a-dangerous-place-to-be-poor-black-and-a-woman-47287.

South African History Online. 2012. "This Day in History: Thursday 20 August 1959." Accessed 19 February 2015. http://www.sahistory.org.za/dated-event/andrew-khehla-lukhele-president-national-stokvels-association-johannesburg-born-johannes.

Spencer, Lynda Gichanda. 2013. "The House of Mothers: Constructing Alternative Forms of Mothering in Kagiso Lesego Molope's *The Mending Season*." *English Academy Review: Southern African Journal of English Studies* 30 (1): 52–64.

Spencer, Lynda Gichanda. 2014. "Writing Women in Uganda and South Africa: Emerging Writers from Post-Repressive Regimes." Unpublished doctoral thesis, Stellenbosch University.

Spencer, Lynda Gichanda, Dina Ligaga, and Grace A Musila. 2018. "Gender and Popular Imaginaries in Africa." *Agenda* 32 (3): 3–9.

Stampfl, Barry. 2014. "Parsing the Unspeakable in the Context of Trauma." In *Contemporary Approaches in Literary Trauma Theory*, edited by Michelle Balaev, 15–41. London: Palgrave Macmillan.

Steffen, Therese. 2012. " 'Leben unter dem Schleier': Afroamerikanische Texte und Kontexte." In *Verschleierter Orient – Entschleierter Okzident? (Un-)Sichtbarkeit in Politik, Recht, Kunst und Kultur seit dem 19. Jahrhundert*, edited by Bettina Dennerlein, Elke Frietsch and Therese Steffen, 181–201. München: Wilhelm Fink Verlag.

Steinberg, Jonny. 2008. "Crime." In *New South African Keywords*, edited by Nick Sheperd and Steven Robins, 25–34. Johannesburg: Jacana; Athens: Ohio University Press.

Steiner, Tina. 2017. "The Stranger's Gaze: Defamiliarizing the Local in Hawa J. Golakai's Crime Novels *The Lazarus Effect* (2011) and *The Score* (2015)." In *Kulturbegegnung und Kulturkonflikt im (post-)kolonialen Kriminalroman*, edited by Michaela Holdenried, Barbara Korte and Carlotta von Maltzan, 101–118. Bern: Peter Lang.

Stiebel, Lindy. 2002. "Black 'Tecs: Popular Thrillers by South African Black Writers in the Nineties." In *Readings in African Popular Fiction*, edited by Stephanie Newell, 187–192. Bloomington: Indiana University Press.

Stubbs, Julie. 2012 (2007). "Beyond Apology? Domestic Violence and Critical Questions for Restorative Justice." In *Gender and Crime: Critical Concepts in Criminology, Volume IV: Gender, Crime, and Punishment*, edited by Sandra Walklate, 339–357. Abingdon: Routledge.

Titlestad, Michael, and Ashlee Polatinsky. 2010. "Turning to Crime: Mike Nicol's *The Ibis Tapestry* and *Payback*." *The Journal of Commonwealth Literature* 45 (2): 259–273.

Tlhabi, Redi. 2017. *Khwezi: The Story of Fezekile Ntsukela Kuzwayo*. Johannesburg: Jonathan Ball Publishers. Kindle.

Twidle, Hedley. 2012. " 'In a Country Where You Couldn't Make This Shit Up'?: Literary Non-Fiction in South Africa." *Safundi: The Journal of South African and American Studies* 13 (1–2): 5–28.

Ulicki, Theresa. 2011. "'Just the Way Things Are': Gender Equity and Sexual Harassment in the South African Police Service." *Transformation: Critical Perspectives on Southern Africa* 76: 95–119.

Vale, Helen. 2010. "Margie Orford: Crime Writer With a Mission." *Sister Namibia*, April 2010. https://sisternamibiatest2014.files.wordpress.com/2017/07/margie-orford-crime-writer-with-a-mission2.pdf.

Van der Merwe, Chris, and Pumla Gobodo-Madikizela. 2008. *Narrating Our Healing: Perspectives on Working through Trauma*. Newcastle, UK: Cambridge Scholars Publishing.

Van Marle, Karin, and Elsje Bonthuys. 2007. "Feminist Theories and Concepts." In *Gender, Law and Justice*, edited by Elsje Bonthuys and Catherine Albertyn, 15–50. Cape Town: Juta.

Vincent, Louise. 2008. "The Limitations of 'Inter-Racial Contact': Stories from Young South Africa." *Ethnic and Racial Studies* 31 (8): 1426–1451.

Vincent, Louise, and Sam Naidu. 2013. "Vrou Is Gif: The Representation of Violence against Women in Margie Orford's Clare Hart Novels." *African Safety Promotion Journal* 11 (2): 48–62.

Visser, Irene. 2011. "Trauma Theory and Postcolonial Literary Studies." *Journal of Postcolonial Writing* 47 (3): 270–282.

Visser, Irene. 2014. "Trauma and Power in Postcolonial Literary Studies." In *Contemporary Approaches in Literary Trauma Theory*, edited by Michelle Balaev, 106–129. London: Palgrave Macmillan.

Visser, Irene. 2015. "Decolonizing Trauma Theory: Retrospect and Prospects." *Humanities* 4: 250–265.

Walton, Priscilla L. 2013. "'The Girl Who Pays Our Salaries': Rape and the Bestselling Millennium Trilogy." In *Rape in Stieg Larsson's Millennium Trilogy and Beyond*, edited by Berit Åström, Katarina Gregersdotter and Tanya Horeck, 21–33. London: Palgrave Macmillan.

Walton, Priscilla L., and Manina Jones. 1999. *Detective Agency: Women Rewriting the Hard-Boiled Tradition*. Berkeley: University of California Press.

Warnes, Christopher. 2012. "Writing Crime in the New South Africa: Negotiating Threat in the Novels of Deon Meyer and Margie Orford." *Journal of Southern African Studies* 38 (4): 981–991.

Wicomb, Zoë. 1998. "Shame and Identity. The Case of the Coloured in South Africa." In *Writing South Africa: Literature, Apartheid, and Democracy, 1970–1995*, edited by Derek Attridge and Rosemary Jolly, 91–107. Cambridge, UK: Cambridge University Press.

Wiener, Mandy. 2012. *Killing Kebble: An Underworld Exposed*. Johannesburg: Pan Macmillan South Africa.

Worthington, Heather. 2011. *Key Concepts in Crime Fiction*. London: Palgrave Macmillan.

Index

Aaron, Michele   24, 34, 45, 67–69, 109
acquiescent femininity   114, 117, 119, 123, 131
Adhikari, Mohamed   90
Africa, Adelene   79, 187, 223
agonistic solidarity   139, 151–155, 167
Albertyn, Catherine   204
Altbeker, Antony   15n20, 208
Amid, Jonathan   14, 113, 127, 194
amnesty   10, 11n12, 56, 90, 205
Andrews, Chris   7, 27n8
anti-apartheid struggle   11, 17–18, 78, 85, 87, 91, 217, 219
apartheid   1–2, 3n4, 7–11, 14n17, 14–15, 17, 24n4, 27, 35–36, 39, 39n16, 41, 43n19, 46–49, 59, 62, 89–91, 95, 104, 121, 137, 139, 148, 154, 159, 162, 181, 191, 203–206, 208, 213

Baartman, Sarah   94, 145
Balaev, Michelle   25–27
Barber, Karin   9–10
Benjamin, Walter   164n14
Bertens, Hans   143
Bhabha, Homi   148
Biko, Hlumelo   35–36, 36n13
Black men   84, 97, 104
black widow spider   93, 112, 127
Black women   3, 34, 42, 47, 63, 79, 89, 95–96, 113, 118, 157, 170, 177, 183, 189, 195, 197–198, 204, 209
Black, Shameem   15
Bohnet, Iris   218
Bonthuys, Elsje   134, 165, 200
Boonzaier, Floretta   19n21
Boraine, Alex   35–36
Borer, Tristan Anne   11, 27, 56, 90
Borzaga, Michela   25–28
Braude, Claudia   138
Breysse, Serge   85
Brink, André   12
Bronfen, Elisabeth   24, 29–32, 34, 45, 59n35, 64–66, 70–71, 87, 99, 199, 215
Brown, Adam   80n2
Büchler, Andrea   165
Butler, Anthony   11, 39n16, 41, 206

Butler, Judith   20, 77, 212
Butler, Pamela   176

Cape Town   51–52, 58–59, 85, 89, 91, 141, 162, 168–169
Cawelti, John   9
Chandler, Raymond   137, 176
Chetty, Rajendra   27n8
chick lit   168, 175–180, 189
child abuse   159
Christensen, Matthew   16
Christian, Ed   148
citizenship   100, 104, 129, 163, 219
Cock, Jacklyn   104
Collins, Patricia Hill   4, 94
Coloured men   51, 183
Coloured women   84, 89–91, 97–98, 148, 172, 181, 210
Colvin, Christopher   26–27
Comaroff, Jean and John   15, 52, 65n40, 0042278–81
corporate crime   186–187, 187n20, 189, 205
Cottier, Michelle   165
counter-violence   77, 130–131, 219
Crenshaw, Kimberlé   3

D'haen, Theo   143
Dankwa, Serena   81–82, 103, 114
Davis, Geoffrey   14n17
De Crescenzo   14n5
De Kock, Leon   6, 8n9, 14–16, 29, 84, 86, 96–98, 211
Decoteau, Claire Laurier   202
Desai, Jigna   176
detective   2, 6–7, 13, 20, 23, 33, 40–46, 60–63, 99–112, 133–212, 214, 01185217–220
detective novel   13, 28, 38, 50, 101, 139, 169, 191, 210
Dietze, Gabriele   4n5
Dlamini, Nhlanhla   41
Doak, Jonathan   165
Doane, Mary Ann   96
domestic violence   43, 112, 121–124, 131, 143
Driver, Dorothy   116, 116n28, 118
Drummond, June   138

Du Bois, W.E.B.   23, 31, 175
Du Toit, Louise   17–19, 22, 24n3, 32, 37, 51, 73, 82n5, 219
Durban   39, 191, 197
Dyer, Richard   3n4, 181, 197

Eastern Cape   28
Ebert, Teresa L.   83, 104, 136, 157
ecological crimes   100–101, 129, 197, 201, 204–206
education   113, 117, 126, 131
education system   35–36, 128
Edwards, Martin   23
Erasmus, Zimitri   90, 95, 147
ethics   22, 24, 34, 42, 48, 50, 63–64, 66–68, 72, 77, 108–112, 121–128, 151–152, 155, 159, 187, 190, 200, 220
Every, Kate   54, 72

Fasselt, Rebecca   171
feminist crime fiction   6, 42, 49, 62, 111, 125, 128, 130–132, 134–137, 151–157, 169–175, 178, 189, 192–199, 210–212, 219
femme fatale   76, 84, 87, 93, 96, 98–100, 112, 135, 177
Ferriss, Suzanne   176
Fletcher, Elizabeth   50, 56n30, 63
Frenkel, Ronit   8–10
Freud, Sigmund   41, 93
Frizzoni, Brigitte   77–78, 99, 157

Galusca, Roxana   189
Gates, Henry Louis Jr.   3n4
Gavin, Adrienne   76, 134
genetic engineering   106, 129
genre bending   157
genre blending   175–180
Gentry, Caron   80n2
Gobodo-Madikizela, Pumla   24, 26n7, 27n8
Goldblatt, Beth   11, 27, 90
Goltermann, Svenja   24
Gqola, Pumla Dineo   16, 19–20, 75n1, 90, 145
Graham, Shane   12
Green, Lelia   200
Green, Michael   14n17
Greyling, Mike   79
Grunebaum, Heidi   90

Haffejee, Sadiyya   79
Halberstam, Judith   81–83, 88–89, 103, 106, 115, 124, 130, 192, 194, 199
Hamber, Brandon   17, 106, 207
Hanson, Helen   76, 96
Harris, Marla   16, 111
Hayner, Priscilla   10–11
hegemonic masculinity   81–82, 98, 114, 118–119, 127–128, 130–131, 194
Henry, Claire   76, 94, 117
Hilmes, Carola   76
HIV   35–37, 114, 117, 122, 130, 191–192, 201–204, 212–213
Honig, Bonnie   151–157
Hooks, Bell   89, 118n31, 146, 177
Horsley, Lee   87
Hudson, Barbara   164–167, 180, 185–186, 188, 200, 202, 211, 218
human trafficking   51, 56, 101, 129, 189

imagined violence   83, 107
intersectionality   3, 7, 115, 141, 161, 195, 204, 214
investigative journalism   15, 15n20, 51, 168, 188–189, 191, 194, 208, 211

Jewkes, Rachel   17, 114, 117, 122–123, 130, 146n8
Jezebel   94
Johannesburg   43n20, 79, 100–101, 217
Jones, Manina   2n1, 23n2, 135–137, 164, 210
justice
   alternative   13, 76, 100, 106–108, 134, 163–167, 180–189, 01130199–211
   restorative   12, 134, 163, 165, 208
   retributive   100, 106, 129, 219

Kinsman, Margaret   23n2, 135
Klein, Kathleen Gregory   23, 134, 136
Knight, Stephen   2n1, 13, 135
Krüger, Gesine   11
Kuzwayo, Fezekile   213

Lacan, Jacques   31, 151
LaCapra, Dominick   25n5, 40–43, 48, 58, 60, 71, 216
land restitution   161–163, 167

INDEX 243

Le Roux, Elizabeth 7, 8n8, 8–9
Lewis, Desiree 18, 78, 93–94, 120, 145, 170
liberation movements 8, 90, 129
Ligaga, Dina 10, 221
Lorde, Audre 178
Lugones, Maria 4

MacKenzie, Craig 8–10
Madikizela-Mandela, Winnie 78
Mäntymäki, Tiina 77, 80
Maras, Steven 200
Martin, Caitlin 54, 62
Matzke, Christine 13, 149
Mbeki, Thabo 201, 203, 209
Mbembe, Achille 163, 163n13
McClintock, Anne 43, 75, 120, 156, 195–196, 198
McEwan, Cheryl 17
McFadden, Patricia 178
McGuire, Matt 7
Meintjes, Sheila 11, 16–18, 27, 90
Mengel, Ewald 25–28, 43n18
Messerschmidt, James 82, 82n5
migrant detective 171–172, 180, 189
missing children 52, 183
Moffett, Helen 17–18, 56
Mohanty, Chandra Talpade 3, 214
Mokgoro, Yvonne 116
Morford, Mark 141n5
Morrell, Robert 17, 83, 83n6, 114, 117, 122–123, 130, 146n8
Morris, Rosalind 14, 27n8
Motsemme, Nthabiseng 47, 215
Mühleisen, Susanne 13, 149
Munro, Brenda 78
Munt, Sally 135, 157, 175
Murray, Jessica 55–56, 117, 123
Murray, Sally-Ann 62, 125
Musila, Grace 10, 221

Naidu, Sam 7, 9, 13–14, 50, 53, 55, 63, 66, 69, 180
Narkadien, Zahrah 91
nation as family 119–121, 129
nation-building 8, 196, 203n25, 215
noir 13, 76, 84–85, 87, 93–94, 171
norm 3, 5, 30–32, 45, 75–77, 80–81, 100, 103, 105–106, 120, 125, 128, 136, 150, 164, 167, 193, 197, 219–220

O'Mahony, David 165
O'Rawe, Catherine 76
outlaw 102, 135

Patterson, James 101
perpetrator 2, 5, 7, 13, 18–20, 51, 54, 61–62, 66, 75–132, 149–150, 159–161, 165, 180, 183, 185, 187, 192, 205, 207, 214, 219–221
Pietermaritzburg 190, 192, 204
Pillay, Anu 18
Place, Janey 87
Plain, Gill 23, 134–135, 137, 146, 178
Polatinsky, Ashlee 85–86
Pollock, Griselda 66, 70, 98, 158
popular literature 2n1, 9, 16, 76, 83, 85, 110, 117, 175, 204, 221
Posel, Deborah 3n2, 11, 138, 159, 161–162, 185, 203–205
postcolonial 3, 5, 13, 24–28, 36, 53, 148
postcolonial detective 148
post-transition 7–9, 13, 16, 35, 138, 167, 213–214, 219
Pretorius, Antoinette 50, 62, 138

queerness 4n5, 18, 57, 81–82, 82n3, 87, 89, 115, 119, 137, 168, 172, 178–179, 193, 199

race 3n4, 7, 16, 18, 26n7, 39n16, 41, 43n19, 47, 65, 65n40, 79, 93, 105, 121, 144n6, 144–145, 147–148, 153, 155–156, 161, 165, 167–170, 173, 175–176, 181, 189, 195, 197–198, 204, 214, 219
rage 83, 89, 106–108, 111, 129, 190, 192–194, 196–197, 219, 221
Raine, Adrian 109
rape 17, 19, 24n3, 52, 56, 75–76, 89–90, 92, 94–96, 143, 146, 185, 202–203, 213, 215, 220
Rautenbach, Anneke 211n26
reader identification 94, 99–100, 108–109, 111, 125, 131
real crime 15–16, 22, 51–52, 111, 211
Reddy, Maureen 135
re-enactment 28, 62–63, 66, 148
representation 3, 5, 22, 29–34, 44–46, 63–72, 77, 94–98, 124–125, 167, 181, 199, 215
representational practices 2, 28–29, 39, 64, 217

revenge   2, 20, 50, 53, 71, 00404 75–78, 84, 91, 94, 100–101, 106–107, 117, 129, 187
Rijsdijk, Ian-Malcolm   85n10
Riordan, Ellen   117
Robins, Steven   90
romance genre   2n1, 101n21, 176
Röser, Jutta   77
Ross, Fiona   11, 26–27, 32, 54–55
Rzepka, Charles   13

Samuelson, Meg   8–10, 88, 90, 215
Sapphire   89, 115
Savage, Tyrone   12n15
serial murderer   53, 87, 100–101, 110, 137, 194, 208
silence   12, 20, 31, 34, 47, 49, 53, 90, 111, 121, 142, 144, 156, 178, 214–216, 219
Simpson, Graeme   3n2, 11, 161, 205
Singh, Jaspal   27n8
Sjoberg, Laura   80n2
slavery   4, 51, 58–59, 62, 91, 91n15, 94, 147, 148n10, 162
Slovo, Gillian   138
South African Police Service (SAPS)   141, 143–144
Spencer, Lynda Gichanda   10, 120, 176, 178, 221
Stampfl, Barry   25n5, 25–26
Steffen, Therese   23, 31
Steinberg, Jonny   15n20, 82n4
Steiner, Tina   169, 175, 180–181
stereotype   4, 16, 23–24, 30, 53, 72, 80n2, 89, 94–95, 105, 115, 120, 130n34, 130–131, 145, 147–148, 156, 170, 177, 179, 181, 187, 189, 196, 199, 220
Stiebel, Lindy   8n8, 14n17
stokvel   116
Stubbs, Julie   123

thriller   5, 13–14, 85, 101, 112, 128, 220
Titlestad, Michael   8, 85–86
Tlhabi, Redi   90, 213–221
trauma   7, 20, 22, 24–28, 35–38, 40–43, 46–49, 53, 0034657–64, 72–73, 98, 117, 140, 157–159, 185
true crime fiction   211, 213–221
truth   3, 3n2, 6, 10, 24, 29, 50, 90, 95, 101, 133, 156, 165, 205, 211, 214, 217

truth-finding   7, 28, 108, 137–138, 157–163, 180–189, 209, 217
truth-telling   11
Truth and Reconciliation Commission (TRC)   6–7, 10–13, 15, 24–28, 32, 34, 37, 54–55, 62–63, 72, 81, 90, 100, 106, 118, 127, 129, 137–138, 152, 154, 159, 165, 167, 205–207, 214, 216, 219
Turshen, Meredith   18
Twidle, Hedley   211n26

ubuntu   116, 118–119
Ulicki, Theresa   143–144

Van der Merwe, Chris   24, 26n7, 27n8
Van Marle, Karin   165, 200
Vetten, Lisa   79
victim   2, 4, 7, 11–12, 19–20, 22–74, 78–79, 95, 98–99, 108, 114, 119, 122, 128, 134–135, 137, 150, 158, 161, 165, 180, 00998 182–187, 189, 196, 199–202, 207, 214–217, 220
victim-avenger   76
vigilantism   74–75, 78, 80, 107, 112
Vincent, Louise   50, 55, 65n40
violent female masculinity   77, 81–83, 86–89, 97–98, 100, 102–106, 111–119, 128, 130, 219
Visser, Irene   25n5, 25–27, 27n8

Walton, Priscilla   2n1, 23, 23n2, 72, 135–137, 164, 210
Warnes, Christopher   15, 63
White men   90, 95–96, 105, 154, 158, 165, 172, 211
White women   48, 59, 89, 100, 113, 129, 158–159, 176, 190, 195, 198, 209
Wicomb, Zoë   90, 147
Wiener, Mandy   15n20, 187n20
Wilson, Richard   106, 207
women of colour   3, 24, 31, 65, 83, 94, 134, 145, 166, 176, 181
Worthington, Heather   13, 134–135

Young, Mallory   176

Zuma, Jacob   36, 213, 215, 217
Zupančič, Alenka   151

Printed in the United States
By Bookmasters